CHARLES W.
COLSON

CHARLES W.
COLSON

A Life Redeemed

Jonathan Aitken

WATERBROOK
PRESS

CHARLES W. COLSON
PUBLISHED BY WATERBROOK PRESS
2375 Telstar Drive, Suite 160
Colorado Springs, Colorado 80920
A division of Random House, Inc.

ISBN 1-57856-510-3

This book is copublished with Doubleday, a division of Random House, Inc.

Library of Congress Cataloging-in-Publication Data
Aitken, Jonathan, 1942–
   Charles W. Colson : a life redeemed / Jonathan Aitken.—1st ed.
        p. cm.
   ISBN 1-57856-510- 3 (WaterBrook Press) ISBN 0-385-50811-5 (Doubleday)
Includes bibliographical references and index.
   1. Colson, Charles W. 2. Baptists—United States—Bibliography. 3. Evangelists—United States—Biography. 4. Ex-convicts—United States—Biography. I. Title.

BX6495.C5687A35 2005

2004062137

286'.1'092—dc22

Printed in the United States of America
2005—First WaterBrook Press Edition

10 9 8 7 6 5 4 3 2 1

To Michael and Sylvia Mary Alison

Contents

Acknowledgments

I acknowledge with great thanks all those who have made this book possible.

Michael and Sylvia Mary Alison, Charles Colson's oldest British friends, first introduced me to the subject of this biography in 1987 and first suggested I should write about him in 1997. Sadly, Michael passed away as the book was nearing completion. Nevertheless, he and Sylvia Mary gave me so much encouragement during my biographer's journey, and so much of their own letters, papers, and recollections about Colson in the early days of Prison Fellowship, that this book is gratefully dedicated to them.

It would be invidious to single out for special thanks the most important contributors to this biography from among the numerous interviewees listed in the Source Notes. All of them are quoted in its chapters, and most of them contributed invaluable threads of insight to the tapestry of my understanding of Colson's life and personality.

Nevertheless, I must express exceptional appreciation to all members of the Colson family who between them gave me more than two hundred hours of interviews and allowed me to read numerous private letters and papers. Their nervousness at knowing that this was going to be a "warts and all" biography was tempered by an openness and willingness to "tell it like it was" to the author. The same appreciation, multiplied many times over, is due to Charles W. Colson, who was generous with his time and punctilious in keeping our agreement that all editorial control should rest with his biographer.

Various collections of papers were made available to me and my research assistants. My thanks are due to the staff of the Nixon Library at Yorba Linda, California; to the staff of the Billy Graham archive at Wheaton College, Illinois; to the staff of the Library of Congress; and to the Federal Archivists at Laguna Niguel, California, and Washington, D.C. To Mrs. Nancy Bursaw I express special gratitude for allowing me access to her personal collection of letters and papers relating to Charles W. Colson, her first husband.

Several members of the staff of Prison Fellowship Ministries in Reston, Virginia, were particularly helpful in response to my biographer's questions regarding facts, figures, and papers. I would like to thank Al Lawrence, Val Merrill, Nancy Niemeyer, and Kim Robbins for their kind assistance.

I express my gratitude to the changing team of secretaries on both sides of the Atlantic who typed and retyped the manuscript of the book or who helped me with research and administrative support. They were: Jackie Cottrell, Helen Haislmaier, Helen Kirkpatrick, Megan Ring, and Jean Sinclair. The heaviest burden of transcribing the tapes of my interviews was borne by Pamela Spearing, whose enthusiasm and efficiency were a great blessing to me.

Finally, I thank my publishers and editors at Doubleday and Waterbrook. Special gratitude is due to Eric Major of Doubleday, who commissioned the biography; to Michelle Rapkin, who succeeded him as Vice President of the Religious Affairs Division; and to Trace Murphy, my editor, whose insights and suggestions made great improvements to the final text.

The final responsibility for all opinions, judgments, and factual statements in the book is, of course, my own.

Jonathan Aitken

Prologue

Easter in Texas

As a chilly dawn cast its first rays of light across the hill country of central Texas on Easter 2004, Charles W. Colson was waiting in a strange yet familiar place. The strangeness was supplied by glinting coils of barbed wire held aloft by iron pillars; double-banked lines of twenty-foot-high steel fencing; blinding searchlights; and fortified watchtowers manned by sentries with rifles. The familiarity came from his twenty-seven previous Easters, all of which had begun with Colson waiting in similar situations for armed guards to arrive and let him in.

The guards, true to form, were late. As a result there was a need for patience, a quality Colson does not possess in abundance. There was ample time to observe the wind swirling through Gatesville County's gray-green grasslands flecked with patches of bluebonnets, or to watch the rivulets of rainwater trickling down the reinforced wire meshing of the perimeter fence.

Noticing that a woman in his party was shivering, Colson took off his raincoat and put it round her shoulders, leaving his trim, six-foot-one-inch frame exposed to the elements. At odds with his surroundings, he looked the epitome of elegance, dressed in a Brooks Brothers blazer, a red-and-blue silk tie, pressed gray flannel trousers, and highly polished leather shoes. Colson's attire and demeanor suggested that he could be an Ivy Leaguer, a New Englander, a former officer in the armed forces, a partner in a white shoe law firm, or a successful leader in the worlds of money, influence, and power. In his time Colson had been all these things and more. But today there were two other clues to his life and mission. The first was the Bible he held in his right hand. The second was the quiet comment he made to no one in particular: "You know, there's nowhere I'd rather be on Easter morning than here in these tombs of modern society."

As gates were unlocked and security passes checked with interminable thoroughness, there was more time to observe the inside of this particular tomb—Mountain View. The name could be for a ski resort or a real estate development, but here in Texas, the state Department of Corrections had chosen it as the title for a high-security jail incarcerating over six hundred women inmates. Colson's term, "tomb," seemed singularly appropriate as a label here, for Mountain View resembled a moonscape punctuated by mausoleums. Emotionally Colson was soon sent into a sepulchral mood. The first of the mausoleums, or cell blocks, on his itinerary was death row.

In nearly three decades of prison ministry, Colson has visited over eight hundred prisons in forty countries and at least seventy death rows. Inevitably, his times with men and women under sentence of death are emotionally searing. This one was especially so. A senior prison officer explained in an advance briefing that there were eight women in the condemned cells, but one of them, Agnes Miller,* was likely to be executed later in the year. "She's come to the end of the road in her appeals. She has no chance of a reprieve. So she's the next one up," said the officer in a Texan drawl as metallic as the sound of his jangling keys.

Colson came face-to-face with Agnes in a whitewashed visitors' room overlooked by guards watching from behind a glass panel. To get there, he and his party passed through three sets of electronically controlled iron doors, each with the words DEATH ROW painted on its lintel. "Subtle directions in here," Colson remarked dryly.

Agnes herself was subtle too, but in a profound way that reflected the tensions between the peace of acceptance and the palpitations of fear that she was feeling at this most fragile of times in her life's journey. She was a highly intelligent, vivacious, and attractive African-American woman of thirty-nine, with elaborately pleated hair. It emerged from the conversation that she had committed her crime eighteen years ago, when she was twenty-one. She said she had changed a lot during her time on death row. "Have you come to know the Lord?" asked Colson. "Yes sir, I love the Lord," said Agnes, touching her Bible. She said the passage that spoke to her with special power at this testing time was Isaiah 43:1–5. In it the Lord promises to protect those whom he loves and calls by name even though

---

*This name and the names of most prisoners in this book have been changed.

they pass through floods, which will not drown them, and flames, which will not scorch them. Agnes asked her visitors to pray for her mother and father. So Colson said prayers for them in words of great beauty, also asking for God's mercy, God's peace, and God's grace to be granted to "Agnes, our sister in Christ."

Colson's party of four companions for this death row visit (among them this author) included a young folksinger named Kelly Minter, who sat on the floor of the visitors' room playing gentle gospel music on her guitar. The tuneful lilt of her songs brought tears to the inmates' eyes. Agnes, taking on the role of an etiquette-conscious hostess, offered her chair to Kelly several times, but the singer preferred strumming from her cross-legged position. Two other death row prisoners joined Agnes in the room with Colson. One of them, Maria, had prepared a little speech. "Mr. Colson, I want to thank you so, so much for all you've done for me," she began.

"What have I done for you?" asked Colson with surprise.

"I'm talking about Angel Tree," said Maria, "and those wonderful Christmas presents Angel Tree gives every year to my three kids. That's been my only way of doing something for them at Christmastime to show them I love them. So I want to thank you personally, from the bottom of my heart."

Colson, who was visibly moved, explained how Prison Fellowship, the ministry he founded in 1976, now distributes six hundred thousand Christmas gifts a year, labeled "With love from Mom" or "With love from Dad," to the children of prisoners.

"It's one of the best things we do, but the idea didn't come from me," he told Maria. "It came from a lady who, like you and like me, had been in prison. She knew as a mother how awful it feels to be so helpless over Christmas when you're in jail, so she put up the idea of giving presents to prisoners' kids, and the Lord blessed it."

After more prayers and conversations with the inmates of death row, some of them on a one-on-one basis in individual cells, Colson moved to the main body of the prison and into the chapel. It was packed with about 350 women dressed in their all-white prison uniforms. When Colson rose to give the main address of the service, he strode onto a platform festooned with colorful banners saying, *This is God's House of Freedom* and *I am the Resurrection,* and he seemed to have the physical vitality of a man half his seventy-three years. Speaking without notes, in a resonant, baritone voice accompanied by expressive gestures, he began with an extension of his earlier comment outside the prison gates comparing prisons to tombs.

"Easter isn't about parades, bunnies, chocolate rabbits, and fancy bon-
nets. It's about the empty tomb. And you and I know about tombs, because
prisons are the tombs of our society and we're in one now. But you and I
also know that the only way to come out of these hellholes, these tombs, is
by knowing the risen Lord."

That opening created a risen audience as the ladies of Mountain View
leapt from their seats shouting hallelujahs and amens. Colson quieted them
down with a personal analysis on whether the resurrection of Jesus was a
mythical conspiracy of untruths invented by his disciples. "Ladies, you are
all too young to remember Watergate," he began.

"Oh no we're not!" chuckled an elderly lady with white hair at the back
of the hall. "I'm old enough to be that grandmother of yours."

Few if any of her fellow inmates got this joke,* to which Colson, by now
in full flow, did not respond.

"The great scandal of Watergate really started when everybody tried to
cover up for themselves after March 21, 1973. That was when John Dean
told Nixon that there was a cancer in the presidency, and then he ran away
to make a deal with the prosecutors," declared Colson, turning from politics to polemics as he added: "Jesus had Judas. Nixon had John Dean. Because of both those betrayals, twelve men came under pressure. Those of
us around Nixon at that time could have been called twelve of the most
powerful people in the world. But we twelve powerful men couldn't hold
a lie together for two weeks. We couldn't support a secret that wasn't true.
The pressure was far too much for us."

Building on this analogy, Colson turned up the heat as he continued:
"Look what pressure Jesus' disciples came under! They were persecuted,
tortured, brutally murdered, stoned to death. But none of them snitched.
None of them copped a plea by confessing to their tormentors, 'We've been
part of a conspiracy to tell lies about the resurrection.' They were willing
to die for something they knew to be true. No one ever gives up their lives
for what they know is untrue. But the disciples were willing to give up their
lives because they knew that resurrection of Christ is true. So do you and
so do I. He is risen!"

The Watergate references seemed to fascinate the inmates of Mountain
View, some of whom evidently had more than a passing acquaintance with
conspiracies, snitches, plea bargains, and prosecutors piling on the pres-

---

*Colson achieved great notoriety while a White House aide for allegedly saying in
1972, "I would walk over my grandmother for Richard Nixon."

sure. But Colson quietly changed the current of his oratory to a lower voltage in order to connect with those prisoners (usually a majority in any prison) who were in denial about their crime.

"When I first got entangled in the Watergate scandal, I said to myself, 'I'm not a bad guy,' " explained Colson. "I didn't feel I was a bad guy, because I thought I hadn't done any worse things than the Democrats had done. But when I came to know Christ I was appalled by my sinfulness. And as I realized that Jesus died on the cross for me, so that my sins could be forgiven, I knew that out of gratitude I had to give my life to him. That is why God sends me into prisons. That's why I'm in this prison today—to serve him, to live for him."

The chapel fell quiet, and in the stillness Colson launched an appeal to his audience: "Ladies, I want *you* to live for *him*," he said. "I know it's not easy, I've been in prison. I know the temptations—the drugs, the deals, the homosexual stuff—but I want you to turn your back on all of that." He gave a circular swing of his arm, half turning as he gazed up at the cross on the altar. "Because if you do give it up and live for the one who died for our sins, then out of gratitude to him you will want to join me in these words of prayer.

"Jesus, you're holy. I'm guilty . . . ," he began in an extempore flow of supplication, which ended: "So, Lord, bless these ladies, and thank you for their willingness to open their hearts to you. Bless them on this Easter day in a special way. Pour your grace out on them and on their families, and show them how much you love them and we love them, through Jesus Christ, our Lord and Savior. Amen."

In an almost supernatural way Colson was able to tune in to an invisible wavelength that bonds offenders in jail with ex-offenders who come back into jail. On that Easter Sunday morning, former prisoner 23226 Colson touched hearts that most other preachers could never have reached.

Mountain View was not the only stop on Colson's weekend travels. In the last forty-eight hours he had been to four other prisons as part of the Prison Fellowship's nationwide crusade, Operation Starting Line, which aims to bring the gospel to every single inmate of America's penal institutions over the next ten years. In Texas alone, Operation Starting Line has a systematic plan of campaign for Christian volunteers of all denominations to visit 160,000 prisoners in the Lone Star State's 119 jails over two years. Raising the money, training the volunteers, and running the organization for such a massive enterprise are formidable tasks. Yet they are essential to the cause that Colson has given his life to since starting Prison Fellowship twenty-seven years ago.

Some thoughtful observers of Prison Fellowship have in the past expressed fears that its impetus might falter or even fade away when the time comes for Colson to relinquish the leadership of the ministry. These anxieties are now starting to recede, after the appointment of a chosen successor, fifty-year-old Mark Earley, the former attorney general of Virginia, who now runs the day-to-day operations of the ministry as president of Prison Fellowship. On this tour of Texas prisons, Colson took an almost paternal pride in his protégé's preaching to the inmates. After the two men shared the morning's heavy schedule of sermons, Colson told a friend: "This Easter is different. The ministry doesn't need me anymore. Mark is so gifted that my heart lifts every time I hear him speak. He can lead Prison Fellowship superbly well long after I'm gone."

For all Mark Earley's leadership abilities, he is the first to say that Colson, the chairman, will be needed at the helm of Prison Fellowship for the foreseeable future. Passing the torch may take years of transition. But the colorful, charismatic founder of the ministry and his quieter heir apparent are a good team. They are branching out together into new fields, such as a teaching ministry for the Centurions (one hundred handpicked Christian leaders) in biblical worldview educational programs. This is a relatively new Colson passion, with the ambitious purpose of changing the culture of secular American society. The mere fact that Colson has started it with such gusto at the age of seventy-two suggests that he has lost little of his appetite for Christian evangelism. His energy and enthusiasm for this big-picture goal is impressive.

So also is his attention to small-print details and the control of them. This aspect of Colson's character was well illuminated by the next episode on his Easter schedule.

In between leaving Mountain View and getting to his next and crucially important Easter Sunday destination, the Carol Vance Unit at Sugar Land, near Houston, there was a glimpse of what might be called Colson the control freak. There are times (and this was one of them) when this cap still fits the hyper-controlling former USMC officer, law partner, and special counsel to the president of the United States for whom glitch-free scheduling and zero-defect command of detail were once daily imperatives.

The schedule for the 220-mile journey between the Mountain View and Sugar Land jails was a tight one. Phase one was a fast drive to Waco airport. Phase two was a 170-mile flight on a Learjet from Waco to Sugar

Land. Phase three was a short trip from Sugar Land airport to the Carol Vance Unit, for one-on-one meetings with major donors and prominent politicians before the Easter service started. Prison Fellowship staffers had gone ahead to be on duty at every juncture of this itinerary, and Colson kept them on their toes with frequent calls from his cell phone.

The first and very minor glitch came when the driver of the van carrying Colson and his five companions took a wrong turn inside the Mountain View prison perimeter, which resulted in an extra circuit of the parking area. This forty-second detour was enough to make Colson decide that he should take over the navigation for the rest of the journey. So he sat up front with a map and directions, calling out mileages and left or right turns to the driver while simultaneously calling up various Prison Fellowship staffers ahead of him on the route to check that every last detail had been attended to.

One detail beyond anyone's control was the weather. Colson's arrival at Waco airport coincided with a thunderstorm. The Learjet pilot said he could take off in it, but he didn't think he could land in it at Sugar Land, because the visibility was even worse there. Colson the meteorological expert now came to the fore. After studying various charts and screens in the weather center at Waco, he decided to take off as soon as possible, heading for either Hobby or Bush International Airport in the Houston area before they too closed down because of visibility problems. Various Prison Fellowship aides waiting in cars at Sugar Land were called and ordered to head for the alternative landing grounds of the chairman's aircraft.

As the Learjet (on loan from a local supporter) bucked and tossed through the stormy skies of Texas en route to its uncertain destination, Colson kept busy on his cell phone asking his men on the ground where exactly they were and issuing them new instructions. Frequent questions and instructions were also issued to the pilot and copilot, who had to keep the door of their cockpit open for this purpose. As Colson was in the backseat of the aircraft, his requests were sometimes hard to hear, so they had to be relayed to the pilots by his close friend and major Prison Fellowship donor Dallen Peterson, who was occupying the seat nearest to the cockpit. The trialogue between Colson, Peterson, and the pilots eventually became a little strained: "Would you mind telling Mr. Colson we're kinda busy up here?" said the captain. That veiled rebuke produced a welcome silence in the passenger cabin until his next announcement: "Hey, there's a gap opening up in the cloud bank and I think we're going to be able to get through it and come down at Sugar Land."

"Sugar Land!" exclaimed Colson, seizing his cell phone to issue coun-
terorders to members of the team on their way to Hobby or Bush. Thanks
to their first round of orders being countermanded, there was no reception
party at Sugar Land. But after a flurry of fresh calls from the chairman, a
local volunteer living near the airport was recruited as his stand-in chauffeur. So the hanging-around time on the ground was minimal, even though
Colson kept looking anxiously at his watch and making more calls throughout it. "Oh well, Chuck gets like that some days," said Dallen Peterson
philosophically.

Colson's anxiety to reach his destination on time was understandable,
for the InnerChange Freedom Initiative at the Carol Vance Unit at Sugar
Land stands out as one of his most interesting and innovative creations in
his role as a criminal justice reformer. In terms of prisoner rehabilitation,
Sugar Land is America's most successful penal institution. Colson got the
idea for it from visiting APAC, a Christian-run prison in Brazil, in the early
1990s. His proposal for repeating the APAC formula in a Texas jail was
supported by Governor George W. Bush and by the head of the state Department of Corrections, Carol S. Vance, in April 1997. The regime at
Sugar Land, known as the InnerChange Freedom Initiative (IFI), which the
jail's 311 inmates—all volunteers but not all Christians—sign up for, is
based on "restorative justice" principles aimed at bringing about behavioral, moral, and spiritual changes in the lives of those doing the course.
Restorative justice is another of Colson's major interests, which he has
championed through the Justice Fellowship arm of Prison Fellowship and
in his book *Justice That Restores*. Every prisoner in the IFI unit at Sugar
Land (and at the other new IFI jails run by Prison Fellowship in Iowa, Minnesota, and Kansas) has to follow the path of repentance, restoration, and
public apology to victims that is described in the gospel story of the corrupt tax collector Zacchaeus. The regime is compulsory, not only while an
inmate is incarcerated but also for another twelve months of post-release
mentoring in the community. There is nothing soft or easy about the program, but every IFI prisoner has volunteered for it and has gone through a
competitive selection process run by PF in cooperation with prison chaplains.

An IFI prisoner's day, which at Colson's insistence starts at 5:30 A.M. (an
hour earlier than for inmates in other Texas jails), consists of life-changing
and life-enhancing skills training. It is also full of Christian devotional activities, such as chapel services, prayer meetings, hymn singing, Alpha Course
sessions, and Bible reading. These features caused the *Wall Street Journal* to

scoff at the IFI unit as a "Bible boot camp" back in 1997. Such cynicism was originally shared by many of the Corrections Department officials who run the security and administration of Sugar Land IFI. However, their skepticism has steadily diminished in light of the unit's results. According to a recent independent study by the University of Pennsylvania, inmates released from this IFI prison over the last seven years have reoffended at the rate of 8 percent. This compares to the 67 percent reoffending rate that prevails across the totality of prisoners released from American jails.

In light of the growing political and media interest in these remarkably low repeat-offending statistics, it was not surprising to find Colson in an upbeat mood on Easter Sunday afternoon as he showed his visitors, including Congressman Tom DeLay, the majority leader in the U.S. House of Representatives, around the facility. "You can argue with faith but you can't argue with the consequences of faith. That eight percent reoffending figure speaks for itself," said Colson. And several of the IFI inmates wanted to speak for themselves. One of them, Jason Edwards, told Colson that a copy of his 1976 autobiography, *Born Again,* was on his bedside table and that he read it every night "because it's been such a great inspiration to my life."

After listening to this and several other testimonies from IFI inmates, Colson swung into inspirational mode himself as he delivered his second Easter sermon of the day.

"The whole world is now watching IFI to see if what is happening here is truly God's work," Colson told the prisoners. "I believe the Lord's hand is upon you. Show your gratitude to him by living for him. Don't you dare let him down when you get out of here! Stay faithful to him, and he, in his great love, will be faithful to you."

The amens and hallelujahs in the men's prison, where two-thirds of the inmates are African-Americans, were just as fervent as they had been in Mountain View women's prison a few hours earlier. But the big difference was the joy on so many of the men's faces and their obvious commitment to the IFI course they were following.

Congressman Tom DeLay was one of several VIPs in the audience who took in the importance and the promise of the IFI experiment. "I have visited many prisons but this one is completely different," said the House majority leader. "It is clean, there are no unpleasant smells, you get lots of smiles, and good feedback from the inmates. Many people in Washington are positive about this place and are impressed by its remarkably low repeat-offending statistics."

DeLay explained that his interest in IFI had been affected by Colson's latest best seller, *How Now Shall We Live?* He added that after reading it, he had invited the author to be the first speaker in a series of talks on Capitol Hill known as the Majority Leader's Lecture Series. Colson's lecture had apparently made a big impact on several members of Congress.

Later in the evening Colson was making a big impact with a speech to a hotel room packed with Houston-based supporters of Prison Fellowship. Many of them work as voluntary mentors to released inmates, helping them to find jobs and new roots as they adjust to the world of freedom in their home communities. Others are donors who produce the $650,000 a year it costs Prison Fellowship to run the IFI course at Sugar Land. Fired with enthusiasm for the success of his project as it reached its seventh anniversary, Colson made an upbeat speech and introduced a number of former inmates who gave a human face to the repeat-offending statistics. They included Robert Sutton, a paroled ex-murderer who had been in the prison when Governor George W. Bush opened it in 1997.

"Last year Robert came with me to a meeting in the Roosevelt Room of the White House," declared Colson. "When I introduced him to President Bush, the president greeted him like an old friend, embraced him in front of the cameras, and congratulated him on becoming a law-abiding citizen, all thanks to IFI."

Three and a half decades before that White House meeting with President Bush, Colson began working there as special counsel to President Richard M. Nixon. Within three years, Colson became second only to Nixon himself as the object of media notoriety and political hatred. He was vilified as one of the most wicked architects of Watergate and loathed for his arrogant, overbearing style of political ruthlessness. His reputation, as much as his actions, led to his indictment in 1973 on Watergate-related criminal charges. After entering a plea of guilty he was imprisoned, disgraced, demoralized, and finished. No one would have predicted that he might one day return to the White House as a regular visitor and confidant of another president. Even more unbelievable would have been the idea that Colson would reemerge in the public life of America as someone famous, only this time for good deeds and moral leadership. His demonization in the 1970s has been replaced by lionization in the 2000s—at least among the nation's 65 million evangelical Christians, who often claim that he has been "anointed by the Lord." That label aside, Colson has lived to see his reputation transformed and his life redeemed. By any standards it is a remarkable turnaround, which his admirers say could have been accomplished only by the hand of God.

Colson's redemption has not gone unquestioned. When he came out of prison in 1975 and published his best-selling autobiography, *Born Again,* his conversion was greeted with far more secular cynicism than applause. Much of that skepticism has receded after twenty-eight years of public ministry accompanied by impeccable financial and personal rectitude. Yet some doubts remain. As recently as two years ago, Henry Kissinger asked this author, "Are you sure Colson is for real?"

Kissinger's question was answered with a confident affirmative based on deeper knowledge than the research for this book. For I have known Colson for over seventeen years and have special personal reasons for being able to make a positive judgment on the authenticity of his post-conversion life and ministry.

The Colson and Aitken paths first crossed in 1988 when I was a young British Member of Parliament. At the time of our meeting I was combining my duties as a backbencher in the House of Commons with writing a biography of President Richard M. Nixon.* Colson was an excellent source for that book, and a good relationship grew between us, subsequently strengthened by visits to each other's homes on both sides of the Atlantic.

Although friendly toward Colson, I did not share his evangelical faith or fervor. Far from being "Born Again," I was merely a nominal member of the church-reticent wing of Anglicanism. Perhaps for that reason our relationship did not deepen much below the level of personal cordiality and political gossip. Colson was interested in my political career, which prospered in the 1990s when I became a defense minister and chief secretary to the Treasury in the cabinet of Prime Minister John Major. During that turbulent era of British politics there was media speculation that I could emerge as a possible leader of the Conservative Party. As a result of coming under intense journalistic scrutiny, I had a spectacular fall from grace. In the course of an ill-judged civil libel action against *The Guardian* newspaper, I was caught telling a lie while giving evidence in court. A press campaign to have me prosecuted for perjury resulted in my indictment on this charge in 1999. I pleaded guilty to it and was sentenced to eighteen months' imprisonment.

Nixon: A Life by Jonathan Aitken (Washington, D.C.: Regnery Publishing, 1993).

On the day that my world fell apart during the libel case, Colson, by co-incidence, was on a visit to London. He witnessed my public humiliation in the headlines and on the television news. Although we had not been in touch with each other for some time, Colson's immediate reaction was to come alongside me as a friend and spiritual counselor.

"I just want you to know that my heart goes out to you, that you're in my prayers, and that I consider myself your friend," began one of his first letters. "Your greatest test will be right now, Jonathan. You can let circumstances shatter you as I saw you quoted in the press or you can decide that adversity will be your greatest blessing . . . As you know, I have looked back on Watergate and thank God for it. Through that crucible I came to know Christ personally and discovered that in the darkest moments of my life He was working to produce what I would later see as the greatest blessings of my life."

These sentiments, and the follow-up actions that accompanied them, were characteristic of Colson. He has a natural empathy with those going through the agony of a breaking experience, and a natural inclination to witness to them in their time of trouble. Around the world there are numerous individuals, unknown and well known, whose wounds have been healed with the help of Colson the Good Samaritan. I am one of them.

Under Colson's guidance, and with the help of a group of prayer partners convened by his closest friend in Britain, Michael Alison, I traveled along a road of pain, penitence, and prison. In the course of these spiritual searchings I eventually made a commitment to a new life in Christ. When I came out of jail in January 2000 I studied at Oxford University for two years, reading Theology at Wycliffe Hall. I have subsequently devoted my life to authorship and prison ministry.

Although there are obvious similarities between the trajectories of my career and Colson's, I shy away from such comparisons because his life of service is so infinitely greater than mine will ever be. However, I recognize that our shared experiences have given me, as an author, some unusual, possibly unique insights into Colson's story. As a result, it is told in the ensuing pages by a kindred spirit—although not by an uncritical one. For there are aspects of Colson's life that were deeply unattractive. As a result, this is a "warts and all" portrait of the man. It is not religious, political, or personal hagiography. It stands or falls as a work of historical biography.

As a result of my biographer's journey through the first seventy-four years of Colson's life, I have come to believe that he is a far more significant figure in the history of twentieth-century America than many contemporaries have realized. In the Epilogue I have attempted to explain why this is so. For Colson's footprints on the sands of time go predictably deep in the spiritual fields where he has worked since his Christian conversion. There he has made an enormous impact on prison ministry, church unity, evangelism, discipleship-teaching, and authorship. Less predictable but no less important is Colson's impact in secular fields such as prison reform, politics, and presidential election campaigns. Few men who influenced the presidency of the United States in the 1960s are still doing so in the 2000s. Yet this is true of Colson. Anyone who expected that his contribution to politics would end when he left the Nixon White House in 1973 would have been surprised by the following two Colson vignettes from the presidential election of 2004.

Three weeks before the two presidential candidates were to debate on television, George W. Bush invited Colson to the White House for a private meeting. In part their encounter was a recognition of Colson's importance in helping Bush build the "moral majority" that was to prove so crucial to the election result. For in recent years Colson has become a confidant to the forty-third president, and to his principal political adviser, Karl Rove, on faith-based issues such as international human rights, the war in Sudan, religious persecution in North Korea, AIDS in Africa, sex trafficking, prison reform, and partial birth abortion.

Important though these issues were to many moral-majority voters in 2004, this particular meeting, held at 1:00 P.M. on September 15 in the Executive Office Building of the White House (by surreal coincidence in the same suite of offices where Colson often talked with Richard Nixon), was more related to politics than to faith.

The president wanted to know how Colson thought the campaign was going. So far so good, was the essence of Colson's reply, as he gave an upbeat assessment of the election from his perspective as a Christian leader, a Florida voter, and an old political pro who, thirty-two years earlier, had played the Karl Rove role in Nixon's reelection.

As the discussion moved to the upcoming debates with John Kerry, Colson offered George W. Bush some prescient advice: "Whatever you do, Mr. President, don't make the mistake that my boss made in 1960. Before his first debate against JFK, Nixon got tired. He made his tiredness worse by campaigning on the morning of that debate. As a result, Nixon looked exhausted. That was why he lost the first debate in the eyes of the television audience. So please, don't overtire yourself, Mr. President."

George W. Bush was politely dismissive of Colson's counsel. Brushing it aside, his response in effect was that tiredness wasn't a problem for him. In reality, however, the forty-third president did allow his campaigning schedule to overtax him. Ignoring Colson's advice, he added to his fatigue on the morning of the first debate against John Kerry by taking time out for a visit to Florida victims of the September hurricanes. The net result was that on the night of the debate Bush came across as tired, tetchy, and more than a touch petulant. Opinion polls declared that he had been outscored by John Kerry. "How we wished that Colson's warning had been listened to by the president," a senior White House aide told this biographer. "From that time on he took Colson's advice and changed his schedule to make sure he rested up properly before the next two debates. That made a big difference."

While his positive contribution to George W. Bush's reelection remained private, Colson also made a public and embarrassingly negative appearance in John Kerry's campaign. This occurred when the Democrats were attempting to discredit Vietnam veteran–turned–author John O'Neill on account of his book, *Unfit for Command*, which had cast doubts on Kerry's military record. In the course of their discrediting efforts, the Democrats discovered that there had been a Colson-O'Neill connection dating back to the 1970s, when Colson had brought O'Neill into the Oval Office to see President Nixon. The purpose of the meeting was for Nixon to enlist O'Neill's support in countering Kerry's antiwar activism. At that time Kerry was a twenty-seven-year-old former navy officer who had become a thorn in the administration's side because of the powerful evidence he had given to a Senate committee regarding Vietnam War atrocities.

Extracts from the 1971 White House tapes, extensively replayed on many radio and TV channels in 2004, showed both Colson and Nixon to have been full of hostility toward the young Kerry:

COLSON This fellow Kerry they had on last week . . .

NIXON Yeah, yeah.

COLSON Hell, he turns out to be really quite a phony.

NIXON Well, he is sort of a phony, isn't he?

COLSON Well, he stayed, when he was here.

NIXON Stayed out in Georgetown.

COLSON You know he's just the complete opportunist.

NIXON A racket, sure.

COLSON We'll keep hitting him, Mr. President.

These reminders of the dark side of Charles Colson in his White House years reignited old flames of controversy around him. He had to take considerable criticism for his past hostility to John Kerry. However, if the full story of the Kerry-Colson relationship had been known, both men might have been seen in rather different light.

More than two decades after Colson had promised to "keep hitting" John Kerry, their paths crossed at the 1993 National Prayer Breakfast in Washington, D.C. Colson was in the audience as a national Christian leader. Kerry was on the platform as a United States senator delivering a homily on the New Testament reading of John 3:1–21—the story of Jesus' meeting with Nicodemus.

Colson was deeply moved by Senator Kerry's remarks on the reading's themes of the search for faith and renewal by the spirit. Returning to his Prison Fellowship office immediately after the prayer breakfast, Colson wrote this letter to his former adversary:

February 5th 1993
Dear Senator Kerry,

Some years ago you and I were on opposite sides. I suspect from your point of view that's the most charitable way it could be put.

But I must tell you, we certainly are not today. In the twenty or so years that I have been attending the National Prayer Breakfast, I have never heard a more articulate, unequivocal presentation of the Gospel than your scripture reading. It was the highlight of this Breakfast—and perhaps of any I have attended.

I suppose we all have to live with our stereotypes; I certainly have. But whatever stereotype I have of you is totally changed.

I write this letter asking your forgiveness for any ways in which I hurt you in the past; and to express great joy over your Christian conviction and the courage with which you expressed it to the National Prayer Breakfast.

I hope our paths will cross under what I suspect now will be very happy circumstances. God bless you.

Yours in His service,
Charles W. Colson

Suprisingly, Colson's letter received no reply from John Kerry. However, several weeks later Colson was contacted by a political reporter from the *Boston Globe*. The reporter said he had been told by Senator Kerry that

Colson had "apologized" to him. Could Colson please comment on his apology? The reporter made it clear that the story had been given to him with a hostile political spin by the Massachussetts senator. Colson turned the other cheek, staying silent about the true contents and context of his letter.

Whatever this episode may say about John Kerry, taken as a whole it reveals far more about Charles Colson. The unattractive stereotype of the president's hatchet man is preserved for all to hear on the 1971 White House tapes. Yet Colson's 1993 letter to Kerry is transparently sincere in its sentiments. Who can doubt that the tough, hardball-playing, "We'll keep hitting him, Mr. President" Colson of his White House years, and the gentle, forgiveness-seeking Colson of his Prison Fellowship years, are figures who have traveled from two opposite poles of the spiritual compass?

This polarization is intriguing. Few figures in contemporary society have in their lives stirred up greater passions—negative and positive, secular and spiritual. Even though he has now become America's best-known Christian leader after Billy Graham, people still ask: "Who is the real Charles Colson, and what is the full story of his life before and after his conversion?"

This biography hopes to provide the answers.

CHAPTER ONE

An Unsettled Upbringing

Parents and Childhood

In the beginning was the energy, a life force so enthusiastic that everyone noticed him as a boy with leadership qualities, who never did things by halves, and who rarely knew when to stop. Whether it was collecting nickels and dimes for the war effort, selling ads for the school magazine, or playing practical jokes on his friends, he had exceptional drive that combined zeal, ingenuity, and humor. Yet the *levitas* in his nature was balanced by a *gravitas* shown in the self-discipline he applied to achieving the academic goals of his schoolboy years. So even in his earliest days there were intriguingly polarized characteristics in the young Charles Colson. It did not need an expert in genetics to deduce that they flowed from his radically different parents.

No mother could have had a more appropriate nickname than Dizzy Colson. The nineteenth-century British prime minister Benjamin Disraeli, who acquired the same sobriquet, coined a phrase to describe his parliamentary opponent William Gladstone: "Inebriated by the exuberance of his own verbosity." It was a cap that would have fit well on Inez Ducrow Colson. For Dizzy Colson was a twentieth-century American eccentric who never stopped talking, showing off, spending money, or striking attitudes that she hoped would shock her friends and relatives. Colorful anecdotes of Dizzy abound throughout the story of her son's life.

When Dizzy made her first visit to the White House in 1969 to see Charlie, as she always called her son, in his office as special counsel to the president, she was unusually dressed for the occasion. She wore a light overcoat, but beneath it she was clad in nothing more than her underwear and a slip. When she explained to a startled cousin how she justified this bizarre ensemble, Dizzy declared: "But no one ever lets you take off your topcoat in the White House!" History does not record whether Mrs. Colson ever tested her theory of the disrobing customs at 1600 Pennsylvania Avenue in the Nixon years or whether she simply invented the story to shock her straitlaced relative. The latter seems more likely since Dizzy was not given to understatement either in dress or in words.

One post–White House occasion when Dizzy might have found it difficult to overstate her own role in the proceedings was the Washington movie premiere of the film of her son's best-selling autobiography, *Born Again*. Surrounded by Hollywood stars, Beltway celebrities, the sister of the president of the United States, and a theater full of heavyweight figures from the worlds of politics, journalism, and religion, most mothers might have been content to bask in reflected glory from a backseat. Not Dizzy. Although she was under strict instructions not to talk to the press and had even been assigned a minder to ensure her silence, Inez Ducrow Colson was not one to hide her light under a bushel. She escaped from her minder, Mrs. Beth Loux, by slipping into a stall in the ladies' rest room and slipping out again underneath one of the partitions separating the toilets. By the time Mrs. Loux had discovered that her charge had bolted even though her toilet door was still closed, Dizzy was in full flow, giving an interview to the style correspondent of the *Washington Post*. The main feature of the interview was Mrs. Colson's ethically incorrect opinion of her son's role in Watergate and of his efforts to blacken the character of Daniel Ellsberg. "I'm proud of what Chuck tried to do to that communist Ellsberg. . . . I wish *he* would get up and say, 'I'm proud.' . . . I never want to hear Chuck saying, 'I'm sorry,'" she declared. Apparently oblivious to the new Colson message of Christian contrition and change, Dizzy professed to be mystified by the book's title. "I born him first. I had him baptized as a baby. I don't understand this 'Born Again' business," she told reporters.

It was not the first or last time that Charles Colson found himself at loggerheads with his mother. "The problem was that he and Dizzy banged smack into the middle of each other's energy fields," was how one member of the family summarized their turbulent relationship. The collisions between filial chalk and maternal cheese sometimes had awkward consequences. With the looks of a Bette Davis and the effervescence of a Goldie Hawn, Dizzy had a flamboyance in her character that was the antithesis of her son's self-discipline. Immensely attractive in her expansive personality, she combined generosity of spirit toward underdogs with financial recklessness about overdrafts. One of her many iron whims was a determination to be on the move. This included house moves, for in the 1930s and 1940s the Colsons had at least fifteen different addresses in the Boston area, a velocity of change that caused young Charlie to attend eight schools before reaching the age of twelve.

Some of this switching of abodes may have been due to Dizzy's peripatetic restlessness of spirit, but the more fundamental cause was the constant fluctuation of the family finances. These cash flow problems were usually caused by Dizzy's chronic overspending on clothes, flowers, furniture, and household decorations—of which only the very best would do. Some of Charles Colson's most painful childhood memories concerned the aftereffects of his mother's extravagance, when forced sales of the family furniture were required because her bills had mounted too high. The shock of coming home from school and finding complete strangers carrying chairs out of the living room left its scars on the adolescent Colson. The anxieties created by the debt crises and rent shortfalls of his youth resulted in a careful frugality with money in his adult life.

Visits from debt collectors were not the only insecurities to trouble young Charlie. Another perplexity was his mother's sense of humor. Extraordinary though it sounds, Dizzy enjoyed pretending that her son was not her son at all. With a straight face she would tell her friends that she had really given birth to a daughter, who had been accidentally swapped by a maternity nurse in the hospital for the boy baby she now had to bring up. So elaborate were the details of this fantasy that some people actually believed it. Although Charlie himself was not among the believers, he was understandably unsettled by the frequency with which his mother repeated and varied the story in ways that could only have been hurtful to a young boy. As he recalled it: "This was my mother's favorite gag. Of course, I knew she was saying it half in humor, but it always left me feeling uncomfortable. Even to me she would say, 'I never wanted a boy. I really wanted a little girl and I had one.' Then she'd go on and explain how in the next room in the hospital there'd been a Mrs. Peterson who'd had a girl and that the hospital had mixed up the babies. 'So you really belong to Mrs. Peterson and her little girl is really my daughter,' she used to say."

A modern child psychologist might make interesting observations on the wisdom of these maternal jests, particularly since their negative impact was compounded by Dizzy's reluctance to express the love and pride she inwardly felt for her Charlie. These failings corrected themselves when she spoke of him with loving admiration to other people. Yet the direct lines of communication between mother and son were curiously flawed, as the latter recalls: "My mother would never say to me, 'I am really proud of you and what you're doing.' She never said, 'You're wonderful,' or, 'I love you.' I can't ever recall my mother saying things like that to me . . . she never really understood me or my work . . . we just never clicked."

Fortunately for the young Charles Colson, he clicked happily with his other parent, his father, Wendell Ball Colson, with whom he had a good rapport and many similarities of both character and appearance.

The Colsons came from Scandinavian stock. Wendell's father arrived in America in the 1870s as an immigrant from Sweden. He became a successful musician, celebrated for his cornet solos with the Boston Symphony Orchestra, but his life and career were ended by a virulent flu epidemic in 1919. Wendell was seventeen at the time of his father's death and he dropped out of high school in order to support his widowed mother. Throughout his remaining teens and twenties, Wendell worked as a bookkeeper for a Boston meatpacking plant, earning around $32 a week. However, he was determined to better himself, for he spent his evenings studying at night school until, after twelve years, he achieved professional qualifications in law and accountancy.

In the middle of these exertions Wendell met the colorful Inez, or Dizzy, Ducrow, a beautiful twenty-one-year-old Bostonian whose penchant for fantasy extended to the claim that she was descended from the British aristocracy. The British part was true. Her parents emigrated from Birmingham, England, in about 1900 and never relinquished their U.K. citizenship, even though they resided in the United States for over forty years. Aristocratic lineage would have been harder to establish, for Dizzy's father was a silversmith, a trade that in nineteenth-century Britain was not usually associated with the nobility and gentry unless they were its customers.

The marriage of Wendell Colson and Inez Ducrow at Saint Andrew's Episcopal Church, Orient Heights, in 1926, seems to have been inspired by that random arrow of Cupid known as "the attraction of opposites." In temperament and behavior, the bride and groom were poles apart, but perhaps Dizzy's intuition told her that she needed the qualities of stolidity and stability in a husband. Although Wendell must occasionally have wondered whether his down-to-earth normality was equal to the task of keeping his exotic wife rooted in reality, their forty-eight-year marriage was a happy one. Despite those creative fictions about the mix-up with Mrs. Peterson's daughter in the maternity ward, one of the most joyful moments of the marriage must surely have been the birth of their only child, Charles Wendell Colson, on October 16, 1931. To be born during the years of the Depression in one of North Boston's poorer residential districts meant growing up in an environment tinged by economic hardship and food shortages. Although the Colsons never went hungry, because Wendell held down a steady job in the food industry throughout the Depression, many of their neighbors were not so fortunate. One of Charlie's earliest memories was of his mother cooking subsistence meals for people down the street who had nothing to eat, and of giving away her best coats to unemployed women who were cold in winter.

Wartime memories also loomed large in the Colson boyhood. He was ten years old when Pearl Harbor was attacked, and he remembers how fear stalked the streets of Boston in 1942–43 over expected Japanese or German bombing raids and submarine attacks. His father was appointed an air raid warden with the duty of going out on night patrol to check that everyone in the neighborhood had put blackout curtains over their windows so that enemy pilots could not see any lights on the ground. Charlie himself contributed to the war effort at the age of eleven, when he organized a schoolboy house-to-house collection to buy a jeep for the U.S. Army. As the leader of this fund-raising campaign, Charlie sold his model aircraft collection to swell the coffers, and was chosen to hand over the check to an army officer—an event recorded for posterity by a photograph published in the *Boston Globe.*

Also recorded for posterity was an early example of Colson's talent for public speaking and fund-raising. In the course of the campaign for collecting donations to the jeep fund, Charlie addressed his fellow sixth-grade classmates with a speech whose pencil-written text has survived in his family archives. "What I am about to say I want to be assured as a plea not as an offer," began the eleven-year-old orator. "There will be no reward for your donations and work, nothing but the satisfaction of knowing that you are helping our boys. . . .

"The war now rests on the shoulders of the American people. If the people of the conquered countries had another chance they would gladly give their money, their homes, yes, even their lives. We, the people of the United States, are the avenging sword of freedom destined to liberate the impressed [*sic*] world. This can be our destiny if we give this cause our fullest cooperation."

Although a little flamboyant for an audience of ten- and eleven-year-old schoolboys, Colson's first speech displayed some early promise of political leadership. It also revealed some early skills in the art of news management, since a version of the text appeared in the *Boston Herald*. Even to have attempted such an address while in sixth grade suggests a certain precociousness. This may have stemmed from the self-assurance that came from his overprotected home life as an only child. The privations of the Depression followed by the uncertainties and food rationing of the war were the ostensible reasons why Dizzy did not have any more babies. Her decision may also have been influenced by the exceptional pain she suffered in childbirth from her son's high forceps delivery. Like many an offspring without siblings, Charlie was cosseted by his parents. Yet his mother's cosseting seemed negative because she was excessively critical and overbearing in her maternal attentions. By contrast, his father was a more positive source of support and encouragement. Described by a contemporary as "the straightest of straight arrows . . . a lovable, kind old bear of a man with a wonderfully calm and easygoing tolerance which he sure needed to cope with Diz," Wendell was the rock on which his son's character was built. For Chuck, as his father preferred to call him, absorbed his core values from his dad and regarded him as a role model of diligence, dedication to the job, and patriotic duty.

In spite of the paternal emphasis on these values, Chuck grew up with a well-tuned appreciation of the absurd. Both his parents had a keen sense of humor, especially Wendell, who loved playing practical jokes within the family. This was a peculiarity that Chuck inherited. His boyhood was packed with slapstick episodes, such as letting off stink bombs in movie theaters, pulling away the legs of the hall table in a country club in order to leave a hapless cousin holding an unsupported surface laden with silverware, and hiding snowballs in the caps of train drivers. This humorous activity went deeper than the syndrome of "Boys will be boys," for as later chapters will show, Chuck's penchant for juvenile capers lasted long into adulthood. The child that was father to the man had a strong streak of comic, as well as serious, energy within him.

Perhaps the most serious legacy of his childhood was a reverence for academic achievement. Chuck was deeply impressed, when he was eight years old, at going to watch his father receive his degree from Northeastern Law School, formally dressed in gown and mortarboard. That graduation ceremony, and the long hours at night school he knew had preceded it, imprinted on Chuck a highly developed sense of the importance of education.

Browne & Nichols

That priority was reinforced by his parents' willingness to make financial sacrifices to give their son the best possible start in life. Chuck's earliest education had taken place in a swift succession of seven public elementary schools in various neighborhoods where the Colsons were renting a house. When he was eleven, his parents opted for scholarship and stability by moving him to a well-known private day school in Cambridge, Massachusetts—Browne & Nichols. Originally established to educate the male children of Harvard faculty members, B&N (as it was known) was not in the same crème de la crème social class of such New England private schools as Andover, Exeter, and Groton. However, the broader social backgrounds of its pupils and the intellectual families from which many of them came made B&N an outstanding academic school. It was expensive too. Its fees of approximately $600 per term put a strain on the Colson family finances, but it was Dizzy who pushed hardest for it on the grounds that only the best was good enough for her Charlie.

Arriving at Browne & Nichols in September 1942, Colson was soon recognized as a clever and hardworking schoolboy. Recording an IQ of 159, he came top, or almost top, of his classes in Latin, French, History, and English. One early indication of his skills as a writer came when he was set an essay assignment requiring the description of an unusual house. At that time, the Colsons had temporarily moved into a renovated barn with a high roof whose eaves were populated with bats. Chuck and his father embarked on a joint exercise that combined essay composition with bat extermination.

"What my dad and I did was turn the roof lights out, position ourselves in the rafters and then, when the bats started flying, we would open fire on them with .22 scattershot guns," recalled Colson. "We hit plenty of bats but some of them fell through the beams down to the rooms on the ground floor where we had guests staying. They were very surprised to be bombed by dead bats! Then my grandfather climbed up to the roof to find out what was happening and we mistook his noise for more bats so we almost shot him too. The whole story made a very humorous essay. When I handed it in to my professor, he gave me an A, and I remember him being very complimentary about it and saying, 'Colson, you really should become a writer.' "

Although Colson did not turn his hand until he was in prison thirty years later to the writing that was to produce twenty-three books in eleven languages with worldwide sales of over 10 million copies, he did exercise his abilities on schoolboy journalism. When he was in tenth grade, he unsuccessfully applied for a post on the editorial team of the Browne & Nichols newspaper, the *Spectator.* His response to this rejection was to launch a rival publication, the *Spec,* with the help of a fellow pupil, Jonathan Moore. The *Spec* was regarded as being so much livelier than its established competitor that in the spirit of "We'd better let them join us before they beat us," Moore and Colson were offered posts on the *Spectator's* editorial team after all. The offer was accepted and swiftly resulted in a reverse takeover, for in no time Chuck Colson became editor in chief of the *Spectator,* with Moore his deputy. Jonathan Moore was Colson's best friend at Browne & Nichols. In some ways they were an odd couple. Moore described himself as "a skinny little kid with a bad eye problem, rather shy and confused by my many hang-ups. I was in awe of Colson at first because he was a year older than me. I saw him as a natural leader, bursting with drive and confidence. In retrospect, I think he may have gone out of his way to be generous in his friendship to me because I was such an obvious underdog."

Colson was an obvious overdog. Photographs of him at the age of sixteen give the impression of a rather pretentious, self-satisfied youth whose chubby features protruding over his stylish collar and bow tie make him look like a cat who has recently consumed several dishes of cream. There were many reasons why his contemporaries, like Moore, felt somewhat overwhelmed by him. One was his car, a British Morris Minor given to him by Wendell and Dizzy. Colson equipped it with an accessory that suited his persona—a truck bullhorn. Moore recalls scenes of Colson's progress down Boston's Memorial Drive going west toward Route 2. With a blast or two on the bullhorn he would make the traffic ahead of him divide like the Red Sea before Moses. Then he would shoot through the empty middle lane, leaving behind him a trail of irate motorists realizing they had given way not to some gigantic juggernaut towing a trailer, but to a diminutive Morris Minor with a schoolboy laughing at them from behind the wheel.

Laughter was a big ingredient in the life of the teenage Colson. He was a life enhancer, forever having fun, playing jokes, and being the life and soul of every available party. Yet he had a caring side to him too. An incident recalled by several of his classmates involved a highly charged scene when the school's English teacher, Mr. Paul Marsh, accused one of his pupils of cheating in an essay. The charge was plagiarism and the evidence pointed clearly to the boy's guilt. However, before painful disciplinary measures could be applied to the plagiarist, Colson rushed to his defense. In the manner of an impassioned courtroom attorney pleading with the jury for a not guilty verdict, Colson produced a plethora of possible excuses and explanations for the malefactor's behavior. The arguments in his plea suggested that the boy had subliminally absorbed the plagiarized passages many years earlier; that he had retained them in his memory from a radio broadcast; or that he had innocently believed that copying another writer's work was an acceptable essay writing technique. So popular with the class were these creative defenses that the plagiarist escaped with a warning. It would not be the last time that Colson argued with eloquence for leniency on behalf of an underdog in trouble.

Although he was only an average athlete and football player, Colson made himself a force to be reckoned with at Browne & Nichols by displaying a talent for business and journalism. His power base was the *Spectator.* Although some contemporaries, with the wisdom of hindsight, later came to see his teenage seizure of school media power as an early example of the dirty tricks for which he became notorious in the Nixon administration, at the time Colson breathed new life into the moribund and money-losing newspaper.

"Colson made it a testy, zesty, much-talked-about paper," recalled his deputy, Jonathan Moore, "and he turned it around by sheer obsessive hard work. He was a control freak, who could lose his temper, and he quite often did, but he also did a lot of storming around in gales of laughter. If you were on his team you felt the warmth of his inclusiveness."

In 1947–48, the *Spectator* won the Columbia Journalism Awards' interschool gold medal for best school magazine of the year. His track record as an editor was an early example of Chuck Colson's drive, energy, and can-do spirit, but it also revealed one of his less attractive characteristics—arrogance.

Toward the end of Colson's reign at the *Spectator,* the paper had built up a considerable cash surplus, largely on account of the editor's ability to sell advertising space to school contractors. Pre-Colson, the magazine's highest-ever advertising revenues had been around $500. In 1947–48, those revenues tripled, to over $1,500. Colson had proprietary ideas on how the surplus he had created should be spent. He produced ambitious plans for a bigger and better paper. Unfortunately, the teacher at Browne & Nichols responsible for school publications, Mr. Woodhead, was more cautious, which led to a clash of wills between the two. Unable to accept that his plans for expansion were being vetoed, Colson lost his temper dur-

ing an angry exchange of words with Mr. Woodhead and hurled a book at
him. The editor in chief was immediately marched down to the principal's
office and suspended from school for two days. Despite this punishment,
the incident inflated rather than deflated Colson's ego, for his classmates
threatened to go on strike in sympathy with the suspended martyr, and he
returned to school with a hero's welcome.

A similar sense of bumptious invincibility characterized Colson's most
successful activity at Browne & Nichols—debating. Thanks to coaching
from his father and encouragement from the teacher in charge of debating,
William Thomas, Colson won a place on the debate team at the age of fourteen. Two years later he was the team's captain and its prizewinning star,
regularly carrying off interstate and interschool championship awards. One
of the key ingredients behind those triumphs was Colson's self-confidence.
The Browne & Nichols 1949 yearbook recorded the debate team's triumphs with this tongue-in-cheek comment on its captain: "Chuck's success
as a debater is due to the fact that he feels anyone who disagrees with him
is insane."

Rejecting Harvard

The adjective "insane" may also have been used by several early Colson admirers, including his mother, his teachers, and the dean of Harvard, to describe the most surprising decision of his schoolboy years—the rejection of
a Harvard scholarship. There was, however, method in his apparent madness.

Browne & Nichols, located in Cambridge, Massachusetts, only a few
hundred yards from the campus of Harvard, thought of itself as a prepara-
tory school for its revered university neighbor. So in the eyes of the school
and of his doting parents, Colson's success in winning a scholarship to Harvard was the zenith of academic achievement. Chuck himself had other
ideas. For at the same time as applying to Harvard, he had applied for, and
won, a Naval ROTC scholarship to Brown University.

As he weighed the pros and cons of the two scholarships, Colson felt increasingly attracted to Brown. He had some good friends there. He liked
the feel of the smaller but still prestigious Ivy League atmosphere of
Brown. More significantly, the NROTC scholarship would pay for his full
board and tuition, whereas the Harvard scholarship paid only tuition fees.
These economic advantages of Brown were important at a time when the

Colson finances looked fragile, for Wendell had lost his job as vice president of General Seafoods and was struggling to make the grade as a Boston lawyer. Even more important was Colson's urge to escape from the narrow confines of Cambridge, where he had been based in home and in school for nearly ten years. The short walk up the road to Harvard seemed far less exciting than the forty-mile drive to Providence, Rhode Island, where Brown, the seventh-oldest university in the United States (founded 1764), was located.

In addition to all these substantive arguments and counterarguments, which Colson carefully annotated on yellow legal pad paper (a habit that stayed with him, whenever he made important decisions, for the rest of his life), there was the wild card ingredient of loving to surprise. Perhaps it was another characteristic inherited from his mother, but this time Dizzy was on the receiving end of a stage-managed shock. "It was my mother's dream that I should go to Harvard," recalls Colson, "partly because of the education there, of course, but also because it would make her so happy socially to be able to talk to her friends about her son at Harvard. So I must admit I enjoyed giving her the news that I was not going there. She really was shocked. She raged at me in that temper of hers. But my mind was made up."

Colson's next shock was delivered to the dean of admissions at Harvard, who, in June of 1949, interviewed him in the administration building overlooking Harvard Yard. Surrounded by university memorabilia and seated behind an elegant old colonial desk, the dean delivered his good tidings of great joy. "I am very happy to inform you, Mr. Colson—you are a fortunate young man—that the Board of Overseers has granted you a full scholarship to Harvard University."

The dean paused, expecting Colson to respond with elated acceptance. Instead, savoring the dean's aghast expression, Colson replied: "But I haven't really decided, Dean, whether I will be coming to Harvard."

"I can't imagine anyone turning down a scholarship to Harvard," responded the irritated dean, his temper worsening as Colson explained he had opted for Brown, a university traditionally regarded as a poor Ivy League cousin by Harvard men.

In his autobiography, *Born Again,* Colson portrayed this Harvard episode as an audacious act of rebellion against the values of Bostonian elitism and Eastern intellectualism. In fact there were more personal reasons of choice and economic self-interest governing his preference for Brown. Nevertheless, it was true that the young Charles Colson had an interesting chip on his shoulder, which seems to have been created by a combination of social insecurity and social compassion. The insecurity came partly from the ups and downs of the relationship with his mother, and partly from being a "Swamp Yankee." This was a label given to the poorer white Protestants of old Boston, who had never been accepted by the upwardly mobile denizens of the Harvard and Brahmin establishments living in the smart residential districts in and around Beacon Hill. Instead, this lower strata of society, which included the Colsons, had been left behind to jostle "in the swamp" of the old city alongside the Italians, the Irish, the Jews, the Slavs, and other ethnic groups. Chuck Colson's resentment at his family's rejection by the elite was greater than his enthusiasm for joining it. Climbing sideways and forward to middle-class Brown, in preference to soaring onward and upward to upper-class Harvard, was a small gesture of protest by an independent-minded schoolboy already forming his own agenda.

That agenda included an early interest in social justice, probably absorbed from his parents' charitable activities. For not only did Colson see his mother doing her cooking for the hungry in the Depression; more interestingly, in view of subsequent events, he also observed his father righting wrongs for prisoners. Wendell Colson did a great deal of pro bono legal work on behalf of Massachusetts prisoners with wrongful-conviction appeals. He was a regular prison visitor, and he organized debating teams in prisons for competition. These initiatives were carried out under the auspices of the United Prison Association of New England.

The remarkable father-and-son parallelism in their concern for prisoners was not appreciated by Charles Colson until he was going through Wendell's papers after his death and saw how much time his father had devoted to this cause. Wendell's compassion for prisoners flowed from his Christian ethics, which he instilled into his son's upbringing. Yet although the Colson family followed these ethics, none of them were Christian believers. Surprisingly, Dizzy sometimes said to her teenage son, "You ought to be a minister." This may have been a mysterious intuition, but at the time her motives for making the suggestion were social rather than religious. Mrs. Colson was proud of being a member of the Episcopal Church and even prouder of her acquaintance with its diocesan bishop, Bishop Fisk, who she thought would be a splendid role model for her Charlie. However, she had no believing relationship in Christ, and neither did her husband or her son. None of them ever read the Bible (which Dizzy insisted had been carved, word by word, on tablets of stone), and their extremely rare visits to church were purely nominal. So religious belief had no part to play in the early upbringing of Charles Colson.

As he left Browne & Nichols to spread his wings as a college student, the eighteen-year-old Charles Colson was the supreme self-believer, buoyed up by his own cleverness, brashness, self-confidence, and pride. These were the youthful characteristics that powered him forward to the new worlds he hoped to conquer: Brown University, the U.S. Marine Corps, and a girl named Nancy Billings.

CHAPTER TWO

Student Days

Frat Life and Love Life

"Conceited, overweight, and rather forward with his questions," was the immediate impression Nancy Billings had of her future husband, Charles Colson, when they met for the first time. They were both seventeen-year-old high school seniors attending a Christmas dinner dance (tickets, $3.50) at the Concord Country Club near Acton, Massachusetts, on December 18, 1948. Nancy's negative feelings toward her dancing partner did not last long, for thirty-six months later they were engaged to be married.

The Billings family was a cut or two above the Colsons in social and economic status. Nancy did her best to disguise this at the Concord party when Chuck made his opening conversational gambit. "What does your father do for a living?" he asked.

"He's a chemist," replied Nancy, piqued by the temerity of such an inquiry from a young man she had met only a few moments earlier. Her answer was an understatement because her father, Howard Billings, was no ordinary chemist but executive vice president and treasurer of the large Boston medical research corporation Arthur D. Little.

"My dad is a lawyer on State Street," continued Chuck. By implication this was an overstatement of his father's standing in the Massachusetts legal profession, for Boston's State Street, the prime office location for many a famous international law firm, was not Wendell Colson's normal milieu of practice.

Other tensions arising from the differences in the two families' backgrounds continued to arise. At first, Mr. and Mrs. Billings did not allow their daughter to accept Chuck's pressing invitation to a New Year's Eve party and other early offers of dates. However, Nancy was allowed to attend the Browne & Nichols production of Gilbert and Sullivan's *Iolanthe* on March 18, 1949. Soon afterward, she was invited for dinner at the Colson home, which amazed her by its showy opulence. "I was a little country girl who grew up in a small town, in an old house full of antique furniture. Everyone I knew lived in homes like that. So I was astonished by the home Chuck's parents live in," she has recalled. "It was fabulously modern. You walked in the front door and it was like one big, enormous fishbowl of a room, with plate glass windows all around it, and those windows were all ablaze with color from over a hundred red geraniums in full bloom. I had never seen anything like it in my life! I thought the Colsons must be extremely rich to live in such a house. It all came as quite a shock."

Another shock came when Nancy was introduced to Chuck's enthusiasm for practical jokes. The couple was dating regularly throughout the summer of 1949 and Chuck was invited to Nancy's eighteenth birthday party. As the family sat down at the table, a beautifully iced cake was produced. Chuck put on an act of wrinkling his nose and suggesting that the birthday girl should take a good sniff of the icing to make sure it was OK. As an obedient but puzzled Nancy lowered her nose toward the cake, Chuck suddenly pushed her face deep into its cream-and-marzipan coating, laughing uproariously. Mrs. Billings was not amused by this slapstick humor at the expense of her daughter and her confectionery, but Chuck laughed on. It says much for Nancy's growing feelings for her admirer that she laughed too, though later she commented, "This was not exactly my idea of intimacy."

The summer of 1949 was an idyllic time in the lives of the young dating couple. Television was the revolutionary news medium that glued them to the small screen for much of their courtship. The Colsons did not yet own a TV set, so Chuck spent long hours in the more affluent Billings family living room, mesmerized by flickering black-and-white images of newscasts from Ed Murrow or live broadcasts of Senator Joe McCarthy's hearings on alleged communist penetration of the U.S. Army. Nancy preferred entertainment programs like Ed Sullivan's *The Toast of the Town*. They were both captivated by the epic baseball pennant race of '49, starring giants like Joe DiMaggio and Ted Williams. Away from the Billings' RCA Victor television (price, $375), the couple enjoyed playing LP records, going to drive-ins to see movies like *A Streetcar Named Desire*, starring Marlon Brando, and eating hamburgers at a new chain restaurant called McDonald's. Like many young people of the postwar period, they were neat and formal in their appearance. Nancy was a typical bobby-soxer with a perm that created short, elfin curls around her ears. Chuck was a noticeably natty dresser, his slightly overweight physique tidily turned out in a blue blazer, gray flannel trousers, a button-down Brooks Brothers shirt, and white shoes. He looked the part of the college boy he was about to become.

In September 1949, Colson began his freshman year at Brown University. Arriving on campus in his navy blue high school graduation suit, at first he was awed by Brown's venerable surroundings of Corinthian columns, Latin inscriptions, flagstone quadrangles, and statues of Roman emperors. But it did not take him long to throw off his feelings of shyness and to throw himself into the new excitements of college life with tremendous zest. However, in his early months, he directed most of his energies to extracurricular activities rather than to academic work. As a result, for the first time in his educational endeavors, Colson became a bad student; so bad that he was at the bottom of his class and suffered the indignity of being put on academic probation.

The principal diversion from his studies was fraternity house life. Within weeks of his arrival on campus, Colson was talent spotted by the Beta Theta Pi fraternity, whose rushing (recruiting) chairman was twenty-two-year-old Bill Maloney—later to become a general in the U.S. Marine Corps. Maloney saw in Colson a kindred spirit who would be a full-blooded participant in the "joyful enthusiasm" that was said to be the keynote of brotherly life at Beta Theta Pi. There were seventeen fraternities on the Brown campus, each with forty to fifty students living and eating together in their houses and adjacent dormitories. If the members of Beta Theta Pi had any characteristics in common, besides joy and enthusiasm, they might have included love of parties, love of country, a shared conservatism in their political views, their social attitudes, and their dress code, and a driving ambition to succeed in adult life.

"As soon as Chuck arrived on campus, we liked the cut of his jib," said Bob Torok, a key player in the rushing process and a later Colson roommate. "He was a natural fit for us, particularly at a time when we were trying to upgrade the image of Beta Theta Pi. He was a man's man: quick, well-dressed, imaginative, patriotic, and full of outgoing energy." Bill Maloney took a similar view of the new recruit, who was initiated into the fraternity on October 19, 1949. "As a freshman Chuck could make you tired just by watching him," he recalls. "He was superbright but not a springbutt. If you'd asked me back in those days who I thought was the most likely to succeed among my college contemporaries, without a doubt Chuck would have been top of my list."

The qualities that make a fraternity brother admired by his peers are not necessarily the qualities that lead to success in the wider world, and there were certain characteristics in the young Colson that might have been seen as warning lights for his future. He could be insensitive about knowing when to stop or pull back when his over-the-top excesses went too far. An unfortunate incident in this vein was the hazing of "Chocolate Drop." Thirty years later it had serious legal repercussions for Colson in the aftermath of Watergate.

"Chocolate Drop" was an eighteen-year-old African-American student, Theodore R. Newman, from Washington, D.C., who arrived at Brown as a freshman in 1951. By this time Colson was a junior, leading the charge on one of the stranger rituals of college life—hazing. Newman had the physical peculiarity of being wider at his hips than in any other part of his body. Colson found this amusing and made Newman's pear-shaped posterior a butt for jokes and then a butt for beating. "He was a sweet young man but I'm afraid I hazed him mercilessly, nicknaming him 'Chocolate Drop' because his shape reminded me of one," he has recalled.

Nearly three decades later Colson, by then a convicted Watergate defendant and ex-prisoner, was required to attend a hearing in the Court of Appeals in the District of Columbia, to decide the question of whether or not he should be disbarred from practicing law. His legal team was optimistic because the D.C. Bar Association had already voted not to disbar him. As soon as the judges hearing the case took their seats on the bench, Colson whispered to his lawyers, "Forget it, we're going to lose. The chief justice is 'Chocolate Drop'—the kid I hazed at Brown University." True to this prediction, the court, led by Chief Justice Newman, duly overturned the bar association's ruling and disbarred Colson.

Back at Brown in the 1950s, the good life at Beta Theta Pi was untroubled by any thoughts about future reversals of fortune. "It was almost like Camelot. We lived from weekend party to weekend party," recalled Bob Torok. "It was the age when men didn't swear in front of women, when we wore blazers, shirts, and ties in the evening, and when we honored all the great values. Just about the only things that went on happened when someone had too many beers or the practical jokes got a little out of control."

Another fraternity brother, Tom Glidden, who later became Colson's roommate, took a slightly harsher view of their community lifestyle. "It

was a pretty shallow existence," he recalled. "Ours was a somewhat snob-
bish fraternity. We were middle-class boys trying to ape Ivy League elitism.
If you didn't wear the right Ivy League clothes and the right kind of tie,
Beta Theta Pi didn't want to know you. We were primarily a party house.
Going to school in the week was something that had to be endured. What
we lived for were the weekends. What did we do on the weekends? We
joked and we drank. Chuck Colson, I would say, was the biggest rascal of
us all."

About the only rascally trouble Colson got himself into in his fraternity-
centered world occurred when he was fined for "dirty rushing" in his senior year. The problem was that Colson, who had been made rushing
chairman for Beta Theta Pi, became a little too imaginative in his efforts to
recruit the finest freshmen for his fraternity house. So he broke the rules
that prohibited taking potential candidates off campus to the fleshpots of
New York for party weekends in the early weeks of their first semester. He
also invented challenges for new recruits that were a step or two outside
the boundaries of acceptable Ivy League taste. One such challenge, imposed on the shyest of freshmen, required him to obtain the imprint of a
breast in a custard pie from a student at Simmons College, a straitlaced establishment for the education of the well-bred young ladies of Massachusetts. Under Colson's orders, the custard pie imprint of a bosom (modestly
encased in the unmistakable contours of a brassiere) was acquired and
brought back in triumph to the cheering brothers of Beta Theta Pi.

This was not an isolated example of these young men's enthusiasm for
pranks connected with ladies' underwear. Nancy remembers feeling "horribly embarrassed" when, on a visit to the Beta house, she discovered that
her bra had been purloined from her suitcase, signed in red ink by every
member of the fraternity except Chuck, and then hauled up the house flag-
pole to be flown like a captured set of colors. No wonder she disliked what
she in retrospect described as "the shady side of frat life—the drinking and
playing of jokes that could be crude or hurtful to people."

However, at the time, Nancy, like Brer Rabbit, lay low and said nothing.
It was a self-effacement that worried some of her contemporaries. "Nancy
was the sweetest and prettiest of gals but if she had a fault it was that she
was too passive, too accepting, too tolerant," said one Colson roommate.
"We worried sometimes that nothing that Chuck could do or say ever
seemed to rouse anger in her." A little blindness in love is understandable,
particularly since Chuck was constantly demonstrating higher romantic
qualities when away from the temptations of cakes and custard pies.

Throughout his student days he was impeccable in his loyalty to Nancy, spending every weekend in her company and never dating any other girl. Their courtship, aside from attending fraternity house parties, usually took the form of walks and picnics *à deux* on the North Shore of Massachusetts. Sitting on the rocks for hours at beauty spots like Gloucester and Marblehead, just talking and watching the waves, was the activity that most appealed to both of them, particularly to Chuck, who found that proximity to water had a pleasantly soothing effect on his restless energy.

At one stage, early in their relationship, Nancy began to wonder if they had enough interests in common to make them compatible as a couple. "I was keener than he was on books, paintings, music, and intellectual exploration," she recalls. "I used to worry that Chuck might not have much of a sensitive side to him. I remember talking to him about my concern that anything to do with art, nature, or beauty seemed to pass him by. I knew that the ocean was important to him, as it was to me, as a source of inspiration. But I was surprised that most cultural activities like reading, poetry, novels, or going to concerts or exhibitions never really interested him."

Colson's lack of a cultural hinterland in his life, whether real or imagined, was not a serious obstacle to the progress of his romance with Nancy. As a symbol of his growing love and commitment, he presented her with his fraternity pin in October 1950. Eleven months later, on Labor Day 1951, he took her to a carefully chosen rock overlooking the ocean, and there, on an idyllic late summer evening, he proposed to her. He was nineteen and she was just twenty.

The next step was shopping for a diamond engagement ring, which Colson took out a bank loan to purchase. Then came introductions of each other's families. The first dinner, hosted by the Billings for the Colsons, was not an unqualified success. Although Wendell was the perfect guest, Dizzy indulged herself with an excess of flamboyance. She arrived, dressed to overkill, in an haute couture creation that would have been the envy of many a Paris fashion model, but it was far too exotic attire for a family supper in an unpretentious country town like Acton. Mr. and Mrs. Billings were no less startled by Dizzy's loud and incessant laughter, by her large consumption of wine, and by her boisterous conversation. Yet despite these initial surprises, the two families liked each other and bonded in a steadily strengthening relationship. Chuck and Nancy's relationship was strengthening too, so much so that they announced that they wanted to get married before Christmas. This was no doubt partly due to a growing desire for matrimony, but it was also due to Colson's growing sense of impatience. He was the quintessential young man in a hurry. At this moment in his life he was bored with Brown and chafing at the bit—although even more for the battlefield than for the marriage bed. However, with characteristic ingenuity, he thought he had found a way of reaching both goals ahead of schedule.

"I was afraid the Korean War was going to end before I could be sent out there," he later recalled. "So I came up with the idea of getting commissioned before graduating. I told Nancy that if I could get my commission I would give up my last semester in college, marry her, and then go to Korea."

Fortunately, perhaps, Colson's impatience was crushed by a higher force in his life than either Mars or Cupid—the senior officers of the NROTC. They would not countenance the idea of one of their best and brightest cadets dropping out of college six months before graduating. So Colson's two dreams of fighting in Korea and getting married to Nancy were both put on hold until after his graduation and commissioning day, scheduled for June 1953.

Midshipman Colson

The NROTC was pivotal in the life and development of the young Charles Colson. The scholarship he had won to Brown paid for his tuition, worth $600 a semester, and gave him an additional $50 per month for personal living expenses. In return, an NROTC scholar, known as a midshipman, was required to attend military drill training once a week, to wear uniform on campus on drill days, and to do eight weeks of formal military service on a ship or a naval shore establishment during the summer vacation.

Colson relished his Midshipman's duties. On his first summer vacation, in 1950, he was assigned to the battleship USS *Missouri* along with his fellow Brown NROTC student Tom Glidden, who was one of three triplets (the other two were called Dick and Harry) from Pennsylvania. Glidden had initially taken a poor view of Colson from their early encounters on campus. "I thought he was just a dilettante. He looked like a yak with his burr haircut, big hips, and big round face. He didn't seem to be serious about anything except drinking beer and partying." On board the *Missouri*, Glidden revised his opinion. "Colson knuckled down to all the tough duties we midshipmen were given. He was great at polishing the brasses and 'holy stoning,' which meant scrubbing the ship's teak deck with a pumice stone. We slept in crew quarters up in the fo'c'sle, next to each other in canvas bunks eighteen inches apart, and we talked many a night away in our discomfort, as we were both too big for those bunks. That was when we agreed to become roommates in the next semester."

The fifty-eight-thousand-ton USS *Missouri* was the last battleship to be commissioned in World War II. Its firepower was awesome, with sixteen-inch guns that could land shells the size of a Cadillac on targets forty miles away. On the morning of June 25, 1950, while Colson was scrubbing the decks, the news came over the ship's loudspeaker that North Korean troops were pouring across the 38th parallel and attacking U.S. military bases. The Korean War had begun.

"Holy smoke," Tom Glidden said to Colson. "This is going to change our lives." The first change was that the *Missouri* altered course and headed at her top speed of thirty knots for Korea via Panama. The nineteen-hundred-strong ship's company, including Midshipman Colson, spent every waking hour preparing for action. "It was terribly exciting being on a great battleship getting ready for war," he recalled. "I and the other midshipmen were extremely disappointed to be taken off at Panama. We begged to be allowed to stay. Obviously that wasn't likely to happen as we were just a bunch of kids who would get in the way, but even so it was an arresting moment for me to realize that I was in the military and that the military was going to war. After that I dreamed of going to Korea every day until I graduated. I just could not wait. If there was a war going on, then I wanted to be over there fighting for my country as soon as possible."

Before any such dreams could turn into reality in the life of nineteen-year-old Colson, he first had to decide into which branch of the armed forces he would be commissioned. Although most NROTC cadets were destined to serve in the navy, one out of every fourteen midshipmen ended up in the marine corps. Strongly influenced by Bill Maloney, who came back from Korea to visit his old fraternity brothers in early 1951, Colson made a brash application to join the USMC to their representative at the NROTC office on campus.

"Midshipman Colson, sir," he said to the duty officer, a Lieutenant Cosgrove. "I'd like to inquire about the marine corps."

"You are a bit premature, Colson," retorted Cosgrove. "First we will have to see whether you are good enough for the marine corps."

For weeks afterward Colson smarted under the suggestion that he might not be "good enough" for the marines. He applied himself intently to the finer points of drill, polished the brass on his uniform as never before, spit-shined his shoes, and strove to present himself as the epitome of a future marine officer. This self-improvement effort succeeded. Eventually he was summoned to Lieutenant Cosgrove, who glowered fiercely at him and said: "Colson, we think you're good enough."

Colson's acceptance by the USMC needed careful presentation to his parents, for in the spring of 1951 the Korean War was at its bloodiest. So he made a special trip back home to explain the decision to his father over a man-to-man scotch in the cocktail lounge of Boston's Copley Plaza Hotel. "I was concerned that my dad would try and talk me out of it, but he didn't wince," recalls Colson. "Instead, he just said, 'I don't want to stop you from doing something you think is right. I'll worry about you when you go off to war, but it's your decision and I'm right behind you.' That was the sort of father-and-son relationship we had."

In contrast to Wendell's supportive reaction, Dizzy voiced strong objections—on the idiosyncratic grounds of dress rather than danger—urging him to stay in the navy because the cut and color of a naval officer's uniform would make him look far more elegant at parties.

Colson was so keen to go to the war that in the fall of 1951 he and his roommate Tom Glidden sought out Major Richard Jescke, the senior marine officer in charge of the NROTC program at Brown. The two nineteen-year-olds requested that they be drafted immediately for combat duty in Korea. "Forget that foolishness and nonsense," Jescke told them. "Your job is to prepare to be marines and to get your commission."

Colson's military preparations for the marines were not entirely easy. First, he had a dentistry problem because his lower teeth were not fully aligned with his upper teeth. Eventually, after six months of wearing a brace to pull his lower teeth back, he passed this part of his physical, but his bite has never been right since. Then he had a problem with his sight. The marine corps required that officers have twenty-twenty vision. Colson's eyes were not up to this standard. However, when he took his optical test a helpful assistant to the doctor in charge whispered, "Just cover your bad eye both times." Colson took his advice and passed.

In the hundred-degree heat of a Virginia summer the officer cadets were subjected to the boot camp ordeal for which the marines are famous. The climax of their training was the Quantico assault course, a death-defying journey at the double through water jumps, wall climbs, rope swings, barbed-wire fences, and many other obstacles. Colson, complete with rifle, helmet, and eighty-pound equipment pack on his back, completed the required two circuits of the three-mile course well ahead of the time limits, but on reaching the finishing line he collapsed, fainting and vomiting from heatstroke. As he lay retching on the ground the major in charge of the assault course addressed him scornfully. "If you can't carry your weight, Colson, we'll get someone else to carry your backpack to the barracks for you—but marines don't do that."

"You sonofabitch," Colson snarled under his breath. But in his anger he summoned up the strength to run another couple of miles in the boiling heat to the barracks, carrying all his equipment. He must have pleased the major in the end for Colson finished at the top of his class in basic training at Quantico. "Those kinds of experiences, and I had many of them, taught me guts, perseverance, and determination," he recalls. "I learned to do things I just didn't believe were possible. The marine corps took me in as a flabby college kid and turned me into a man."

Scholar and Debater

In a further demonstration of his growing maturity, Colson came back from his summer boot camp with a changed attitude to his studies. Ashamed of being on academic probation, he returned to the work ethic of his school-days at Browne & Nichols, suddenly discovering a new enthusiasm for political philosophy. The professor teaching his course at Brown was Guy Dodge, a New Deal liberal who at one time had been a state chairman in the Democratic Party. Colson, brought up by his staunchly Republican father (a Wilkie supporter) to believe that all Democrats were thieves, clashed frequently with Dodge in the class discussions on Hobbes, Bentham, Locke, Jefferson, Burke, Nietzsche, and Marx. It became a regular habit of the professor to round off his lectures by saying, "Well, now it's time for the opposition point of view. Let's hear from Mr. Colson." The opposing viewpoint was evidently well argued, for Colson was awarded straight A's throughout his last two years of political science and philosophy. He remembers Professor Dodge with gratitude. "He was a great communicator and a great teacher. Although I don't think I ever agreed with any of his utopian and paternalistic ideas, he was a formative influence on my own political beliefs because of our intellectual debates."

From political theory Colson moved smoothly into political activism. In his final year he was Brown's top debater, and he was elected secretary of the student governing body. There was nothing intellectual about his election platform for office. "Men of '53, this is an open letter written as frankly and sincerely as possible," he declared in a statement to the electors printed in the *Brown Daily Herald.* "I am running for Secretary of our class because I feel a sincere and conscientious effort must be made to improve our spirit and unity. . . . To achieve this goal I will work for more beer parties, social outings, 'big' weekends, 'name band' weekends and, of primary importance, a great Junior Prom Weekend." On this populist program of bread and circuses Colson swept to victory with over 60 percent of the vote.

The student politician also found the energy to become a student scholar. Galvanized by his enjoyment of Professor Guy Dodge's political seminars, Colson began to work hard at all his subjects. As a result, his academic performance did a complete turnaround. Instead of being bottom of the class, on probation, he moved to top of the class in his senior year, consistently receiving A's for his essays and course work. By the time of graduation Colson had risen so fast that he was awarded a liberal arts degree with honors. It was a result that astonished his classmates, one of whom jokingly compared his achievement to that of Lazarus.

It is likely that Colson, the twenty-one-year-old university student, was unaware of the miracle of the raising of Lazarus, for his life on and off campus was a religion-free zone. Nancy, who had been a dutiful attendee of Sunday school since the age of six, did occasionally try to talk to him about devotional matters. "I was astounded that Chuck knew absolutely nothing about the simplest of Bible stories," she recalls. "He hadn't even heard of the Good Samaritan or the Prodigal Son. All he did was to make fun of people who thought belief and faith were important." A similar memory is retained by Bob Torok, the only one of Colson's Beta Theta Pi roommates who was a regular churchgoer. "I can remember Chuck and the other guys yelling at me and making disparaging remarks when I broke away from playing cards to go off to a service," he recalls, "but it was just ribbing. It was kind of common ground among us that we honored God and country and the values that went with it."

While the motto of Brown University was *In Deo Speramus*—We Hope in God—throughout his college years Colson was not in the habit of hoping in or even thinking about God. He considered himself a "deist," although in his lexicon the term did not mean having any sort of meaningful relationship with the Lord. Nevertheless, he remembers an episode toward the end of his time at Brown when, as a result of "a strange stirring," he was moved to do something unusual. "I suddenly felt I needed to be in a church. I don't know how or why this happened. I just found myself walking into Saint Stephen's, which is the Anglican Episcopal church on the Brown campus. I sat down there and had a quiet time of prayer and meditation. I didn't know who I was talking to but I knew there was a God and that he was hearing my prayers. I also remember thinking, How can God listen to everyone's prayers at the same time?"

This was the only recorded example of religious curiosity in the life of the young Charles Colson.

Graduation, Commissioning, and Marriage

As his years at Brown drew toward their idyllic conclusion, Colson may well have had a warm glow of deistic feeling that God's in his heaven and all's right with the world. For in one glorious weekend in June 1953, he attended his graduation ceremony, he was commissioned as an officer in the United States Marine Corps, and he was married to Nancy Billings.

Of the three ceremonies, the first two went without a hitch. The Brown graduation followed the traditional Ivy League pattern. Immediately after receiving his degree scroll, designating him a bachelor of arts with honors, Colson posed for photographs with his parents in full academic plumage of gown, mortarboard, and blue silk hood. Then, like all the other NROTC cadets, he had to change for the commissioning parade into military uniform, which in his case meant dress whites. After having his gold bars pinned on his shoulders by the commanding officer, Second Lieutenant Colson, USMC, marched off the parade ground. As he received his first salute from a marine sergeant, to whom he handed over the traditional dollar, Colson felt he was experiencing the proudest and most important moment of his life.

Two days later he was enjoying an even prouder and more important experience—being a bridegroom. His love for Nancy had deepened during his years at Brown, and so had her feelings for him. "I think what I adored most about Chuck was that he was so caring," she has recalled. "Of course, there were lots of other things I liked, such as his tireless energy, his good looks, his ambition, and his absolute certainty that he was going to succeed. There were one or two things I didn't quite like too, such as his chain-smoking and his drinking. But the most attractive thing of all was that he could be so kind, so gentle, so compassionate, and so caring. Those were his best qualities."

Though the wedding had been meticulously planned, at the last minute

a cloud suddenly loomed over it when Nancy's father developed a mysterious illness. He became disoriented, distressed, silent, and totally unresponsive in his facial expressions. The local doctor diagnosed him as
traumatized over losing his only daughter. This was medical nonsense.
Months later he was correctly diagnosed as having suffered a stroke, but at
the time, the belief that her father was undergoing some sort of psychological trauma on account of her wedding must have cast its shadow over
Nancy's feelings.

The marriage ceremony took place at 4 P.M. on Tuesday, June 3, 1953,
in the Congregational church at Acton, Massachusetts. The officiating minister was Nancy's uncle the Reverend Royden Leonard, incumbent of a
Unitarian church in Connecticut. As the local paper, the *Acton Colonial,*
reported the scene: "The bride wore an heirloom, princess lace veil with
her organdy gown that was embroidered in a sculptured rose pattern. She
carried a single white rose and a white spray of stephanotis with her white
Bible."

The groom was wearing the formal dress blues uniform of a U.S. Marine Corps officer. In his high-neck collar, deep blue jacket, and red-striped
trousers, Nancy thought he looked too militaristic for a country wedding.
She had suggested that he should settle for a dark gray business suit, but
the newly commissioned Second Lieutenant Colson would have none of it.
Not that their respective wedding clothes mattered anyway. "Frankly I
couldn't have cared less by the time the great day arrived," said Nancy. "I
would have been just as happy if we'd both worn cheesecloth."

The reception after the service, held in the backyard of the spacious
eighteenth-century Billings family home overlooking Acton Green, did not
entirely live up to the tone of dignified ceremonial conveyed by the *Colonial's* description of the occasion. Colson, escorted by his best man, Tom
Glidden, was extremely nervous that his fraternity brothers might be planning to use the occasion for an elaborate practical joke of the kind that he
had practiced on other bridegrooms. Uppermost in his mind was a tearful
scene at the wedding of a Marshall Field scion in Chicago when the Beta
Theta Pi humorists had presented the bridal couple at their reception with
a shotgun. So Colson was much relieved when the surprise of his wedding
was merely the arrival of a four-hundred-pound brown-and-white cow,
lightly tethered to one of his classmates, David Livingstone.

The cow was unaccustomed to being led into a tent with two hundred
wedding guests. She became excitable and far from well behaved ("Very
smelly," said Nancy). Yet her large presence added much laughter to the oc-

casion and did not detract from the general happiness, even when the cow's irate owner, a local farmer, arrived to recover his prize milker from the rustlers, with whom he exchanged frank words.

The cow was a joke, unplanned by Charles Colson, but all his other plans had come to fruition like a fairy story with a happy ending. In his four years at Brown University there were times when he came across as abrasive, brash, insensitive, and overexcitable in his enthusiasm for following the whims of fraternity house joie de vivre. Yet in the era of the World War II generation he was following, Colson had also developed a maturity with deeper ballast. He had a gift for bonding in male friendship. His patriotism and his *Semper Fi* faithfulness to the marine corps were rock solid. His formidable intellect, when backed by his even more formidable energy, had shown it could win him glittering prizes. He had been loyal and lucky in love. As Colson, the newly married husband, honors graduate, and marine officer, left the Brown campus for the last time to head for his first military posting, at Camp Lejeune in North Carolina, he must have been counting his blessings with justified pride and happiness.

CHAPTER THREE

The Marines

First Year as a Second Lieutenant

S econd only to my conversion, it was the most important experience of my life and the greatest influence on the formation of my character" was Charles Colson's overview of his two years of active service in the U.S. Marine Corps, 1953–55. The judgment is a fair one. For it was in this character-building period that Colson defined his leadership abilities, changed the direction of his career plans, and discovered new depths and values within himself. It is also possible that the first seeds of his conversion, which took place two decades later, were planted by a fellow marine when they were sailing together on a secret and potentially dangerous mission aboard a U.S. warship off the coast of Guatemala.

Second Lieutenant Colson's introduction to military life as a commissioned officer did not begin auspiciously, for he was troubled by health and housing problems. Immediately after receiving his commission, he was posted to Camp Lejeune, a sprawling complex of training facilities on the swampy coast of North Carolina. Arriving here at the end of June 1953 with Nancy, his bride of less than a week, he was told there was no military housing available. This was due to the expansion in numbers of the USMC under the pressures of the Korean War, from which a disturbing number of marines were returning each week in pine boxes. Colson's first duty was to find some off-base housing to rent in the neighborhood. This proved difficult. The only accommodation he could afford on his salary of $285 a month was a two-bedroom apartment overlooking the ocean on Topsail Island, a tourist summer camp located an hour and a half's drive from the base. In the interests of economy, Colson shared the apartment and the rent with another marine, Second Lieutenant Harry Jenks, who had also just been married immediately after his graduation from Brown. The two couples did not have much time for their honeymoons. At 4 A.M. every morning, Colson would get into the Chevrolet sedan given to him by his parents as a wedding present, drive to the base with Jenks, do a full day's training in the sweltering heat, and then drive home, arriving at around 9 o'clock. "It was a pretty rugged summer," recalls Colson, "crazy and exhausting. It was the sort of routine you can only do when you are twenty-two years old."

Halfway through his first training course Colson was afflicted with hives, an itchy rash caused by an allergy. Hives can become life threatening if the rash affects the lungs and leads to suffocation. This happened three times to Colson, who had to be rushed into the base hospital and given adrenaline injections to restore his breathing. After the third suffocation attack the doctor warned him that if his allergy continued to be a problem he would have to apply for a medical discharge. Colson, whose heart was set on a career in the marines, flew into a panic and left the hospital telling the doctor, "Don't worry, you'll never see me in here again." This self-suggestion treatment worked wonders, for Colson never again suffered from hives.

After eight weeks at Camp Lejeune, Colson was ordered to Quantico for five months of basic training. Already hardened to the worst Quantico could throw at him, as a result of his previous experiences of its assault course while a Brown NROTC student, Colson took the tough regime in stride. At the end of this intensive training, he came through at the top of his group of young officers, proud of the peaks of physical fitness he had attained and enjoying a new level of self-confidence as a result.

One episode that did dent Colson's self-confidence began when he received an urgent message that his father was in a Boston hospital, terminally ill with stomach cancer, expected to live for only a few more days. On being granted compassionate leave, Colson was dismayed to find that the fastest way to get from North Carolina to his father's bedside would be a bus trip of forty-eight hours. But then a marine aviator called Captain Mack volunteered to fly Colson to Boston in his training aircraft, an ancient World War II Beechcraft utility transport plane with twin tails. At the last moment they were joined by an obese Catholic padre weighing well over three hundred pounds, who had great difficulty squeezing himself into the Beechcraft seat.

All went well until they had to make a refueling stop at a New Jersey naval air station, where they were advised not to proceed to Boston because of heavy electrical storms in the New York area. Yet Captain Mack defied the advice, claiming to have great experience of flying through thunderstorms, and took off for Boston, only to encounter far worse weather conditions than had been forecast. As the plane flew over New York City, it was hurled about in the turbulence of the storm like a dinghy in a typhoon. To make the situation more dangerous, the wings iced up, causing the plane to lose altitude. Then, to make it catastrophic, both engines cut out. Captain Mack had forgotten to switch them over to the number two fuel tank.

There was no way of telling how long, if at all in those icy conditions, it might take for the fuel lines from the second tank to restart the engines. As the plane plummeted, Captain Mack ordered his passengers to strap on their parachutes and jump. As Colson harnessed himself to his parachute, the copilot came back into the cabin and flung open the side door. But the overweight padre was far from ready. At first he could not get out of his seat. He was stuck there, eyes closed in prayer, fingers on his rosary beads. Colson yanked him out of the seat and tried to strap him into his emergency 'chute, but the terrified cleric was clumsy and unresponsive. As Colson wrestled desperately to fit his copassenger into his harness, it became clear that the padre was simply too fat for the parachute. So he prayed on while Colson swore on. Deciding that he could not leave his companion behind, Colson began dragging him toward the open door of the aircraft with the intention that they should jump together on one parachute. The padre's prayers became more fervent—but they were answered. First one engine and then the other spluttered back into action.

After landing at Boston, the padre held up his rosary beads and said: "You see, son, it was better to do it my way!" If Colson had been converted on the spot, it would have been understandable, for this seemed to be his day for miracles. A few minutes later he was told that his father was not suffering from stomach cancer but from some minor and benign abdominal obstruction. But as it was, the only lasting impact of these ups and downs on Colson was that for the next seven years he refused to fly again.

When he was posted back to Camp Lejeune, this time with base housing costing $60 a month, Colson was given his first taste of leadership. He was made commander of Machine Gun Platoon A in the Weapons Company of the Second Battalion of the Eighth Marine Regiment. Colson was exhilarated by his experiences of being in command of fifty enlisted men. He drove his platoon hard in training, leading them from the front, as he would have to do in combat. But he also loved the caring side of leadership, steeping himself in the roles of paterfamilias and personal mentor to the men under his command.

"I never found an occupation I enjoyed more," he recalls. "I had a platoon of wonderful kids, most of them between seventeen and nineteen years old. They had all sorts of personal and home problems, which they would come and talk to me about. I tried to be a father figure to them and I took a real concern for their welfare, writing letters for quite a few of them and advising them in a paternal sort of way on the most intimate matters. Also I used to look at them with the realization that their lives could be in my hands when we were together in combat. It was part of my leadership ethos to accept that the decisions I would make about my men on the battlefield might well determine whether they would live or die. That was a very sobering reality."

In fact the chances of Colson and his platoon having to face death in battle had receded considerably with the ending of the Korean War. After the armistice was signed on July 27, 1953, the Pentagon's embryonic plan to create a third division of the marine corps was canceled and the pressure of numbers at Camp Lejeune and other USMC bases began to ease.

Within the Colson family, however, numbers were on the increase. On April 4, 1954, Nancy gave birth to a seven-pound-three-ounce boy in the naval hospital on the base. He was officially named Wendell Ball Colson II, but because the obstetrician had hailed his entry into the world with the greeting "Hello Buster," for many years afterward his private nickname within the family was simply Buster.

The birth of Buster brought enormous joy to the Colson and Billings families. The proud father took a week's paternity leave from his military duties and amazed Nancy by his hitherto untried domestic and nursing skills. A cavalcade of doting grandparents, aunts, uncles, and cousins came down to visit. The most doting of all was Wendell Sr., blooming with patriarchal happiness at having his firstborn grandson named after him. Wendell sat down and wrote Chuck and Nancy a four-page letter of grandparental thoughts on the new baby. It contained the wise but subsequently unheeded recommendation "The only advice I am going to give you, Chuck, is to grow up with your son. So many times men miss that opportunity." One opportunity that Chuck Colson did not miss was the chance to enjoy a good number of toasts and festive drinks at the time of his son's birth. This was natural, but his old fraternity house weakness of not knowing when to stop having fun at a party turned one joyful event into a knockout blow.

About two weeks after Buster was born, Colson accepted an invitation from his company commander, Captain Joseph Holzbauer, to come over and celebrate. Leaving Nancy and the baby behind, Colson imbibed with enthusiasm and returned home at three o' clock in the morning very much the worse for wear. Crashing his way into the house, Colson badly frightened his wife, not only by his lack of bodily control but also by his desire to lift Buster out of his crib. "He was so drunk that I actually feared for the safety of our child," recalled Nancy. She felt drastic measures were required. So, picking up her heaviest frying pan, she struck her spouse on the back of his head with all her strength. The blow poleaxed Colson. "For a moment I had visions of spending my life in jail for murdering my husband," said Nancy. Relieved to see that he was still breathing, she left him unconscious on the kitchen floor until morning. When he eventually woke up, his contrite apologies were not immediately accepted. Reinforcements arrived in the shape of Captain Holzbauer, who pleaded with Nancy to forgive his drinking companion. "Don't be too hard on Chuck—he's just had a baby," was the CO's request. It was not the most sensitive of excuses. "But I'm the one who's had the baby," retorted Nancy.

Matrimonial harmony returned to the Colson household well before the next drama in their lives, which started on June 2, 1954, with a 4 A.M. telephone call and the military order "Report at once to the barracks with your seabag packed. Emergency. You will be gone for an unknown time to an unknown destination." When Colson reached the barracks, he rounded up his platoon. They were put on buses and driven to the Morehead City naval base, where they embarked on a troopship, the USS *Mellette,* an old World War II rust bucket with a maximum cruising speed of eleven knots. Not a word was said about their mission, but Colson noticed that the ship was being heavily loaded with live ammunition. In training, ammunition travels on a separate ship from personnel, so the USS *Mellette*'s loading arrangements meant that its mission was on a war footing.

After the ship sailed, the officers were called into the wardroom for a briefing. The captain told them they were taking part in a highly classified mission, Operation Hard Rock Baker, which would involve an invasion of Guatemala. This small South American country's leftist government, headed by President Jacobo Arbenz Guzmán, was about to be overthrown in a CIA-inspired coup, designed to prevent Guatemala from becoming a bridgehead for communism on the continent. President Eisenhower, who had authorized the coup, was sending in the marines to protect American citizens who might be caught up in the revolution. The military orders warned that the planned amphibious landing in Guatemala was likely to be opposed by armed communist guerrillas.

Colson's platoon was less trained than most because of a sudden influx of seventeen-year-olds who had arrived straight from boot camp. Training them on board ship was difficult at the best of times, and made worse by seasickness. The voyage to Guatemala required going round Cape Hatteras, where the Gulf Stream meets other prevailing currents, creating one of the roughest patches of water in the world. Billeted in the fo'c'sle of the ship, Colson's men bore the brunt of the *Mellette*'s pitching and tossing through high waves. All fifty of them were laid low with seasickness and were unable to get up for training drills until their ingenious platoon commander arrived one morning with white pills that he declared to be "a miracle cure for seasickness, just invented by the navy." In fact the pills were aspirins. Colson had his own theory about seasickness, which reduced it to a mere problem of psychological disorientation. The theory seemed to work. "Once these guys thought they had a cure, most of them were fine," he recalls. "Within twenty minutes of taking the aspirin, forty of them or so were back on their feet."

Homesickness rather than seasickness was Colson's personal problem. He wrote letters home to Nancy on almost every single day of the mission. His correspondence to her is touching in its intimacy and revealing about the seeds of change that were starting to germinate within him. "I don't have to tell you, darling, how much I miss you and Buster," he wrote on the third day of the voyage to Guatemala. "Being away from home for the first time since we were married has convinced me of one thing for certain—that my values have changed over the past few years. In college the only measure of happiness in life I thought really important was success and money. I think I have learned that a happy family and a happy home life are so much more important."

This theme of yearning for hearth and home is echoed and reechoed in many of Colson's letters from USS *Mellette*. "I hate, detest, abhor, despise being away from you and Buster and our home," said his next letter. "I just don't see how I could ever go through life wondering when I was going to have to leave on another trip, or maneuvers, or war. . . . I know one thing for certain, leaving my family is hell."

Colson seemed to have protested rather too much on this subject to his brother officers. When the *Mellette* was still only fifteen days out of port, he started to gripe impatiently in the mess about his longing to be back home. Then, as he described the scene to Nancy,

*One lieutenant who came up through the ranks very quietly and
pleasantly told me that he had spent nineteen months in Korea
away from his wife and two children while I was in college. Nothing more needed to be said. I felt two inches high. . . . I am very
grateful to that fellow for shutting me up when he did before I
made more of a thoughtless fool of myself. Lord knows I have never
been called upon to make any sacrifices in return for the wonderful
life I have lived in the past twenty-two years. I'll try to keep my
thinking straight every time I think of complaining.*

While Colson was straightening out his thinking, the USS *Mellette* was
going in circles. A task force of American warships had now reached
Guatemala and began steaming around its coastline in full sight of the
shore. The show of strength had the desired effect on the communist
forces, which faded away into the hills. As tensions eased and a noncom-
munist leadership asserted itself, the prospect of beach landings by U.S.
Marines under hostile fire faded also. However, the Pentagon decided
it would be prudent to keep its forces in the area as a precautionary measure. So the USS *Mellette* stayed on station. As the days at sea lengthened,
Colson began to discover that he had a low threshold of boredom and
a high level of impatience. These were not the best qualities for a ship-
bound marine. "Life aboard ship becomes more depressing each day," he
confided to Nancy. "The lack of contact with the outside world is so dis-
couraging."

Shipboard Spiritual Searchings

In his restless searching for a better life in or out of the marines, Colson's
thoughts intermittently turned toward God. This was a surprising development for a young man who had never previously shown any interest in
spiritual matters. Yet the evidence of it is clear. In the almost daily
husband-and-wife correspondence that was exchanged while Colson was
patrolling the waters around Guatemala, by far the most surprising theme
was religion. Colson's letters on this subject are a historical as well as a
spiritual surprise. For in his own accounts of his life prior to his conversion, written during the aftermath of Watergate in 1973, Colson always
gave the impression that only the rarest and vaguest of religious searching
ever troubled him. In broad terms this is accurate, but when one focuses

on his spiritual thinking during the ship-bound months of June and July 1954, a rather different picture emerges.

The religious dimension in the Colsons' correspondence was introduced by Nancy in her first letter after her husband had set off from Camp Lejeune for his unknown destination. "Please, Charlie, while you are away, learn to respect other people's religions and don't tease them about it simply because you see no sense in it," she wrote. "We are all ultimately striving for the same thing and there may be several approaches to that goal for all we know . . . religion can have so much meaning." Colson, who in his college days had a history of ribbing classmates for preferring churchgoing to bridge playing, made an uncharacteristic response: "What you said in your letter about other people's religions really hit home with me. There is a great deal to faith. One couldn't exist without it. I feel much closer to religion than I ever have. We have so much in the world to be thankful and humble for. Every now and then I just stop and give thanks to God for giving us such a healthy child. Lord knows, my darling, how any couple could be as lucky as we have been, so very fortunate in everything."

This seems to be a rather different Charles Colson from the man to whom Nancy addressed her please-don't-tease-people-about-their-religions letter. From then on, his correspondence is sprinkled with spiritual references:

"These are really long days around here. After hearing from you today, I went to say a prayer of thanks for yours and Buster's safety."

"One of the times I feel very close to you is when I go out on deck at night and say a prayer for yours and Buster's care and health and I know you are standing there with me."

Colson felt such stirrings when he looked out at the night sky from the deck of the USS *Mellette*. One evening, when he still believed he would have to lead his men onto the beaches of Guatemala, he thought about their lives and gazed up in wonder at the luminous heavens. "That night," he wrote, "I suddenly became as certain as I had ever been about anything in my life that out there in that great starlit beyond was God. I was convinced that He ruled over the universe, that to Him there were no mysteries, that He somehow kept it all miraculously in order. In my own fumbling way I prayed, knowing that He was there, questioning only whether He had time to hear me."

These supernatural searchings were followed by religious observances and spiritual discussions. Soon, in true Colson style, a religious action plan was being formed. He summarized his thoughts to Nancy:

*I went to church services on board (where else!) yesterday and
really, wholeheartedly, enjoyed it. If nothing else, this cruise has
given me endless hours for meditation. One recurring thought has
bothered me—perhaps I have not paid enough interest in my life to
religious thinking. Perhaps it is something I have really missed. I
think for Buster's sake we should introduce a little religion into our
lives. It's something we have neglected and there are times like this
when one surely needs it. It's a great comfort when things get you
down. Maybe just saying Grace once in a while would expose
Buster to it. I wish I had seen more when I was younger. I have
been talking to Brad Allen at great length about it. He has devoted
his life and thinking to religion. He has shown me a lot of sense to
it all that I had neither seen before nor had occasion to think
about.*

Who was Brad Allen? Like Colson, he was a marine second lieutenant,
full name Norbert Allen. He had committed his life to Christ some years
earlier. A graduate of Columbia University who had been through basic
training at Quantico with Colson and who had taught him to play chess,
Allen must have stood out in that church-reticent culture of the U.S. military in the 1950s. For all Colson's contemporaries in the marines agree that
in those days, religion was virtually a taboo subject. "You just didn't ever
talk about it. Religion was a private matter. Off-limits in conversation," recalls General Bill Maloney, the marine who had come back to Brown from
the Korean War and inspired Colson to sign up for "the best"—the USMC.

Brad Allen was different. He did converse about religion. He got
through on spiritual matters to Charles Colson, who had almost forgotten
his existence until these letters written on board the USS *Mellette* were unearthed in the course of the research for this biography. "I remember Brad
Allen now and I realize that I have underestimated his importance in my
spiritual journey," says Colson. "He was scary smart; a very bright guy. He
didn't fit the marine picture. He was quiet, introverted, and he had an
eclectic personality. We talked a lot, but we were not real buddies. It made
an impact on me that he wanted to leave the marines and become a minister. He may well have tried to evangelize me, but that never registered in
my consciousness. After that time with him, my awareness of God faded
as personal interests crowded my life."

Colson's shipboard mentor did become a minister in the Episcopal

Church but died at a young age in a car accident. If it is true that he planted some of the first spiritual seeds in the heart of the young Charles Colson, then Norbert "Brad" Allen served God well.

Platoon Commander and Military Policeman

As the summer of 1954 wore on, the tensions in Guatemala eased still further. The CIA's undercover operatives in that country—by coincidence they included the young Howard Hunt, who, eighteen years later, was to play a pivotal role in Watergate as Colson's recruit to the Nixon White House—reported sufficient political tranquillity for the patrolling task force of U.S. warships to be dispersed. So on July 7, the USS *Mellette* docked in Vieques.

Colson decided to put his platoon through its paces the day after they came on shore, but alas, with negative results. "I had an inspection yesterday morning and found that most of my people looked terrible," he wrote to Nancy.

> *Rusty rifles and dirty dungarees. I was furious. . . . I needed to teach them a lesson so yesterday, after the regular working day was over, I took every one of them on a hike with full packs, rifles, etc. We took no breaks and brought no water with us. We covered nine miles in two hours flat, up and down hills. All but eleven of the fifty people I took collapsed before we got back to camp and we had to send a jeep back out after them. No one was hurt, just tired. I guess I'm not as young as I used to be. I was really puffing at the end. When we got back I restricted them, which means they can't go to San Juan this weekend. I hated myself for doing it, but they needed the lesson.*

Descriptions like this may leave the impression that platoon commander Colson was a harsh martinet with his men, but other passages in his letters home reveal a tough but tender mixture in his character. For example, he anguished over a seventeen-year-old marine who was following immediately behind him on a rope-climbing exercise up the side of a warship in the task force. When Colson reached the deck, he turned and stretched out his arm to pull his follower to safety. Unfortunately the boy lost his nerve, slipped, and fell all the way down. Even though there was no serious injury, Colson regarded the incident as his "worst experience in the marines" and castigated himself for a failure of understanding and leadership.

A second episode illustrating the compassionate side of Second Lieutenant Colson involved another seventeen-year-old member of his platoon, who was court-martialed for falling asleep while on sentry duty. Colson felt that the charge should never have been brought against a young man who was normally exceptionally conscientious. So he prepared a detailed defense, working on the case for several days. "I am fully convinced he is innocent and I am trying my best to get him acquitted," he wrote to Nancy. "I hope I can fight the system of military courts, which are very bigoted in their ways. I will do my best. I really feel sorry for some of these youngsters who get into serious trouble because no one really takes an interest in them."

No one could accuse Colson of not taking an interest in his men. Against the odds, he won the court-martial case for his somnolent sentry. This was not an isolated example of his willingness to challenge the system when he felt an injustice or an unfair ruling had been imposed on a member of his platoon. His letters were full of caring descriptions of his men's personal problems, often sympathetic to the difficulties they faced under the highly pressurized conditions of life on board a warship preparing for a potentially dangerous amphibious landing.

"I want to spend every minute with them when I see their dirty, weary faces looking in bewilderment at what is going on," he lamented.

> *It's a crime to take 17-year-olds into the Marine Corps. We have made them men prematurely in the long month that's just passed. Maybe it's a good thing—if we sent them all back to civilian life I don't think there would be a juvenile delinquent in the bunch of them. They are all men now, not the same people I took with me out of Morehead City. I have fifty-five men: three of them Latin Americans, four Negroes, many Southerners, Yankees, Catholics, Protestants and all. It's a real cross section of the American people, from all types of homes and no homes. They are wonderful kids, every one of them. Maybe they are the thing that makes this such a great nation. I'll never again listen to anyone who scorns "the younger generation."*

Colson had a tendency to romanticize about his men, and also about his commanders. He hero-worshiped General Lewis B. "Chesty" Puller, a legendary USMC warrior who had risen from the ranks as an enlisted man and in 1954 was commanding the Second Marine Division, whose units had been sent to the coast of Guatemala. The only man in history to have been decorated with five Navy Crosses, Chesty Puller was in theater, ready to lead from the front if the invasion planned in Operation Hard Rock Baker took place. "I would have walked off a cliff if he so ordered me," wrote Colson, whose letters describe several encounters with this authentic twentieth-century hero (he is still immortalized by the marine corps, which to this day calls its bulldog mascot Chesty). "We are getting up at 4:30 in the morning for an inspection by General 'Chesty' Puller . . . everyone is dashing about wildly trying to impress the old boy," wrote Colson.

By this stage of the training cruise Colson was as tough as marines come, but he was at pains to reassure his wife that his admiration for Chesty did not run to emulating the general's famous drinking habits. "Since that night with the Holzbauers the thought of getting drunk has sickened me," he explained to Nancy. "Perhaps I realize how childish all of that really is. I hope I'll continue to feel that way. I don't mean to join any temperance union but it is much wiser to control your drinking. Doesn't sound like the old Beta House days, does it?"

To Leave or Not to Leave?

As the USS *Mellette*'s journey round various ports, islands, and training bases in the Caribbean continued, Colson's letters reflect a growing tug-of-war in his mind between a future life of excitement in the marine corps and a future life of prosperity in civilian life. On the one hand, he loved the thrill of danger, and his letters sparkle into vivid prose whenever he described episodes such as rock-climbing exercises, training assaults, amphibious landings into simulated minefields of pyrotechnics, or fighting brush fires. On the other hand, his letters convey the restlessness of a young man constantly searching for pastures new. After his successful court-martial defense, he wrote with enthusiasm about becoming a naval justice lawyer. Then he floated the idea of going into law practice with his father, or of becoming a businessman with Grace Lines or Cargyll. Money worries may have been at the root of some of these thoughts about his career. The Colson family budget was stretched at this time, particularly when Wendell Sr. and Dizzy, hit by one of their perennial financial crises, could no longer keep up with the payments on their wedding present. As a result, the monthly car payment had to be met by Nancy out of her husband's paycheck. It gave her some difficulties with the housekeeping budget. When news of the problem reached Colson on Vieques, he replied anxiously: "Nancy darling, *please* don't skip on food money. You mentioned eighty to ninety cents a day, which just doesn't sound sufficient . . . it won't hurt us if we aren't able to save anything this summer . . . be sure that you spend enough to take good care of Buster and yourself. Please don't cut short on things you need."

Colson may have been short of cash but he was never short of confidence. Amid all his messages to Buster and endearments to Nancy, his letters bounce with optimistic plans for buying a house, investing his gratuity,* going to law school, or even starting a vegetable garden. The idea of failing at any of these enterprises never entered his head. "I have enough confidence to do anything when I get out," he wrote to Nancy. "I know without question I can make a success of whatever I do in civilian life."

Not one to hide his light under a bushel, Colson evidently radiated his ebullient confidence in his future prospects to his brother officers. One of them, his occasional spiritual mentor, Brad Allen, teased him about his materialistic values. As Colson explained to Nancy:

> Brad Allen was kidding me last night about my future after the Marine Corps. He said it was certain that I would live in New York City. It couldn't be elsewhere, he said, since I am a "typical, ambitious, young executive type" with an Ivy League background. We will live in Westchester County, you will be the typical suburbanite wife, Buster will go to the best private schools and you and I will be host and hostess at all the country club functions. Then I'll have a fatal heart attack by age fifty. Within a few years, all our native ideas and ways will be absorbed into the mass way of life of suburban New York. How dismal!

Although during the next fifty years of his eventful career Colson fully lived up to his aspirations not to become a stereotype, in the months immediately following his conversations with Brad Allen, he did return to the mold of a typical marine officer. One reason for this reversion to type was the excellent reports received from his superiors toward the end of the Caribbean training exercises. Colson proudly told Nancy:

---

*A gratuity is a cash grant given in that era to military officers when they completed the term of duty they had signed up for.

I got my semi-annual report yesterday. As you know, these re-
ports are vitally important to a career officer. They stay in his per-
manent record and have a great influence on promotion and duty
assignments. Every category on mine was listed as "excellent and
outstanding"—the highest rating of the seven categories you can
get. Both the Colonel and Captain Holzbauer marked me and they
added comment sheets, which is unusual. One of them said: "He is
a reliable, capable officer who shows extremely advanced maturity
by his demeanor and ambition." I was truly flabbergasted. They
also recommended I be promoted as soon as possible.

With reports like these, it was hardly surprising that Colson felt encouraged to continue his career in the marine corps. To make him feel even better, the USS *Mellette* was heading back to its base port at Morehead City
at the end of August, which meant a blissful reunion with Nancy. Their
love had grown during this three-month period of separation, as their letters testify. One of Nancy's billets-doux expressed the depth of their relationship in this way:

The time has gone both rapidly and slowly. We both have been
busy and not allowed ourselves to miss each other too much in a
way, but at times it seems so strange and different to be away from
you. . . . No one could ever wish for a more wonderful or more
thoughtful and loving husband than you are to me, my darling. I
can never tell you how much I appreciate it. Don't ever let me slip
up and fail to live up to what you expect of me as a wife, my Char-
lie. I always want to do everything possible to make you happy.

Nancy did make her Charlie ecstatically happy after his return, although
she was surprised to hear him declare soon after entering the house, "I
want to hug the washing machine too." He would no longer have to do his
own laundry in the field with his scrub board, his GI soap, and his thirty-
cent PX scrub brush, in cold water that would not suds up.

Although he was well blessed by the delights of home and family life back
at Camp Lejeune, it was not long before Colson once again began feeling
restless. The problem was a repetition of the tension he had experienced on
board ship, caused by the difficult choice he was facing between a career in
the marines and a career in civilian life. The timetable for making this choice
was accelerated by a Pentagon decision to allow Colson and other young of-

ficers on three-year commissions to seek their discharges after only twenty-seven months. At this time Colson's career prospects in the marine corps could hardly have looked brighter. He was promoted to first lieutenant and made acting executive officer of his weapons company. He also had a short spell as acting company commander when Captain Joseph Holzbauer was away on bereavement leave. To be a company commander at the age of twenty-two, even on a temporary basis, was unheard of. Colson did the job well, which may have helped him to get the formal rating of number one in the linear list of officer promotions in his year. This meant that he would be first in line for the next promotion in the marine corps hierarchy.

Yet this early taste of success soon turned to ashes when, in January 1955, Colson received orders to go to supply school for training to become a supply officer. This was his idea of a posting to hell. He had joined the marines to be an infantry officer, a fighting man. Suddenly, as a result of a rule change requiring that all infantry officers have a secondary MOS, or military occupational specialty, Colson saw himself being turned into a bureaucrat. From the marine corps' vantage point, the posting made good sense. There were not many lieutenants with an IQ of 159, so the view from headquarters was that Colson's brainpower would make him good at paperwork. Colson saw it differently. He could anticipate himself getting trapped in the USMC's world of bean counting rather than bullet firing, working behind a typewriter rather than shooting in combat. So he protested vigorously.

Military hierarchies do not look kindly on junior officers who balk at their orders and challenge the authority of senior officers. Colson knew this but he pressed on regardless. He complained to his company, regimental, and divisional commanders. He even wrote a letter of protest to the commandant of the USMC. He lodged three formal appeals against his posting, but the marine corps denied him each time. So a disgruntled First Lieutenant Colson served the required three months at supply school and in April 1955 was posted as supply officer in the Marine Air Wing at the New River naval air station, adjacent to Camp Lejeune.

Colson's job as supply officer consisted of ordering spare parts for marine corps helicopters. He hated it. "I had loved what I was doing for most of my first two years as a marine," he recalls. "Then all of a sudden I ended up doing something I totally disliked. I was in a typical administrative job, just pushing paper. I couldn't stand it. I was unhappy and disappointed. I wanted to leave. So I spent most of my last three months as a marine writing letters to find the best route out."

Colson's chosen route to the exit was an examination for the JMA (Junior Management Assistance) program, designed to help young college graduates find executive jobs in government. The examination was highly competitive: fifty-two thousand applicants took the exam but only five hundred were allocated JMA positions. Colson, always a better examinee than a student, scored top marks and was awarded a job in the Navy Department. He was on his way.

In June 1955, almost exactly two years after he had been commissioned, Colson was transferred to the reserves and was given permission to go on inactive duty so that he could move to Washington for his internship with the Department of the Navy. He did not find his final days in the marine corps an easy experience, for emotional reasons.

"Although I would have been unhappy staying in, I was unhappy when the time came for me to go out," he recalls. "I had always loved those evenings on the base when they would sound the retreat, lower the colors, and the dress parade would march off. I loved all that stuff and I felt a great debt to the marine corps for what it had meant to my life. Also, I was pretty uncertain about what the future held for me. I knew I was going to a job in the government but I had no real idea what that involved. I was sad about leaving behind a lot of friends who'd been good to me. So one way and another I found leaving Camp Lejeune and the marines very painful." On Colson's final morning of active duty, he went through a ceremonial leave-taking of his commanding officer at New River naval air station, a Colonel Anderson. After the ceremony, Anderson, who had put himself through a night-school law program at George Washington University while stationed at the Pentagon, strongly advised Colson to follow his footsteps and take exactly the same course.

Colson subsequently described Colonel Anderson's advice as "highly influential on me at that vital moment." Although he had considered law school before, Anderson's recommendation made it crystallize in his plans as a firm blueprint for action. The JMA program had never meant anything more to him than a means to an exit. Now it was a means to an end. Colson was crossing the Rubicon, headed in a new direction. He had become clear in his mind that he would obtain the educational qualifications to become a lawyer. As he saw these events with the wisdom of hindsight many years later: "I now recognize it was a good thing that I didn't stay in the marines. It was also a good thing that the marines were so stubborn in their insistence that I should become a supply officer. For that moment of disappointment became a moment of decision. It opened my eyes to new horizons and new opportunities."

CHAPTER FOUR

A Political Operator

The Restless Bureaucrat

Charles Colson was unsuited for the role of a government bureaucrat. Impatient in his temperament, unorthodox in his methods, and hyperactive in his energy, he soon became a frustrated square peg in the sleepy round hole of the Junior Management Assistance (JMA) program. Yet the very qualities that made him a critic of the torpid pace of life within the Washington bureaucracy brought him to the attention of other unconventional figures in the system who had an eye for talent. As a result, Colson was soon rising to positions of considerable power for a young man in his twenties, first within the Navy Department and later as a key congressional aide on Capitol Hill. Despite the high pressure of these jobs, he never faltered in his commitment to his principal ambition of becoming a fully qualified lawyer before the age of thirty. However, his home and family life came under severe strain during this period as a result of his long office hours by day and his long law school hours at night.

The JMA program required its interns to attend lectures on government administration during the mornings and to carry out assignments in government offices during the afternoons. Colson found the lectures boring and the assignments meaningless. "I quickly discovered that those afternoon assignments on what was called 'job training' were a complete farce," he has recalled. "I did nothing except sit in an office with fifty desks in it filled by people drinking coffee, talking to one another, shuffling papers, but basically doing nothing. I had nothing to do myself. I only had to fill in one or two forms to do with printing orders for the Navy Department, sending stuff off to a printer. Very soon I was saying to myself, I just can't take four years of doing this. So I began to think of quitting."

Quitting was not so easy, given Colson's financial responsibilities. He was on a salary of $360 a month, which was roughly the same as his pay in the marines, but his costs of living were higher, largely because of a mortgage. With a deposit of $5,000, provided by a gift from Nancy's parents, and a $12,500 loan available to veterans under a housing plan created by the GI Bill, the Colsons bought a small redbrick house without air-conditioning on Seventeenth Street in North Arlington, Virginia. In an identical house next door lived a government employee in his mid-fifties who Colson came to know quite well; they often walked to the bus stop together and had neighborly conversations over the fence on weekends. Suddenly the neighbor died of a heart attack. The Colsons attended his funeral. As the casket was carried into the church, Colson suddenly felt "a terrible chill as I started thinking that his life could be my life, stuck in Washington, in the government bureaucracy, pushing papers around all day long, and living in a little house in a little suburban street. It seemed so dull compared to being a platoon commander in the marines. I said to myself, God, don't let me fall into the same trap and become a government employee."

With such musings, and with his frustrations over the pointless inactivity of the JMA program growing daily, Colson started to dread going to work. "It was a horrible time for me," he recalls. "I just couldn't adjust to this lifestyle. I knew that this was not the place I wanted to be. I reckoned I would rather be out on the street selling shoes or something to put myself through law school."

Some three months after starting work in Washington, Colson sought an interview with the head administrator of the JMA program, Dorothy Mead Jacobsen. In a conversation that he has subsequently described as "treading a fine line between frankness and rudeness," Colson poured out all his frustrations, vigorously expressing his preference for selling shoes on the street rather than filling in forms for Jacobsen's office. To his surprise, Jacobsen gave him a sympathetic hearing and a positive response. "That's very interesting," she said. "Well, as it happens, we've just had a call from the secretary of the navy's office. Someone's gone off on sick leave for three months. They want a bright young intern to help out up there on the procurement side. Maybe you'd be some good at that." The following day, Colson was interviewed by William H. Moore, executive assistant to the assistant secretary of the navy. Asked what he thought of the JMA internship program, Colson gave a frank and forthright answer. "Good, that's just the sort of attitude we need in this office," said Moore. "You're hired—start right now."

Colson had landed on his feet. On that first afternoon, he was asked to review a huge export contract between the U.S. and Indian governments involving the sale of warships. Nancy recalled seeing her husband off in the morning for what was expected to be a routine day of JMA lectures and assignments, and then welcoming him home in the evening with his seersucker suit drenched in perspiration as he gabbled excitedly about his promotion into the world of multimillion-dollar international arms deals. From then on, it was roses all the way. Within a matter of weeks he had been formally appointed to the post of assistant to the assistant secretary of the navy. Despite the difficulty in getting his tongue round such a sibilant job title, it was an exalted role for a twenty-four-year-old, even though it was the bottom rung of the ladder in Moore's office. Colson's principal responsibilities were reviewing major contracts put out to tender by the Navy Department. "Whenever problems or political pressures arose, I would write a brief for the secretary of the navy advising him whether or not such and such a contract had been properly bid for, whether the navy had got the specifications right, or whether there were any problem areas that had been overlooked," recalls Colson. "Those contracts were often worth hundreds of millions of dollars for items as big as aircraft carriers, cruisers, naval aircraft, and communications systems."

In the complex world of defense procurement, political and business pressures can play an important role. Colson reported to William Moore and to Raymond Fogler, who had been president of the retail chain W. T. Grant before Eisenhower appointed him assistant secretary of the navy. A gentle, self-effacing man of sixty-five, Fogler liked his youthful aide and gave him steadily increasing responsibilities. Colson shouldered them with enthusiasm. He enjoyed mastering the contractual details of big defense contracts and was flattered by the attentive visits to his office from CEOs of major defense corporations as well as admirals of the stature of Hyman Rickover, some of whom addressed him as "sir." This was heady stuff for a marine lieutenant just a few months out of active service, but Colson took it all in his stride. Long after he had left the Navy Department, he was remembered for the quality of his work there. In 1960, Dorothy Mead Jacobsen, the administrator who had sent him to the secretary of the navy's office in 1954, wrote to Colson saying: "You will be interested to know that whenever Bill Moore wants someone for his office, he always says, 'Please get me another Colson.' So far we haven't been able to oblige."

One of the reasons Colson so much enjoyed his job at the Navy Department was that it was highly political, involving skillful handling of calls and other pressures from congressional aides and Beltway lobbyists. A particularly active caller to his office was Bradford Morse, the administrative assistant to the senior senator from Massachusetts, Leverett Saltonstall.

The economy of Massachusetts, Colson's home state, was heavily dependent on defense corporations. The three largest employers in the Boston area were General Electric, maker of torpedoes; Raytheon, which specialized in defense electronics; and Harrington & Richardson, which made rifles. There were also many smaller defense contractors with factories around the state, including a shipyard at Quincy that had built some of the U.S. Navy's finest warships. Moreover, Leverett Saltonstall was the ranking Republican on the Senate Armed Forces Committee, a body that took a keen and sometimes oppressive interest in meting out pork-barrel defense contracts. So one way or another, there were good reasons for the frequent calls to Colson from Brad Morse, who was usually most concerned, on Saltonstall's behalf, about procurement issues.

On Capitol Hill

Brad Morse was one of those Capitol Hill staffers who liked to work two telephones at once and who fibrillated with energy and enthusiasm for getting things done fast. He found a kindred spirit in Colson. The two men worked hand in glove to solve numerous problems. A typical example of their collaboration involved the Massachusetts-based machine gun and rifle manufacturer Harrington & Richardson. The company made panic calls to Senator Saltonstall's office one morning in the spring of 1956 to say that they were going to have to lay off five hundred workers on their assembly line because a contract they had been awarded some months earlier had become mired in the bureaucracy of the Navy Department. Morse called Colson and asked for his help. Within twenty-four hours, the bureaucrats at the contracts branch concerned had been berated into fast-track action, the jobs at Harrington & Richardson had been saved, and the key players in the company and on Capitol Hill who had been involved in this drama were mightily impressed with the troubleshooting skills of Charles W. Colson. Against the background of this and similar episodes, when a vacancy occurred for the number-two post of executive secretary in Saltonstall's office, it was no surprise that Brad Morse put forward his new friend Colson for the job. Leverett Saltonstall, an aloof and patrician New Englander of the old school who had first won election to the U.S. Senate in 1944, accepted

Morse's recommendation. The appointment was a big step up for the twenty-five-year-old Colson in terms of salary and status. He was rising fast.

Colson began work as executive secretary to Senator Saltonstall on August 16, 1956. On the day of his arrival, the senator and Brad Morse set off for the Republican Convention in San Francisco, which was to nominate Eisenhower and Nixon to run for a second term. "You're in charge," said the senator as he departed. So Colson found himself in immediate command of Saltonstall's office in the Old Senate Building on Capitol Hill. He did not like the atmosphere he found there.

"The place was an absolute snake pit," he recalled. "Saltonstall was a grand old man, a prominent Yankee, a Boston Brahmin, and a former governor of Massachusetts. He had many fine qualities, but running an office was not one of them. He never fired anyone in his life, so his office was staffed by a bunch of neurotic old women who had continuous fights over things like where to put the flowerpots or whether their seniority in the office was determined by their longevity or their responsibilities."

One of the most cantankerous characters on Saltonstall's team was his stenographer. On Colson's second day in the office, she announced she would resign unless the new man in charge fixed a malfunctioning light in the ladies' room immediately. "Fine, you can leave at once then," was Colson's response. As the lady flounced out in high dudgeon, the new executive secretary became anxious that the senator might not be best pleased when he returned from the Republican Convention to discover that his personal typist had been fired. These worries proved groundless. Saltonstall was delighted. "I've been wanting to get rid of her for years," he said.

Although he had to sort out other personnel problems, Colson was liked and respected by most members of the staff. "Mr. Colson was definitely a leader. He ran our office well," recalls Evelyn Slater, who was on the Saltonstall payroll as a constituency caseworker for eleven years during the 1950s and 1960s. "He made a good impression on me from day one by his very nice appearance. Very much the marine, I'd say. I was also impressed by his attention to detail and his enormous capacity for hard work."

In fact, Colson did not let on to his colleagues just how hard he was working. He left his home in North Arlington at seven-thirty every morning and arrived at Saltonstall's office by eight-thirty. An eleven- or twelve-hour day was normal for senior staffers when the Senate was in session, but when Colson finished he had to go over to George Washington University Law School for night classes. As it was, his late arrivals meant he missed about half the classes, normally a heinous offense resulting in dismissal from the university. However, the dean of the GWU Law School, Ed Potts, was keenly interested in Republican politics. So he reached an understanding with Colson that his absences would be overlooked provided he caught up on the required cases and achieved good grades. Colson kept his side of the bargain and scored consistently high grades. But the cost was high. He would get home at nine or ten o'clock, have a sandwich, and go straight down to the basement, where, night after night, he would work until one or two in the morning, rising again at seven. It was a punishing regime and it took its toll on Colson's relationship with his wife and children.

Family Life

No man carrying the double workload that Colson imposed upon himself could possibly have qualified for that most coveted of paternal labels, "a good father." Nancy bore the brunt of his absences from the family, and the gap was also filled by the Colson grandparents, Pop and Diz (as Wendell Sr. and Dizzy were known within the family). They moved into the attic bedroom (which Diz immediately redecorated in a vivid chartreuse) of the house in North Arlington just after the birth of Christian, on April 12, 1956. Wendell Sr. had once again been diagnosed as terminally ill, this time with six months to live. The diagnosis was wrong, and Wendell lived for another seventeen years. At the time, however, Nancy lovingly shouldered the burden of having her in-laws staying with them, saying, "If he's only got six months, he'd better spend them with his only son."

Nancy subordinated her life to her husband and her family, which expanded with the arrival of a third child, Emily, on September 2, 1958. Bringing up three small children, cooking for them as well as the grandparents, and doing a lot of home entertaining for her husband's circle of political friends created pressures at times, but Nancy never complained. Once or twice, Chuck suggested to her that she should read more political books and articles to keep up with his life in the Senate, but this was not her world. One night at the end of a Colson dinner party, a departing guest said to another: "Nancy's a very sweet woman, isn't she?" The other guest, Brad Morse, replied, "Yes, but perhaps a little too sweet for Chuck." It was a harsh but perceptive comment from the man who at that time was Colson's closest friend.

With his salary and status moving upward, Colson in 1956 bought a four-bedroom Mount Vernon–style Colonial house in Evening Lane, Alexandria, for $33,950. During the course of the move into the new home, Colson showed that he had not lost his parents' compassion for the underdog. An elderly black man who was carrying paving stones to build a new patio for the house suddenly collapsed unconscious. Colson leapt out of his chair, ran to the man ("Faster than I'd ever seen him run in his life," said Nancy), carried him inside the house, cradled his head in his arms, poured brandy down his throat, and eventually revived him. Nancy remembers how the other workmen stood gaping with astonishment, for that was not the way white men usually treated black men in Virginia in the 1950s.

Young Wendell, Chris, and Emily loved the house in Alexandria and filled its spacious rooms with the joys and laughter of childhood. But Nancy was suffering from pangs of emptiness and unfulfillment, although she did not fully recognize the problem at the time. In the mid-1950s, the Colsons occasionally went to church, usually at Nancy's insistence, for she was determined to give Wendell an early grounding in Sunday school. The services they attended had little, if any, meaning for Colson. Nancy, who was a practicing Episcopalian, did sometimes feel deeply stirred by the liturgy and the sermons. One Sunday at the Episcopal church in Alexandria, she broke down in the middle of the service. As tears flooded out from her, Chuck was kind and solicitous but he could not understand what was troubling his wife. Nancy was none too clear about the causes of her sadness either. "Although I didn't put it into words," she recalls, "I guessed the real reason I felt lost was that Chuck wasn't home enough."

Colson was not on his wife's wavelength so far as his absences from home were concerned. He had his own agenda and he saw nothing wrong with it, nor with his work schedule that began at 7:30 A.M. and often ended long after midnight. With the wisdom of hindsight he took a different view: "I realize now what a serious mistake I made. I've often said to my kids, 'Don't make the same mistake as I did and cut yourself off from your family.' At the time I got used to believing that I'd got my priorities right. I was the one who went back to work, got through law school, and brought home the paycheck. Nancy accommodated me and became both a full-time mother *and* father. As I've reflected back on all this, I can see that my contribution to our family life was almost zero. Even on vacations, I used the time to catch up with my studies for my law degree and for the Virginia bar exams, which required even more work. So when I took my three-week vacation, I literally holed myself up in a room and studied from six in the morning to ten at night. I didn't allow any interruptions, not from the kids, not from Nancy, not from anyone. It was probably one of the great devastating blows to our marriage but I just didn't see it at the time."

Administrative Assistant

All Colson saw in his late twenties was the career imperatives of life as an ambitious Senate staffer. If he relaxed at all, it was in the office over a drink or, better still, over a practical joke. He also had an eye for a pretty girl. The old maids in the Saltonstall office were gradually being replaced by younger women who were more attractive and more efficient. (One of these new recruits was twenty-seven-year-old Patty Hughes, who came as a receptionist from the office of retiring senator Ralph Flanders of Vermont.)

The Saltonstall team became a lively, life-enhancing crowd. The fast-lane gusto of Brad Morse and Charles Colson was balanced by the statelier pace of the senator's son Bill. He remembers his father's most famous aide as "quite a party man. He liked a cocktail or two in the evening. He was a heavy smoker. His language could become marine-oriented under pressure, but he sure liked to relax, to have fun, and to organize some quite elaborate jokes." One of the jokes Bill Saltonstall remembers involved a phone call to Brad Morse when he was hosting a somewhat overrelaxed gathering for drinks in the Old Senate Office Building. The caller on the line was an officer of the Capitol Police, who said he had received reports that a lewd and drunken party was in progress. He was on his way to investigate. Only when a nervous Morse had hushed his guests, put away the bottles, and made everyone put on coats and ties was it revealed that the call had been a hoax instigated by Colson.

In 1958 Brad Morse moved to a new job in the Veterans Administration, and Colson succeeded him as Senator Saltonstall's number-one aide. This promotion made Colson, at twenty-seven, the youngest administrative assistant in the U.S. Senate, at a salary of $16,500—five times what he had been earning in the marines three years earlier. His rise was getting noticed. A cover story in *Newsweek* in June 1958 about young people in high positions reported that Colson was one of the best and brightest rising stars on Capitol Hill.

With an election looming eighteen months ahead, when Senator Salton-stall would be seeking a third term from the electorate of Massachusetts, Colson reckoned his first task was to raise the political profile of his boss. One of his first creative moves in this direction, which used both Salton-stall's prestige as the ranking Republican on the Senate Armed Services Committee and Colson's know-how as a former assistant in the procurement office of the secretary of the navy, led to the senior senator from Massachusetts filing a series of bills to reform the government's defense procurement process. Colson, the true author of these proposals, was savvy enough to realize that a defense procurement reform, however meritorious, was likely to prove as dull as dishwater to the average voter unless an unusual angle to it could be found. So he unearthed the absurd case of an eight-page specification for U.S. Air Force Ping-Pong balls that cost five times more than their off-the-shelf equivalent because they had to conform to cumbersome official specifications.

After Saltonstall had delivered a Colson-crafted speech on the floor of the Senate about these overspecified Ping-Pong balls, the case became a national sensation. *Time* and *Newsweek* both covered the story with full-page spreads. Saltonstall was interviewed on all the network news programs and at far greater length by the Massachusetts media. His bills received extensive and favorable editorial comment and led eventually to a root-and-branch reform of defense procurement. All this could not have been better publicity for a senator seeking reelection. The episode also showed that Charles Colson had a natural flair for political showmanship.

The 1960 election was dominated by its two young presidential candidates, Richard M. Nixon and John F. Kennedy. Colson knew both of them surprisingly well. Kennedy was the junior senator for Massachusetts and had frequent meetings and dealings with the senior senator's bright young administrative assistant in the office down the corridor. "I liked JFK personally. We had a good friendly relationship," recalls Colson. "He was very engaging and very witty. His charm was enormous, especially where women were concerned. His conquests in the office were blatant and notorious but that was all part of his dashing persona. However, for all his mystique, when he was a young politician I looked at him pretty closely and said to myself, He's shallow; he's not really concerned with the gut issues that worry the voters. I noticed that Kennedy, like quite a few liberals, would make a big superficial show of welcoming ordinary little guys on the state delegations into his office, but once they were gone, he'd express just a touch of disdain for them because they were lower-class. So I always saw him as a lightweight, a playboy. I didn't think he would ever become president."

For all their mutual cordiality, the Kennedy magic never captivated Colson, because he was a hard-core ideologue passionately committed to the cause of populist Republicanism. Colson's hero, from the same ideological stable, was Vice President Richard Nixon. Colson looked up to him as a champion of the small man's interest at home and as an international statesman on the world stage. He thought Nixon had the intellectual and political gravitas that Kennedy lacked. As vice president, Nixon presided over the Senate and had an office adjacent to its chamber throughout most of the 1950s. This gave Colson the opportunity to see his hero at close quarters and to form an admiration for him that was to have profound repercussions on both their lives during Nixon's presidency.

The initial sources of Colson's hero worship for Nixon were their similar backgrounds and their shared ideology. Both of them had been born on the wrong side of the tracks, to parents who had been forced to wrestle with continuous financial difficulties during their children's insecure upbringing. Both of them were clever scholarship boys who had fought their way to good schools while harboring residual feelings of resentment toward the liberal and social elites they believed were typified by Harvard University. Both of them were interested in serious discussion of political philosophies and ideas, not as an intellectual exercise but in order to implement the resulting policies. Both of them regarded power as a goal for which they were prepared to fight with sharp swords forged in the hottest furnaces of political ruthlessness.

None of these elements in the chemistry of bonding between Richard Nixon and Charles Colson were spoken about in the late 1950s. The two men were separated by a yawning chasm between their respective political statuses, not to mention an eighteen-year age gap. Nevertheless, they were in contact enough to recognize each other's qualities. Nixon noticed Colson as a comer in the world of Senate staffers and cooperated with him in a television project that was innovative and original for its time.

The project, dreamed up by Colson, consisted of Senator Saltonstall conducting fifteen-minute interviews with big-name interviewees in his Senate office, then sending the tapes out as a public service broadcast to all the television stations in Massachusetts. The idea caught on, the interviews won good audience figures, and it was all grist to the mill of Saltonstall's reelection campaign. Nixon agreed to be the star interviewee in one of the programs.

Saltonstall was not a natural television performer, so Colson was accustomed to doing most of the producing, directing, script writing, coaching, and editing by himself. In contrast to the wooden senior senator from Massachusetts, the vice president, in this friendly fireside chat between two Republicans, put on an impressive performance. "I was awed by Nixon's dazzling ability," recalls Colson. "He had a complete mastery of all the issues, he was quick in his mind and brilliant in his responses." As they talked together after the recording, Colson could not help continuing to make a comparison between the formal relationship he had with his senator and the instant rapport that sprang up in his conversation with the vice president. "Saltonstall was a genuine aristocrat and a fine man," says Colson, "but he was not intellectually deep, he was not quick on issues, and he liked to stay aloof. Nixon, on the other hand, had an instinctive feel for issues, he got to the heart of things very fast, and he was warm and easy to work with." Not everyone took such a favorable view of Richard Nixon, but Colson was a true believer in him from the beginning.

As the preparations for the 1960 election got under way, there was a moment when a safe seat in Congress was Colson's for the asking. The story of how this came about, and why Colson turned down the opportunity when it was offered to him on a plate, sheds interesting light on some aspects of his character, his skills as a political operator, and his ambitions.

In early 1960, Edith Nourse Rogers, a long-serving Republican congresswoman from the Fifth Congressional District of Massachusetts, suddenly died of pneumonia. The local GOP leaders were thrown into consternation because her death occurred just five days before nominations closed for the election. Rogers's name was already printed on the ballot as the GOP candidate. Under Massachusetts electoral law the only way a name on the ballot could be changed was if sufficient numbers of stickers with an alternative name were printed, distributed to the voters, and then pasted on top of the nominated candidate's name on the ballot. Getting this done in the five-day time frame was a challenging problem, especially since there was no agreement on who the new Republican candidate should be.

Colson liked challenging problems. Using his clout as Senator Saltonstall's administrative assistant, he convened an urgent meeting of the GOP's selection committee in Boston to choose the new candidate. However, Colson himself had already decided who the new candidate should be. He called his old friend Brad Morse, who was now in place as the number two at the Veterans Administration, and said to him: "How would you like to be the congressman?" A surprised Morse said he would, but started to doubt whether it could be done. "Don't worry. I'll fix it," said Colson confidently. "Just get on an airplane and come to Boston in time for the meeting tomorrow."

The meeting of the Fifth District GOP leaders and financial backers did not go entirely according to plan. Brad Morse's plane was delayed. Colson found it difficult to sell him as a candidate, partly because of his absence but more because a prominent member of the selection committee, Ralph Bonnell, wanted to be the candidate himself. After several hours of discussion at Boston's Union Club in a traditional smoke-filled room (to which the chain-smoking Colson was a substantial contributor), the committee was deadlocked. However, it emerged in the conversation that Nancy Colson's parents lived in the Fifth District, a coincidence which could allow Colson to be put forward as a local or favorite son candidate. Suddenly a draft Colson movement began within the committee. It was so well supported that it became obvious that he was being offered the nomination. Colson had to work hard to stop his own bandwagon from rolling. "Look, fellas, you know I'd like it, but you're making a mistake," he told the committee. "I'm not the strongest candidate. The strongest candidate is Brad Morse." After several more minutes of Colson's powerful advocacy for his old friend, Morse was eventually nominated. The meeting ended with the Republican state chairman saying, "We'd better get our skates on and place an order for Brad Morse stickers." Colson surprised him by saying: "Don't bother. I ordered those stickers myself this morning. They'll be ready by four o'clock." By the time Brad Morse arrived at the airport, he had the nomination and the stickers—which were distributed across the Fifth District that evening.

This episode, which Bill Saltonstall, the senator's son, has described as "a typical piece of Chuck's wizardry showing how he was always five jumps ahead of everyone else," explains why Colson was building a reputation as a tough and clever political operator. Yet perhaps the most interesting question to be asked about this story is, why didn't Colson seize the moment and accept the offer of a safe congressional seat? No doubt his loyalty to Brad Morse played a part in his decision, but it seems extraordinary that a young man who loved politics and was well suited for the job, with his speaking skills and his experience of life on Capitol Hill, should have closed the door on what many would have regarded as an appointment with destiny. Colson himself has had no regrets or doubts about the path he took in that smoke-filled room. "I just knew that elected office wasn't for me," he says. "I didn't think that was where I could do the best job. I didn't think I had the patience for it. I didn't like the front side of politics. I liked the back side of it, being kingmaker, orchestrating things, getting things done, and serving my ideals in that way."

Campaign Manager

Throughout the election year of 1960, Colson was working hard to serve and to save Senator Saltonstall, whose prospects for reelection were not looking good. The polls were showing him running ten points behind his expected Democratic opponent, Foster Furcolo, the governor of Massachusetts.

Furcolo was given the full Colson treatment in the run-up to the primaries, with devastating effect. "We knew there were quite a few skeletons in Furcolo's cupboard. It was my job to get them out of the cupboard and into the press—and I did," recalls Colson. "I managed to stir up a lot of controversy about him even though he was a fairly successful governor. I also managed on the quiet to do quite a few things to build support for the young Democratic mayor of Springfield, in the western part of Massachusetts, Tom O'Connor. My thinking was that O'Connor would have a brutal primary fight with the governor, damage him, and then make it easier for Saltonstall to beat him. Unfortunately, we did far too good a job, because Furcolo got beaten by O'Connor. So now we were up against a fresh, clean-shaven, handsome young Kennedyish candidate against whom Saltonstall, sixty-four years old and looking older, seemed tired and out of date. All the polls and the pundits said we would lose. So as we started the campaign it was clear that we had an enormous fight on our hands."

By virtue of being Senator Saltonstall's administrative assistant, Colson became his campaign manager. Under his leadership, most members of the Saltonstall office team on Capitol Hill were moved up to Massachusetts in the last three or four months before the election. They included Patty Hughes and a new recruit, Jonathan Moore, Colson's old friend from their years together at Browne & Nichols. Moore's talent for schoolboy journalism had led to him getting a job with the United States Information Agency. He was persuaded to leave his post in the USIA office in Liberia by Colson, who needed his skills in Massachusetts for a different kind of propaganda.

While remaining a Colson admirer, Moore was not afraid to challenge and criticize his boss. One incident that caused a flare-up between them concerned a campaign press release that Colson had drafted. "I objected to that press release on grounds of truthfulness," recalled Moore. "Chuck was infuriated with me. He moved heaven and earth to argue me into backing down. About halfway through the argument I said to him, 'What the heck. I think it's wrong, but you're the boss. You can send out any press release you want.' That really drove him nuts. I don't know whether it was his conscience or whatever, but he tried harder and harder to get me to agree, but I wouldn't go along with him. Eventually he lost his temper completely and kicked a wastepaper basket across a room so hard that he left a big dent in it."

There were other outbursts of temper under the pressures of the campaign. Colson is remembered for throwing over a chair in a restaurant after a ferocious argument with a long-standing Saltonstall supporter named Doris who had criticized some tactical maneuver or other for being unethical. "Doris got really under his skin, but she was probably right," recalls Jonathan Moore. "The problem was that Chuck's electioneering ethics were as different from Saltonstall's ethics as it was possible to imagine. Chuck often used to say to the staff, 'The senator doesn't want to know about this,' and that gave Chuck a deserved reputation for doing things that were considered shady. 'Cutting corners' would be the most euphemistic way of putting it. He was a rough-and-tumble man who could be ruthless for getting what he wanted."

For all Jonathan Moore's reservations about some electioneering tactics, he was full of admiration for Colson's strategic thinking, which he said was always "several jumps ahead of the opposition." Since Colson was only twenty-nine years old and had no previous experience of political campaigning, his successful strategies were all the more surprising. However, he had taken lessons in the arcane art of electioneering from Steven Shadegg, a brilliant Republican campaign manager who against all the odds had masterminded a stunning 1958 Senate victory by the conservative Barry Goldwater, in the Democratic state of Arizona. Under Shadegg's tuition, Colson bought up all the billboard space in Massachusetts months ahead of the election. He created a network of interest groups across the state that Saltonstall consulted as regular sounding boards for his Senate speeches, and using an early equivalent of the word processor, he started sending personalized letters from Saltonstall to thousands of constituents.

Colson's most important innovation in the age before television commercials had become part of elections was to make a half-hour film on

Saltonstall and distribute it to TV stations and movie theaters across the
state. The film, which played on Saltonstall's seniority and his effectiveness
in winning jobs for Massachusetts, was a big hit. All of a sudden there was
a new interest in Saltonstall and what he had achieved as a senior statesman in national politics. The polls started to narrow.

Intriguingly, the groundbreaking television film project on Saltonstall
had been suggested to Colson by Ted Reardon, John F. Kennedy's legislative assistant in the Senate. Apparently Kennedy did not have any particular empathy with the Democratic senatorial candidate, Tom O'Connor,
whereas he was close to his fellow Harvard graduate and fellow patrician
Leverett Saltonstall. So in all sorts of quiet, subterranean ways—the film
was one—Kennedy, the Democratic presidential candidate, did his best to
help Saltonstall, the Republican, win reelection.

However helpful Kennedy was being privately, all the electoral mathe-
matics suggested that Kennedy's Democratic Party coattails would be extremely unhelpful to Saltonstall on polling day. It was certain that in the
presidential election, Massachusetts would fall to Kennedy by a huge plu-
rality. So Saltonstall's biggest problem was how to persuade voters to split
their tickets. The resourceful Colson ran a billboard campaign with the slo-
gan "Massachusetts for Kennedy and Saltonstall," with backup reminders
that every federal goodie that had come to the state in recent years had
been due to Saltonstall-Kennedy cooperation. Colson also put out several
bogus mail shots from supporters of this split-ticket approach and organized a breakaway group of Democrats for Salty in O'Connor's hometown.
As election day loomed, O'Connor's lead faded. He and Saltonstall went
into the last week of the campaign running neck and neck.

Colson realized that the key to victory would be the voting intentions of
the huge Irish bloc in the Massachusetts electorate. So he went for the
jugular with a secret strategy unknown to Saltonstall. First, after much
arm-twisting and hard drinking, Colson inveigled six prominent Irish Democrats into signing a letter endorsing the split ticket of Kennedy and
Saltonstall. Then he ran off three hundred thousand copies of the letter and
moved into a small Boston hotel, renting several rooms there, where he in-
stalled some twenty young volunteers in a makeshift office behind locked
doors. The volunteers addressed plain envelopes to every Irish-sounding
name that could be found in the Massachusetts phone books. Three days
before the election, all three hundred thousand envelopes had been addressed and filled, ready for delivery to an out-of-the-way post office where
a friendly postmaster had agreed to process the bulk mailing.

Secrecy was essential to this plan, for it would be fatal if this mysterious mail shot could be traced to Saltonstall's campaign manager. It had to look like a genuine letter from Irish-American Kennedy supporters to their fellow Irish-Americans across the state. For this reason, Colson handpicked his volunteers, swore them to secrecy, and kept them incommunicado in the hotel rooms, whose locks had even been changed to cordon them in.

All these well-laid plans came perilously close to ending in disaster. As the secret operation was completed and the letters were being moved from the hotel to the post office in a couple of station wagons, the volunteer in charge of the project asked to speak to Colson privately. The two men went for a walk in the hotel corridor. "Chuck, I'm worried about one of our girls," said the head volunteer, a Harvard freshman named Tom Winter. "Her father is an avid party man and she thinks we're being disloyal to Nixon. I overheard her talking about going to Republican headquarters to tell the chairman what's going on here."

It was worse than that. The girl became hysterical in her indignation over this betrayal of the official GOP presidential candidate, even though the mail shot's sole purpose was to save Saltonstall's Senate seat for the Republicans in a state where Nixon had no chance. One of Colson's close friends, Don Whitehead, reported that he had heard the girl screaming, "Colson is a son of a bitch! He is not going to get away with this. I am going to report him to Chick McLean, chairman of the Republican State Committee. I am going to the press. I am going on the radio. I will not let this happen."

Colson was shattered. He could see that his unorthodox methods might anger Nixon loyalists at GOP headquarters. A leak to them would probably mean a leak to the press, which would be a catastrophe.

With disaster staring him in the face, Colson became even more unorthodox in his methods. He dipped into his wallet and took out his airline credit card (in those days the best credit card available) and $100 in $10 bills. Don Whitehead also chipped in with a $10 contribution. The money and the credit card were handed over to the head volunteer. "Tom, take this girl out tonight and get her loaded," Colson told Winter. "Keep her diverted, whatever you have to do, until election day."

The diversions were remarkably effective. Not only was the girl kept quiet for the next forty-eight hours, her relationship with Tom Winter lasted for many years. As a result of her conversion from potential leaker to established lover, the mail shot landed safely in the mailboxes of the Irish-American community. Its results brought joy to the Saltonstall camp on election night. Although in the presidential election count Kennedy won

Massachusetts by 500,000 votes, in the Senate race Saltonstall romped home with a majority of 310,000. This meant that approximately 800,000 Massachusetts voters who wanted to elect a Democratic president had split their tickets and voted for a Republican senator. It was a triumph for Colson's strategy.

As the good results poured into Colson's office from the precincts on election night, he knew by ten-thirty that victory was assured. So he called Saltonstall at home to congratulate him and to bring him to Boston's Shoreham Hotel to deliver his acceptance speech. The candidate and the campaign manager met on the sidewalk just outside the hotel. At such a glorious moment, great jubilation might have been expected, or perhaps at least a hurrah and a hug from the victor for the aide who had delivered the election. But that was not the Saltonstall style. As Colson recalls the scene: "I'll never forget what happened. It was a brisk November night and Saltonstall had on his Chesterfield coat and his felt hat. As we met on the sidewalk he just shook my hand and said, 'I'm much obliged.' I thought to myself, I've just given a year of my life to this election, I'm utterly exhausted and elated, and that's all he can say? But that was Saltonstall's way. It was the caste system. I was the hired hand, I'd done my job well, so 'much obliged' was all that needed to be said."

The coldness of Saltonstall's thanks might have upset Colson more if he had been intending to remain in the Senate as a professional staffer. But he was already on the move with new ambitions. While the election campaign was in progress, Colson had received his law school results. They were excellent by any standards and amazing for a night student who had carried the draining workload of being a senator's administrative assistant and an election campaign manager. Colson graduated eighth in his class of 120 at George Washington University. He was awarded a Juris Doctor degree (at the time, the equivalent of a Doctorate in Law). He had also been appointed to the Order of the Coif, one of the highest law school academic awards. In addition he passed the Virginia bar exam and was granted licenses to practice law there and in the District of Columbia.

With all these good results in the bag, several top law firms approached him with job offers. Staying on in the Senate was also an option. But Colson had made his plans, and they were characteristically bold ones. He left the Saltonstall office in December 1960 with a new goal in life. It was to start his own law firm.

CHAPTER FIVE

Colson and Morin, Nancy and Patty

Early Setbacks and Successes

In 1961 Charles Colson cofounded the law firm Colson and Morin, which was to become the focal point of his ambition for the next eight years. Although the partnership brought him considerable financial rewards, a wide circle of influential friends, and was the launching pad for his appointment as a White House aide, Colson's early steps to success were often thwarted by economic and personal difficulties. When the law firm opened its doors for business, the going was hard. Perhaps this should have been expected, for Colson, to put it mildly, was an inexperienced lawyer. He had only just graduated from night law school and taken the bar. He had no knowledge of how to practice law, no clients, and virtually no money. These disadvantages did not deflect his vaulting ambition. Yet even Colson's get-up-and-go brashness might have faltered at the hurdle of instant law practice had he not bonded so deeply in friendship with Charles H. Morin.

Son of a former Internal Revenue Service official from Springfield, Massachusetts, Morin had graduated from Harvard in 1943 and served with distinction in the Korean War as a CIA officer. Although eight years older than Colson, Morin came from a similar outsider's background, for his Irish-French Canadian parentage and his middle-class origins kept him some distance from the establishment of Boston.

Colson was introduced to Morin in 1959 by Brad Morse, with the words "Chuck is one of the smartest guys I have ever met in my life. When he finishes at night school, he will have a great career as a lawyer." Intrigued, Morin invited Colson to dinner at his home. Their first social encounter was not a success. The urbane and widely traveled Morin was a wine connoisseur. On a visit to Burgundy, he had persuaded a reluctant vineyard owner to part with one of the last bottles of his finest postwar vintage. This was a magnum of Clos de Vougeot 1947. It was exhibited like an icon upon the sideboard of Morin's dining room, awaiting homage from wine buffs with palates as expert as their host's.

Enter Colson, attending his first and very nearly his last supper chez Morin. Observing that glasses were standing empty, Colson decided that his assistance was needed with the service. Undeterred by his ignorance of the difference between a *premier grand cru* and a *vin ordinaire,* he appointed himself wine steward. Taking up his duties with his customary energy, Colson uncorked the biggest bottle of wine he could find. This was the holy magnum of Clos de Vougeot. Colson dispensed it freely, filling up the guests' glasses to the top. Morin's eloquent words on discovering this act of sacrilege are best left veiled under that catchphrase made famous by the Nixon presidency, "expletives deleted." Despite this inauspicious opening of their relationship, Colson and Morin began discussing the idea of starting a three-man law partnership, the third man being Brad Morse— who dropped out because of his sudden election to Congress through the Colson-inspired maneuvers described in the previous chapter.

As a two-man partnership, Colson and Morin were short of the resources required to finance a new law firm. Colson put up $5,000 from his savings. Morin, even though he was already a partner in a small family legal practice, could not afford to put up any money at all. They soon discovered that their capital was not even enough to buy the office furniture, until, to their considerable relief, a salesman introduced them to the concept of monthly leasing payments. The next problem was finding clients. Colson proved a talented if unorthodox businessman. As Morin amusingly recalled in an after dinner speech to the Becket Fund almost forty years later: "Those who say Colson has changed are not getting it right. He has always been an evangelist! When we were starting out in 1961 with tiny offices, he was very evangelical. Believe me, there is no better training for being an evangelist than hustling for clients for a two-man law firm. If we came across prospective clients searching for the way, we were the light! If they were short of loaves and fishes—no problem. We spoke with the tongues of prophets—spelled either way."

Profits were quite a worry in those early days. Initially, Colson had considerable success in bringing in new clients. One of the first he signed up was the gun and rifle manufacturer Harrington & Richardson, for which he had done favors in his days as Senator Saltonstall's aide. Another defense industry client was Craig Systems, founded by the inventors of the bazooka. Swords were followed by plowshares when Colson landed an account with the New England Council—a trade association of regional industries, including manufacturers of agricultural machinery. Morin was busy too, bringing in significant clients such as the mutual fund group Federated Investors. So by the end of the first year, the partners felt they were doing well enough to pay themselves $25,000 each.

However, at the end of the second year, shortly before Christmas 1962, times were becoming harder. Colson and Morin spent a long evening in their Boston office, shirt sleeves rolled up, a bottle of scotch in front of them, and the ledger books of their young firm spread out on the rented conference table. Sometime after midnight, Morin, deep shadows under his eyes and anxious furrows across his brow, came to a gloomy conclusion: "We still owe ten thousand for the furniture, the payroll is up to twenty thousand a month, we are hiring too many people, and the big firms are putting up blocks to us. I don't see enough business to get us through." At the time, Colson could not find convincing answers to his partner's doom-laden prediction that the firm would have to close. But two days later he wrote Morin a seven-page letter of spirited exhortation. Colson did not lack a talent for inspiration as he expounded his philosophy for fighting back with determination:

> *Charlie— I have noted with much distress the downcast tone of your voice. Unfortunately I've been down also. Since we are both manic depressives, only disaster can result from us both being down at the same time—hence permit me a brief bit of political philosophy. . . .*
>
> *As with any business, there are ups and downs—and they also come in bunches. You and I cannot but make a success of C and M. All the ingredients are there. In fact, considering that we have been in operation only one year, I think the results are fantastic, since the first year is always the hardest. But there are bound to be rough spots.*

The letter continued by setting out a litany of business woes, such as companies that had not paid their bills, relationships that had become strained, and clients who had turned "slippery." Then, in a passage that may have contained a hint of his later gift for delivering sermons, Colson gave his partner a pep talk.

Real greatness is measured not by how well a man can take his
successes (any idiot can handle this) but rather how well reverses
can be turned to one's advantage. You and I, being sensitive guys,
get somewhat morose when a few things don't go just as we want
them. But our greatest asset is optimism, a positive outlook and
real determination. These are things, Charlie, that make the differ-
ence and if we have a streak of tough luck we just have to push
harder. This firm is going to be the most successful in the East or
I'm going to break my ass. If we lose all our clients and go flat
broke, I'm going to keep going because we have everything it takes
to make it. If you and I ever despair, we have had it because the
Spirit makes the difference—and now I'm about to add a little spir-
its myself!

Morin must have wondered whether his partner had refreshed himself
rather too liberally as the next two pages of the letter unfolded. After declaring, "We could easily double our business," Colson listed "good possibilities." They included some of the most important names on the New
England business scene, among them Grumman Aircraft, Raytheon,
McPherson Instruments, and New England Electric. Alongside each name
Colson set out reasons why the company might be persuaded to transfer its
legal business to Colson and Morin. He concluded his letter:

If we are aggressive and positive, with our abilities we can't
miss, and contrary to your statements last week our empire will not
collapse. To the contrary, we've done remarkably well and will do
better—so keep your spirits up! See you soon.

> *Your ever loving partner,*
> *Chuck*

The optimistic scenario set out in this letter was not a case of whistling
in the wind. Over the next four years, eleven of the nineteen prospective
clients on Colson's list became actual clients. It was a good batting average
given the fierce competition from rival law firms, and it owed much to Colson's indefatigable networking among the corporate friends he had made
during his days as a Senate aide. One of them was Lew Evans, executive
vice president of Grumman Aircraft. He bonded closely with Colson and
transferred much of his company's legal business to the firm. Another significant client was Simplex Time Recorder, a manufacturer of clocks and

punch cards located in the small town of Gardner, Massachusetts, where it was by far the largest local employer. The proprietor of Simplex was Curtis Watkins, a strong-willed businessman who, on the day Colson and Morin visited him, was in a state of enraged shock because his nominee had been unexpectedly passed over for a patronage post he thought was his by right—postmaster of Gardner.

All the more weighty reasons why Simplex Time Recorder might need new corporate legal advisers were put on one side while its chairman raged about the personal injustice he felt at his man being rejected for the postmastership of his company's and his own hometown. All Colson and Morin could do was to promise to make representations to the White House for a change of mind regarding the next postmaster of Gardner.

Driving back to Boston, empty-handed in terms of new legal business, Colson had a bright idea. Stopping at a pay phone, he called Curtis Watkins and asked him what percentage of mail handled by the post office in Gardner originated from Simplex Time Recorder.

"At least eighty percent of it," said Curtis Watkins.

"In that case, why don't you say you're going to send all your company mail through the post office in Fitchburgh?" suggested Colson, referring to the neighboring town and postal district. "That might change some minds."

"Colson, you are a genius!" exclaimed Watkins.

The threat of removing 80 percent of the mail revenues from Gardner's post office was more than enough to make the postmaster general's office in Washington reconsider the appointment of a new postmaster for the town. Soon afterward, the job was offered to and accepted by the nominee of Curt Watkins. As a result, Watkins transferred the entire legal business of Simplex Time Recorder to the law firm of Colson and Morin.

One other story of Colson's original or, as Morin would later say, "evangelistic" methods for winning new business for their firm involved a chance encounter on a train journey. It happened on a day when all flights between Washington and Boston had been canceled. Colson managed to get a seat on the crowded train to Boston and found himself alongside a fellow passenger who was perching uncomfortably on his suitcase in the aisle. They fell into conversation. Colson discovered his neighbor was Sam Bass, the owner of a small computer company, Control Logic, which held some interesting patents but had no money to develop them. Before the train reached Boston, Colson was perching on the suitcase and the more comfortably seated Bass had agreed to become a client of the firm. Morin quickly turned himself into a securities lawyer, raising $300,000 for Control Logic in a private placement. A grateful Bass for many years paid Colson and Morin a $6,000 annual retainer. Within the firm it was suggested (unsuccessfully) that since Colson had displayed such natural skills as a traveling salesman he should in future make all his journeys between Washington and Boston by train.

Breaking the Color Bar

In light of such successes, the law firm began prospering, to the extent that the founding partners could no longer cope with their workload. Colson was in the office fourteen hours a day, six days a week. His Sundays were given over to the partnership too, for socializing with clients almost invariably took precedence over relaxing with the family. Under such a regime Colson's rapport with Nancy came under increasing strain. He could not find enough hours in the day to be a good lawyer and a good husband too. As a result of his priorities being so law-firm-oriented, the Colson marriage was fast becoming a dysfunctional relationship. As the legal work continued to expand, the two partners decided they must take on a third lawyer. They sought advice on whom to recruit from the outgoing U.S. attorney for Massachusetts, Elliot Richardson, a Republican appointee who had relinquished his post a few months after the inauguration of a Democrat president, John F. Kennedy, in 1961, and who was later to serve in four cabinet posts. Over a drink in Boston's Parker House bar, Richardson recommended a candidate for Colson and Morin.

"If I were you, I'd take the most brilliant young assistant U.S. attorney in my team," said Richardson. "He's the one I trusted with all the big cases, all the complicated tax cases, all the difficult litigation. This guy works around the clock, he's really smart—a superb lawyer."

"Who is he?" asked Morin, who thought he already knew all the superb lawyers in Massachusetts.

"Joe Mitchell," replied Richardson.

"Elliot, you can't be serious. C'mon!" said Morin.

"What's the matter, Charlie?" asked a mystified Colson. "The guy sounds great—just what we need!"

"Chuck—he's a Negro," said Morin.

"Oh, darn it!" said Colson.

This dialogue may read strangely in the racially tolerant climate of twenty-first-century America. However, in the 1960s, racially intolerant attitudes were the norm in Boston's legal profession. In the city's charmed circle of prestigious law firms, not a single one employed a black lawyer. The color bar was real. After further reflection on Elliot Richardson's recommendation, Colson and Morin acted boldly. The abilities of the candidate, they decided, were more important than the prejudices of the profession. Although they took the precaution of sounding out their leading clients before the appointment was made, they signed up Joseph S. Mitchell Jr. as the firm's first associate. No business was lost as a result of the arrival of a black lawyer in the office. Joe Mitchell, in private practice, lived up to the high reputation he had enjoyed as an assistant U.S. attorney. More important, the color bar that had been operative for over two centuries in Boston's established law firms was broken by Colson and Morin.

Although the newly recruited Joe Mitchell liked Charles Colson, who he later described as "very energetic, with an excellent mind and an oddball sense of humor," the last quality did not appeal, with good reason, to Joe's wife, Doris. She recalls a darker side of Colson. "He was cocky, brash, and full of unpleasant ideas. As soon as I heard about the Watergate break-in I said, 'That's Chuck!' But I admit I had a bias against him ever since the cross burning."

Cross burning? In the leafy suburbs of Boston in the 1960s? It happened on the night of the midterm congressional elections in November 1962. Pleased by the results and well refreshed by alcohol, Colson and Morin decided it would be a good moment for a little nocturnal humor at the expense of their black associate. Joe Mitchell had just bought a new house in Newton, an exclusive suburb five miles west of Boston's city center. It had a fine lawn leading up to the front porch. Colson thought this would be the ideal site for a housewarming with a difference. As Joseph and Doris Mitchell and their young children slept peacefully in the early hours of the morning, the founding partners of Colson and Morin tiptoed onto the lawn and erected a large brushwood cross. As Doris Mitchell remembers the episode: "Suddenly there was a crackling noise and then a great blaze lighting up the whole house. The cross was huge, at least six feet by four feet; I can't think where they got the wood for it. At first all I could see was men running around in hoods and raincoats, but then I knew it was Colson because he laughed so loudly. He was obviously half potted. I came out with buckets of water to pour on the flames and I was furious. I was terrified too that my small children would wake up and be badly frightened."

Colson and his fellow Ku Klux Klan impersonator could not have known that two decades earlier, Doris's parents had seen their Mississippi home burned to the ground in a real KKK arson attack that began with a cross burning in their backyard. No wonder Doris Mitchell was not amused. "To this day I'm still mad at Chuck," she says. "At least Charlie Morin was quick to see that the joke had misfired. He apologized and asked my forgiveness. He often said he was sorry about it for years afterwards. But Chuck never apologized."

In those days, Charles Colson was a far from sensitive soul when his quirky sense of humor was in the ascendant. He played many jokes within the firm. Some of them were amusing. One rather shy young associate was attempting to court Morin's attractive secretary, Pat Owens. Unfortunately, his romantic ardor was quenched early in the wooing proceedings by his alcoholic consumption. He collapsed into total insensibility and spent the night on Owens's sofa without anything happening. The next morning he confessed that he had absolutely no recollection of the night's events. Colson imaginatively filled this memory gap. He confidentially warned the young man that Pat Owens was living in fear that she might be pregnant. This phantom-pregnancy joke was kept going for weeks as Colson thoughtfully presented the terrified young man with a succession of books with titles such as *The Responsibilities of Fatherhood* and *How to Bring Up an Unwanted Child*.

Even Charles Morin did not escape Colson's penchant for elaborate hoaxes. In January 1962, Colson received a letter from the secretary of the Interstate Commerce Commission requesting "a frank opinion of the moral character of Charles H. Morin, who has filed an application for leave to practice before the commission." Enchanted by this golden opportunity to make mischief, Colson solemnly replied to the commission that he realized "my responsibility as a lawyer and as a citizen demands a completely forthright answer in response to an official question from a government agency." The letter went on to warn the commission that Morin often failed to pay his bills at the country club, got himself involved with strange women in New York, physically abused his wife, and was anti-Semitic. When a pink carbon copy of this letter crossed the desk of Hannah Campbell, a straitlaced office secretary, she flew into a panic and tried to recover the original copy from the local post office. Eventually, a delighted Colson revealed that the pink carbon was a spoof and that he had sent an impeccable letter to the Interstate Commerce Commission praising the upright moral character of his partner.

Liquor may have played its part in these office comedies. Although the partners worked long into the night as a matter of course, they observed a rule known as the 6 P.M. Mandatory Quit—a break for drinks, often followed by dinner at a nearby restaurant, El Bodegón. Usually they went back to work after these refreshments, but sometimes they went out to play. Stories abound of Colson's joie de vivre on such evenings. He would walk over anyone for a practical joke. Several of his pranks involved Joe Mitchell. One evening Colson was so delighted to find Mitchell's Chevrolet parked on a slope that he released its hand brake, with the inevitable result that the car careered down the hill, eventually crashing into a wall. This was an expensive escapade, for the morning after it the partners had to buy their associate a new car.

It might have been thought that Joe Mitchell would become a little weary, if not upset, by such manifestations of Colson's humor at his expense. Not so. The two men maintained a warm personal relationship throughout their years together in the law firm, which ended when Mitchell was elevated to the judiciary in 1966 as an associate justice in the Superior Court of Massachusetts. From this vantage point, eight years later, Mitchell wrote an eloquent letter to his fellow justice Judge Gerhard Gesell, asking him to be lenient when Colson came before him for sentencing at the time of Watergate. "Charles Colson and I spent many thousands of hours together," wrote Mitchell.

> His mind was one of the greatest and most brilliant that I have ever encountered in dissecting problems and effecting practical solutions. He unselfishly shared his wisdom and insight with us who were his constant companions. But far beyond this, Charles Colson was a sensitive and kind human being. While our social philosophies were not always in agreement there was never anything as a friend he would not extend himself to do. . . . The goodness of men like Charles Colson is often lost in the controversy that surrounds them. As one who bathed in the beauty of the goodness of Charles Colson I would like it so recorded.

Polarizing Opinions

Not everyone shared Joe Mitchell's favorable views on "the goodness of Charles Colson." One of his enemies was the formidable Senator Margaret Chase Smith of Maine. Not only did she take a negative view of the rising young lawyer, she made a formal request for him to be investigated by the FBI.

The background to this episode was that Colson, after resigning as Senator Leverett Saltonstall's administrative assistant in 1961, nevertheless remained in his post as secretary to the New England senators' committee. He retained this appointment at the request of Saltonstall, supported in turn by several senators on the committee. However, Margaret Chase Smith had a different view. She thought it was wrong for Colson to attend the monthly meetings of the New England senators as their committee secretary while simultaneously representing several New England corporations as their legal counsel. The first Colson knew about Smith's opposition to him was when he received a call in his law firm office from the deputy director of the FBI, Deke Deloach.

"I'm a friend of yours, Chuck, so I thought I'd better let you know that Senator Margaret Chase Smith has made a formal request to the bureau to have you investigated," began the FBI man.

"Investigated for what?" demanded Colson.

"Conflict-of-interest allegations," replied Deloach, going on to explain Smith's concern about the New England senators' committee. Colson's next call was to Senator Leverett Saltonstall, asking, "Get me out of this!" By mutual agreement Colson vacated the post of secretary to the New England senators' committee a few days later.

This setback was of no lasting importance. New business was pouring into the law firm so fast that Colson was relieved at not having to spend his valuable time on non-fee-earning activities for the New England senators. Colson and Morin, having originally been cold-shouldered by the Boston legal establishment, were now on the brink of joining it. The initial move in this direction came in 1962 when a former chairman of the SEC, Edward Gadsby, became the first name partner in the firm that was relaunched as Gadsby Colson and Morin. This was the first of six name changes in five years. Between 1962 and 1967, the firm was variously known as Colson and Morin; Gadsby Colson and Morin; Gadsby Hannah Colson and Morin; Gadsby Maguire and Hannah; Gadsby Maguire Hannah and Merrigan; and finally Gadsby and Hannah—which still flourishes today. Throughout these high-velocity changes in nomenclature, the founding partners, Colson and Morin, always retained a controlling interest, even when their names vanished from the letterhead. At first Colson resented his status as an invisible partner. When it was first proposed that

Morin's name be eliminated from the brass plate, Colson angrily scribbled him a note:

> *I'm rarely sentimental but if "Morin" is to be dropped, so is "Colson." Please so advise the others. As the founders of this outfit we can call the shots on future names. The fact is that you and I stay or go together. Screw them all! I love ya—*
>
> > *Chuck*

In fact, financial logic was driving the name changes. Edward N. Gadsby, as a former SEC chairman, had opened the door to a lot of prestigious securities business. Paul Hannah, the former general counsel to Raytheon, had brought that huge defense manufacturer's legal account to the firm, in the process introducing Colson to the dynamic young president of Raytheon, Tom Phillips, who ten years later would play a pivotal role in his conversion. Another key partner was Richard Maguire, a Kennedy White House aide who, as a former treasurer of the Democratic National Committee, introduced a number of good clients from the other side of the political fence. Throughout these years, Colson himself remained a tireless business getter, sometimes using unorthodox methods, as the story of the firm's first international client demonstrates.

Back in the days when the partnership was still struggling to make ends meet, Colson was introduced to Moises Benaceraff, a wealthy property entrepreneur from Venezuela. At the time of his introduction, the partners were warned that Benaceraff was the sort of South American big shot who might be underwhelmed when he saw the small size of his prospective law firm's Washington office. Colson came up with an ingenious idea for handling the problem of first impressions. In the same building as Gadsby Colson and Morin were the headquarters of the Organization for Veterans of Foreign Wars. Colson approached the marine corps general who headed VFW. Could his spacious office be borrowed for a meeting with an important foreign visitor? "Permission granted," said the general.

Surrounded by flags, medals, and military memorabilia, Moises Benaceraff was impressed. Clearly he was dealing with a large and prestigious law firm at the heart of the American establishment. Unfortunately, the business he wished to entrust to Colson looked like mission impossible. Benaceraff wanted to obtain a $12 million U.S. government loan guarantee in order to build a high-rise luxury apartment building in downtown

Caracas. This was a tall order, since the only source for such a loan guarantee was the U.S. State Department's Agency for International Development, whose remit was to finance construction of housing for the poor.

Undeterred by any misgivings about the use of U.S. taxpayers' money to
build apartments for the rich, Colson set up a meeting with the State Department official who knew his way through the maze of sections and sub-
sections of the relevant AID loan-guarantee statutes. This official, Ed Wise,
advised that the Benaceraff apartment building could be granted a loan
guarantee by the U.S. government, provided that a highly complex series
of steps was followed to obtain the necessary mortgages, indentures, bond
issues, and underwriting in compliance with the small print of the legislation.

In spite of this encouraging advice, Colson and Morin came away from
the meeting somewhat despondent because it had become clear that the
highly specialized expertise needed to follow the procedures described by
Wise was beyond the range of their own abilities. *"Grande problema* for a
small law firm," said Morin dolefully as they rode back to their office in a
taxi. Colson had other ideas. He turned the cab around and went back to
the same official in the State Department with an ingenious proposition:
"Would you be interested in joining an up-and-coming law firm?" Colson
asked Ed Wise. Following that original headhunting approach, Wise had a
new job, and Benaceraff built his luxury apartment block, with the U.S.
government providing the loan guarantee for it. As for Colson, he earned
his firm over $300,000 over the next three years from his new Venezuelan
client.

Although Colson was outstanding in his drive to get business, opinions
differed within the partnership on his abilities as a lawyer. Charles Morin
rated him highly. "Chuck had one of the smartest legal brains I ever saw,"
he has recalled. "He went to the vital point in a case at once, and he was a
clever cross-examiner." By contrast, a later partner, Robert Owens, described Colson as "a second-rater at the law. He was too aggressive, too
boastful, too brash, too impatient."

Colson was certainly impatient, and although he never admitted it to his
partners, he was often bored by the minutiae of legal documentation and
pleadings. However, when the rare opportunity to try a challenging and interesting case in court came his way, he had both the intellectual ability and
the moral zeal to fight it to a finish. Two interesting cases, one a big fee
earner and the other pro bono, well demonstrated the capacity of Colson
as a trial lawyer.

Grumman v. Renegotiation Board was a groundbreaking case that resulted in Colson's being upheld in the Supreme Court on a substantive point of law involving the interpretation of the Freedom of Information Act. The Grumman Aircraft Corporation had fallen foul of the Renegotiation Board, an independent federal agency that had sweeping powers to compel companies executing government contracts to repay profits the board deemed to be excessive. Grumman, represented by Colson, argued that its profits on a fighter aircraft project were not excessive at all and that the Renegotiation Board's demands for a repayment of several million dollars were extortionate and unfair. Colson sued the board on the argument that they had given insufficient reasons for their excessive-profits allegation against Grumman. The board, unused to having its high-handed ways challenged, refused to disclose any additional information or reasons. Colson argued that they were obliged under the Freedom of Information Act to disclose all their procedures and reasons. The board replied that they had already put into the public domain by press releases and official announcements everything Grumman or anyone else needed to know about their agency.

Grumman lost the case at its first hearing, before the District Court. By the time it was heard by the Court of Appeals, Colson had trawled through every announcement made in the *Federal Review* by the Renegotiation Board. "I discovered that three quarters of the board's announcements had been related to housekeeping matters such as salary increases for board members," he recalled. "So I read out every one of their announcements to the Court of Appeals and then, instead of any sort of peroration, I simply said in a very deadpan way: 'Counsel for the agency has said that the board released everything my clients needed to know. Let the record speak for itself.' "

The Appeals Court ruled in favor of Grumman, and its judgment was upheld by the Supreme Court. Colson's tactics paid off well and brought a great deal of new business from Grumman into the firm. One exceptionally lucrative assignment given to Colson at this time was representing Grumman in the battle to win the contract for building the lunar excursion module on the space flight to the moon. It was his finest hour as a Washington lobbyist and lawyer when Colson delivered that huge contract to his clients.

Although he loved pulling off big deals, money was not the only motivator in Colson's career as a lawyer. He often displayed a steely determination to fight cases for pro bono clients assigned to him by the court. One such client was a teenage juvenile delinquent, Ricky Austin, charged in 1963 with burglary from a convent. It was the boy's fourth offense and the police evidence against him appeared to be strong. Colson could easily have turned the case over to an associate or followed the all too common practice of a cursory investigation and a guilty plea. But when the prosecution lawyer called to suggest a plea bargain, Colson replied: "I need time to find out whether the kid is guilty or innocent."

"Of course he's guilty. He was arrested, wasn't he?" retorted the prosecutor. Nettled by this attitude, Colson went to Ricky Austin's home, talked to his parents, walked with him around the scene of the alleged crime, and unearthed evidence of harassment by the arresting officer toward the boy. After this painstaking investigation Colson said to his client: "I believe your story. I am ready to take it to trial." After much preparation, Colson appeared in court on the day of the trial, only to be met by a total surrender by the prosecutor, who withdrew the charges. After this victory, Colson took Ricky Austin out onto the courtroom steps, sat him down, and gave him a civics and personal morality lecture, saying: "I want you to learn some lessons from this. The law isn't just there to arrest you when you do wrong. It is also there to protect you when you are in the right."

According to Austin, "Mr. Colson had a long talk with me. He made it clear, as no one had done before, that my life was headed for disaster. He spoke of honesty, truth, ambition, and obligation to others in terms that since then I have heeded." Austin, who corresponded with Colson for some years after the case, went on to stay clear of crime for the next decade of his life and secured a steady job at the Smithsonian Institution. He wrote the words quoted above in a letter he sent in 1974 to the probation officer who was preparing reports for Judge Gesell prior to Colson's sentencing.

Ricky Austin's case illustrates one feature of Colson's character that became well known after he had served his prison sentence but that was hardly known at all when his career was soaring upward. This was his instinctive sympathy for, and his willingness to go the extra mile for, an underdog in trouble. It may be speculated that this characteristic could have been inherited from both his mother, who ran a soup kitchen of sorts during the Depression, and from his father, who had a long history of pro bono legal work for prisoners in Massachusetts during the 1930s and 1940s. Whatever the source of this urge to help the unfortunate, it made its appearance at regular intervals in Colson's life story long before he got into misfortune himself.

As a counterbalance to his habit of sympathizing with underdogs, it was noticed that Colson could often be difficult and abrasive toward those he considered to be posturing as overdogs. This category of personages was not confined to his opponents. Colson had little or no tolerance when it came to suffering fools gladly. Even within the circle of his law partners he was considered by some to be an arrogant member of the team, cocksure in his certainties and aggressive in his attitudes. Others who worked closely with him saw almost everything he did through rose-colored spectacles. This ability to polarize opinions was to be a continuing feature of his upward progress. "It's the story of his life," said Charles Morin. "No one has ever been neutral about Chuck. You either loved him or loathed him. Personally I always loved the guy and still do."

There was no love lost between Colson and one of the most significant of his later partners in the law firm—Paul Hannah. They clashed as personalities and in frequent memo wars on matters ranging from postage stamps to partner remunerations. One of their more entertaining battles concerned some litigation between a Colson client and a client represented by John Murtha, the senior partner of Murtha, Cullina, Richter and Pinney, an old-fashioned law firm from Connecticut. Colson favored an attacking approach to the litigation. Hannah, who was a friend of Murtha's, tried to get the case settled in private correspondence, to which Colson took strong objection. Getting angry with one particular letter from John Murtha to Paul Hannah, Colson composed a blistering reply to Murtha.

Dear John,

I have had on my desk for over a week your letter of October 18th to my partner Paul Hannah. I have been trying to think of something clever to say in reply.

I have also been trying to restrain my temper and, after a week of careful thought, I have decided simply to tell you that in my opinion, you are one of the most insufferable s—— I have ever known, and if you ever have the misfortune to see me face to face, I am going to break your nose.

Sincerely yours,
Charles W. Colson

When a copy of this aggressive epistle landed on the desk of Paul Hannah, he went ballistic. In fury, he protested to the other partners about Colson's insulting rudeness to his friend, the distinguished senior lawyer from Connecticut. Colson could not contain his laughter. The letter, ostensibly written to Murtha, had never been posted. Colson was merely up to his old tricks with carbon copies. The recipient he had wanted to infuriate was Hannah. It was a tease that succeeded brilliantly, but it did nothing to promote good working relationships within the partnership.

Perhaps these tensions were more of a spur than a spoiler. For whatever the frictions between individuals may have been, the firm as a whole was making good money. By the mid-1960s, Colson and Morin, now finally renamed Gadsby and Hannah ("Chuck—Sic Transit Gloria Mundi—Chas," was a note scribbled by Morin to Colson on a copy of the announcement), had twenty-five partners and billings over $2.5 million. Colson was earning over $100,000 a year—a sum equivalent to approximately $1 million in today's money. However, in the middle of all this success, Colson had been passing through a period of torment. It was so serious that his loving wife feared he might be contemplating suicide and his loving partner, Charles Morin, argued fiercely with him, saying, "You can't do this. You will destroy the firm."

What was this all about? In a word, divorce.

Divorce

The strains and stresses in the marriage of Chuck and Nancy Colson had been building up for some time. The journey from teenage sweethearts in the late 1940s to deadened noncommunicators in the early 1960s was filled with many joys and sorrows, and faults on both sides. If Nancy had failings, they may have lain in the areas of being too sweet, too submissive, and so oriented toward the children that she failed to keep pace with her husband's widening horizons and interests. Chuck's faults were those of the overdriven careerist who was so tightly focused on success that he failed to find time for his nearest and dearest. To complicate these problems beyond repair was the fact that Colson had fallen in love with a new nearest and dearest.

The first signs that Colson was taking a romantic interest in Patty Hughes, the attractive receptionist he had hired for Senator Saltonstall's office, came on the night when John F. Kennedy was chosen to be his party's presidential candidate, at the Democratic National Convention of 1960. It was a tense evening for Colson, given the concerns about the effect of JFK's coattails on the reelection of "Salty." So Colson imbibed many too many drinks as he and other members of Saltonstall's staff watched

JFK's acceptance speech at a party in the home of Nancy's mother, Emily Billings, in Acton, Massachusetts. Under the influence of alcohol, Colson began behaving badly, making open advances to Patty Hughes. She was embarrassed and pushed him away. Undeterred by these rebuffs, Colson brought his two-year-old daughter, Emily, out of her bedroom and sat her on Patty's lap in order to get himself into position to make more advances. Nancy was by no means the only person present to feel offended by this behavior. Patty was upset, Nancy's mother was outraged. Even Colson's old friend Jonathan Moore called the amorous lunges "wholly indiscreet and inappropriate," while Jack Quinlan, chairman of Volunteers for Saltonstall, threatened to resign from the campaign if such misbehavior continued. "I just made a complete fool of myself," recalled Colson, who spent the day after the party apologizing to all and sundry.

Patty stayed cool, indeed chilly, toward her unwanted admirer throughout the election campaign. Colson, who was already worried about the state of his marriage, made an effort to breathe fresh life into it by taking Nancy away for what was supposed to be a romantic cruise to Bermuda, soon after the election. Unfortunately, this well-meaning attempt to rekindle love with a shipboard romance turned out to be a disaster. Nancy was seasick, Chuck was miserable, and both of them seemed to have nothing in common to talk about except their children. Soon after returning from Bermuda, Colson confided to his friend Don Whitehead that he just couldn't bear the thought of spending the rest of his life with the stranger Nancy had become to him.

"What shall I do, Don?" he asked in evident anguish.

"When things get as bad as this, they have a life of their own," replied Whitehead. For a long time there was nothing other than platonic life in the relationship between Colson and Patty Hughes. He took her out for dinner a few times, yet there was a Puritan streak in him and a Catholic conscience in her that delayed their deeper involvement. But in time they fell heavily for each other. Eighteen months after Colson's first advances to Patty on the night of the 1960 Democratic Convention, they had become an item.

One evening in the spring of 1962 Chuck took Nancy out to dinner—a rare event for the couple at that stage—at an expensive restaurant in the Virginia countryside. Toward the end of the meal he told his wife that he was seeing Patty regularly and that he had fallen in love with her. Nancy was devastated. She got up from the table and left the restaurant early in a flood of tears.

The following morning, after Colson had left for the office, Nancy's misery was written all over her face. As she struggled with her usual maternal and homemaking duties, Diz and Pop, as she always called Chuck's parents, who were staying in the Evening Lane house at the time, saw that something was terribly wrong. They sat down with Nancy, who poured out everything that Chuck had told her about his passion for Patty. Diz exploded. In a state of militant outrage she sided completely with Nancy and began making war plans to save the marriage. Commander in chief Diz's first shot was to dispatch Pop to Capitol Hill on a search-and-destroy mission. The target was Patty. Although Pop's normally benign nature must have made him feel somewhat reluctant to be deployed as a heat-seeking missile, he nevertheless obeyed orders and locked on to Patty, who at this time was working as a secretary in the office of Congressman Bob Stafford of Vermont. Bursting into the office, Pop had a confrontation with Patty in which inexcusable words were said at such a high volume that doors had to be closed along the corridor. After all this sound and fury, Patty was understandably upset. When she described the upheaval to Chuck, he became furious too. The main targets of his wrath were Diz, who he knew had sent Pop into battle, and Nancy, whom he blamed for revealing matrimonial secrets to his parents. As if this imbroglio were not enough, Diz summoned reinforcements in the shape of Nancy's mother, Emily Billings, who flew down from Boston to join the far from happy throng in residence at the Colson home in Alexandria. Nancy began to feel she was presiding over a sitcom as her in-laws and her mother plotted and planned to get the marriage back on track with what Diz kept calling a "quick fix." It was a vain hope. The reality was that Chuck and Nancy had been growing apart for at least two years and nothing could possibly be fixed quickly—if at all.

The sitcom pressure eased in the next few days, partly because Colson judiciously found it necessary while the quick-fix brigade was in residence at his home to spend exceptionally long hours in his office. However, those office hours were not entirely easy either. When he confided in Charlie Morin about his personal problems, the loving partners had their first ever exchange of angry words. "It was the one and only time we had a serious dispute," recalls Morin. "I had to say to him bluntly, 'You can't do this. You can't walk out on your family. You can't divorce. You'll destroy the firm.' "

This hard-line attitude did not last. Although in the more judgmental era of the 1960s clients had been known to leave law firms where a partner was involved in an acrimonious divorce, in this situation acrimony was avoided. Morin himself became very fond of Patty. After a dinner or two with Chuck in her apartment, Morin said of his smitten partner, "What could you do? Colson was head over heels in love with her. It was a fait accompli."

Nancy did not think of the situation in those terms. When the in-laws eventually departed she sat down with Chuck and tried to persuade him to agree to "Plan A" for saving their marriage. The two main elements in this plan were that Chuck should stop seeing Patty for six months and that the house in Evening Lane, Alexandria, should be sold so that the family could move into a rented town house two blocks from the law firm's Washington office. Nancy regarded Chuck's commitment to Plan A as a great victory. Patty, to her credit, did nothing to stop or object to the Colsons' efforts to get their marriage back on track. She behaved honorably and dropped out of the relationship.

The hope that Plan A would result in a closer bonding of the Colson family because the no longer sinning or commuting husband would be spending more time at home was in vain. Both Chuck and Nancy came to regard the summer of 1962 as the most nightmarish period of their lives. Colson kept his promise of not seeing Patty, but he was utterly miserable without her. What began as an earnest and sincere effort to make the marriage work soon turned to frustration, depression, and manic mood swings.

One close witness to this time of trial was Charles Morin's wife, Elizabeth, who later wrote of it: "Chuck's marriage to Nancy was just visibly disintegrating and nothing they could do seemed to help. Chuck's anguish at the time both for his children and for themselves is still vivid in my memory."

The anguish Colson was feeling made him highly volatile. There were days when he raged in and out of the new town house like an angry bull, keeping strange nocturnal hours and drinking far too much. One night he drove up to the driveway dangerously fast and crashed his car straight into the garage door, which he had omitted to open. On another night, following an earthshaking argument with his wife, something inside Colson snapped. In the middle of the row he called his friend Don Whitehead, who had an apartment with a spare bedroom on Fifth Street NE. "Don, I'm breaking up with Nancy. Can I bunk in with you for a few days?" asked the highly emotional Colson. "I've got to get out right now. Will you help me move?"

Whitehead came over and found Colson in an upstairs bedroom, throwing his possessions into a huge box. "Chuck was so upset he wasn't bothering to pack anything properly," recalled Whitehead. "He didn't take his suits off their hangers or wrap up his bottles. He was in such a hurry that everything was hurled into this darn great box, which was at least six foot long and three foot wide. Into it went shoes, socks, toiletries, a big bottle of Maalox he said he needed for his stomach ulcers, shirts, papers, shaving stuff—you name it—all piled up in one big jumble. Then we had to get the box down the stairs, which wasn't easy because it had no lid and everything kept falling out. As we were struggling down the steps I'll never forget Nancy coming out with tears streaming down her face and saying to me, 'Take care of him, Don.' "

Colson needed a lot of care that night. He had been drinking heavily and his inflamed emotions led him into an abusive argument with the cabdriver. Once he and Don Whitehead arrived at the latter's apartment they had to carry the box up three flights of stairs, past the bedroom door of the property's straitlaced landlady, Mrs. Mitchell. "Unfortunately the box got jammed against Mrs. Mitchell's bedroom door on a U-turn in the stairs," recalled Whitehead. "She was a lady who insisted that her tenants didn't smoke, drink, or swear, and I had this nightmare that we were going to break through her bedroom door, with Chuck drunk and both of us swearing. But somehow we got away with it, although we must have woken her up with a lot of noise."

Colson stayed in the apartment for several weeks. Although he did not always comply with the landlady's rules for abstemious living, for he and Whitehead were both keen consumers of scotch, their bachelor household settled down into a steady routine. "On the face of it Chuck was making a pretty good shot at having a normal life," recalled Whitehead. "He didn't want to talk about the breakup but I could see he was deeply troubled."

So was Nancy. She believed that her husband was hiding himself away incommunicado on his boat on the Potomac. She feared that his depression and his heavy drinking could be harbingers of a suicide attempt. Nancy was wrong about this. Never for a moment did Colson consider taking his own life. Nevertheless, he was a soul in torment, partly because of the pressures of the marital triangle in which he was now ensnared, and partly because for the first time in his thirty-one years he was staring into the abyss of failure.

Nancy felt physically sick for much of that summer. Realizing that she might be on the verge of a nervous breakdown, she received counseling from the minister of the Georgetown Episcopal Church in Washington. It did not help her. One day when she was feeling particularly distressed she noticed that the skirt she was wearing was hanging loosely about her waist. When she weighed herself, her bathroom scale showed that she had lost twenty-four pounds in two months, down from 128 to 104. This weight decline concentrated her mind on new ideas to solve the crisis. She decided that she had to get out of Washington, not only for her own peace of mind but because the children (who were then eight, six, and four) needed to be looked after in a more stable environment. So she and Chuck sat down and devised "Plan B" for saving their marriage.

Plan B required yet another move in little more than six months. The new family abode was a typical New England Cape Cod–style three-bedroom home in Weston, Massachusetts, bought for $32,000 in July 1962. Nancy and the three children took up permanent residence there. Chuck divided his life between Weston, which was within easy driving distance of his Boston office, and Washington, where he rented a one-bedroom apartment near Union Station. For Nancy it was not easy to acknowledge that there were now three people in her marriage, but her priority was to save her family life whatever the personal cost. Her only confidant at this time was the Episcopalian minister in Weston, to whom she often posed the poignant question "Is it possible for a man to love two women at the same time?" The minister was unable to give her an answer.

Colson struggled with the same issue. Gradually he came to the conclusion that the marriage could not be saved. He felt that even if he tried to rebuild the relationship, it would never work, because Nancy would always have a hold over him for his affair with Patty. A clean slate and a fresh start therefore seemed unattainable for them. Feeling desperately torn between the two women in his life, he tried to calm his troubled conscience by living with neither of them. This was not a recipe for tranquillity and it was self-evidently collapsing in failure. Nancy began to think that the failure was more painful to her husband than the situation itself. For a rising star who had never flubbed at any stage in his progress of onward and upward mobility, the realization that he was facing a marital disaster seemed unbearable. The signs of torment manifested themselves again, particularly in sleeplessness, erratic behavior, and heavy drinking. At one point in this saga of agony, Colson said to his old friend Bill Maloney, "If it goes on like this I'll not only ruin Nancy's and my life, but Patty's life as well."

One evening in the spring of 1963, Colson came home to Conant Road and asked for a divorce. Nancy was distraught. She had sincerely believed that her submissive acceptance of the situation would save the marriage and that her calm, rational approach to the problem would eventually bring a solution. So it came as a great shock when she was faced with a request for a divorce. At first she refused on the grounds that she was not ready for a parting of the ways and that she thought her husband was not ready for it either. The firmness of her reply made it her husband's turn to be distraught.

Colson had never in his life taken no for an answer. So week after week, month after month, he persisted in his requests for a divorce. Eventually, in late 1963, Nancy caved in. The reason for her surrender was not Chuck's persistence but his drinking. On his most recent visits to Weston, in the fall of 1963, she had noticed a steep change in his reliance on alcohol, with un-pleasant consequences such as mood swings, instability, and foul breath. She decided that her husband had become incapable of holding on to and supporting their marriage. Although in her heart she still loved Chuck deeply, in her head she knew that something had to give. So with overpow-ering sadness Nancy Billings Colson agreed to give her husband of ten years the divorce he so badly wanted.

The pain of the divorce left scars on both partners, even though they have since had forty years in a good and cooperative relationship as ex-husband and ex-wife. Nancy buried her pain in motherhood, and later in remarriage. Colson came to look back on the breakup as the most miser-able period of his entire life—worse than the time he spent in jail. It was a grim time for him, but there were redemptive consequences from this pe-riod that manifested themselves decades later, long after Colson's life had been transformed by his religious conversion in 1973.

As an established Christian leader, Colson occasionally found himself in-volved in counseling friends who were having marital difficulties. Some of these friends expected to find their counselor sympathetic to their plans for divorce since he himself had been through the same experience. Not so. For Colson became implacably opposed to divorce. He has consistently ad-vised all those who ask his advice against ending their marriages. This hard-line approach has ruptured some good friendships. In the case of one old friend, a prominent politician who was strenuously advised by Colson not to divorce his wife, the counseling session grew so heated that it almost came to blows. Yet Colson remained impervious in the face of his friend's protests, which may well have included protests against alleged double standards. For it is fair to ask the question, how can a man who is divorced himself display such an inflexible opposition to everyone else's divorce? The answer to the question is to be found in the power of the redemptive process Colson has been through. An acceptance of easy divorces is just one of the old attitudes the new Colson now totally rejects. This may in special cases be an overreaction, but the general principle is an integral part of Colson's redemption. His own divorce, at a time when he was not a Christian, in retrospect seemed to Colson, the Born Again Christian, one of the worst sins of which he was convicted. So today he stands firm against all divorce, rejecting it on grounds of scriptural authority and moral principle.

Back in 1962, however, Colson's moral principles were limited to the narrower ground of behaving honorably toward Nancy in practical matters. She received a settlement that included their home, all the money in her husband's bank accounts, an agreement to pay the costs of the children's education, and $1,000 a month in maintenance for the children. This was not a large sum, but it represented 40 percent of Colson's income in those early days of his law partnership.

Once these formalities had been agreed, Colson set off for Mexico with the signed divorce papers. He had to complete a period of residence there before he could obtain what is known in the divorce trade as a "Mexican quickie." It was a frustrating delay, but by early 1964 he was legally divorced, back in Washington, and free to marry his beloved Patty.

Remarriage

Patty Hughes was a thirty-three-year-old young woman of considerable beauty and character. Born in 1930 in the small town of Hoosick Falls, New York, she came from an Irish Catholic family whose forebears hailed from County Cork. Like Colson, Patty grew up in the shadow of World War II. Her father was a blue-collar worker, employed as a painter in the factory of the armaments manufacturer Jones & Lampson, in Springfield, Vermont. Soon after graduating from high school, in 1947, Patty moved to Washington, D.C. She took a job in a florist's shop and lived with her mother's sister, Aunt Marguerite, who had daughters of similar age. Patty's social life revolved around church and baseball. She was a dutiful Catholic, attending mass every Sunday and on all holy days. Her attendance at the ballpark was even more dutiful, for her regular date was a baseball player with the Washington Senators.

Patty was widely praised for her beauty, which helped her to become Vermont's Cherry Blossom Princess at the capital's annual Cherry Blossom Pageant, in the spring of 1953. Among those who noticed her were two senators. One was John F. Kennedy, who dated her briefly. The other, whose interest was more avuncular, was the senior senator from Vermont, Ralph Flanders. When he discovered the Cherry Blossom Princess was from his hometown of Springfield, he offered her a job as a receptionist in his Capitol Hill office. "He treated me like a granddaughter," recalled Patty.

"Over and above the work in his office he was forever encouraging me to come and sit in the gallery and to listen to the debates on this or that bill on the floor of the Senate."

Senator Flanders, an upright legislator from the same traditional New England Republican background as Leverett Saltonstall, was a much-respected figure on Capitol Hill in the 1950s, not least on account of his early opposition to Senator Joe McCarthy. From Flanders, Patty Hughes gained a love and knowledge of politics. Soon after the Vermont senator announced his retirement from politics in 1959, Patty applied for a secretarial job in Saltonstall's office. She was interviewed by Colson, who hired her, he said at the time, because the only other applicant for the job had ruined her chances by wearing purple stockings.

The flames of attraction between Colson and his future second wife were slow to ignite but, by the spring of 1962, they were burning brightly. "I was drawn to Patty because she was so vibrant and glamorous, with a radiant and winsome personality," Colson has recalled. "She was also bright and quick, with a zest for life and a love for politics that were like mine."

The kindred spirits in zest, life, politics, and love were now heading for the altar. Within months of the divorce being finalized, Chuck and Patty were married, on April 4, 1964, in a simple legal ceremony led by a justice of the peace, in the Fort Myers military chapel, adjacent to Arlington National Cemetery, in Virginia. Patty would have loved a big formal church wedding, but Catholic canon law made marriage to a divorced person out of the question. So the nuptials were very low-key. Patty's father and mother had both died in the late 1950s, and Pop and Diz were still adamantly opposed to the marriage—so much so that Diz refused to speak to her son for several years. As a result of these tensions, the only guests present were Chuck's closest friend from his Browne & Nichols school days, Jonathan Moore, and his wife, Katy. Even Moore, who acted as best man, could not help feeling "a considerable discomfort because my wife and I had known and liked Nancy so much."

After the ceremony in the Fort Myers chapel had been completed, the sequence of events for the newlyweds did not go entirely smoothly or conventionally. The Virginia justice of the peace stunned them by saying, "I'm afraid we've got to do this again. I can't legalize a marriage on federal property. We will have to go back to my office." After they had spoken their vows for the second time in the space of an hour, Mr. and Mrs. Colson had to make a social detour to the apartment of Hannah Campbell, a somewhat lonely and possessive secretary in the Colson and Morin office who, behind a public façade of champagne and rejoicing, was privately worried that her influence over Mr. Colson might be on the wane because of the arrival of the new Mrs. Colson. Patty was concerned, so she joked later, that the champagne might have been poisoned.

Once this placatory duty had been performed, the next stop was Saint Matthew's Catholic Cathedral. Patty was happy in love but unhappy about being out of sorts with her church over her marriage. So in their second place of worship in one day, the Colsons knelt alongside the Moores in a second placatory duty, this time of prayer. As Colson looked at his bride a strange feeling came over him. "As I saw Patty kneel and pray, there was a deep reverence in her," he recalled. "It was just such an act of beauty the way she prayed and crossed herself. I thought I simply must find out about this one day to see if there is any truth in this."

This moment of religious curiosity was to prove a fleeting one. Although Colson did vaguely discuss with Charles Morin a few weeks later the idea of receiving instruction in the Catholic faith, nothing ever came of it. No further interest in matters spiritual was apparent in Colson until the time of his conversion experience, eleven years later.

At the end of the wedding day, the prayers at Saint Matthew's Cathedral were immediately followed by a dinner of celebration. However, as the Moores and the Colsons headed out toward their chosen restaurant, yet another unexpected problem interrupted their plans. Jonathan Moore had somehow managed to lock his station wagon (doubling up on that day as the bride and bridegroom's carriage) with his keys inside it. So Colson and Moore had to retrace their steps to the cathedral. In the absence of any available plumbers or tools, they borrowed a coat hanger from the cloakroom attendant and used it as a jimmy to force open the station wagon's window. Only after this "Colson break-in" had been accomplished could the delayed wedding dinner begin. One way and another it had not been the easiest of days, but by the end of it, Chuck and Patty were man and wife. The divorce chapter that had closed was retrospectively described by Colson as "the unhappiest and least attractive part of my life." The remarriage chapter that was about to begin brought him success, happiness, and the most steadfast of partners to support him in both the good times and the bad times that lay ahead for the next forty years.

CHAPTER SIX

The Road to the White House

Nixon Watching

The second half of the 1960s proved to be one of the most productive periods of Colson's life. He prospered greatly in his legal practice. He settled happily into his second marriage. He built better relationships with his children, who were initially unsettled by the divorce. Beyond these immediate personal relationships the most powerful attraction in Colson's world was the elixir of politics. Campaigning, lobbying, maneuvering, and strategizing on the great battlefields of presidential and senatorial elections were the focus of his political energies. He used them well. For in 1969 his drive took him to the mountaintop achievement of being appointed special counsel to the president of the United States, at the age of thirty-eight. Colson's first phase as a political operator had ended in December 1960 when, with mixed feelings, he resigned as administrative assistant to Senator Leverett Saltonstall, soon after masterminding the senator's successful reelection campaign in Massachusetts. The decision to leave Capitol Hill was not an easy one. After much heart searching Colson came to the conclusion that starting a new law firm offered him a better future than becoming one of the brightest stars in the firmament of congressional aides. Yet two years after launching his law firm Colson was nearly tempted back into the political arena when, via Leverett Saltonstall, an approach was made to him to see if he would manage the 1962 reelection campaign of the senior senator from Connecticut, Prescott Bush. It is intriguing to speculate about the future services Colson might have rendered to the Bush political dynasty if he had accepted the offer and won reelection for the father of the forty-first and the grandfather of the forty-third president of the United States. However, it was not to be. Prescott Bush decided not to run, so Colson stuck to the law and played only a cameo role in the midterm congressional elections of 1962, making a brief and fruitless effort to unseat the latest member of the Kennedy dynasty. This was Senator Edward M. Kennedy, who had been appointed to his brother John's vacant Senate seat in Massachusetts in 1961. He won it in his own right in 1962 despite Colson's peripheral contribution to the Republican campaign against him.

Nineteen sixty-four was a disaster year for the Republicans. Their presidential candidate, Senator Barry Goldwater of Arizona, lost the battle for the White House to Lyndon Baines Johnson by the unprecedented margin of 52 electoral college votes to 486. Colson was a sufficiently shrewd political analyst to see this landslide coming. Although he admired Goldwater for his staunchly conservative views, Colson considered him unelectable. So early in 1964 Colson wrote a personal memorandum to Richard Nixon. The purpose of this memo was to urge Nixon to throw his hat into the ring for the Republican nomination on the grounds that he was the only figure in the party who could mount a serious and credible challenge to LBJ.

Nixon, who was playing a waiting game in early 1964 with somewhat transparent coyness, loved Colson's analysis. So the noncandidate invited Colson to meet him at his New York law firm of Nixon, Mudge, Rose, Guthrie & Alexander. In its offices on the twenty-fourth floor of 20 Broad Street, in lower Manhattan, the two men talked together for a whole afternoon about delegate counts, primaries, convention floor tactics, and other vital ingredients in the alchemy of presidential politics. Those politics were in reality a forlorn hope for Richard Nixon in 1964 because Lyndon Johnson was already looking unbeatable. His sure touch in the aftermath of the Kennedy assassination and his Great Society legislative program gave him a powerful lock on the White House. The American electorate evidently liked the idea of going "all the way with LBJ" and wanted continuity of leadership rather than three different presidents in one year. So on that spring afternoon at 20 Broad Street, the only chemistry that mattered for the future was the personal chemistry between Nixon and Colson.

It was illuminatingly summed up by the junior partner in the political discussion. "Nixon and I understood one another—a young ambitious political kingmaker and an older pretender to the throne," wrote Colson. "We were both men of the same middle class origins, men who'd known hard work all our lives, prideful men seeking that most elusive goal of all—acceptance and the respect of those who had spurned us in earlier years." With such feelings in common, it was no surprise that the afternoon's conversation expanded into an invitation to dinner at Nixon's Fifth Avenue apartment.

The journey uptown in a shared limousine further encouraged Colson's growing sense of hero worship for the man he so fervently believed in as a future president when Nixon's musings on foreign policy issues became an impassioned address to his audience of one on the future of NATO and the vital importance of strengthening the Western alliance. This was Colson's first exposure to Nixon's habit of geopolitical strategizing. Like many a later listener to these partly political, partly intellectual expositions of foreign policy, Colson was awed by his host's statesmanship. "I saw at once that here was a brilliant mind at work," he has recalled. "Nixon withdrew into himself, talking almost as though he was alone in the car, yet I caught a glimpse of an idealism, an expertise, and a vision in him which I knew our country needed."

After Nixon the visionary came Nixon the peacemaker in action. As the limousine crawled along Fifth Avenue, the traffic gridlocked when two drivers some six cars in front leapt out of their cars and started a fistfight. To Colson's breathless admiration the former vice president of the United States jumped out of his limousine, parted the fighters, calmed them down, and got the traffic moving again. It was an anecdote Colson retold many times in his White House years. On that evening in New York the drama of the episode and Colson's laudatory comments to Nixon immediately afterward helped cement their warm relationship.

The warmth continued over a convivial dinner. Toward the end of the evening, Nixon told his young admirer, "I can hardly bear the thought of another campaign, seeing all those dull, tired, pedestrian faces all over again." When Colson demurred, Nixon flashed back at him, "Well, if you want me to be the candidate, will you come and run the campaign for me?" Perhaps it was a rhetorical question, not intended to be taken entirely seriously in the cold light of morning. Colson was dispatched to take soundings among a number of congressional leaders and Washington opinion makers to discover whether or not there was any groundswell of support for a Nixon candidacy. This mission, ostensibly carried out entirely at Colson's initiative (a typical Nixonian request), produced disappointing results. Colson remembers Congressman Mel Laird, who four years later was appointed defense secretary in the Nixon administration, being scathingly dismissive about the prospects for a Nixon presidency. "Oh no! He's had his chance. He's history," was Laird's judgment. It was a widely shared consensus. When Colson reported it back to his boss, all dreams of Nixon being the one for '64 faded into oblivion. The only legacy of Colson's doomed initiative to make Nixon the nominee that year was the start of a good rapport between the two men.

This rapport continued over the next four years. It surfaced occasionally, and in interesting ways—for example in 1966, when Colson persuaded both Nixon and the retiring Senator Leverett Saltonstall to back Edward Brooke as the best candidate to fill the vacant Republican nomination in the midterm U.S. Senate election in Massachusetts. That Colson initiative resulted in Brooke becoming the first African-American senator in the history of the United States.

Colson's support, which gave Brooke a vital head start in the fight for the nomination, began on the night Saltonstall confided to Colson that he would not be seeking reelection. "You've got to think carefully how you announce this," Colson advised Saltonstall. "There are two people who want your seat in the Senate. One is John Volpe, the governor. The other is Edward Brooke, the attorney general. They would both make excellent senators, but I see this as a chance for the Republican Party to do something it's never done before in its history and have a black United States senator. That would be a great thing for the country."

Arguing that Brooke's nomination would send a groundbreaking signal to the voters of Massachusetts in the same way that Joe Mitchell's appointment to the law firm had sent a similar message to the legal profession of Massachusetts, Colson persuaded Saltonstall to let him give Brooke advance notice of the retirement statement. "So I called Edward Brooke that night with the news," recalled Colson, "and I said to him, 'Get ready! The Senator is going to make his announcement at ten A.M. tomorrow. You should be announcing your candidacy at ten-oh-one A.M.' "

Thanks to Colson, Brooke seized the initiative in the fight for the nomination. Soon after he had won it, Colson arranged a fund-raiser for him in Washington. Nixon was invited. In the course of the evening, Nixon was photographed with his arm round Brooke, giving him a formal endorsement. It was the first declaration of support Brooke received from any national Republican leader and it helped him to victory in the Senate election a few weeks later. The episode was another example of Colson's boldness in political strategy. It was also the second time that Colson had been instrumental in breaking a color bar in Massachusetts.

As the time came round for the first stirrings in the presidential election of 1968, most seasoned observers had written off Richard Nixon as a contender for the White House. Not Colson. His political antennae told him that Nixon was the dark horse moving up on the rails for the Republican nomination. As a series of unexpected events that spring changed the political betting—among them the Tet offensive, the antiwar demonstrations, and Eugene McCarthy's startling near victory in the Democratic primary in New Hampshire—Colson became more and more certain that Nixon was the one. On the night of March 31, 1968, Chuck and Patty were watching television in their new home in Washington when Lyndon Johnson stunned the nation with his announcement: "With America's sons in the field far away, with America's future under challenge right here at home, with our hopes and the world's hopes for peace in the balance every day, I do not believe that I should devote an hour or a day of my time to any personal, partisan causes, or to any duties other than the awesome duties of this office—the presidency of your country.

"Accordingly, I shall not seek, and will not accept, the nomination of my party for another term as your president."

When Colson heard these totally unexpected words, he turned to his wife and said: "This means Nixon will be the next president."

Life with Patty

Patty Colson was a political confidante as well as a wife. Her years as a secretary on Capitol Hill had given her a feel for politics that was to stand the couple in good stead during the years of turbulence that lay ahead. Soon after their marriage, in 1964 the new Mr. and Mrs. Colson bought a house in Washington: 11 Fourth Street SE, just a few blocks from Capitol Hill. It cost $36,000, paid for with a $27,000 bank loan and a deposit of $9,000 that came from Patty's savings. Colson himself had virtually no resources in the immediate aftermath of his divorce, for he had transferred all the funds in his bank accounts to Nancy. However, he was beginning to earn good money from the law. In 1964, the year of his marriage, he made $80,000, which three years later had more than doubled, to an annual income of $175,000. Yet Colson did not raise his living standards to match the rise in his earnings. He and Patty always lived frugally. This was a legacy from the hard times they had endured in their childhoods, during the Depression. So they continued to budget on the same amount from the day they got married until the day Colson entered the White House five years later, when they had to manage on a $40,000-a-year government salary. These financial ups and downs did not trouble Colson. "I never spent money foolishly," he has recalled. "Anything I had left over at the end of the year I would put away for the kids in investments or real estate so as to be sure that we wouldn't run out of money as a family. Patty fully shared in this philosophy." Much of the credit for the improvement in Colson's prosperity in the mid-1960s was due to Patty. Not only was she a good housekeeper, she was also a good partner when it came to winning clients for the law firm. By the warmth of her personality Patty turned the Fourth Street house into a welcoming base for corporate hospitality. "We had friends and clients staying with us and having supper with us all the time," recalled Colson. "Patty was a great hostess and supportive of my career in every possible way."

More subtly, perhaps, Patty also brought in one or two changes in her husband's character. "Those of our friends who say Patty tamed me were right," said Colson. "I was pretty loud and brash in those days, but under Patty's gentle pressure I calmed down a lot."

One disappointment in the midst of the increasing success was that Chuck and Patty found they could not have any children. So they decided to adopt, only to face a second disappointment when they went for an interview with a Washington adoption agency. The matronly interviewer grilled Colson with uncomfortable intensity. From her line of questioning it became clear that she was wondering whether Colson's lifestyle was too full for more children, since he did not appear to have done too good a job with his first three. "You seem to have a very successful record, Mr. Colson," said the interviewer. "Why do you feel you want more children?" Bridling at the implication of the question, Colson protested that he adored Wendell, Chris, and Emily and that he spent as much time as possible with them. However, now that he was married to Patty, he wanted to bring up a family with her.

"You're very clear about what you want, aren't you?" pressed the interviewer. "I suppose you don't think you have ever failed in anything in your life."

"That's right, I haven't," retorted Colson.

Behind his haughty reply lay a weakness sufficiently obvious to the adoption agency for it to reject the Colsons' application: Colson had become too busy, too self-centered, and too career-oriented to be a good father in the conventional sense of the term during his children's most formative years. Although he pretended to be unaffected by the adoption agency's decision, blaming it on the national baby shortage caused by the pill and legalized abortion, it seems likely that Colson was inwardly shaken by the rejection. For around this time he began turning himself into a much better parent to his teenage children than he had been to them when they were small children.

His eldest son, Wendell, who initially became a withdrawn and reclusive boy in the months after the divorce, gradually noticed a change in his father's approach to family life. "When we were little my father was so busy being hardworking and incredibly successful that he just didn't know how to be a dad," recalled Wendell. "It was only after the divorce that he found time for us. When we came to stay in Washington with him and Patty, for the first time in our lives he gave up parts of his weekends to be with us. Even so, our weekend plans usually revolved around clients who would be asked to join us on the boat or wherever we were."

Colson was not much good at relaxing with his children. He would look at his watch and assign so many minutes to playing time. Then he would direct them to tasks or projects such as practicing how to debate or sanding the dining room floor. "It was always clear that he loved us kids and that he was excited about teaching us things and showing us interesting things," recalled Emily, "but his problem was that he just didn't understand children. Dad was born grown-up. I have no picture of him playing in the mud or messing around. It just wasn't him."

Emily had the most volatile temperament of the three young Colsons. As the youngest in the family, she often clashed with her father. He respected her femininity and her artistic talent but often failed to understand her. When Emily was ten, Colson gave her an easel and asked her whether she would like to take it home to Weston or leave it in Washington. Emily replied that she thought she would keep it in Washington "because there's nothing much to do here." Colson was shocked by his daughter's answer. He gave her a long lecture about how Washington was the national capital, the seat of government, and the place where the president and Congress took great decisions. Emily, for her part, was shocked by her father's vehemence. "He was coming at it from a Washington power perspective and he couldn't understand my ten-year-old's perspective. It was a big gap between us."

Patty worked hard to bridge such gaps and was evidently successful, because Wendell, Chris, and Emily all came to love her as a confidante, good cook, and good stepmother. Mealtimes, however, were not always easy, because Colson was apt to play the stern father and insist that his children eat everything on their plates. One of his disciplinary methods was to tip the unfinished food on their heads. One day when fish (which she disliked) was on the menu, Emily arrived at the table with her head cowled in a blanket in anticipation of having a portion of grilled snapper placed on her hair. Her father, however, doubled up with laughter at the sight of Emily in the blanket, as did Patty, who took away the fish.

One place where Colson did find it possible to relax with his family was on or beside the water, which often seemed to have a benign effect on his hyperactive temperament. He loved to take his sons sailing and enjoyed some of his happiest times as a father with them on his boat. One particular moment when he was sailing with Chris, then aged ten, on a lake in New Hampshire etched itself on Colson's memory because it brought him into a sudden and unexpected communication with God. Colson later described the episode: "As the craft edged away from the dock the only sound was the rippling of water under the hull and the flapping of the sail when puffs of wind fell from it. I was in the stern watching the tiller, Chris in the center, dressed in an orange slicker, holding the sheet. As he realized he was controlling the boat, the most marvelous look came over his cherubic face, the joy of new discovery in his eyes, the thrill of feeling the wind's power in his hands. I found myself in that one unforgettable moment talking quietly to God. I could even recall the precise words: 'Thank you, God, for giving me this son, for giving us this one wonderful moment. Just looking now into this boy's eyes fulfils my life. Whatever happens in the future, even if I die tomorrow, my life is complete and full. Thank you.' "

This understanding of and dialogue with the divine presence was a one-time event in Colson's life during the 1960s. He had plenty of opportunities for spiritual development through Patty, who set an impressive example of regular prayer and churchgoing, but there were no discernible effects on her husband. "From what we children could see at that time, religion was not in the least important to my father," recalled Wendell of his teenage years. "The big contrast in the family was between Dad's attitude and Patty's. She had a serious faith. Even when we took the boat and went on vacation we'd have to pull into port and go to church, but Dad never went with her."

One other person with a serious faith who tried to make an impact on Colson's spiritual development in the early 1960s was Fred Rhodes. He was a self-effacing Washington lawyer serving as minority counsel to the Senate Appropriations Committee. He was also a committed Southern Baptist, a nonsmoking teetotaler, and deeply conservative in outlook and lifestyle. On the face of it there seemed to be little or nothing in common between the introverted fifty-year-old "Dusty" Rhodes and the ebullient thirty-two-year-old, chain-smoking, hard-drinking, irreligious extrovert Chuck Colson. Yet somehow the two men became friends, lunching together regularly at the Lawyers Club in Washington. Sensing that deep down within himself Colson might be yearning for a Christian commitment similar to his own, Rhodes at one of these lunches began talking about the importance of his personal faith. "Oh, I think religion is fine," interjected Colson, "provided one has as little of it as possible!"

Despite this and other rebuffs, Fred Rhodes continued to feel called to talk about the message of the gospel to Colson. An opportunity for this arose, or so Rhodes thought, when Colson invited him and his wife, Winona, for a boat cruise on the Potomac one warm Saturday afternoon in July 1963. The Colson boat was a thirty-foot skiff with a small cabin but a large, 225-horsepower engine. Rhodes's hope of having some quiet time of one-on-one ministry with his host soon evaporated as they were joined on board by three old drinking buddies of Colson's: Jonathan Moore, his contemporary at Browne & Nichols; Bill Saltonstall; and Bob Torok, his Brown fraternity brother and fellow marine.

Skipper Colson was in a mood for practical joking and risk taking. As Winona Rhodes settled herself into a deck chair in the rear of the boat, Colson approached her with a straight face, saying gravely: "It's all right to sit there, Winona, but the only problem is . . . well . . . when we start the engine there can sometimes be an explosion right under where you're sitting. Nothing dangerous of course, but noisy." A white-faced Winona Rhodes shot out of her chair and vanished belowdecks. Soon after the boat roared out of Columbia Island Marina, Bill Saltonstall shouted to Colson, "Hey Chuck, you've missed the marker buoy. I can see rocks coming up ahead."

As Colson spun the wheel to execute a ninety-degree turn, Fred and Winona Rhodes were thrown sideways in the cabin, crashing headlong into the boisterous party of drinking companions up forward. The two ex-marines, Colson and Torok, were having an argument about which of them had been the best marksman back in their boot camp days. Colson declared that the argument would be settled by holding a shooting competition. Thinking that this announcement meant that pistols were about to be produced on deck, the Rhodeses started to feel they had joined a boat cruise from hell. However, to their relief, the shooting competition took place on shore at a rifle gallery in Marshall Hall Park, the good ship *Colson*'s next port of call on the banks of the Potomac.

At the rifle gallery the marksmanship proved even more erratic than the steering. The shooting competition was not won by either of the two ex-marines. To universal surprise the victor was Jonathan Moore, despite the handicaps of having one glass eye, no previous experience of rifle shooting, and even more liquor inside him than his two companions. As Moore's triumph was hailed with much cheering and more drinks all round, Fred and Winona Rhodes made a surreptitious exit from Marshall Hall Park, catching an excursion steamer back to Washington.

Their exit was not the end of the day's dramas. As the steamer chugged its way back up the Potomac with darkness falling, Dusty and Winona's tranquillity was shattered by the noise of a fast-approaching launch, the beams of a searchlight, and the shouts, over a loudspeaker, of "Hey Dusty! Hey Dusty! The marines are coming to rescue you!" The scene that developed was a combination of nautical drama and slapstick comedy. Colson drove his launch amidships alongside the steamer and bellowed the command "Marine boarding party—advance!" The crew of the steamer rushed forward with boat hooks, trying to push the boat away and repel the boarders. Skipper Colson reversed his engines, circled the steamer, and then throttled forward for a second assault. His jovial shipmates yelled marine battle cries and again attempted to board. Some of the steamer passengers cheered while others booed and shook their fists at the invaders. The steamer captain gave several blasts on the ship's horn while his crew wielded their boat hooks, and Colson kept up a running commentary over the loudspeaker. As for Fred and Winona Rhodes, they pulled the blankets over their heads and prayed that the Colson launch would go away—which eventually it did.

The day after these excitements a sheepish Colson dropped round to Rhodes's office in the Senate building to ask, "Dusty, are you still my friend?"

Fred Rhodes said yes, he was, but that it might take a little longer to restore good relations with Winona. As for his evangelistic mission, Rhodes noted dryly: "The episode indicated that it might be premature for me to try to minister to Colson." Fred Rhodes's judgment was correct. In the long term, his intuitive feelings about Colson's hidden spirituality were not as wide of the mark as they must have seemed at the time. For as later chapters will show, Rhodes was to become one of Colson's most influential mentors and partners in his prison ministry. However, in the 1960s, Colson's potential spirituality was submerged at invisible depths. He was far more of a hell-raiser than a believer. Although Colson liked to think of himself as a deist, his real gods were success, money, and power. Of these, political power was gradually becoming the most important, as events in the arena of presidential politics drew him inexorably closer to Richard Milhous Nixon.

Moving Toward Power

Soon after Lyndon Johnson withdrew from the presidential election of 1968, Richard Nixon's bandwagon began to roll, and Colson jumped onto it. In the spring of that year he put out feelers to see if there might be some role for him to play in the Nixon campaign team, but his overtures were not enthusiastically welcomed by the protective ring of insiders around the candidate at that time, particularly John Mitchell and Bob Haldeman. However, an old friend came to Colson's rescue in the shape of Brad Morse, now a third-term Republican congressman.

Back in 1960, a few weeks after Colson had delivered the nomination for the Fifth Congressional District of Massachusetts to Brad Morse, the newly elected congressman had sent his benefactor an effusive letter. "We have both had many friends, CW, but I have never had, nor can I ever expect to have, a friend like you," wrote Morse. "My debt to you is great, Chuck—it can never be fully repaid." Now it was payback time. Morse had just become vice chairman of the influential Key Issues Committee for Nixon in 1968. This committee was entrusted with the job of formulating the candidate's position on election issues, with the help of input from Congress. It was one of the most important tasks in a presidential election year, and the committee was looking to appoint the staff to help them to do it.

After being interviewed by the committee chairman, Senator John Tower of Texas, and others, including Congressmen Gerald R. Ford and Brad Morse, Colson was offered the job of staff codirector of the Key Issues Committee. His fellow codirectors were Alan Greenspan, later to become chairman of the Federal Reserve Board, and Richard Allen, later to become President Reagan's national security adviser. Their first meeting with Nixon was on August 9, 1968, the day on which Soviet tanks were rolling into Prague to crush the dissident Czechoslovakian government of Alexander Dubcek. Once again Colson was awed by Nixon's masterful analysis of the complex foreign policy issues arising from this international crisis. He felt even more certain that he was backing the right presidential candidate.

As a loyal Republican, Colson attended the GOP convention in Miami. By this time, Nixon's progress toward the nomination was so serene that it resembled a stately Spanish galleon coasting to harbor under full sail from a fair wind. Almost the only excitement in Miami arose over the selection of the vice presidential nominee. Colson was strongly opposed to the choice of Governor Spiro Agnew of Maryland. In the hours before Agnew was ratified by the convention, Colson expended much energy on working the phones, doing all in his power to get the decision changed. "I thought Agnew was an absolutely terrible choice," recalled Colson. "He was an in-your-face, abrasive polarizer, which was the last thing we needed when the country was already polarized. I tried to get Nixon to take Governor John Volpe as his running mate instead. He would have brought a lot to the ticket as a Northeasterner, a Catholic, an Italian-American, and a great campaigner. But I couldn't get the idea accepted."

Where Colson was getting his ideas accepted was in his power base at the Key Issues Committee office at 350 Madison Avenue, in New York. From the room he shared with Alan Greenspan and Richard Allen, he poured out position papers that eventually became a campaign manual, *Nixon on the Issues*. A lot of intellectual and political toil went into *Nixon on the Issues*. It was a policy document designed to win support from special interest groups, and the liaison between the candidate and his congressional supporters on the policy commitments was well handled. Colson was a fountain of energy in this enterprise, and in the course of it his ingenious political mind came up with a new idea that was to be the forerunner of the work he was to do in the Nixon White House.

"I quickly saw that there was a great political opportunity to be seized here," recalled Colson. "That opportunity was to develop the issues in the campaign not only in consultation with senators and congressmen but also in consultation with politically influential interest groups. For example, if a maritime issue came on the agenda, then I would get in touch with shipbuilding corporations, the maritime unions, the longshoremen, and so on. I would let them know the president-to-be was interested in their concerns and that he wanted their input in his policy positions. There was a lot of political mileage to be gained in this way, and Nixon picked up plenty of support as a result of it."

There was one bad moment for Colson during the election campaign, when he was publicly accused of buying votes for Nixon by making promises to the securities industry. The controversy arose when Nixon sent out a letter to some three thousand brokers and fund managers in the securities industry, setting out his views on the regulation of mutual funds. The letter attacked the Johnson administration's legislative proposals to impose "wide, sweeping new regulatory powers over the mutual fund industry, which powers would be tantamount to price fixing."

This "securities letter," as it became known, was attacked in the press on the grounds that one of the firms that stood to gain from Nixon's implied pledge to reverse the Johnson administration's proposals for tighter regulation of mutual funds was Investors Diversified Services (IDS). Nixon had been on the board of IDS until early 1968, and Colson's law firm, Gadsby and Hannah, was the registered lobbyist for IDS. When the *Wall Street Journal* identified Colson as the author of the letter, a furor erupted in the press and on the floor of the Senate, with conflict-of-interest allegations against Colson. Senator Thomas McIntyre (D–New Hampshire), who knew Colson from his days as secretary to the New England senators' committee, attacked him personally as a mutual fund lobbyist "who was often in my office with all sorts of ingenious proposals on behalf of his clients to legitimize the undue extraction of money from widows, orphans, and others." Caught in the crossfire of this unwelcome attention, Colson denied that he had written the letter. Close behind him in the denial business was Richard Nixon, who said he had not written the letter either, even though it went out under his signature. The authors, apparently, were the members of the Key Issues Committee. These evasive tactics provoked withering scorn from Senator McIntyre: "Once again the Nixon camp is busily engaged in the denials, cover-ups, and other signs of guilt over getting caught with a hand in the cookie jar," said the senator. "The pattern continues. Mr. Nixon wrote a secret letter. When the secret letter was made public, Mr. Nixon denied that he had written the letter. He said it was written by a committee. The committee had a secret counsel. When the secret counsel was made public, the counsel denied that he had written the letter. And so it goes on."

The securities letter controversy was in reality a very small storm in the election teacup. Many hands other than Colson's had been engaged in making the tea, among them Alan Greenspan, Bryce Harlow, and Brad Morse, all of whom had been involved in drafting and redrafting the letter. As its text was based largely on an interview Nixon had given to *Business Week* some months earlier, and as its position on the mutual fund industry was consistent with the Republican platform, it was not surprising that the controversy soon ran out of steam. Perhaps the only lasting consequence of the securities letter was that John Mitchell blamed Colson for mishandling it.

This was unfair, for Colson had not been engaged in any sort of "secret" operation "to buy votes." Nevertheless the incident did create the first sign of what was to become a lasting enmity between Mitchell and Colson.

Colson was not an admirer of John Mitchell's skills as an election campaign manager and said so rather too forcefully for his own good as Nixon's fifteen-point lead in the polls in August 1968 slipped to a three-point lead by October. As the contest entered its final week in November, the result was becoming breathtakingly close, especially after Lyndon Johnson announced a bombing halt and an alleged breakthrough in the effort to end the Vietnam War. This news put the Democratic presidential candidate, Vice President Hubert Humphrey, ahead by a nose in the race for the White House, according to the pollsters. Many leading Republicans suspected that Lyndon Johnson was up to some knavish tricks in an attempt to swing the election to Humphrey. Bryce Harlow, one of Nixon's closest aides, contacted Colson to ask him if he could check with his best sources inside the Pentagon to find out what the top brass were saying about the authenticity of the bombing halt.

Colson had excellent military connections as a result of representing clients like Grumman Aircraft and Raytheon. He spoke to an old friend, General Wallace Greene, the commandant of the marine corps and a member of the Joint Chiefs of Staff. Greene was remarkably forthcoming. "We, the joint chiefs, advised against it," he told Colson. "The president took the decision away from us. It's very ill advised. We think it's a purely political move to get Hubert Humphrey elected president."

Whatever the motivation for the move, it turned election night into a cliffhanger. As the results came in, the popular vote tally was seesawing both ways, then dead-heating, and finally edging toward Hubert Humphrey by a hairline margin. However, in the all-important electoral college vote count, Nixon was moving ahead in the states that really mattered. By the early hours of the morning, after California, Ohio, and Illinois had swung into the Republican corner, Nixon was the president-elect of the United States. He had been carried to his narrow victory by a surprising number of votes from traditionally Democratic sources such as the blue-collar unions and other working-class interest groups. These were the very constituencies that had been courted by Colson in his strategy on behalf of the Key Issues Committee. It was a contribution whose significance was not lost on that archstrategist of politics Richard Nixon.

Just in case the new president-elect might overlook his long-standing connections with the young Massachusetts lawyer who had first urged him

to run for the presidency in 1964, Colson wrote to him a week after the
election.

> Dear Mr. President-Elect,
>
> Congratulations and Godspeed. Our Nation needs you as never
> before in its history. I am sure that you do not remember the
> evening in March of 1964 when we rode together in your car from
> your downtown office to your apartment through a typical New
> York traffic jam. You spent much of the time telling me of the many
> things you had hoped to do had you been elected President in 1960
> and the many things you hoped you could do if you ever had the
> opportunity again.
>
> What you said that evening impressed me as much as anything
> else in my life, not only because I was flattered that you had taken
> me into your confidence but more importantly because of the sub-
> stance of what you said. Any man who holds to the beliefs you do
> is more than a match for the most difficult problems of the most dif-
> ficult office in the world.
>
> No lawyer likes to admit it when he gives bad advice but I must
> say in recalling the meetings I had with you in the spring of 1964
> that I am very thankful that you did not heed my urgings that you
> run for President then.
>
> Your election is a lesson to every American. Any man who has
> the fortitude to run for President after being defeated twice exempli-
> fies the best that there is in people and in Nations.
>
> With this kind of courage and determination you and your Ad-
> ministration will prevail, no matter what challenges and problems
> you face.
>
> My prayers go with those of millions of others for your personal
> happiness and for the success of you and your Administration.
>
> > Respectfully yours,
> > Charles W. Colson

The references in this letter to "Godspeed" and "my prayers" were mere
figures of speech so far as Colson was concerned, for he had not offered
any prayers in a religious sense since his time with the marines on board
the USS *Mellette*. On the other hand, Colson, like millions of others, was
becoming increasingly troubled by forebodings about the near ungovern-
ability of America, so much so that he was ambivalent about whether or

not he wanted to serve in the new administration. One of the reasons for his uncertainty was a fearfulness about the future. Nineteen sixty-eight had been a year in which the sixties exploded. The passions and poisons that had been fermenting inside American society for most of the decade were boiling over with a fury that traumatized the nation. The ferocity of the antiwar movement, the youth rebellion, the riots on campuses, the fire bombings in the cities, and the assassinations of political figures added up to an epidemic of violence that had not yet run its course. One evening at the Capitol Hill Club, soon after the assassinations of Bobby Kennedy and Martin Luther King, Colson had said to his friend Jonathan Moore: "I am sure Nixon is the best man to be president but almost hope he will lose the election because the next few years are going to be so difficult, with the violent polarization of our society. Whoever is in the White House can't succeed. Purely as a political calculation, it would be better if the Democrats got in and screwed up as badly as they inevitably will in this climate."

There was considerable political prescience in this view, which reflected a mood encapsulated in a line by W. B. Yeats that was much quoted around Washington as the new president prepared to take office:

Things fall apart; the centre cannot hold;
Mere anarchy is loosed upon the world.

As Nixon's inauguration took place among some of the worst and most anarchic scenes of street violence ever to accompany the swearing-in of a new president, Colson's pessimism deepened. What also deepened was his hesitation about accepting an appointment to serve in the government. Colson was obviously a likely candidate for some sort of a post in the administration, given the role he had played in the campaign. However, his willingness to serve was counterbalanced by his enthusiasm for making money in his fast-expanding law partnership. Back in July 1968, when he had accepted the post of codirector of the Key Issues Committee, Colson had taken a four-month leave of absence from Gadsby and Hannah. His partners had agreed to this reluctantly, with considerable skepticism. Even Charles Morin thought he was making a mistake. "I couldn't see any advantage either to Colson or to the firm," said the loving partner. How wrong he was! A few days after the election the *Wall Street Journal* ran a front-page article comparing Colson to the legendary Washington insider Clark Clifford, whose law practice had become one of the most successful in America because of his close relationship with Lyndon Johnson's administration. The *Journal* suggested that Colson had a similar inside track with Nixon and that many companies soon would be beating a path to his law firm's door. The publication of this article turned its predictions into self-fulfilling prophecies. "In no time, the boys in the law firm were being knocked down by the rush of people wanting to do business with us," recalled Colson. "I acquired a lot of new clients in the early part of 1969. In the first nine months of that year I made over two hundred thousand dollars, which would equate to over one million in today's equivalent money. It was a very successful beginning."

Colson was adept in the art of lobbying the new administration. One client from whom his firm earned huge legal fees was Raytheon, the Massachusetts-based defense electronics manufacturer headed by Tom Phillips. Raytheon stood to win multimillion-dollar orders if the Pentagon went ahead with certain plans for missile defense systems. Colson, ably supported by Norman Paul, a new partner in the firm who had formerly been an undersecretary of the Air Force Department, fought in Raytheon's corner in the corridors of power with success. "There was no question that Chuck helped us to get that business," recalls Tom Phillips. "We thought he was very dynamic and very smart."

Similar complimentary adjectives were being applied to Colson by powerful people within the government. The transportation secretary, John Volpe, invited him to become the department's general counsel. Robert F. Ellsworth, a congressman who was acting as an administration appointments scout, called to ask if he would accept a middle-ranking position on the White House staff. Colson said no to these and other approaches but they heightened the conflict within him between big money and big politics. Then the post of assistant secretary of state in charge of legislative affairs was offered to him during an interview with his old friend Elliot Richardson, the undersecretary of state. Colson gave the unexpected reply that he would think about the offer carefully but that a stumbling block might be Vietnam. "I would have great difficulty in defending the administration's position," he told Richardson, explaining in some detail his reservations about the impossibility of the United States winning or even successfully extricating itself from a land war in Southeast Asia.

Despite these doubts over Vietnam, Colson was seriously tempted by the appointment he had been offered, for it would give him full scope to use his old congressional staffer's skills. So he allowed his name to go forward to the White House for political clearance before making the final decision on whether to accept it. In October 1969 Colson was called in for a talk with Bryce Harlow, one of President Nixon's closest counselors. "If you're going to serve anywhere in this administration, you're going to serve here in the White House," said Harlow. Colson, who may have been using the tactic of playing hard to get, made the improbable claim that the job of assistant secretary of state would have more appeal to him. Harlow looked him straight in the eye. "The president needs you," he said. "You may think you like the idea of staying out there making money, but I know you admire the president and he wants you in here right now."

Colson asked why President Nixon required his services.

"Because he's terribly frustrated and terribly isolated," replied Harlow. "He's isolated behind the Berlin Wall of Haldeman and Ehrlichman, who cut him off from a lot of political things. He's frustrated because he needs someone who will come in here with a political mind and do what has to get done. One of these days there is going to be a damn great mushroom cloud erupting over the Oval Office because this president is getting tired of people who won't do what he tells them. He's got the idea that a fella who knows this city and the way it works might be just the guy who will get things done for him. That's why the president needs you."

Bryce Harlow's words were music to Colson's ambitious ears. Up to this point in his discussions about an appointment within the administration, he had been hedging his bets. "I was waiting for the one call, the one telling me that the President needed *me*," he wrote in his autobiography, *Born Again*. Now that call had come. It was repeated to him in concrete form a few days later by the president's chief of staff, Bob Haldeman, who as a conservative Californian was privately doubtful about having an Ivy League university graduate from liberal Massachusetts within the upper echelons of the Nixon White House.

Prior to the meeting with Bryce Harlow in mid-October there had been a somewhat lukewarm exchange of memos about Colson between Haldeman and various members of his staff. In one of these memos Haldeman reported a discussion with the president about "an individual who would work within the DAR, Boy Scouts, VFW, etc., when we want them to support one of our programs." In another similar memo Colson is described as "an organizer of group support. His job would be to organize VFW groups, Boy Scouts, American Legion, etc. . . . . To act as pressure groups for various programs." Both memos end with requests for further and better particulars on the possible appointee, such as "any reading you would feel appropriate on Colson" and "Follow through to see what Colson's qualifications are, etc."

Haldeman's hesitation was swept aside by Nixon's determination to have Colson on board. Although Colson himself continued to have financial qualms about entering the White House, describing himself as "insane" to be exchanging his soaring law firm earnings of over $200,000 a year for a government salary of $40,000, there was never any serious doubt that he would accept the appointment. "I agreed to do it because I really believed Nixon needed me" was how he rationalized his decision. "His request brought out the old patriotism in me, and I agreed to serve." Whether it was service, patriotism, ambition, or a combination of all three, Colson suppressed his doubts about Vietnam as well as about money and signed on. In a formal White House press release dated November 24, 1969, it was announced that "Charles Wendell Colson has been appointed Special Counsel to the President of the United States." He had arrived in the seat of power.

CHAPTER SEVEN

The President's Point Man

Bloc Politics

The winter of 1969–70 could hardly have been a more inauspicious time for Charles Colson to start his career as special counsel to the president of the United States. Richard Nixon, who came to power backed by the smallest percentage of the popular vote since 1912, had inherited the most unpopular war in the history of America and was making no visible progress in bringing it to an end. As a result, the anti–Vietnam War protest movement was intensifying as it injected new passions of extremism into the body politic of the nation. That winter saw an explosion of unrest across campuses and cities, with over twenty-five hundred fire bombings, $21 million worth of damage to property, and forty-three deaths attributable to political violence. The ferocity of these activities and the size of the demonstrations that accompanied them brought out a mixture of anxiety and aggression in Colson. He was not alone in his instinctive reactions. Even some liberal commentators were becoming concerned by the specter of a government unable to govern if the challenge from the streets worsened. As the *Washington Post* columnist David S. Broder wrote on the eve of the Vietnam Moratorium march that brought a crowd of 250,000 antiwar protesters into the streets around the White House, "It is becoming more obvious with every passing day that the men and the movement that broke Lyndon Johnson's authority in 1968 are out to break Richard Nixon in 1969. The likelihood is great that they will succeed again."

Although Colson was more sanguine than the *Washington Post* about the strength of the protest movement's challenge to presidential authority, he was soon drawn into the administration's bunker mentality, which the temper of those troubled times created. Like other White House staffers, Colson was affected by the unprecedented tensions of heightened security, such as having to go to work through a protective military cordon of troops. He was also unsettled by the atmosphere of isolation experienced by many of the president's men as they went about their duties feeling under siege as a result of the relentless drumbeat of hostility from the demonstrators and from some sections of the media. In that polarized atmosphere of political and emotional tension, it was not surprising that the hostility of the protesters became reciprocated by many impressionable young White House staffers, including Colson.

Despite these pressures, Colson's natural ebullience filled him with elation at having arrived where he had so long wanted to be. He started work in the White House on November 6, 1969. Toward the end of that month he was so enamored with his self-described role as "the president's liaison with the outside world" that he sat down and wrote a euphoric memorandum for his own historical records, entitled "Random Notes About the First Three Weeks." The memorandum was critical of many of his fellow White House staffers—"They have practically no knowledge as to how to apply the broader powers of government, i.e. how to get things done"— and laudatory of himself: "I am very impressed by the way in which the White House staff have quickly looked to me as a source of power because of my relationship with outside groups and my relationship with H. R. Haldeman and, therefore, my access to the President," he wrote. It was a complacent misjudgment of his status. Although he did not know it, Colson in those early days was much more an object of suspicion than "a source of power." He had no direct access to the president and his relationship with Haldeman was an uneasy one.

Nixon's chief of staff, H. R. "Bob" Haldeman, was an administrator of formidable ability and a perfectionist of fearsome severity. He thought he had created a zero-defect management system within the White House, whose centerpiece was his "Berlin Wall"—a tightly controlled screening system designed to restrict the flow of people and paper into the Oval Office. Colson's brashness made him eager to jump over that wall. This was to be the source of many frictions between the two men. Throughout his three and a half years of service in the White House, Colson had a difficult relationship with Bob Haldeman, and with his fellow custodian of the Berlin Wall, John Ehrlichman—the president's special assistant for domestic affairs. "The Germans," as Haldeman and Ehrlichman were known behind their backs, reacted negatively to Colson from the day he joined the administration. Initially their hostility stemmed from a perception that the Ivy League–educated newcomer was "just another Eastern lib" with elitist views and arrogant attitudes. A more substantive problem was that Colson's freewheeling ideas and unorthodox methods jarred with their political and managerial conservatism. In addition, Haldeman's somewhat narrow background as a Californian advertising executive and Christian Scientist made him wary, perhaps jealous, of the broader political sophistication that Colson had acquired from his time on Capitol Hill. For in his years as a senatorial aide, he had acquired far more knowledge about how to get things done in Washington than had the group of young men around Haldeman, known as "the beaver patrol."

This praetorian guard of junior advertising executives transformed into White House aides often outdid the chief of staff in its zeal for internal management disciplines, such as "tickler" systems for chasing up memos. However, they had little or no understanding of how to deliver external results in the minefields of politics beyond the walls of 1600 Pennsylvania Avenue. Colson quickly became scornful of the political ignorance of the eager beavers. Unfortunately he did not always confine his expressions of scorn to the private pages of his historical memo writing. The ensuing resentments sowed seeds of mistrust among his colleagues. These tensions were exacerbated by the hostility of a third powerful enemy, in the shape of John Mitchell, the attorney general, who had been critical of Colson ever since the controversy over the securities letter during the election campaign. Mitchell tried to block Colson's appointment to the White House, warning Haldeman, "He's bad news. He'll get the president in trouble."

With all these currents of opposition swirling around him in his early months, it was hardly surprising that Colson found himself excluded from much of the mainstream business of the administration. Despite his high-sounding title of special counsel to the president, he was not allowed to send memos to Richard Nixon, nor did he have access to the Oval Office, except on rare occasions. As a result of always having to work through Haldeman, whom he described as "curt, sarcastic, and demeaning," Colson felt cold-shouldered and isolated. "There was no team spirit," he has recalled. "I was advised by a good friend always to keep my back to the wall. It was an atmosphere in which everyone would double-cross anyone at any time to get themselves into the inner center of power."

Colson yearned to move toward the inner center of power but was continuously frustrated by the Haldeman filter system. He sent up lists and memos to the chief of staff urging that the administration build relationships with organizations such as the National Wildlife Federation, the Audubon Society, and the National Cattlemen's Beef Association. However, these activities were given low priority by Haldeman, and the president also seemed underwhelmed by them. "I think Colson, in his working with the volunteer groups, has failed adequately to get the women's clubs, service clubs, and some of the broader areas of club activity involved," wrote Nixon in a memo to Haldeman. "Will you talk to him . . . to see if we can't begin to mobilize a much broader spectrum of clubs, and get away from the veterans' organizations and the cow punchers which is about all we have been able to touch so far."

Nixon's frustration over the lack of support from special interest groups was as much directed to the ingrained sloth of government bureaucracy as to Colson. Nixon was neither the first nor the last president to become infuriated by the propensity of the nation's bureaucrats to take little or no action in response to an order from the nation's chief executive. One such failure, which was particularly galling to him, was his inability to fulfill a promise he had made in the 1968 election campaign for extra help to Catholic schools. This educational policy was not unconnected with Nixon's political objective to build a larger bloc of support among Catholic voters. One morning in February 1970, Nixon met with a delegation of Catholic school educators. Colson was also present. The nuns, priests, and teachers in the delegation forcefully reminded the president of his election pledge to give aid to parish schools and urged him to deliver on it. Nixon was embarrassed. Parochiaid, as the policy was known, fitted in with his preference for diversity in education. It also reflected his general distrust of a monolithic school establishment, which he felt was more concerned with social engineering than educational excellence. For these reasons Nixon had, for some months, been asking Ehrlichman and Mitchell to prepare a simple executive order creating a commission to study ways to help Catholic schools. Nothing happened, largely because neither Mitchell nor Ehrlichman shared Nixon's sympathies for the Catholic position on Parochiaid, which they though would lead to constitutional difficulties on the church-state issue. Nixon decided he needed an intermediary other than Haldeman to prod Ehrlichman and Mitchell into action. Later that afternoon he called Colson into the Oval Office and told him in front of Haldeman that he wanted the Catholic schools order drafted immediately. A few moments later Haldeman left the room, leaving Colson alone with the president. Nixon went into a slow burn of anger directed against the aides he thought had been stalling over this project. Then, looking out over the Rose Garden, he issued a decisive order to his special counsel: "Chuck, I want you to be my point man on the Catholics," said the president. "I want a commission appointed *now*. I've been thinking about what those people said this morning. I ordered it a year ago and no one pays attention. You do it. Don't take any notice of what Haldeman and Ehrlichman say. Break all the ******* china in this building but have an order for me to sign on my desk Monday morning."

It was a presidential command that brought out the action man in Charles Colson. He rushed back to his modest office in the Executive Office Building, where he and his secretary, Joan Hall (Colson's only staffer), pulled out all the stops to deliver what Nixon had asked for. This was no easy task at the start of a quiet winter weekend when most of the key administration players were out of town. Indeed, Colson initially thought he had been landed with an impossible assignment when he discovered that Bob Finch, the secretary of health, education, and welfare, was vacationing in the South; that the domestic affairs supremo, John Ehrlichman, was on the ski slopes of Colorado; and that the Justice Department official in charge of executive orders had gone away for the weekend, and so had the director of the Office of Management and Budget. Yet by sheer force of energy, Colson cut a swath through all these difficulties. Using his legal training, he personally drafted an appropriate executive order without the assistance of the Justice Department. He tracked down an irritated director of OMB on the golf course and obtained his oral consent to the necessary budgetary approvals. Bob Finch was also persuaded to give his approval over the telephone once he heard that the file had been retrieved from the desk of some middle-level HEW official and been delivered to Colson in the White House. As for John Ehrlichman, he made the mistake of refusing to take Colson's calls, relying on his junior colleague to obey a strictly worded White House staff instruction requiring all executive orders to pass through the office of the special assistant for domestic affairs. Colson, however, took it upon himself to ignore this rule, arguing that he owed his obedience to a higher source of authority than Ehrlichman. "The president had said Monday morning and so, on Monday morning, I placed the order on his desk," was Colson's rationalization of his action. When all these weekend activities became apparent to the highest echelons of the White House, "there was quite a stir," as Bob Haldeman laconically noted in his diary. The stirring went in two directions. Ehrlichman and Mitchell exploded in fury, but Nixon was delighted. At last he had found on his staff an innovator with the get-up-and-go spirit of a fearless challenger to the bureaucracy. "Colson's got the balls of a brass monkey," he said with de-light to his chief speechwriter, Ray Price. It was an unusual presidential seal of approval but it led to new assignments for Colson, together with an expanded staff, larger offices, and the allocation of a White House limou-sine for his personal use.

Within a short time more egos were getting broken by Colson, who rel-ished the bull-in-a-china-shop role that the president was encouraging him to play. As Haldeman noted, this time rather less laconically, in his diary of March 24, 1970, Colson was soon creating another stir: "[Postmaster Gen-eral] Blount and his Deputy, Ted Klassen, trapped me in late morning about White House staff interference in Post Office negotiations, especially by Colson. They were mad." This contretemps concerned another floun-dering Nixon campaign promise—the reform of the United States Postal Service. A presidential commission had recommended that the Post Office Department, in existence since 1789, should be replaced with a new and more cost-effective agency. These reform proposals were at an impasse be-cause of personal animosity between Winston M. Blount, the postmaster general, and James H. Rademacher, the president of the largest postal workers' union. Realizing that the government would soon have a political debacle on its hands if postal reform failed because of union-induced dead-lock on Capitol Hill, Colson received permission from Nixon to intervene directly in the negotiations. What happened next was a foretaste of many similar episodes in Colson's and Nixon's handling of organized labor. Col-son pulled out all the stops to win the union leader's confidence. He invited Rademacher over to the White House for lunch and offered him better terms for postal workers' employee benefits than Blount had put on the table. Despite Blount's mounting irritation, Colson negotiated the new em-ployee benefits unilaterally, even bringing Rademacher to meet Nixon to help close the deal. Eventually the union called off its opposition to the re-form proposals. A vital House committee, which had been deadlocked by a tied vote, reconvened and approved the package by seventeen votes to six. "The only difference," said Colson, "was Rademacher's support."

This was not quite the end of Colson's first success as a bridge builder to organized labor. The reform legislation suffered an unexpected setback when the full Congress failed to ratify the package accepted by the House committee. In an emotional reaction, some of the postal workers called a wildcat strike as a protest. Rademacher, who by this time was working hand in glove with Colson, alerted the White House to the likelihood of a disastrous national postal shutdown if the government did not intervene immediately. Postmaster General Blount, however, refused to take Rademacher's calls or to have any dialogue with the union until all the strikers returned to work. At this rebuff the union's executive council voted for an official national strike, and Rademacher called a press conference to announce it. Just before the press conference started, Colson pulled off a coup. He persuaded Labor Secretary George Shultz to call Rademacher with a promise that the administration would secure full congressional approval for the reform package, including the improved employee benefits that the workers wanted. On the basis of that assurance, and with further encouragement from Colson, Rademacher opened his press conference not by announcing an official strike, but by telling all his union workers to return to work. The deals were kept by both sides, and the reform of the U.S. Postal Service was achieved. As Jim Rademacher said in a subsequent press interview, "Colson was responsible for breaking the stalemate. He went over Postmaster General Blount's head to do it. He is probably the most effective member of the President's staff."

There were many other signs of Colson's growing effectiveness. One was the amount of time he began spending with the president. "The boss is in love," said the wags in the White House, realizing that Nixon was becoming increasingly captivated by both the political brain and the personal bravado of his aggressive special counsel.

In the early months of their relationship Nixon felt comfortable with Colson because they came from similar non-elitist backgrounds, because those backgrounds instinctively enabled them to understand each other's insecurities and resentments, but most of all because they shared a common vision for an original electoral strategy that focused on what eventually became known as "Nixon's new majority." Organized labor was pivotal to this strategy, whose principal objective was to turn blue-collar voters into Nixon supporters. This was original, if not revolutionary, thinking. Up to 1970 the mind-set of politics was that the Republicans were the party of big business while the Democrats were the party of the working man. Colson, however, had sensed that America could be on the brink of a historic shift in the balance of these traditional voter loyalties. His imagination was caught by Kevin Phillips's book *The Emerging Republican Majority* (1969) and by a provocative article, "The Revolt of the White Lower Middle Class," by Pete Hamill, in *New York* magazine. When Colson alerted Nixon to these predictions, he was captivated by them too. Both men intuitively understood that a new political landscape was being created by the domestic consequences of the Vietnam War.

Wars often break the mold of politics. During the late 1960s the Democrats' increasingly strident anti–Vietnam War activists seized control of the party's platform and moved it toward new left policies such as isolationism, the busing of school children, and an amnesty for draft dodgers. These liberal innovations disturbed the conservative elements in organized labor. They were also anathema to Nixon. He needed little persuasion to let Colson try his hand in implementing a game plan that, if successful, had the potential to bring about a sea change in the political allegiances of working-class America. Colson went to work on his game plan with guile and gusto. He had an instinctive grasp of bloc politics. He knew how to use techniques that were standard practice for Democrats in big cities but standard areas of failure for Republicans: cultivation of special interests, attention to pressure groups, and the wooing of union leaders. All were tasks at which Colson excelled.

"My strategy with the union leaders was to win over those who were social conservatives," he has recalled. "So I quickly identified the ones who were opposed to busing, amnesty, abortion, flag burning, and so on, and who were strongly patriotic in their support for a strong president standing firm in the Vietnam War. These were the issues that Nixon felt viscerally about, so I knew that there was a community of interest here that needed to be signaled and symbolized." One of Colson's most successful and symbolic relationships with a labor leader was with Peter Brennan, head of the construction trades union in New York. He came to Colson's attention because of newspaper reports that he and his members had been staging counterdemonstrations supporting the Vietnam War at a time when large numbers of students were marching to protest against it. The clashes between prowar and antiwar demonstrators in the streets of New York were often inflammatory and occasionally violent. This did not stop Colson from seizing a political opportunity. He recommended that Nixon call Peter Brennan to thank him personally for his patriotic support.

When this recommendation crossed the desks of Haldeman and Ehrlichman, they opposed it on the grounds that Nixon should not appear to be condoning the spectacle of muscular hard hats beating up college kids. Also they had run security checks that revealed that some of the leading lights in the construction trades union were unsavory characters with criminal records. Nixon listened to these objections without saying a word. But as soon as Haldeman and Ehrlichman had left the Oval Office, the president said to Colson: "Let's get Brennan on the phone." In the long conversation that followed, Brennan emphasized his union's steadfast support for the president's handling of the Vietnam War. Nixon responded by saying, "Why don't you talk to Chuck Colson here and arrange to come down and meet me? Bring your council with you." Two days later, Peter Brennan and some twenty members of the construction trades council descended on Washington for their appointment with the president. They wore their working clothes, including hard hats. "I had arranged for these guys to go into the Oval Office in their hard hats," recalled Colson, "but at the last minute someone made them take them off. Still, that famous picture of all their hard hats piled up on a table just outside the Oval Office went right across America. It was deeply symbolic and made a tremendous impact."

Brennan and his members went on making symbolic gestures that helped the president. After the unpopular incursion into Cambodia by U.S. forces searching for North Vietnamese arms hideouts, Nixon desperately needed some expression of grassroots support. Brennan supplied it by organizing a march down Broadway of a hundred thousand New York workers carrying banners saying, WE SUPPORT NIXON. The TV networks reported the event as a major news item, which was a powerful counterbalance to the prevailing coverage of antiwar protests.

Colson threw his net of flattery across the whole spectrum of organized labor. He built major alliances with the leaders of the longshoremen's and maritime workers' unions, Teddy Gleason and Peter Hall. He made a personal friend of Frank Fitzsimmons, James Hoffa's successor as president of the Teamsters. This relationship got off to a rocky start when Fitz and five Teamster vice presidents were invited to lunch in the executive mess of the White House by Colson. The Teamsters ordered beer with their Mexican food. Unfortunately they discovered that the White House served just one beer, Michelob, which happened to be the only leading beer in America to be distributed by nonunion labor. However, after some spluttering, personal thirst triumphed over political principle and the Colson-Fitzsimmons dialogue continued—washed down by nonunion beer.

The wooing of the Teamsters by Colson reached its peak a few months before the 1972 presidential election when the union's executive committee held a meeting in La Costa, California, to decide whether it should endorse the Democratic challenger, Senator George McGovern, or the incumbent Republican, President Richard Nixon. Colson was invited to be present for the debate between the pro-Nixon faction, led by Fitzsimmons, and the pro-McGovern faction, led by Harold Gibbons, the Teamsters leader in Saint Louis. Although the union bosses were reluctant to break the Teamsters' traditional ties with the Democratic Party, Colson and

Fitzsimmons argued that Nixon was far more of a kindred spirit to organized labor than the liberal McGovern. After much cajoling in this vein until 2 A.M. the executive committee eventually voted to endorse Nixon. It was a historic change of allegiance. As instructed, Colson immediately called the president with the good news. "Nixon was euphoric!" recalled Colson. "He was waiting up for my call and I could hear the excitement in his voice. He told me to come and see him first thing in the morning. So I got to San Clemente by eight A.M. carrying a late edition of the *Los Angeles Times,* with the headline TEAMSTERS ENDORSE NIXON. Immediately after he saw it, Nixon was so up that he insisted on giving me a tour of the area in his golf cart. So off we went, careering up and down the hill tracks of San Clemente, going round corners at high speeds with the Secret Service in their golf cart behind us struggling to keep up. I had to hang on tight because Nixon was such a terrible driver. It was just his way of showing me that he was over the moon at this endorsement and grateful to me for getting it."

Although Colson had delivered brilliantly with the Teamsters, one powerful union boss whose heart and mind he never managed to conquer was that of George Meany, president of the AFL-CIO. It was not for want of trying. At Colson's instigation Nixon played golf with Meany, called him frequently, gave a dinner in his honor at the White House, and entertained six thousand AFL-CIO members at a barbecue on the south lawn. All these favors did not result in America's largest labor union following the Teamsters with an election endorsement for Nixon from Meany. However, Colson did eventually manage to neutralize the affiliation of this most dyed-in-the-wool of Democratic loyalists with a political dirty trick.

Colson had formed a personal relationship with Jay Lovestone, Meany's special assistant for international affairs. "Lovestone was a brilliant guy, a onetime communist intellectual who had become a superhawk and a superpatriot," recalled Colson. "I used to have him over to the White House every other week. I fed him NSC material and made him a great ally. Through Lovestone I brokered a flow of information between Nixon and Meany which resulted in a lot of AFL-CIO endorsements for the president's foreign policy positions on China, Vietnam, Russia, and SALT."

Getting the AFL-CIO to back Nixon in the presidential election was an endorsement too far for George Meany. Lovestone called it mission impossible. However, he also told Colson that Meany was getting so irritated by the McGovern campaign team that he might just be provoked into refusing to endorse either candidate. Colson saw AFL-CIO neutrality in the election as a great second prize. Lovestone advised him that the way to pull this off was to make Meany really mad with McGovern. The ingenious Colson did not take long to work out a way of making Meany angry. He invented an insult from the McGovern campaign headquarters. One September morning in 1972 Meany was sitting with Lovestone (a coconspirator with Colson in this plot) in his office at AFL-CIO headquarters when a call came through on the speakerphone purporting to be from Gary Hart, McGovern's campaign manager. The voice of Gary Hart was commandingly imperious. Senator McGovern wanted to see Mr. Meany urgently. Would Mr. Meany come round at once—within the next two hours at the latest?

George Meany was used to fawning and flattery from presidential candidates. He was outraged by this peremptory summons from a mere campaign manager. He blew his stack completely. "I wouldn't go across the street to see McGovern," snarled Meany to Lovestone after slamming down the phone. "I wouldn't even do that to spit on that man." So great was Meany's umbrage that within hours he announced that the AFL-CIO would not endorse any candidate in the election. Game, set, and dirty trick to Colson. One of his aides had been ordered to impersonate Gary Hart in the phone call, using a script written, rehearsed, and directed by Charles W. Colson. When the episode was described to President Nixon, he said: "That's the greatest thing I ever heard."

Organized labor's support for the Nixon presidency was built on more solid ground than dirty tricks and charm offensives. The massaging of union leaders' egos was important. But as Colson had anticipated at the start of his strategic operation to win the blue-collar vote, the traditional landscape of politics was undergoing a seismic change. In the midterm elections of 1970 Colson made his first attempt to target, with organized labor's help, four Senate seats, in Maryland, Tennessee, Connecticut, and New York, which he thought could be stolen from the Democrats. He was right. Against the trend, the Democrats lost all four. Perhaps the most interesting of these was the victory in New York of James L. Buckley. He owed his Senate seat as a member of the Conservative Party to the ubiquitous Peter Brennan, who at Colson's instigation organized a switch of traditionally Democratic labor voters into Buckley's camp.

Soon after the midterm elections, Colson sent a memorandum to the president that, seen in retrospect, showed remarkable prescience both politically and numerically. He wrote: "According to Gallup, we received one third of the blue-collar vote in 1968. Yet 54% of the blue-collar vote approves of your handling of the economy. It is obvious that any improvement over 1968, even as much as 5% to 10%, could be decisive in any number of lay industrial states." Richard Nixon, who never forgot the blue-collar roots of his father, Frank Nixon, was impressed by Colson's voter calculations and strategy. So, over the next two years, great attention was paid by the White House to blue-collar interests in swing states such as Michigan, Ohio, Pennsylvania, New Jersey, and Illinois. Colson led the charge in this effort to break the Democratic stranglehold on the labor vote and was resoundingly successful.

When the 1972 presidential election results were analyzed it was seen that 54 percent of union members and their families (the exact percentage pinpointed by Colson in his 1970 memo) voted for Nixon, compared to the 33 percent who voted for him in 1968. In the other main bloc where Colson was trying to engineer a big swing—the Catholic vote—the results were equally spectacular. Nixon had lost the Catholic vote by 22 to 78 percent when he ran against John F. Kennedy in 1960. He had lost it again when running against Hubert Humphrey, by 33 to 59 percent. But in 1972, against George McGovern, Nixon won the Catholic vote by 52 to 48 percent.

These figures show that in the blue-collar and Catholic voting blocs that Colson had targeted in his original strategy as ripe for a change in voter loyalty, Nixon improved his vote shares by 21 and 19 percent respectively. The president's point man had delivered. Since Colson was both the architect and the mechanic of these huge shifts in long-established voter patterns, he may well have deserved Nixon's compliments to "his instinct for the jugular" and to his habit of being "positive, persuasive, smart, and aggressively partisan." A more measured but scarcely less flattering accolade came from presidential historian Theodore H. White, who described Colson in his book *The Making of the President* (1972) as "the cleverest political brain, after Richard Nixon, in the White House."

Playing Hardball

The president's point man pointed himself in many other directions during his first eighteen months as a White House aide. "I never saw anyone in my life with so much energy as Chuck," said his assistant, Henry Cashen. "He would be at his desk earlier than anyone else. He would blast off more memos than anyone else. He always had about sixteen balls in the air at any one time and he would not stop kicking them until he hit an absolute brick wall."

Not knowing when to stop was initially regarded as a great Colson virtue in the eyes of Richard Nixon, although ultimately this quality came to be seen as a vice as the shadows lengthened over Watergate. But in the beginning, Colson's exuberance had in it a touch of the "Bliss was it in that dawn to be alive" spirit of the French Revolution. He was forever coming up with ingenious new ideas for broadening the president's support base and he did not care whose toes he trampled on when it came to implementing those ideas, good, bad, or awful.

One of Colson's earliest assignments was to help out with the lobbying for the Anti–Ballistic Missile Treaty, which was running into so much trouble on Capitol Hill that it looked as though the Senate would vote against its ratification. Such a rejection would have been a devastating blow, not only for Nixon's presidential authority but also for the geopolitical architecture for peace that he and Henry Kissinger were secretly constructing between the Soviet Union, China, and the United States. The ABM Treaty and the wider Strategic Arms Limitation Talks (SALT) were cornerstones of that architecture. So it was all hands to the pump in the administration when the ABM Treaty's ratification vote started sinking in the waters of congressional and media opposition.

Although Colson had been in the White House for only a few weeks when the ABM crisis arrived, he threw himself into the lobbying drive with enthusiasm. One of his first ideas was to form a citizens' committee that would fund and write newspaper advertisements in favor of ABM. Haldeman vetoed Colson's plan with the sharp rebuke "You don't know the first thing about writing ads. That's my business, and I don't need the help of a heavy-handed lawyer."

Colson was too heavy-handed to take Haldeman's no for an answer. Having heard Nixon say, "We've got to get more public support for this treaty," he embarked on a freelance operation of his own, forming a group of Nixon loyalists that he labeled the Committee to Safeguard America. He persuaded former secretary of state Dean Acheson to become cochairman of the committee, along with former senator Henry Cabot Lodge. Colson then sat down to design the ad, which featured the mushroom cloud of a nuclear explosion under the headline "Stop the Arms Race—Support Strategic Arms Limitation by Supporting ABM." When the full-page ad appeared across the country under the aegis of the Orwellian-sounding Committee to Safeguard America, it made a considerable impact, particularly in the home states of senators whose ABM votes were still undecided.

One newspaper reader whose eye lighted on the ad with approval was the president. He tore the page out of the *New York Times* and sent it to his chief of staff with a note saying: "Powerful! This is the kind of stuff we should be doing." Haldeman, the former J. Walter Thompson advertising executive, was mortified to receive a memo from Colson saying that the ad that the president praised had been single-handedly written and organized by a certain "heavy-handed lawyer" in the White House.

One other footnote to the ABM treaty. Because the vote on the treaty was a cliffhanger, several White House aides were asked to twist arms in the Senate. One wavering voter assigned to Colson was Margaret Chase Smith of Maine. In view of her history of disliking Colson, and even reporting him to the FBI with conflict-of-interest allegations seven years earlier, she did not seem a good prospect. But to Colson's amazement Senator Smith listened to him attentively as he argued that the president needed ABM as a vital bargaining chip in the SALT negotiations. She ended the conversation by saying, "You've convinced me. You can tell the president I'll vote for his treaty." Since the Senate vote on ABM was a tie, with ratification achieved only as a result of the vice president casting a vote, Colson's lobbying of Margaret Chase Smith was of vital importance.

A few weeks later as the midterm congressional campaigns of 1970 came to a climax, Colson's activities in forming citizens' committees, placing newspaper ads, and putting pressure on Senators became less edifying. On October 12, 1970, Colson sent Haldeman a draft for a number of ads to be placed by a committee calling itself Committee for a Responsible Congress. In fact, this was a Colson-created front organization whose whole purpose was to attack what he called "Democratic extremists" in the last ten days of the campaign. Colson's selection of extremists included Senators Lloyd Bentsen, Vance Hartke, Harrison Williams, Albert Gore Sr., John Tunney, Joseph Montoya, and Joe Tydings. The story of the campaign against Tydings was an early example of Colson's political ruthlessness.

The ads attacking Tydings had a format similar to those used in campaigns against the other Senate incumbents being targeted by Colson. They ran above the banner headline EXTREMISTS NEED JOE TYDINGS—MARYLAND DOES NOT. The text accused the Maryland senator of condoning crime, undermining national defense, forgiving rioters and looters, and regarding the use of heroin and marijuana by young people as acceptable. The justification for these charges was flimsy, to say the least, for they were often based on quotes that were distorted by selective editing or by being taken out of context. For example, the "condoning crime" allegation was based on Tydings's anodyne statement to *Playboy* magazine that "it cannot be shown in most categories of crime that stiffened sentences, mandatory minimums and the like, have an appreciable effect on crime rates."

When the ads were published, two weeks before election day in 1970, they triggered an explosion of anger among the targeted Democrats, particularly in Maryland, where the race was a close one. The anger increased when it leaked out that the organization funding the ads, the Committee for a Responsible Congress, was a bogus body, linked to the White House. Colson was named in various newspapers as the suspected instigator of the ads and he came close to admitting his involvement in a convoluted answer to a *New York Times* reporter. However, his complicity was forthrightly denied by Nixon's press spokesman, Ron Ziegler, who said, "Any suggestion that the White House had anything to do with the motivation behind the ad, the preparation of the ad, or anything at all connected with the ad, is totally incorrect."

Before anyone found out that Ziegler's denial was itself incorrect, the elections were over and interest in the ads faded. Tydings faded too because he lost his seat in the Senate. However, his bitterness did not fade. For many years afterward Tydings blamed Colson personally for his defeat, and not only because of the ad labeling him as an extremist. In another low blow earlier in the campaign, Colson planted a damaging story about Tydings in *Life* magazine alleging that the senator had improperly intervened with a federal government agency on behalf of a Maryland building contractor who was a client of Tydings. The story was neither proved nor disproved, but the planting of it damaged Colson's, as well as Tydings's, reputation. The furor created by the "extremist" ads and the Tydings controversy brought Colson what he called "great distress at this sudden onslaught of publicity," together with calls for him to be dismissed by the president. There was no chance of such an outcome; Nixon thoroughly approved of this kind of political hardball and had known about Colson's efforts to undermine Tydings well in advance of the appearance of the ads. In fact Colson's reputation was visibly on the ascendant both inside and outside the White House. "A White House Aide on the Rise" was the *Washington Star*'s title for a flattering Colson profile published in June 1971, citing his new staff of four secretaries, three assistants, and his new suite of offices. This was suite number 184 in the Executive Office Building. It was immediately adjacent to the small EOB office that Nixon had begun to use as a working hideaway in preference to the formal grandeur of the Oval Office. In a world where proximity to the president symbolizes power, Colson made the most of his neighborly status. At his staff meetings, junior aides like speechwriter William Safire noticed how often Colson used "the most effective one-up in the White House." Safire recalled that "whenever you raised your voice in objection to a Colson idea he would look furtively at the wall of his office, giving you the impression that he hoped you had not disturbed his neighbor, the president."

There was quite a lot of such posturing as Colson's influence increased. It did not improve his popularity with his colleagues—a fact that occasionally troubled Colson himself. He acknowledged this in a memo to Haldeman's aide Lawrence Higby when he referred to his "continuing and uncomfortable position of being the House Bastard." Haldeman, no slouch himself in the house bastard stakes, later wrote that "Colson, in those days, had an abrasive, boastful and overbearing personality . . . dealing with him was no fun for the White House staffers at any level. If he was superior to them in rank he would bully them. If he was inferior he would smile and remind them that he had 'the ear of the President.' Which he did." The growing closeness of Colson to Nixon's ear worried Bob Haldeman. Bill Safire witnessed a demonstration of this concern one morning in early 1971 when he was attending a meeting from which Colson was summoned next door to see the president. In the hiatus that followed the summons, Joan Hall, Colson's secretary, went to a window overlooking the street between the Executive Office Building and the West Wing of the White House, where Haldeman worked. "In one minute you'll see Bob Haldeman come out of that West Wing basement exit and run up those steps," said Hall. She was right in her prediction. According to Safire, the chief of staff had arranged with the president's duty aides to be tipped off as soon as Colson and Nixon were alone together in order that he could join them so as to "not let Colson end run him with the old man."

Colson's end runs could range far beyond his theoretical area of responsibility, public liaison. Sometimes they backfired on him. For example, when Nixon nominated the obscure Florida judge G. Harold Carswell to fill a vacant seat on the Supreme Court, Colson made himself an energetic player in the lobbying effort to neutralize the growing opposition to this appointment. Like other White House staffers engaged in this enterprise, he soon ran short of good arguments to present to the Senate in favor of this most mediocre of judicial mediocrities. To fill this void, Colson came up with a thoroughly novel argument, which was that the Senate had no constitutional right to challenge the president's nominee. Amazingly, Colson persuaded Nixon to take the offensive with this argument in a letter of protest to a key member of the Senate's Judiciary Committee, Senator William Saxbe. Nixon liked Colson's draft letter so much that without any further staff input he called in his secretary, Rose Mary Woods, and asked her to type it up. Then he signed it and sent it off. The result was a furor.

Colson's (by this time Nixon's) letter to Saxbe contained this paragraph: "What is centrally at issue in this nomination is the constitutional responsibility of the President to appoint members of the Court—and whether this responsibility can be frustrated by those who wish to substitute their own philosophy or their own subjective judgment for that of the one person entrusted by the Constitution with the power of appointment." Although Colson had been able to research some interesting legal precedents in support of his confrontational doctrine of presidential infallibility, this offensive strategy was a political blunder, made worse by a factual error in the letter to Saxbe. The White House's argument was seen as an affront to the Senate's historic power to "advise and consent" on Supreme Court appointments. So Nixon had to take a lot of flack in the Congress and in the media for the position his ingenious aide had persuaded him to take up. The *New York Times* summarized the general reaction when it called the letter "full of bad history and bad law." It was certainly a bad judgment call by Colson, but it did not appear to do him any harm with Nixon.

One episode that did Colson a lot of good with Nixon involved some carefully orchestrated negative publicity for Senator Edward Kennedy. The episode started in December 1970 when Kennedy was visiting Paris as a member of a congressional delegation to the funeral of President Charles de Gaulle. In his off-duty hours, it became known, the junior senator from Massachusetts was dating a film starlet named Maria Pia. Knowing that Nixon enjoyed hearing salacious tidbits of gossip about his political opponents, Colson reported Kennedy's dalliance. "Can you get a picture of him with her?" asked Nixon. Colson called Pat O'Hara, a New York lawyer who specialized in undercover investigative work. Within hours, one of O'Hara's private detectives was on his way to France with $5,000 for expenses in his pocket. Two days later, Colson walked into the Oval Office saying, "I've got a package here from Paris which I think you might enjoy, Mr. President." Nixon opened the envelope. When he saw the photograph of Teddy Kennedy dancing cheek-to-cheek with Maria Pia he could barely contain himself, swiveling round his chair. Once Nixon was facing the wall, he collapsed into laughter. At the time, Colson thought the president's movements curious but put them down to the hilarity of the moment. Many months later, when the secret taping system in the Oval Office was revealed, Colson realized that Nixon had turned to the wall to avoid his glee over Kennedy's exposure being recorded for posterity.

In fact there was more to the Kennedy–Maria Pia episode than presidential laughter. Haldeman's diaries showed that there were at least three additional meetings in the Oval Office at which the photographs were discussed. "P[resident] had Colson bring in the photos and file on Teddy Kennedy's activities," wrote Haldeman on December 5. "P seemed to be pleased with the evidence we have on this and wants Colson to follow up on getting it out." Then on December 19, after two weeks of mailing the photographs to selected journalists and politicians, Haldeman recorded: "Colson reported on Teddy Kennedy question. He's getting more pictures distributed and maintaining the effort on that." On December 28 the photograph is again referred to as part of the agenda when "Colson came in for a two-and-a-half hour talk with P about how to attack the Democrats."

It seems strange that so much of Colson's, Haldeman's, and the president's time should have been devoted to these seedy efforts to blacken Kennedy's already tarnished reputation for extramarital womanizing. One explanation was that Nixon longed to hit back personally at Kennedy, who had got under his skin for his frequent and scathing criticism of the conduct of the war in Vietnam. Another was that Nixon feared the war might turn his occupancy of the White House into a one-term presidency. Already the Democrats were making uncomfortable inroads into Nixon's nationwide base of political support. At the midterm congressional elections in November 1970 the Republicans suffered a net loss of nine seats in the House. They also lost eleven governorships. Although these defeats were balanced by one net gain in the Senate, the overall outlook was uncertain and the critics were becoming increasingly vociferous. So it seemed a good time for the White House to launch a new strategy of tougher political hardball in which two particular targets were singled out for attack. The first was any potential Democratic challenger for the presidency, principally Senators Ted Kennedy and Edmund Muskie. The second target was the greatest bête noire of all in the eyes of Colson and Nixon—the liberal media.

In Combat with the Media

Two weeks after the 1970 election results, Colson sent into the Oval Office his first ever memorandum directly addressed "To the President." It marked a further crumbling of the Berlin Wall's powers of exclusion. For some months Colson had been circumventing Haldeman and Ehrlichman by his personal access to Nixon. Now the circumvention went a great deal further as Colson happily accepted the president's invitation to communicate with him in direct "eyes only" notes and memos.

Colson's first such communication to Nixon was ostensibly a six-page analysis of the political way forward from the 1970 elections. However, the real meat of the new strategy Colson proposed was contained in a section of the memo headed "Recommended changes in the handling of the media." In a key paragraph, Colson advocated a program of "quiet but firm pressure from here on the media." He suggested using the Federal Communications Commission (FCC) to "keep the networks off balance and worried, as they are now, over possible regulatory measures." He proposed meetings with senior executives of NBC, ABC, and CBS, adding caustically, "Most of them are so biased that it will only be marginally effective but we can't be hurt by trying."

Perhaps the most controversial of Colson's recommendations was contained in the seemingly innocuous line "We should work at getting more stations in friendly hands." What he meant was that the White House should work on persuading the FCC not to renew the TV station licenses of media organizations that refused to comply with an obscure section of the Federal Communications Act that, in theory, required broadcasters to give equal time to reporting the administration's views. Colson's prime targets here were the TV stations owned by the *Washington Post,* for he was busy lining up alternative friendly bidders for their licenses.

This memo and the discussions that followed it were a turning point in Colson's relationship with Nixon. Two days later an instruction came down from the Oval Office: "You should assume the lead and take full time responsibility for working with the networks, advertisers, etc., and really put it to them on this equal time matter." Colson was exhilarated by this breakthrough. "Nixon was so taken with my ideas for pressurizing the media that he kept calling me at all hours of the day and night about them," he recalled. "Before I wrote that memo a call at home from the president was a rare event. Suddenly I was on his regular call list. That made me truly a member of his innermost circle."

Colson's ticket to the innermost circle was his willingness to cajole, pressure, or even bully the media in accordance with Nixon's wishes. This was an extremely demanding task since the president's wishes in this area were obsessive to the point of paranoia. Nixon could be extraordinarily thin-skinned in the face of journalistic criticism and often exhibited a venomous pettiness in his urge to retaliate against his tormentors. For example, after one TV interview in December 1970 with Dan Rather of CBS,

Nixon was so angry with what he regarded as the snide and offensive tone of Rather's questions that Colson was summoned to the Oval Office to discuss a counteroffensive operation. "Get a hundred people to call Rather and complain," commanded the president, dictating the precise words the callers should use in their complaints. Colson carried out these orders, which were the origin of a more lasting and heavily orchestrated letters-to-the-editor campaign. For the next two years Colson organized fifty to sixty letters a week to influential newspapers, many of them protesting against anti-Nixon bias in their news coverage. This operation was a failure. For as Colson had to report to his boss after a lengthy monitoring exercise, only about one in ten of their carefully planted letters were selected for publication.

Colson had more success at the boardroom level of media power, particularly when he embarked on a series of meetings with senior executives from the TV networks to discuss the balance of their news reporting. These discussions were none-too-subtly linked to Colson's veiled threats about FCC licenses and powers to enforce equal time coverage under the Federal Communications Act, and the atmosphere at the meetings was often full of tension. A prime example of this occurred at meetings in the Oval Office, in May and June 1971, with top executives of ABC, NBC, and CBS. Nixon and Colson appeared to have worked out a soft-man, hard-man routine, with Nixon saying in tones of gentle weariness, "I know you fellas can't do a damn thing about what goes on in your newsrooms . . . your reporters just can't stand the fact that I am in this office. They have opposed me for twenty-five years, they'll continue to oppose me and I realize there's nothing you can do about it . . . but if you have any suggestions, give them to my principal communications adviser, Mr. Colson." As Colson noted afterward: "As they all knew my attitude to FCC controls and network powers, the president's message to the networks was chilling enough."

Colson's main target when it came to chilling or pressuring the networks was CBS, which Nixon often referred to as "the Kennedy Channel." Armed with reports and surveys that allegedly confirmed the antiadministration bias of CBS Evening News (which in those days had by far the highest audience ratings), Colson had several meetings with CBS's chairman, William S. Paley, and its president, Frank Stanton, at which he complained vigorously of unfair reporting. Although many promises were made by the CBS bosses about investigating Colson's complaints and redressing the imbalance of the newsroom's reports, no real progress was made until the extraordinary episode that later became known to insiders as "the bugging of Stanton."

CBS had got itself into trouble on Capitol Hill with allegations of misleading editing of filmed interviews in a documentary titled *The Selling of the Pentagon*. Appearing before the House Commerce Committee, which had legislative jurisdiction over communications statutes, CBS president Frank Stanton defied the committee's subpoena to hand over the unedited film. This set the stage for a full-scale confrontation between CBS and Congress, which was headed by a clear majority of bipartisan votes in favor of censuring Stanton and to citing him and CBS for contempt. Watching this drama from the White House, Colson could hardly restrain his glee at seeing CBS getting its comeuppance from another branch of government. On the other hand, Colson was shrewd enough to see that if the contempt citation succeeded, as it appeared it would, the enforcement of it (which meant putting Stanton in prison) would have to be carried out by the Department of Justice. This would create new bitterness between the media and the Nixon administration, even though the contempt vote was the initiative of Congress. So Colson saw the problem as a political loser for the White House. Unaccustomed as he was to being in sympathy with a network executive, he hoped that the contempt vote would fail.

In the middle of these musings, Colson received an unexpected call from CBS lawyer Alexander Lankler, asking if the White House could help rescue Stanton. As Lankler was an old friend, Colson enjoyed needling him. "Why should we help Stanton?" he joked. "We'd like to see him in jail for life. Too bad capital punishment is not available."

"Listen, Chuck, this is serious," replied Lankler. "Stanton is really uptight about this. He's honestly afraid he'll go to jail. He's authorized me to tell you that he'll do anything you ask if you help him out of this jam. What Stanton wants is a chance to start helping you guys by making sure CBS is fair in its news coverage. Just help him, he really needs it."

Convinced that Lankler was making a genuine offer, Colson saw an opportunity to solve several problems in one go. So, after clearing his lines with Nixon, he called Lankler with a cunning proposition. The White House, Colson told the CBS lawyer, would be prepared to help Stanton, but not as a deal or a quid pro quo. However, *after* the vote in Congress, if Stanton would care to come round to the White House and show his appreciation, Colson would be glad to see him.

Lankler jumped at this guileful approach. The no-deal deal was done.

With some difficulty Colson persuaded the House Republican leaders, Gerald Ford and Les Arends, to withdraw GOP support for the contempt citation. As a result, Stanton escaped. Two days after the vote, on July 15, the CBS president was sitting in Colson's office. Unknown to Stanton, the conversation was bugged. On Colson's instructions the Secret Service wired his office, taping a microphone under his desk. The conversation went magnificently from Colson's point of view. Stanton was in a mood of obsequious sycophancy. As Colson took him through a long catalog of familiar complaints about unfair news reporting by CBS, Stanton agreed with almost every item on the administration's list of grievances, saying: "That's terrible. We've got to put a stop to that sort of thing." Or, "We simply can't have that happening. No wonder you fellows have been upset with us."

Colson, reveling in the knowledge that every word of Stanton's climb down was being recorded, could hardly bear to stop. Eventually, after some ninety minutes of groveling by the CBS chief, Colson emphasized that the administration had not asked for this meeting, was not asking for any favors from CBS, and was seeking not fairness, but "occasional fairness," from its news division. Did Stanton agree with this summary and did he have anything more to say? Frank Stanton agreed completely and concluded: "You know, Chuck, there will be instances when you have major news stories coming up that our people may not fully appreciate the significance of. All you have to do is call me and I will see that they are very adequately covered. Furthermore, if there are any more instances like those that you have demonstrated to me this morning, I personally want to know about them and I will see they don't happen again."

For a short period Stanton was as good as his word. Indeed, Colson was soon writing triumphalist memos to Haldeman, such as "Stanton has clearly passed the word on . . . CBS is being most responsive" and "I don't know that I can stand it. CBS yesterday gave us a sickeningly favorable report on the casualty situation. . . . I don't know what's next but at the rate they are going they might even start having Cronkite praise the Vice President. I'll bet this is really paining these guys."

Stanton's pain increased still further when Colson, through Alexander Lankler, let slip the information that the July 15 meeting had been preserved for posterity on tape. But after a few months this entente cordiale collapsed. One of the causes of the collapse was a Nixon-Haldeman decision, unknown to Colson, to have CBS correspondent Dan Schorr investigated by the FBI as a way of putting pressure on his news reporting. Colson later characterized the moves against Schorr as "sheer idiocy . . . it probably did more than anything else to hurt Nixon with the press and was a major factor in causing many journalists to pursue Watergate."

Nixon was both fascinated and infuriated by journalists, although the latter emotion was usually in the ascendant. "The press is the enemy," the president often said to his aides. "They are all against us." Colson disagreed with this sweeping generalization and said as much in a memo that nevertheless still managed to pander to many of the prejudices of his boss. "It is good politics for us to kick the press around, or rather see that they are kicked around," he wrote to Haldeman. "It is also a good thing to make people question the credibility of the little band of intellectual snobs known as the Washington Press Corps . . . but to point out that the whole press establishment is anti-Nixon is in my mind very dangerous."

Dangerous or not, the antijournalist mind-set was a feature of the Nixon White House. Even though Colson was too intelligent and experienced an observer of politics to believe in it, he went along with it whenever the president's orders required him to do so. So when he was told to involve himself in bullying tactics or discreditation operations against media organizations, Colson saluted and obeyed, even when the president's requirements were as eccentric as they were in the episode of the phantom best seller.

One morning in early 1971 Colson was summoned to the Oval Office to receive an unusual order from the president. "Chuck, I want this on the best-seller list," demanded Nixon as he slammed down a green-and-black-jacketed book on his desk—*The News Twisters,* by a little known New York TV critic, Edith Efron. As Colson took the book back to his office for a quick perusal, he "soon saw that it was destined to preserve the author's obscurity," he recalled. "It was full of charts and graphs showing the anti-Nixon bias of the TV coverage of the 1968 campaign. Well done and scholarly, but it was definitely not bedtime reading material, still less best-seller material. But an order from the president was an order that had to be obeyed."

At a meeting of his staff later that morning, Colson inquired if anyone knew how to get a book on the list of national best sellers. The question was greeted with puzzled silence. But by midafternoon one of Colson's enterprising assistants established that the best-seller list was compiled from weekly phone surveys of several key New York bookstores. Colson swung into action. Once he had identified the New York bookstores concerned, he diverted $8,000 raised from Nixon loyalists to his ingenious friend Pat O'Hara, the Manhattan lawyer who some months earlier had obtained the photographs of Senator Edward Kennedy with a starlet in Paris. O'Hara recruited a team of student volunteers who were sent round the bookstores of New York to buy up every available copy of *The News Twisters.* The operation was successful. The following Monday morning Colson strode proudly into the Oval Office and laid a copy of *Time* magazine on the president's desk. To Nixon's delight, *The News Twisters* had reached the best-seller list.

One other Colson initiative directed partly at the media was his idea that Nixon should start a carefully planned program of personal telephone calls to stroke influential opinion formers. "In accordance with our discussion in your office—I have prepared a list of the 100 people you might from time to time choose to call," wrote Colson in a memorandum to the president dated January 18, 1971. "In preparing this list I have attempted to follow the criteria you outlined, that is people you know, who are influential, who would from time to time appreciate a call from you, and in most cases people you could call without any specific reason."

The list Colson submitted covered labor leaders (Peter Brennan, Teddy Gleason, Jay Lovestone, and George Meany), Catholics (the cardinal archbishops of Chicago, Philadelphia, and New York), celebrities (Pearl Bailey, Bing Crosby, Bob Hope, Elvis Presley, and John Wayne), and sports figures (Peggy Fleming, Billy Casper, Woody Hayes, and Ted Williams). However, by far the largest category was journalists and media, with forty-six names out of the hundred, covering a wide spectrum of columnists, editors, and TV commentators. It is not known how many of the names recommended by Colson actually received calls from the president, but the operation was quickly discontinued, possibly because of the Ben Bradlee episode.

Bradlee, the editor of the *Washington Post,* was the recipient of two or three "stroking" calls from Nixon in early 1971, at his home on Saturday mornings. The first of these presidential telephone initiatives got off on the wrong foot because Bradlee thought the deep-voiced caller was Art Buchwald playing a joke. Even after this misunderstanding had been ironed out, Nixon's efforts to build bridges to the editor of the *Post* proved counterproductive. At both ends of the line the conversation seemed stilted, purposeless, and without any intellectual foundation. Bradlee himself was singularly underwhelmed by the White House's carrot-and-stick approach to himself and other journalists. "We thought these PR techniques were bizarre in their lack of subtlety," he recalled. "It was like they were running some sort of sleazy hotel in the Caribbean. 'Give 'em a free trip and fill 'em up with booze if they're for us. Buy 'em off if they're neutral. Knee 'em in the groin if they step out of line.' It was just so darn unsophisticated."

It was not quite as bad as that! Yet Colson was at the heart of all this antimedia activity. The hostile us-against-them mentality that lay behind it was largely his creation. Because of it he became the president's point man on a wide range of political and public relations issues. In early 1971 Nixon appointed Colson to be in overall charge of the administration's public information and communications strategy. This was a humiliating blow for Herb Klein, a longtime Nixon associate who headed up the White House Office of Communications. To save face, Klein was allowed to remain titular head of this office. However, he had to take his orders from Colson; so did the staff, most of whom were fired or swept away into other parts of the administration by the ruthless new broom.

An example of Colson's ruthlessness at this time concerned John Scali, a foreign policy expert and ABC news commentator, who was selected by Nixon for a key role in the restructured Office of Communications because he was "a tough political nut cutter." Colson brought Scali into the Oval Office to see the president, who offered him the job. Scali said he longed to accept it but could not do so for health reasons. He explained that he had been hospitalized recently for surgery on his bleeding ulcers. He feared that the pressures of working in the White House would cause the problem to recur. Colson, who never liked to take no for an answer, persuaded Scali to have a full medical examination by the president's personal physician, Commander Bill Lukash. Returning to his office straight from the meeting between Nixon and Scali, Colson called Lukash with an order to make sure the physical produced the result the president wanted.

"Commander, we have a special little assignment for you," began Colson. "It concerns a guy named John Scali the president wants to come and work for us. But Scali is worried about a problem with his ulcers. He is afraid the job he's been offered will reactivate the problem. So your duty is to give him a thorough physical and to tell him he's in great health, his ulcers are fine, and that the job will be good for him."

"Aye aye, sir," replied Commander Lukash. A fellow White House aide sitting in Colson's office listening to this call on the speakerphone was John Whitaker, the president's adviser on environmental health issues. "My God, Colson," said Whitaker in shocked tones as the call ended. "You really are the monster they say you are."

Whether he was a monster or not, Colson's ability to deliver what the president wanted was formidable. His ruthlessness became legendary and turned him into one of the heaviest political hitters of the Nixon administration. There was a step change in his importance and status. By the summer of 1971 the "big three" of senior White House aides—Haldeman, Ehrlichman, and Kissinger—had become the "big four," with Colson as the new entrant to the president's inner circle. He was now in a position to be tested to the full by the episode of the Pentagon Papers and by the subsequent saga of Watergate.

CHAPTER EIGHT

Watergate

The Pentagon Papers

Charles Colson's involvement in Watergate was major in terms of its political immorality, but minor in terms of its criminal illegality. He was a significant contributor to the creation of the climate in which Watergate could happen. Because he made his contribution by words rather than by deeds, he was usually one step removed from the worst excesses. His misjudgments, his aggressive attitudes, and his encouragement of the darker instincts in Nixon's character made Colson a key Watergate player, but even so, the record shows that his participation in the actual events and criminal activities that led to the resignation of the president was far less than has often been claimed.

For Colson, the slide toward Watergate began with the publication of the Pentagon Papers. Nixon's explosive reactions to the security leak of these classified documents brought about a sharp change in the attitudes of many presidential aides, some of whom became sucked into a downward spiral toward illegal activities. Colson was one of the most important figures to be affected in this way. However, his initial reaction to the leak of the documents was to argue for a restrained response by the White House. He was soon swept away from this position on the flood tide of the president's wrath.

The saga of the Pentagon Papers burst upon the world on June 13, 1971, when the *New York Times* ran a front-page story headlined VIETNAM ARCHIVE: PENTAGON STUDY TRACES THREE DECADES OF GROWING U.S. INVOLVEMENT. There was no good reason why this journalistic scoop should have become the watershed in Colson's life that eventually resulted in his going to jail. For all the media ballyhoo that accompanied the *New York Times's* disclosures, they were yesterday's news. The Pentagon Papers took the form of an academic research project commissioned in the early 1960s by Robert McNamara, defense secretary under President Kennedy, with the title "The History of U.S. Decision-Making in Vietnam." The study, carried out by the Rand Corporation, was based on an archive of secret documents drawn from the Defense Department, the State Department, the CIA, the White House, and the Joint Chiefs of Staff. These documents contained a wealth of material that was embarrassing to the Kennedy and Johnson administrations. However, since the study ended in 1968, nothing that had happened in Vietnam since Nixon's inauguration was published. The new presidency was therefore untainted by the publication of the Pentagon Papers.

Colson understood this more clearly than any other senior member of the administration. At a time when several of the president's closest advisers, particularly John Mitchell and Henry Kissinger, were going ballistic with their recommendations that the U.S. government should take on the *New York Times* and other newspapers in an all-out legal battle in the courts, Colson composed an eight-page memorandum advocating a different strategy. It began on an unusual note of moderation. "I think you know that I am very impulsive by nature. I tend to plunge hard into the issue of the moment and like to join battle on every hot topic," wrote Colson. "However, because I feel the issues are so profound, I am in effect advocating what is for me a very uncharacteristic caution."

Emphasizing his view that the Pentagon Papers could have an important, if not decisive, impact on the coming presidential election in 1972, Colson urged a long-haul exploitation of the damage to the Democrats rather than a short-term battle against the press. "The heartland isn't really aroused over this," he wrote. "It is not the kind of issue that will last. People just don't give a damn if we beat the New York Times in the Supreme Court or the New York Times beat us." Continuing in this vein, Colson recommended that there should be no escalation in the administration's criticism of the press and no attacks on newspapers by administration spokesmen. Instead, he urged a change of emphasis, away from the publication of the documents and onto the theft of the documents.

Warming to his theme, Colson's memorandum recommended going for the jugular of the man who stole the Pentagon Papers—Daniel Ellsberg, a forty-year-old Rand Corporation employee who had been a member of the team of researchers working on the study Robert McNamara had commissioned. "The prosecution of Ellsberg . . . could indeed arouse the heartland which is at present not very excited over the whole issue. First of all he is a natural villain to the extent that he can be painted out," wrote Colson. "Second, a prosecution of Ellsberg can help taint the press. If he indeed conspired with members of the press and he is painted black they too will be painted black."

Wielding his black paintbrush with vigor in the concluding pages of his memorandum, Colson advocated using an Ellsberg prosecution to discredit individual Democrats who were foolish enough to defend the leaks, and to ensure that members of the Democratic Party kept fighting among themselves over their deep divisions on the Vietnam War. "I have not yet thought through all of the subtle ways in which we can keep the Democratic party in a constant state of civil warfare, but I am convinced that with some imaginative and creative thinking it can be done," he wrote.

Although Nixon would normally have jumped at Colson's ideas for keeping the Democrats "in a constant state of civil warfare," on this occasion the president showed little interest in playing domestic political hardball. For Henry Kissinger had managed to persuade Nixon that the Pentagon Papers crisis would strip him of his reputation as a world statesman. "It shows you're a weakling, Mr. President," said Kissinger. "The fact that some idiot can publish all the diplomatic secrets of this country on his own is damaging to your image as far as the Soviets are concerned and it could destroy our ability to conduct foreign policy."

Colson thought Kissinger's fulminations over the Pentagon Papers were wildly excessive. However, they prevailed over all other more moderate counsels. "Henry managed to convince Nixon that the leaks would bring down the geopolitical house of cards he had so elaborately constructed by playing the Chinese against the Soviets," recalled Colson. "He feared that his top-secret mission to Beijing might be called off. So Ellsberg became the symbol of the sinister, revolutionary forces who were undermining the administration and who had to be stopped."

In June 1971, less than a dozen people in the world knew that Nixon was planning a top-secret mission to China. Colson was one of them as a result of his membership of the *Sequoia* group. This was the cabal of confidants Nixon regularly invited to cruise down the Potomac with him on the presidential yacht, the *Sequoia,* on balmy summer evenings. Dining one night on the *Sequoia* over fresh corn on the cob and New York strip steaks with Nixon, Haldeman, Ehrlichman, and Kissinger, Colson was startled when the president winked at him and asked, "Do you think, Chuck, you'll get me an SST to fly to China?" This was a teasing reference to

Colson's unsuccessful efforts to lobby Congress for funds to build a supersonic-jet passenger airliner. It was the first Colson had heard of the China initiative. Kissinger bridled at the disclosure of this tightly held secret. Nixon teased him for his reaction. "Relax, Henry, relax," chided the president. "If those liberals on your staff don't stop giving everything to the *New York Times* I won't be going anywhere. The leaks, the leaks, that's what we've got to stop at any cost."

"At any cost." Those words were not just a figure of speech. As the summer of 1971 wore on, Nixon descended into a mood of darkening paranoia toward Ellsberg and other liberal antiwar activists who had at one time served on Kissinger's National Security Council staff. The president's rantings against these real or suspected leakers of classified documents often took place when Colson was present in the Oval Office. As a result Colson later had to face accusations that he planned fire bombings and burglaries for Nixon in the aftermath of the Pentagon Papers disclosure.

The allegation that Colson was the author of a plan to firebomb the Brookings Institution in Washington, D.C., was one of the most bizarre byproducts of the Pentagon Papers saga. The background to it was Nixon's obsession that two former NSC aides, Leslie Gelb and Morton Halperin, had cached certain files at Brookings that could be used as a Pentagon Papers analogue for the first eighteen months of the new administration's decision-making processes on Vietnam. Nixon lashed out wildly in his frustration over the government's inability to find the files allegedly stored at Brookings. "I remember Nixon shouting, 'I want these ******* documents back and I want a team that can break into these places and get them,' " recalled Colson. "He was really putting the heat on Haldeman to develop a team of people who would carry out burglaries. That was over the line, and I wish I'd had the courage to say, 'No, you can't do that, Mr. President.' But I just kept quiet, and so did Haldeman. Afterward Haldeman chose the course of not doing what the president had asked him to do. I never did anything either, despite what the press said."

The press, largely on the basis of testimony during the Senate hearings on Watergate from John Dean, two years later, gave huge headlines to the sensational claim that Colson had ordered the firebombing of Brookings. This order was said to have been given to Jack Caulfield, a former New York policeman turned White House investigator. Caulfield allegedly reported the order to John Dean, but Colson himself resolutely denied the story. According to his own account, Colson came out of the meeting in the

Oval Office saying to Haldeman, "What are we supposed to do about the documents at Brookings?"

"Call Ehrlichman, he knows what to do," replied Haldeman.

When Colson called Ehrlichman, he replied, "I'll send Jack Caulfield round this evening. He's the one who'll know what to do." Colson had never before dealt with Caulfield and had no idea what his responsibilities were in the White House. All he knew was that Caulfield had been Nixon's protection officer in the New York Police Department during his years as vice president. So when Caulfield arrived in his office, Colson repeated what Nixon had said about the need to recover the papers at Brookings. Caulfield's response—he had already discussed the subject with John Ehrlichman—was simply, "Fine, I'll take care of it."

"I really honestly thought that Caulfield would call in a few days' time and leave word that the secretary of defense had revoked the security clearances of Brookings," recalled Colson, "because that would have forced them to return any classified documents they had. That was the first thought I'd had in my mind despite what Nixon had said."

Caulfield, however, had other thoughts. A week later he sidled up to Colson in the men's room of the Executive Office Building and whispered: "It's going to be very difficult to get those papers back unless we can create a diversion."

"What do you mean?" asked Colson.

"Well, what we used to do in the NYPD when we needed to recover documents from a building was that we would stage a fire. Then, in all the confusion with the firefighters and fire engines, we would go in and get what we wanted."

Colson was startled. He had never heard of such incendiary diversions by police officers. The idea of trying one at Brookings had never entered his mind until Caulfield mentioned it in the EOB rest room. Instead of knocking the plan on the head then and there, Colson shrugged his shoulders and said: "Jack, I don't know how you're going to do it, but all I know is that the president wants those papers back."

These whispered exchanges in the rest room do not reflect particularly well on Colson. But nor do they reflect particularly badly on him. If he had been a pillar of moral rectitude, perhaps he should have voiced his instant disapproval. On the other hand, he made no suggestion that the Brookings Institution should be firebombed. Nor did he initiate, authorize, or support any such plan. He simply assumed that the responsibility for recovering the papers from Brookings, and the methods of doing it, were matters for John Ehrlichman.

The next time Colson heard about this harebrained scheme (which was never taken any further) was when it hit the headlines two years later in the course of the Senate Watergate hearings in 1973. John Dean, basing his evidence on flawed reports from Jack Caulfield, told the Senate committee that Colson had given an order to blow up Brookings. Dean said he had been so disturbed on hearing the news of this alleged order that he had immediately flown on an air force plane to San Clemente for a meeting with John Ehrlichman. At their meeting, Dean had urged Ehrlichman to countermand Colson's "order."

Colson was astonished by this version of events and strongly denied ever having suggested, or ordered, the bombing of Brookings. But in the hysteria of Watergate, his denials were disbelieved. The story was repeated so often that the mud stuck. No charge in Watergate relating to Colson received more media attention or did his reputation more damage.

The damage went on being repeated in books and TV programs about Watergate for nearly three decades. "I just had to grin and bear it. I knew the story was wrong. But who was going to believe me?" said Colson.

The first indication that someone who really knew the truth believed him came on October 1, 2002. Colson was working in his office that afternoon at Prison Fellowship's headquarters when he took an unexpected call from Jack Caulfield. It was the first time the two men had spoken since their conversation in the men's room of the Executive Office Building of the White House, thirty-one years earlier. After some lengthy small talk, which seemed to be going round in circles, Caulfield declared that he wanted to say something important. "I'm getting to the age when I want to be sure that my accounts are straightened out with the man upstairs," he explained. "I need to see you to apologize." Colson demurred, saying a meeting really wasn't necessary.

"Do you know what I'm talking about?" pressed Caulfield.

"Yes," replied Colson, "I know exactly what you're talking about. I appreciate your apologizing. You're a big man. I forgive you." With these words, gracious on both sides, the Brookings firebombing account was corrected.

Six weeks later, in November 2002, Jack Caulfield, in an interview with this biographer, said that his phone call to Colson had been motivated by "a sense of conscience." After making allegations about another member of the White House staff, Caulfield explained that his NYPD badge had been numbered 911. In the aftermath of 9/11, he felt an emotional and moral urge to iron out his relationship with Colson and set the record straight. Caulfield described Colson as "one of the good guys now . . . but those times were days of madness. Yet even in all that madness no one ever came close to firebombing Brookings, and no one ever ordered me to do that."

Although the Brookings story consisted of far more fiction than fact, it was nevertheless symptomatic of the ends-justifies-the-means thinking that prevailed in the White House in the weeks after the Pentagon Papers were published. Concern for the protection of national security was at the heart of that thinking, but in their pursuit of that legitimate objective the aides closest to Nixon became unbalanced by the ferocity of their overreaction. Kissinger, who felt particularly vulnerable to criticism because Daniel Ellsberg had been a member of his staff in 1969, described his former protégé as "the most dangerous man in America today . . . he must be stopped at all costs." Nixon evidently agreed, telling Colson that Ellsberg's activities amounted to treason. "I want him exposed, Chuck," ordered the president. "I want the truth about him known. I don't care how you do it, but get it done."

"Yes sir, it will be done," said the eager Colson, who subsequently played a crucial role in the recruitment of a leading member of "the Plumbers." This was the team of special operatives Nixon had been demanding ever since the beginning of the Pentagon Papers saga. Their mission, which had originally been directed to the detecting and plugging of leaks, took on a new momentum in far more dangerous directions once the team had been joined by an ex–CIA officer recommended by Colson. This was E. Howard Hunt.

Enter Howard Hunt

The fateful appointment of Howard Hunt to the White House staff would never have been made without Charles Colson. The two men knew each other because they had been, respectively, vice president and president of the Brown University Club of Washington during the 1960s. At that time Hunt was a senior CIA officer nearing retirement, with a sideline in writing pseudonymous espionage novels. When Colson was appointed to the White House staff, Hunt sent him a fulsome letter of congratulations, saying, "This is the best news since the moon landing." Colson reciprocated by inviting his admirer to occasional lunches in the White House mess.

Hunt later described these encounters as "almost inspirational experiences." At one of these lunches in late 1970, Hunt told Colson he had taken early retirement from the agency, and added, "I am just across the street working for this public relations firm, Mullen Associates. I have time on my hands. If you have any projects you want me to handle, I can do them. As you know I ran covert operations for the CIA."

Colson remembered the conversation in July 1971 when John Ehrlichman was setting up the team that became known as the Plumbers. Nixon was continuing to put the heat on his senior aides for plumbing results. Late one night in a meeting with Colson and Haldeman the president blew his top. With reddening face and fists pounding the desk he returned to his familiar theme of wanting immediate retaliatory action against Ellsberg, and bellowed, "I don't care how it's done. I want these leaks stopped. Don't give me any excuses. Use any means. Bob, do we have one man here to do it? I want results. I want them now."

Writing retrospectively in his memoir, *Born Again,* Colson came to see that "it was at that moment that the Nixon Presidency passed a crossroads." However, it was Colson who took the first fateful step on the wrong side of that crossroads by recruiting the "one man" who met Nixon's job specifications. Haldeman, who was well used to dealing with his boss's explosions of spleen, often operated a policy of benign neglect when unacceptable orders came his way from an overwrought president. He and Ehrlichman had been ignoring Nixon's thinly veiled requests for burglaries and black bag jobs for some time. Colson, however, was the superobedient ex-marine type whose attitude toward orders from his commander in chief was to salute and say, "Yes sir, Mr. President, I'll go out and get it done." And he did.

Colson called Hunt at Mullen and discussed the surprising vacancy that was opening up at the White House for, in effect, a specialist in burglaries. "He seemed a smart guy, fanatically loyal, and a true conservative believer," recalled Colson. "As he'd done covert operations for the CIA, he must know how covert operations get done." Colson taped his call to Hunt, which began with a discussion of the Ellsberg case and continued:

COLSON Let me ask you, Howard, this question. Do you think, with the right resources employed, that this thing could be turned into a major public case against Ellsberg and coconspirators?

HUNT Yes I do, but you've established a qualification that I don't know whether it can be met.

COLSON What's that?

    HUNT Well, with the proper resources.

COLSON Well, I think the resources are there.

    HUNT Well, I would say so absolutely.

COLSON Then your answer would be we should go down the line to nail
        the guy cold.

    HUNT Go down the line to nail the guy cold, yes.

Colson sent a transcript of this dialogue to Ehrlichman with a note: "The more I think about Howard Hunt's background politics, disposition, and experience the more I think it would be worth your time to meet him." Colson also recommended Hunt to Nixon, in an Oval Office conversation on July 1, 1971. "He's hard a nails. He's a brilliant writer. He's written forty books on espionage," Colson told the president. "His name is Howard Hunt. He's here in Washington now. He just got out of the CIA. Fifty. Kind of a tiger."

Six days later Colson took his tiger to a meeting with John Ehrlichman. As a result of that meeting Hunt was recruited as a $100-a-day White House consultant and installed in a small office on the third floor of the Executive Office Building. His first assignments involved clandestine research into material from the Pentagon Papers that could be unfavorable to leading Democrats; into Senator Edward Kennedy's alleged sexual misbehavior at Chappaquiddick; and into President John F. Kennedy's alleged complicity in the assassination of the South Vietnamese president Diem in 1961. These tasks were directed by Colson.

Hunt was in awe of his new taskmaster. "One had a sense that Colson was a dynamo around which spun large and powerful wheels," he wrote. "This sense of dynamism which pervaded Colson's office reflected the kinetic energy of the man himself. Everything about Colson moved at super speed, not a moment to be lost. To and from the men's room he even carried papers to read."

If Colson had been more experienced in the murky world of clandestine operations, he might have been well advised to pause in the midst of his frenetic activities and to ask some probing questions about his new recruit. He would have been wise to have inquired more carefully into Hunt's antecedents and those of the Mullen public relations company. If Colson had made those checks he might soon have asked the question, who exactly is Howard Hunt working for? To this day there has never been a satisfactory answer to this intriguing inquiry despite exhaustive investigations by congressional committees, authors, lawyers, and journalists.

It is now established that Mullen was not an authentic public relations company at all. It was a front for the CIA, with some of its offices staffed, run, and paid for by the agency. Its owner, Robert Bennett, and several of its employees, including Howard Hunt, were men with close links to the CIA. Some of them filed regular reports to the agency. They also received technical and logistical support from CIA outstations. It may be significant that Howard Hunt was placed in his job at Mullen on the personal recommendation of the director of central intelligence, Richard Helms.

What was this curious collection of CIA characters doing in the Mullen office just across the street from the White House? Several seasoned observers, including Senator Howard Baker, Bob Haldeman, John Ehrlichman, and Jim Hougan, the author of *Secret Agenda,* all concluded that Mullen was being used to spy on the Nixon White House for the CIA. Hunt's self-promotion to Colson may add credence to that theory. The background to the theory was the well-known anxieties within the CIA about Nixon's plans to restructure the intelligence community in his second term. Those restructuring plans would have meant huge cutbacks in the budget and operations of the CIA, which was not a part of the intelligence world admired by the president. However, since the double-edged activities of Mullen in general, and Hunt in particular, remain shrouded in mystery, it would be indulging in conspiracy theories to speculate at any length on the impact of the CIA on Colson's story. All that can be said is that Colson may well have been leaked against, covertly operated against, and unjustly smeared by the CIA as the Watergate saga unfolded. On the other hand, since Colson had been just as active as any undercover agent in the murky waters of leaks, clandestine operations, and smears, the opposite side of this argument is that Colson's worst enemy during this period was not the CIA but himself.

Although Howard Hunt never worked directly under Colson, in his first few weeks on the White House payroll he took on several odd jobs and assignments for Colson's office. Then, in the late summer of 1971, Hunt started to report to and take his orders from Egil "Bud" Krogh, head of the secret unit of leak detectors known as the Plumbers. It consisted mainly of young White House aides but it included one other experienced member of the world of covert operations, ex–FBI agent G. Gordon Liddy. Hunt soon bonded with Liddy, whom he introduced to Colson during the summer of 1971.

The Plumbers were working on their first covert operation, which was to be a break-in of the offices of Ellsberg's psychiatrist, Dr. Lewis Fielding.

Masterminded by Hunt and Liddy, with technical support and disguises obtained from the CIA, the mission to steal the medical files of the leaker of the Pentagon Papers required funding. Colson was the source of the money ($5,000), which he obtained form Joe Baroody, a Washington public relations executive, who in turn got it from Milk Producers, a trade association of dairy farmers that had offered funds to help White House campaigns. Colson's involvement in this financing of the break-in began when John Ehrlichman asked him to produce $5,000 in cash.

"What's it for?" asked Colson.

"Don't ask. It's a national security matter," replied Ehrlichman. Colson later became aware from a conversation with the head of the Plumbers, Egil Krogh, that the funds were needed for travel expenses in connection with a covert information-gathering operation on Ellsberg. Although he did not know the exact details of the covert operation, Colson was a long way from being completely in the dark about it. Three weeks before the burglary Colson had asked Hunt to send him a memorandum on steps that might be taken to neutralize Daniel Ellsberg. "I provided such a memorandum," wrote Hunt, "one line of which suggested acquisition of psychiatric material on Ellsberg from Dr. Fielding's files."

Whatever he knew or did not know about the Plumbers' plans, Colson delivered the $5,000 in cash to Egil Krogh, who handed it over to Hunt and Liddy the night before the break-in with the words "Here it is. Now for God's sake don't get caught." Four days later Hunt reappeared in the reception area of Colson's suite of EOB offices. Taking a set of Polaroid photographs from his pocket, Hunt said: "Chuck, I'd like to show you these. They concern what I was doing over the weekend."

"What are they?" asked Colson.

"This was our covert operation," began Hunt as he started showing Colson the first picture of the damage he and Liddy had done to Dr. Fielding's office during the break-in. Colson leapt away from it like a scalded cat. "Howard, get that stuff out of here," he snapped. "Do not tell me anything like this. I don't want to be involved. You do whatever your job is, but don't come round here telling me what you've done. I don't want to hear anything about it." With that, Colson strode into his office, closing the door sharply behind him.

Hunt attributed this sharp rebuff to "the principle of compartmentation," which he approvingly noted was evidently just as fully maintained in the White House as it had been in the CIA. However, the only compartment of interest to Colson was one that kept him hermetically sealed off

from the dirty work of the Plumbers. He was not the only senior figure trying to keep his distance from the Fielding break-in. The wanton destruc-
tion of the psychiatrist's office had been in inverse proportion to the
material brought back from the psychiatrist's files, for not a single piece of
paper about Ellsberg was ever found by the burglars. When John Ehrlichman was shown the photographs of the broken furniture and smashed filing cabinets he said angrily: "This is far beyond anything I had ever
authorized."

Colson, who had authorized nothing, did not come into the spotlight for
his role in the affair for nearly two years. His lawyer's caution had kept him
one step ahead of the sheriff in terms of legal participation in the Fielding
burglary. Yet it would be morally disingenuous for Colson to claim ignorance or noninvolvement in the crime, as he himself has subsequently acknowledged. "If I had been the prosecutor I would have tried to get a
conviction against me for conspiracy in the Fielding break-in. I would have
pleaded guilty to that because I provided the money for it. Did I do it
knowingly in the sense that I knew how the money was going to be used?
No, not technically. But although I did not know the Plumbers were going
to break in, I knew they were going to get those files. I knew they were going after derogatory information about Ellsberg and to find out what his
psychiatrist had on him. So in that way I was probably a guilty party to the
conspiracy."

Although the Ellsberg break-in was a separate and different episode
from the Watergate break-in nearly a year later, in terms of moral and public perception the two crimes were destined to become inextricably linked.
For a start the same two "hardmen"—Howard Hunt and G. Gordon
Liddy—masterminded both burglaries. Second, and more important, the
operations crossed the same Rubicon of illegality. For by condoning what
the hardmen had done in Dr. Fielding's office, Colson and other top aides
in the White House were signaling that burglary under the cover of national security was acceptable. From there it was only a small step for Hunt
and Liddy to conclude that if the president's men were willing to condone
crime for national security purposes in 1971, it would not be too much of
a stretch to condone it again in 1972 for political purposes. Colson was one
of the creators of this wrongheaded moral climate. His hubris caused him
to become enmeshed in the interlocking scandals that became known by
the generic term "Watergate" even though he was innocent of the specific
crime of the Watergate burglary. Because of that hubris, Colson fostered

the disastrous relationship with Howard Hunt that led to his own down-fall—and also the downfall of the president of the United States.

Hatchet Man and Confidant

On October 16, 1971, Charles Colson celebrated his fortieth birthday. The anniversary approximately coincided with the peak of his White House career. For as newspapers and magazines were reporting, Colson had become what *Newsweek* called "the man who is in." Such outsiders' accounts of his rising eminence were more than matched by insiders' chronicles of the time Colson spent alone with the president. According to the White House logs of the period, only Bob Haldeman enjoyed greater access to the Oval Office. But while Haldeman's relations with his boss were brisk and businesslike, Colson's were far more personal and discursive. This was partly because Colson understood and nurtured the darker side of Richard Nixon.

Although Nixon the president was jealous of his privacy, paradoxically Nixon the man could be surprisingly unguarded with his intimacy. This tended to happen when he was alone, and in the right mood, with an individual he instinctively believed he could trust. Colson began moving toward such a position of trust because he impressed his boss by hard work and can-do attitude. In his primary role as the president's point man for public liaison, Colson delivered impressive results. During his first two years at the White House he established strong links with over 150 special interest groups, some fifty of which he brought into the Oval Office for presidential audiences. These were often far more than glad-handing occasions. As the story of the Catholic schools order indicated, Colson was adept at the necessary executive and legislative follow-throughs requested by interest groups. In that context he was personally responsible for such measures as the school library funding program; revisions to the Davis-Bacon Act, the Hatch Act, and the Communications Act; and a steady flow of initiatives tailored to please Nixon's "new majority" constituencies in the unions and the ethnic blocs. These ranged from the establishment of the construction industry collective-bargaining council to the Right to Read program for bilingual education. All this was good work but it did not impress Nixon so much as Colson's willingness to do bad deeds.

Before the Pentagon Papers, Colson's bad deeds were in the twilight zone of political hardball. Tough and at times quite seedy, like the episode of the Kennedy photographs, they never crossed the line into illegality. However, as the pressures of the anti–Vietnam War protest movement intensified in their impact on the political landscape, so Colson's dirty tricks became dirtier. "Those who say I fed the president's darker political instincts are only fifty percent correct," recalled Colson, "because fifty percent of the time he was feeding my darker instincts."

Misinformation and gathering political intelligence that could be used against opponents were priority items on their mutual agendas, particularly during most of 1971, when the principal Democratic challenger for the next presidential election, Senator Edmund Muskie, was leading Nixon in the polls. One evening when Nixon and Colson were watching TV news reports of Muskie campaigning in the New Hampshire primaries, the president said: "Wouldn't it be kinda interesting if there was a committee of Democrats supporting Muskie *and* busing? Couldn't you arrange that one, Chuck?"

Arranging that one should have been mission impossible. The compulsory busing of schoolchildren (a policy aimed at desegregating schools by transporting children from racially unmixed residential areas to racially mixed schools) was anathema to the Catholic and ethnic groups that made up Muskie's strongest base of support among registered Democrats. But Colson was the ultimate can-do political operator, particularly when it came to forming artificial pro-Nixon committees with Orwellian titles like Citizens' Committee for Peace and Freedom, Americans for Winning the Peace, and Committee to Safeguard America—all Colsonian creations. So by pushing, shoving, paying, and pressuring, he somehow managed to unearth enough oddball New Hampshire voters to form the committee Nixon had dreamed of. Thus Democrats for Muskie and Busing duly came into existence and published a hundred thousand leaflets with funds provided by Colson. The false propaganda coup produced many disaffections among conservative Democrats, to the discomfiture of Muskie and to the delight of Nixon.

Behind their mutual enjoyment of such subterranean machinations lay an interesting personal chemistry between Colson and Nixon. Despite their powerful positions, both men felt they were insecure outsiders at the insiders' court of the East Coast liberal establishment. They shared a visceral dislike of political and social elites, particularly the charmed circle of the Kennedys. The positive qualities Nixon and Colson saw in each other included razor-sharp intellect, a deep sense of patriotism, and a dedicated commitment to the values of hard work and discipline. Their common frailties included an inner shyness, which they cloaked in a carapace of exaggeratedly macho talk and outwardly combative posturing.

Nixon once told his closest friends, Bob Abplanalp and Bebe Rebozo, that he recognized a lot of himself in the young Charles Colson, whom he often addressed in private as "boy." For his part Colson hero-worshiped his president with almost filial devotion. With the pained feelings of an understanding son he empathized with Nixon's rages of hurt and anger over criticism that seemed to both of them to be unfair. Colson also had an intuitive feel for the frustrations of his complex boss, including his urges to hit back at opponents and media tormentors. So although they were an odd couple, they were an understandable one—at least to themselves. Observers of the Nixon-Colson relationship were often harsh in their assessment of it. Bob Haldeman later offered the view that Nixon "enjoyed a feeling of release by talking tough with his iron man bully." John Ehrlichman thought that Nixon, when his wilder ideas of retaliation were blocked by the cautious custodians of the Berlin Wall, needed "to rummage around in his bag of personnel until he found the guy who would do this or that dastardly deed. Someone who would salute him and say, 'Yes, Mr. President, sir,' and get it done. That someone was usually Colson." The Watergate special prosecutor Leon Jaworski, after listening to many tapes of Nixon and Colson plotting political hardball, likened their conversation to "a couple of cheap ward leaders talking in the rear room of the neighborhood dive." There are seeds of truth in all these comments but in terms of a rounded portrait they are more caricatures than characterizations. For they miss the important point that there was depth as well as darkness in the relationship between the president and his hatchet man.

There were two deep areas in which Nixon and Colson bonded. One was political strategy. The other was personal trust. On October 27, 1971, both areas came to the fore in a series of confidential discussions and private conversations that illuminate the almost telepathic mutual understanding that had grown up between the two men. On that day the telepathy started in the cabinet room of the White House, where Nixon had convened his top staffers to hear a presentation from John Ehrlichman and his briefing team on the options for domestic policy in 1972. Twenty minutes into the presentation, the president was squirming in his chair with a mixture of irritation and incomprehension. The academic nature of the briefing on the Domestic Council's detailed proposals for revenue sharing, health insurance, and taxation options evidently left him cold. After asking a perfunctory question or two at the end of the presentation, Nixon turned to Colson and said: "Chuck, tell them about the politics, tell them what's happening in the country, give them your analysis of the 1970 election results and the lessons we should learn from them."

Colson was surprised. Nixon had not prepared him for this request. "But I knew exactly what he was doing," recalled Colson. "He was using me as his foil. We had gotten to know each other so well and gotten so used to reading one another's minds that we could throw the ball back and forth in meetings without any advance warning." So Colson launched into the strategy he had already sold to his boss. He began by talking about the urban Catholic vote—where it was, the states it could swing, the issues it could turn on. He highlighted the alienation of conservative-minded blue-collar voters. He analyzed the makeup of the Wallace vote in 1968 and how it might move to Nixon in 1972. He concluded with an impassioned plea on behalf of the needs and aspirations of the forgotten middle-class households on incomes of around $12,000 a year—people who had bought a small home in the suburbs to be near good schools for their children and who were now feeling crushed by busing, high taxation, and elitist disregard of their priorities.

When Colson sat down Nixon slapped the table, saying, "That's it. He's got it." Turning to John Ehrlichman, he asked: "Now what have we got that will meet these problems? Can we come up with a plan that will get around the constitutional problems and allow us to stop the busing and start the aid flowing to parochial schools?" With heads nodding from John Mitchell, Bob Haldeman, George Shultz, and John Connally, Nixon gradually swung the support of the meeting behind Colson's agenda.

After the Domestic Council had dispersed, Colson was summoned to the Oval Office, where he found the president sitting at his desk with an impish grin on his face. "We showed them, didn't we, Chuck?" said Nixon gleefully. "I don't understand why Ehrlichman comes in with all these charts and academic discussions that don't amount to a damn. The important thing about today's meeting was that we got Connally and Mitchell on board. Did you see the way they warmed up on aid to parochial schools? Congratulations, boy, you handled it beautifully. I think we're on the road now. By the end of the year we'll have the policies we want."

Colson was becoming used to Nixon's curious methods of getting his subordinates to agree with what he wanted. Instead of calling in John Ehrlichman and dictating the agenda he required the Domestic Council to follow, Nixon would go to great lengths to avoid a confrontation. His technique was to tiptoe delicately around the subject, talking softly himself, while using Colson as his big stick. Later on that evening of October 27 the president and his special counsel walked back to the residence together, both glowing with the satisfaction of a job well done. Suddenly Nixon began talking about a subject he normally avoided like the plague—his personal spiritual beliefs.

"You know, Chuck, what we did today is not only good politics but it is the right thing," said the president. "All this business of revenue sharing and new government programs—that's not what's important in America today. What's really important in our country is to restore some fundamental values, some belief in family, in the country, and in God." Nixon then launched into a highly uncharacteristic discourse on his faith. With considerable embarrassment in his voice he told Colson that he really did believe in God; that he knew there was a relationship between God and man; and that he had made this discovery early in life through his Quaker upbringing. Relating his personal credo to the issue of aid to parochial schools, Nixon went on: "You know, Chuck, I have thought seriously about converting to Catholicism. I've had some talks with Julie about it. I might have done it if I wasn't afraid that people would say it was political. I know what the media would say if I did it. They would say there goes Tricky Dick Nixon trying to win the Catholic vote. But you know I have had some really sincere feelings about doing it."

Colson was silent as this stream of consciousness poured out of the president. "You know, what I like about Catholicism is that it is unswerving, stable, and solid in its teachings of traditional morality," continued Nixon. "Catholics don't go off preaching all these half-cock social issues. They stay with the fundamentals of man's obedience to God. They don't get involved in politics or do-goodish issues. That's not the function of the Church."

Colson, who had hardly given a moment's thought to God or to the functions of the church in his life, was completely out of his depth. He recognized that Nixon was reaching out to him with unusual intimacy by sharing these spiritual confidences. Not for the first time, Colson had a sense that the president of the United States was speaking to him as a personal friend rather than as a political adviser. Some weeks earlier a writer, Rod McLeish, had told him that one of the president's closest friends had heard Nixon describing Colson as "the closest thing he had found in his life to a son." Yet even with such a rumored paternal endorsement ringing in his head, and with such intimate spiritual revelations pouring into his ears, Colson could not respond with the warmth Nixon may have hoped for. "I put up a barrier," Colson has recalled. "I always stayed formal with him and kept the shutters up. I don't exactly know why. I think the fact he was the president kept me in awe of him."

Colson's awe for Nixon took some fairly extreme forms. He read *Six Crises,* an early Nixonian memoir, no less than fourteen times. He was quoted in the *Wall Street Journal* as saying, "I would do anything Richard Nixon asks me to do—period." No wonder the *Journal* headlined the article in which this quote appeared "Nixon's Hatchet Man." It was a cap that fit all too well. The White House tape transcripts that have so far been released are peppered with references to Colson's ingenious hatchet-wielding enterprises. They included ordering Internal Revenue Service investigations into Nixon's political opponents; using the Secret Service to keep leading Democrats under surveillance for political purposes; manipulating senators into holding hearings on the origins of the Vietnam War and the Diem coup in order to embarrass the Kennedy administration; making plans to finance a black political party that would take votes away from the Democrats; and funding false signs and billboards for display at rallies addressed by Senator Muskie. In fairness to Colson it should be said that most of these strategies originated from the president. "Kick the ass of the agencies . . . use Colson's outfit to snake out things. He'll do anything, I mean anything," was one typical Nixon instruction. Or as he refined it rather more circumspectly in his memoirs: "Colson's activities were in many cases prompted by my prodding." Most of the time, the prodded one reacted with zealous obedience. However, he occasionally backed off, as in the case of a particularly zany presidential suggestion that news reporters should be hired as White House intelligence agents. "We have to be very careful not to get caught in doing it," warned Colson.

By the summer of 1972, some five months before the presidential election, the chances of getting caught were rising because a virus of "anything goes" immorality had infected both the White House and the Committee to Re-elect the President (CREEP). A week before the fateful Watergate break-in Colson went to a meeting at CREEP, whose offices were located just across the street from the White House, at 1701 Pennsylvania Avenue. The purpose of the meeting was to devise a plan to keep Hubert Humphrey in the contest for the Democratic nomination. If the plot succeeded it would ensure a bitter debacle for the Democrats at their Miami convention.

Hubert Humphrey's strategy for the convention was due to be discussed by him and his close friend Dwayne Andreas at the Waldorf-Astoria hotel in New York the following day. "Tell me Andreas's suite number and I'll tell you everything that is said at the meeting," interjected John Mitchell, puffing contentedly on his pipe. As the former attorney general was smiling as he made this remark, Colson decided it was a humorous aside, not to be taken seriously. Given Mitchell's track record for authorizing clandestine intelligence gathering, burglaries, and dirty tricks, this was a rash assumption. It looked even rasher a few days later when Colson heard the news that four men, one of them indirectly connected to himself and the White House, had been arrested for breaking into the offices of the Democratic National Committee at the Watergate complex.

A Third-Rate Burglary

Saturday, June 17, 1972, started peacefully for Charles Colson. He began the day with a swim in the new pool that had just been built in the garden of his home in McLean, Virginia. Then he enjoyed a long spell of sunbathing on the patio with Wendell, Patty, and their houseguests, Bill and Ginny Maloney. Colonel Maloney, the Brown University contemporary who had persuaded Colson to apply for the U.S. Marine Corps twenty-one years earlier, was just back from Vietnam, feeling much in the mood for R&R. Colson too was unusually relaxed because Nixon was away from Washington, unwinding in Key Biscayne, Florida, in the company of Bebe Rebozo and Bob Abplanalp. So with no possibility of summonses to the Oval Office in prospect, it felt like an exceptionally laid-back weekend for Colson, until his serenity was shattered by a disturbing phone call from John Ehrlichman.

"Chuck, you've heard about the burglary at the Democratic National Committee, haven't you?" he asked. Colson had heard this apparently minor news item earlier in the day on the radio. Wryly he thought to himself, Poor old Larry O'Brien. As if he didn't have enough problems without getting his office vandalized by a street gang of young District hoodlums. They won't have found any money to steal there. Everyone knows the Democrats are broke.

Colson began repeating these thoughts to Ehrlichman, who cut in abruptly: "Where's your friend Howard Hunt these days?" The question seemed a complete non sequitur to Colson, who replied, "He's working at the committee, I guess. I don't know really. I haven't seen Howard in a couple of months. Why, what's up with him?"

"I don't know," said Ehrlichman, "but are you sure he's not working for us?" ("Us" in this context meant the White House staff, who had come to regard the Committee to Re-elect the President as a rival organization. It was a distinction that was real to Nixon aides although lost on the wider public.) There was something about Ehrlichman's tense tone that unnerved Colson. He felt as though an iron hand was clutching at his stomach. But he managed to answer calmly and correctly. "I'm sure he's not working for us. He came off our payroll in March."

"Thank God," said Ehrlichman. "The D.C. police have just notified me that Hunt's name turned up on something found in the pocket of one of the burglars, a check to a country club. Thank God you haven't seen him. I'm afraid he may be somehow connected with this thing. If I hear anything further I'll let you know."

Colson walked away from the phone muttering expletives. He sat down alongside Patty and Wendell with a sinking heart. He remembered that Hunt and Gordon Liddy had come into his office about four months earlier telling him they were trying to see John Mitchell to get his approval for a budget for intelligence and security work. But that was for convention security in Miami. Surely Hunt couldn't be involved in anything so stupid as a break-in of the Democratic National Committee? Or if he was, surely he wouldn't be so clumsy as to let one of the burglars have one of his own checks in his pocket? As these fears started to churn around in Colson's mind, one stark conclusion dawned on him. He said to himself, Whatever has happened, if Hunt is involved, then I know I will be dragged into it. I got him into the White House. I am his sponsor. I am going to be in the firing line.

All these thoughts were visibly troubling Colson as he sat by the pool. The silence was eventually broken by Patty, asking him, "What's the matter?"

"Honey, I have a feeling that in the next few days I'm going to be lambasted in the newspapers," answered her husband. "We're going to take hell. Apparently Howard Hunt had something to do with a break-in at the Democratic National Committee, and if he did, I'll be dragged in. If those jackasses at CREEP had anything to do with it there'll be all hell to pay and I'll be the fall guy."

Next morning, Colson rose early to study the reports of the burglary in the Sunday editions of the *Washington Post* and *New York Times*. After reading them, he heaved a huge sigh of relief. Although the *Post* ran the story on its front page under the banner heading FIVE HELD IN PLOT TO BUG DEMOCRATS' PARTY OFFICE, there was no mention of Howard Hunt. Colson did not recognize a single name or face among the five burglars, whose mug shots were prominently published. However, one of them, James McCord, was reported to be an employee of the Committee to Re-elect the President. This disclosure was enough to make Colson spend most of that Sunday sulking and brooding over the possible political consequences for himself. If this was a CREEP operation and if Hunt was involved, he felt a growing certainty that he, Colson, would be the target for brutal attacks by the press. The thought made him angry and defensive.

Meanwhile, down in Key Biscayne, Nixon was getting angry too. Although the president had no prior knowledge of the break-in, he strongly suspected that Colson had been behind it. As he wrote in his memoirs, "I had always valued [Colson's] hardball instincts. Now I wondered if he might have gone too far." At the time Nixon's response was rather less measured. In his rage he hurled an ashtray across the room and made at least two calls to Colson on the afternoon of Sunday, June 18. "I was clearly suspect number one with the president," recalled Colson. "At that time in my life I would gladly have organized the bugging of a political opponent, but the plain fact was, I had nothing whatever to do with it. I think I got this through to the president."

In fact, Nixon disbelieved Colson. Although the president did not directly accuse his prime suspect of organizing Watergate in those calls of June 18, confining himself to a general tongue-lashing of those who had masterminded the operation for their "goddamn stupidity," nevertheless the White House transcripts show that Nixon maintained his doubts about Colson's innocence for three more days. It was only after exhaustive further inquiries that the president could say to Haldeman with audible relief in his voice, "Thank God that Colson wasn't responsible."

At the 8.15 A.M. senior staff meeting in the White House on Monday, June 19, the icy atmosphere indicated that Nixon was not alone in harboring suspicions that Colson was the man to blame for the break-in. As aghast aides studied the *Washington Post* story, bylined with the unfamiliar names Robert Woodward and Carl Bernstein and headed GOP SECURITY AIDE AMONG 5 ARRESTED IN BUGGING AFFAIR, it was Don Rumsfeld, then a rising young star in the administration, who summed up the general feeling in the room by staring at Colson and saying: "If any jackass across the street or here had anything to do with this, he should be hung up by his thumbs today. We'd better not have had anything to do with this. It will kill us." Immediately after the senior staff meeting, Ehrlichman beckoned Colson into his office. In the ensuing conversation the two men assured each other they knew nothing more about the break-in, and Hunt's possible involvement in it, than when they had last spoken on the phone on Saturday. This was untrue in Ehrlichman's case, for he had been in frequent contact with Haldeman about the burglary over the weekend. Jointly they had formed the view that Colson was to blame and must take the rap for Watergate. This approach began to emerge when Ehrlichman, soon after declaring, "Let's get the facts," called the attorney general, Richard Kleindienst, in Colson's presence and said, "Dick, this break-in business. I had a report Saturday that one of the men assigned to Colson's unit here, a fellow by the name of Howard Hunt, may have been in some way involved. Can you check it out? The president will need a full report."

The words "one of the men assigned to Colson's unit here" struck a chilling note. Colson saw it as a move by Ehrlichman to slide out from a problem that he himself had created. After all, Hunt had been working for Krogh and the Plumbers under Ehrlichman's direct control. Hunt had been transferred from Colson's office to the Plumbers some three months earlier. Now it looked as though Colson was being set up as the fall guy for whatever Hunt had been up to over the Watergate burglary. From that moment onward, Colson was preoccupied with the fear that he would soon be dragged into the fast-exploding furor over Watergate because of his association with Hunt. Returning to his office in the EOB, Colson's first move was to try to discover what connection, if any, Hunt still had with the White House. His first disturbing finding was that Hunt's name was printed in the current White House master phone directory and that his extension was listed as 2742—the same number as Colson's office. The explanation for this situation dated back to Hunt's first month on the White House payroll, when he had made an arrangement for Colson's secretary to take his messages. The phone book had never been corrected even though Hunt had moved on to other offices and phone extensions. In a reaction that was half comic, half panic, Haldeman's housekeeping aide, Bruce Kehrli, immediately recalled every single White House phone directory. He had them delivered to Colson's office with orders that Hunt's name and extension be excised immediately. "I could hardly believe my eyes when I stepped into my outer office later that morning," recalled Colson, "for I saw half a dozen girls from my staff surrounded by a huge mound of several hundred cardboard-covered, loose-leaf phone directories. They were dismantling them all, one by one, replacing the page on which Hunt's name and my extension number were recorded. I couldn't imagine a better way of drawing attention to the problem."

The problem quickly disintegrated into farce because those secretaries on Colson's staff who were not engaged in removing Hunt's name from the White House directory soon found themselves answering calls from reporters asking to speak to Howard Hunt, after being helpfully put through to Colson's extension by the White House switchboard. "Where is Howard Hunt?" the reporters wanted to know. Colson was asking the same question. Haldeman told him to speak to John Dean, the White House counsel. "Hunt has been ordered out of the country," said Dean. Colson exploded into obscenities. "John, that is the dumbest ******* thing that I have ever heard in my life," he shouted. "That could make the White House a party to a fugitive-from-justice charge."

Dean went over to a phone and countermanded the instructions that had been given to Hunt a few hours earlier. The panic factor was rising. Meanwhile, in another part of the Colson offices, a frantic search was under way for the memo that had terminated Hunt's service agreement with the White House. This document was vital since all other evidence, such as the phone directory and a safe belonging to Hunt discovered in an unused office, suggested that Hunt was still a current employee. Colson's aide Dick Howard eventually found the missing document, which had indeed terminated Hunt's $100-a-day consultancy on March 30, 1972. When Colson took the memo in his hand he kissed it and gave a whoop of triumph. His joy was short-lived. The following day the *Washington Star's* lead story carried the headline: COLSON AIDE—BARKER TIED.

According to the *Star's* story, Barker, one of the Cuban burglars who had been arrested on the scene of the crime at the Watergate break-in, was directly connected by the discovery of the Hunt check in his pocket to Colson's aide Howard Hunt. After that the dam burst. The White House had been denying all knowledge of what press secretary Ron Ziegler called "a third-rate burglary." Now there appeared to be a direct link from the burglars to Hunt and Colson. It was an unfair example of guilt-by-association journalism, but who cared about fairness when the hounds were in full cry? The *Washington Post* carried a major story headlined CAST OF CHARACTERS IN WATERGATE BREAK-IN. There were seven names, with full biographies and photographs—Colson, Hunt, Liddy, Barker, Martinez, Sturgis, McCord. The last four were the actual burglars, while Hunt and Liddy were their controllers. Colson, whose ignorance of the Watergate break-in was genuine, might just as well have been caught red-handed with the burglars in the offices of the Democratic National Committee in the small hours of the morning on Saturday, June 17.

As the TV networks, the news magazines, and the rest of the media followed the Washington papers in lumping the same seven deadly sinners together as the leading players in the cast of Watergate, Colson's misery knew
no bounds. His son Chris recalls grim scenes at home during this period of
Colson angrily tearing up offensive newspaper clippings and burying his
head in his hands. He was close to becoming clinically depressed and seriously considered resigning. Indeed he would have handed in his resignation before the end of June had it not been for the fact that Nixon went to
extraordinary lengths to console him. For, once the president had established that Colson had no prior knowledge of the break-in, he made a huge
personal effort to shore up the sinking spirits of his beleaguered aide.

When the early media attacks were at their hottest, Nixon called Colson
into his EOB office on June 20 and said to him, "Chuck, you must not let
this get to you. They're not after you. They're after me. We must not let
them divert us. That's what they are trying to do." Later that evening the
president called Colson at home and said to him, in the tone of a father
consoling a dejected son, "Look, Chuck, the important thing for you to remember is that I have great confidence in you. You are strong and you can
take it. I know how it is but don't let it bother you. You just relax with your
wife and have no fears. I'm behind you."

After the call ended, Colson turned to Patty, saying with emotion, "You
know, he really is a decent, kind, and considerate man . . . you know what
that call was about, all twenty-five minutes of it? It was just to cheer me
up. What a great guy he is." The president's motives may have been less al-
truistic than Colson thought. Although Nixon did have a streak of compassion in him for young aides in trouble, by this time he had embarked on
the cover-up, having instructed Haldeman to get the CIA to block the FBI's
investigation. So he may well have been pouring out his presidential sympathy as a device for keeping Colson on the side and in silence. Colson, by
contrast, was only too keen to help the FBI. "I want to lay out everything
I know to the bureau," he told John Dean on June 19. "I want to get it all
on record and to clear my name. Everyone round here ought to do that. I'd
like to volunteer." As a result of volunteering, Colson was interviewed by
the FBI on June 26. Questioned by two agents from the bureau's Alexandria office, who read him his rights before the interview began, Colson explained how Hunt had been taken off the White House payroll in March;
how Ehrlichman had told the news of the Watergate burglary to him in a
phone call on June 17; and how he had no prior knowledge of the break-
in. The FBI men looked suspicious, if not incredulous, but Colson was un-

perturbed. "It didn't worry me that anything I said might be used against me. I had told the truth."

For all the interest of the media, the truth about Watergate was a long way from coming out. This was because it was being deliberately suppressed by Nixon and a tight circle of aides, which now excluded Colson but included John Dean. It was Dean's job to delay and obstruct the FBI's investigation of the break-in so that nothing would disturb the president's anticipated election victory in November. So skillful was Dean in his management of the cover-up that he was able to reassure Nixon on September 15, "I think I can say that, fifty-four days from now, that—uh—not a thing will come crashing down to our surprise." This promise was delivered. Because the cover-up was working, Watergate remained a Beltway story. Of the 450 or more journalists based in Washington bureaus of newspapers or TV stations, fewer than fifteen of them worked on Watergate. The exception was the *Washington Post,* whose energetic team of reporters, led by Bob Woodward and Carl Bernstein, put Watergate stories on the paper's front page for 79 of the 146 days between the break-in and the election. However, even the *Post* saw Watergate primarily as a campaign issue, for in the two weeks following the election they ran only one Watergate-related story. It was the persistence of Senator Sam Ervin in setting up a committee to hold Watergate hearings that brought the saga back to the front pages. During the election period, when he was under fire from Woodward and Bernstein, Colson was tense and unsettled. However, like Brer Rabbit, he lay low and said nothing. This was not an easy posture for him. Not only was he on the receiving end of continuous attacks from the *Washington Post* for his alleged role in Watergate, he was also getting unnerved at being on the receiving end of several disturbing communications from Howard Hunt. Feeling a moral obligation not to keep his friend dangling in suspense, Colson responded to Hunt's plaintive appeals for help by sending anodyne messages through third parties. The implication of these messages was that everything was on hold until after the election. Much the same signal was being transmitted regarding Watergate, to friend and foe alike. Before the phony peace could end and the real hostilities could begin, the "third-rate burglary" was in abeyance. The election had to take precedence. That was why Colson's energies were totally focused on re-electing Richard Nixon for a second term as president of the United States.

CHAPTER NINE

Winning and Leaving

Doubts Before the Campaign

C harles Colson was the coarchitect of Richard Nixon's victory in the 1972 presidential election. Although this battle ended in a landslide, Nixon spent much of the previous year worrying about the possibilities of defeat. His pessimism appeared to be well founded. Halfway through his first term, with the Vietnam War in deadlock, the stock market in free fall, and the economy in bad trouble, Nixon was a deeply unpopular president. The polls confirmed his poor prospects. Senator Edmund Muskie, the chief Democratic contender for the White House, was leading Nixon in the Harris Poll during the spring of 1971 by forty-seven points to thirty-nine. In the Gallup Poll that same summer, Nixon's popularity had fallen to a lower level than that of any president since Harry S. Truman at a comparable point in his administration. No wonder that Nixon, in those dark days, so often turned for political reassurance to Colson, his in-house optimist, creative thinker, and chief political strategist. Colson was never a doubter. His game plan for winning the election had four main ingredients—cultivating key voter blocs; discrediting opponents; neutralizing the economic issue; and burnishing the image of Nixon the global peacemaker. He set out these objectives in a memorandum drafted November 4, 1971, titled "The President's Posture in the 1972 Campaign." The most unusual idea in Colson's strategy was that Nixon's impending visits to China and the Soviet Union would enable him to avoid campaigning and rise above domestic politics wearing the mantle of a world statesman. "The President must remain very Presidential, self-assured, and above the battle," wrote Colson. "He probably cannot get away with refusing to answer political questions in press conferences in the coming year but, whatever he does, he should dust them off lightly and quickly. He should show a distinct lack of concern with politics."

Being unconcerned with politics was not a natural occupation for Richard Nixon. However, in public he went along with the recommendation, playing his lofty role on the world stage to full effect while privately deploying Colson as his right-hand tactician in the grubby minutiae of vote getting. Yet however hard Colson tried to cultivate the blue-collar and ethnic voting blocs that were crucial to the new majority strategy, both he and Nixon were worried by one huge and imponderable conundrum. It was, what will happen to the Wallace vote? Until that question was answered no one could be sure which way the tide of the election might turn.

The Shooting of Wallace

On the afternoon of May 15, 1972, Colson was chairing a forward planning group of presidential staffers in the Roosevelt Room of the White House, immediately across the hallway leading to the Oval Office. Suddenly one of Ron Ziegler's young assistants from the press office rushed in, shouting, "George Wallace has been shot." For months Colson had seen a third-party candidacy from Governor George Wallace of Alabama as a threat to Nixon's reelection. If the conservative blue-collar voters Colson had so assiduously been cultivating were to swing the busing issue to Wallace instead of to Nixon in the key Northern states such as Ohio, Michigan, New Jersey, Illinois, and Pennsylvania (all of which had given Wallace between 8 and 12 percent of the poll in 1968), then the election could easily tilt to the Democrats. If Wallace was dead, as the first news flash suggested, then that threat was over. But if the governor was alive, as subsequent reports confirmed he was, then the Republican vote could be eroded even further by a backlash of sympathy for a Wallace candidacy. That sympathy might swell into an avalanche if the assassin turned out to be a fanatical pro-Nixon zealot.

These political calculations were weighing heavily on Colson's mind as he walked into Nixon's office a few minutes later. The president's mind was evidently on the same wavelength, as he showed by a tasteless exhibition of sick humor. "Well, you've really blown it this time, boy, haven't you?" was Nixon's greeting. "He's going to survive. You didn't finish off the job; that's not like you, Chuck." Colson was shocked, but before he could react Nixon was off on a secondary line of thought, saying: "Goddamnit, you don't suppose this was someone trying to help us, do you? It's got to be a McGovernite. It's got to be a left-wing fanatic. What the hell is wrong with the FBI; why haven't they told us something?"

Over the next few hours Nixon was at his worst, with Colson not far behind him. Their main preoccupation was a desire to establish the left-wing credentials of the assassin. Colson, from the president's EOB office, made numerous frustrating calls to the senior FBI official on duty in Washington, Mark Feldt, and later to the newly appointed FBI director, Pat Gray. All this time Nixon kept pacing up and down the room like a caged lion, letting off angry growls of threats and orders as he raged over the dearth of information on the attacker's identity and background. Eventually, the FBI reported that they had surrounded and sealed off the Milwaukee apartment of the assassin, whom they named as Arthur Bremer. Nixon immediately asked: "Is he a left-winger, right-winger?"

COLSON Well, he's going to be a left-winger by the time we get through.
  NIXON Good. Keep at that. Keep at that.
COLSON Yeah, I just wish that, God, that I'd thought sooner about planting a little literature out there . . .
  NIXON *[laughs loudly]*
COLSON It may be a little late, although I've got one source that maybe . . .
  NIXON Good!
COLSON You could think about that. I mean, if they found it near his apartment, that would be helpful.

This unedifying extract from the White House tape transcripts shows the lengths to which Colson was prepared to go in order to please the president. The "one source" referred to was the ubiquitous Howard Hunt. Colson called him late at night on May 15 for a discussion on Bremer and his motivation for shooting Wallace. Although they talked about planting left-wing literature, Colson did not order Hunt to take any action. For by that time the FBI had found in Bremer's apartment genuine literature that established him as a supporter of the Black Panthers and an enrolled member of the Young Democrats of Milwaukee. It was also established that Bremer's bullet had lodged in Wallace's spine, paralyzing him for life. Those items of news meant that the only political consequence of the day's events was that the threat of a third-party candidacy from the governor of Alabama was over. Colson could feel reassured that the reelection of the president was now a near certainty, but he could not feel proud of his re-actions and comments on the Wallace shooting as preserved for posterity on the White House tapes.

Coasting to Victory

Colson did not need to plant left-wing literature on Nixon's opponent once the Democratic Party nominated Senator George McGovern as their can-didate. Among the White House staff, Colson had been the first to predict that the liberal antiwar senator from South Dakota might beat his better-financed rivals—Kennedy, Muskie, and Humphrey—in the race for the nomination. When his prediction came true, Colson rejoiced and so did Nixon. For McGovern was a hopelessly inept candidate, encumbered with left-of-center policy commitments that alienated huge numbers of tradi-tional Democratic Party voters.

During the election, Colson played a key role in deciding campaign strategy through his role as chief coordinator of the "Attack Group," a White House committee that met every day to decide on tactics, schedules, and press briefings. Colson's objective was to keep the Democrats per-manently on the back foot by hammering away at the unpopular posi-tions McGovern endorsed—in favor of busing, an amnesty for draft dodgers, liberalized abortion, and pot smoking. Planting questions to harass McGovern on these less than central policy issues proved a fruit-ful exercise because of the candidate's weakness for answering the criti-cisms of surrogates rather than restraining himself to reply only to the president. So day after day Colson exulted as the news bulletins portrayed McGovern as a defensive incumbent rather than as an aggressive chal-lenger.

Colson was also busy mounting some successful challenges of his own to voting blocs that traditionally supported the Democrats. He formed De-mocrats for Nixon with John Connally, publishing several lists of promi-nent figures who signed up under this banner—a move that brought about massive defections from McGovern. Another initiative was to woo votes of blue-collar ethnic groups, particularly the Italian-Americans, Polish-Americans, and Greek-Americans. Colson's carefully chosen front man for his campaign was a thirty-six-year-old former garbage man, Mike Balzano. As a result of reading an article about Balzano's progress, through truck driving, garbage collecting, and night school, to a Ph.D. in political philosophy from Georgetown University, Colson summoned him to the EOB. The Italian-born Balzano was amazed to be offered a $23,000-a-year appointment as a White House aide. "It was quite a step up the ladder from being a forty-seven-dollar-a-week garbage man," recalled Balzano, "but Colson was one helluva persuader and one helluva leader. He sent me all over the country as his ambassador to spread the message that Nixon really cared about us blue-collar guys from ethnic backgrounds. So at Colson's bidding, I was out there day after day at union meetings, factory gates, workers' picnics, and on TV chat shows, telling my story and saying, 'When the hell has any other president ever had a blue-collar representative?' It went down big, I can tell ya. That new majority in 1972 was the real thing and Colson deserves most of the credit for it."

As the pace of the election heated up, Colson was in overdrive, firing on all cylinders with an enthusiasm that was not always matched by his occasionally flagging team of staffers. One Friday morning in mid-August, the day after Nixon had been nominated by the Republican Convention, Colson returned unexpectedly to his White House office to find that about half the members of his staff had decided to take a long weekend. Incensed at this lack of zeal on the part of his subordinates, Colson called in one of his junior secretaries and dictated an intemperate memo that was destined to make headlines around the world.

"There are seventy-one days left between now and the election," Colson's memo began.

> Every single one of these is a campaign day, and for those of you who have not been reminded of this lately, every day has twenty-four hours. I hope it will be possible for each one of us to have some time during the campaign occasionally to recharge the batteries; an occasional Sunday afternoon may be possible but don't count on it. . . . Many of you have been through political campaigns before. For those who have not, a campaign is a twenty-four hours a day, seven days a week job. Do not be lulled into a false security by the polls which show the President well ahead at the moment. They will change. Make every day count. Think to yourself at the beginning of each day, "What am I going to do to help the President's re-election today?" and then at the end of each day think what you did in fact do to help the President's re-election.
>
> I will be expecting maximum output from every member of the staff for whom I have any responsibility. I will be very intolerant of

less than maximum output. I am totally unconcerned with anything other than getting the job done. If I bruise feelings or injure anyone's morale, I will be happy to make amends on the morning of November 8th, assuming we have done our job and the results are evident.

I can well understand that many of you may have gotten the wrong impression of me since so many erroneous things have found their way into print lately. Just so you understand me, let me point out that the statement in last week's UPI story that I was once reported to have said that "I would walk over my grandmother if necessary" is absolutely accurate.

The secretary who took down this dictation, twenty-four-year-old Holly Holm, swallowed deeply as it ended and plucked up the courage to ask her boss, "Mr. Colson, you don't really want this to go to all the staff, do you?"

"Of course, Holly," replied Colson. "They will know most of it is tongue-in-cheek, but it will make the point."

The point was soon being made to a far wider audience. The memo was leaked to the *Washington Post,* which printed it in its entirety. Legions of newspapers took up the story across America and as far afield as Britain, France, and Australia. Art Buchwald enjoyed himself with a spate of satirical grandmother columns, while down on the Lyndon B. Johnson ranch in Texas, the thirty-sixth president of the United States carried a clipping of the memo around in his back pocket, pulling it out for weeks afterward to tell friends, "By God, that's the kind of man I wish I'd had on my staff. That's the way to get things done. I sure don't mind paying my taxes when there's a man like that in the White House."

Although the coverage added greatly to Colson's notoriety, it should be recorded that he never quite said the bombastic words attributed to him. The grandmother allusion first surfaced in a front-page profile of Colson published by the *Wall Street Journal* on his fortieth birthday, October 16, 1971. In that article, which also marked the first appearance of the phrase "hatchet man" in relation to Colson, a friend was quoted paying him a string of compliments. However, the friend added, "But be careful, he's tough enough to run over his own grandmother."

A few weeks later Colson was interviewed by a student contemporary from Brown University for the alumni magazine. The question was asked, "Chuck, an old classmate of yours tells me you're so tough that you'd run over your grandmother if necessary. Is that so?"

"No," responded Colson, "I'd run around her." The magazine printed the exchange correctly but a UPI report misquoted it and the rest is journalistic history.

One lot of people Colson would gladly have walked over during the election campaign were the leading players in the Committee to Re-elect the President. Like most of the senior political aides from the White House who attended the Attack Group, Colson came to regard CREEP as a crowd of incompetent amateurs. One of his frequent sayings at the time was "Oh well, we'll have to win the election *in spite of* those clowns over the road at CREEP." This scornful attitude developed partly because Colson thought CREEP's ailing chairman, John Mitchell, had lost his grip, but more because of his undisguised contempt for the organization's deputy director, Jeb Magruder. A year or so earlier when Colson took charge of Herb Klein's Office of Communications, Haldeman offered him Magruder as a senior staffer. Colson rejected the suggested appointee with the brusque retort "I wouldn't give him house room."

"I'll send him over to CREEP then," said Haldeman.

"At least he can't do any harm there," replied Colson. It was one of his less prescient judgments.

Unknown to Colson and most other White House personnel, Magruder had been doing enormous harm by authorizing a series of James Bond–style clandestine operations against the Democrats with code names like Sandwedge One, Sandwedge Two, and Gemstone. All of them were for the purpose of gathering campaign intelligence. Some involved juvenile dirty tricks and others crossed the line into criminality. Magruder claimed later that one of the reasons why the Gemstone plans to burgle the Democratic National Committee office in the Watergate building had gone ahead was that Colson kept putting CREEP under pressure to deliver more and better intelligence. Given Colson's hectoring style and impatience toward Magruder, the generality of the accusation has the ring of truth to it. However, Colson is unlikely to have been so stupid as to involve himself in the specifics of such a high-risk, low-reward CREEP operation. Or, as Nixon cynically told Colson a week after the burglars had been caught, "I knew you had nothing to do with it. If you had, it would have been a success."

In the sixteen weeks between the Watergate break-in and Election Day, the Attack Group had considerable success in keeping the president elevated above the increasingly dirty swirl of allegations about the burglary's links to laundered money, campaign law violations, and criminal conspiracies involving the White House. The scandal came close to Nixon but somehow stopped short of his office, cut off perhaps by the imaginary wall so many Americans like to build around their presidents. The temporary immunity from the Watergate fallout was helped by Nixon's compliance with Colson's earlier recommendations on presidential posture during the campaign. Colson, who argued that Nixon had been counterproductive in the midterm elections, "because he stepped off his presidential pedestal to campaign like a county sheriff," had to fight hard to keep his boss away from the fray. Throughout September and October Colson needed to beg the president to stay on his leadership plateau and to do the bare minimum of physical campaigning in order to keep his party workers happy. Nixon probably knew that this above-the-battle posture was right. Nevertheless he fought hard against it. "Haldeman and I frantically struggled to keep him out of the campaign by creating events to fill his calendar," recalled Colson. "This was a surprisingly difficult task. I had to spend many hours keeping Nixon busy as he was continually restless."

Some of the president's restlessness may have been due to his growing worries about Watergate. Colson was worried on this front too, partly about his own reputation, which was taking a hard pounding from the *Washington Post,* or *Pravda* as he started calling it, and partly because he deduced from the White House private polls that Watergate was beginning to have an adverse affect on the election. The scandal was not hurting Nixon in relation to his huge lead over McGovern. However, Colson's reading of the poll data was that large swaths of the electorate were getting turned off from all politics and politicians because of Watergate. He predicted in the last days of the election that voter turnout would be disturbingly low. He was right. When the nation went to the polls on November 7, 1972, the lowest percentage of the electorate for twenty-five years cast their ballots.

Colson woke early on election day, full of jitters that the victory would turn out to be wrong. He was irrationally fearful that Nixon's twenty-five-point lead would disappear under a last-minute wave of apathy, with millions of Nixon's supporters not bothering to vote because they were assuming a landslide. Nixon, for whom coasting to an easy victory was a new experience, evidently suffered from similar forebodings. In the last forty-eight hours before the polling stations opened, Nixon called Colson twelve times to check the last-minute reports from key states and to analyze the latest statistics from the Harris and Sidlinger poll computers.

By 6:30 P.M. on election day, Colson's jitters had evaporated. His analysis of the early returns from New Hampshire and Kentucky convinced him

that the president would win, and win big. At 8:05 P.M. Colson called
Nixon with a prediction that he would have a victory margin of just over
60 percent, taking at least forty-seven states. This was remarkably accurate, since the final tally gave Nixon 60.7 percent of the total vote and
every state in the Union except Massachusetts. It was the second-greatest
landslide in the history of presidential elections.

By 11 that night, Colson and Nixon agreed that the result was clear
enough for the reelected president to accept his victory in a televised address at his campaign headquarters. So Nixon came to the Sheraton hotel
in downtown Washington and delivered a curiously stilted acceptance
speech whose most notable feature was its cold ungraciousness to the an-
nihilated McGovern. It was not the only example of graceless behavior that
night by Nixon. Perhaps because he was in acute pain on account of a tooth
he had broken while eating dinner, he failed to express any sentiments of
gratitude to his supporters. He made an abrupt exit immediately after his
speech without even stopping in the VIP room to thank his leading party
workers and contributors. A few minutes after this joyless departure, Colson was summoned to the White House to see the president, who was
alone in his EOB hideaway office with Bob Haldeman, analyzing the latest
returns from around the country.

"Good job, boy, good job," said Nixon, waving Colson to a chair. "Sit
down and have a drink with us." Haldeman did not raise his head from the
figures he was adding up but he scowled as the scotch and sodas arrived.
Colson felt that the chief of staff was jealous and resentful that Nixon
wanted to savor his hour of triumph with another colleague. "Here's to
you, Chuck," said Nixon, raising his glass and downing most of its contents
in one swallow. "Those are *your* votes that are pouring in, the Catholics,
the union members, the blue collars—your votes, boy. It was your strategy
and it's a landslide."

This was just about the only celebratory remark Nixon made for the rest
of the evening. He was in a surly and vindictive mood, maintaining a harsh
spirit of bitterness toward McGovern as he struggled to compose the traditionally gracious victor's telegram to the vanquished opponent. "How
can I say something nice after he compared me to Hitler?" he kept saying
as he crumpled up draft after draft. Haldeman's mood was worse. He
snapped and snarled at Colson, who soon deflated into numb silence. It
was the strangest of scenes for three men who had been the creators of a
glorious victory.

At 2:30 A.M., just as the wire services and the networks were closing down for the night, Nixon ordered three plates of ham and eggs. He did not enjoy his nocturnal breakfast, because of his broken tooth. Colson did not enjoy it either, because he was worried about Patty and Wendell, whom he had left stranded in his own EOB office for nearly four hours without food or drink. Eventually, like mourners parting after a funeral, Nixon, Haldeman, and Colson made their exits. As the president departed he paused at the top of the EOB's gray cement steps leading down to the driveway and said, "Chuck, I just want you to know. I'll always be—" Colson interrupted him. "Thank you, Mr. President," he said. "Tomorrow will be a good day." Unfortunately, that was not how tomorrow turned out.

A Bitter Aftertaste

At eight the next morning, Colson was woken by the shrill peel of the White House phone beside his bed. His head was throbbing from the number of scotch and sodas he had consumed with the president a few hours earlier. Groggily he picked up the receiver, to hear the crisp tones of Steve Bull, the president's aide-de-camp, saying, "Chuck, sorry, but he wants you in his office right away." Colson slowly pulled himself out of bed. By the time he reached the White House the senior staff were assembling in the Roosevelt Room for a meeting with the president. When Nixon entered, looking amazingly fresh and well rested to Colson's bleary eyes, the audience rose to clap enthusiastically. They did not realize that they were applauding their executioner.

Nixon spoke for only twelve minutes. He expressed no elation over the election results. His thanks were perfunctory, his demeanor appeared chilling and remote. The main body of his remarks focused on the political history of nineteenth-century Britain. Quoting from Robert Blake's biography of Disraeli, Nixon recalled how Disraeli had called his greatest rival, Gladstone, "an exhausted volcano." The president continued, "I believe men exhaust themselves in government without realizing it . . . we need new blood, fresh ideas. Change is important." Bringing his address to a close with all the warmth and humanity of an abattoir manager, Nixon said, "Bob will explain the procedures we've worked out . . . today we start fresh for the next four years . . . we must not lose a day. Bob, you take over."

Haldeman took over with a ruthless display of how to lose friends and destroy influence among your most loyal supporters. He announced that every member of the staff was required to submit his or her resignation immediately. Mimeographed forms for this purpose were promptly distributed. Haldeman also asked everyone to submit a full list of files in his or her possession. As an afterthought, he added, "This is, of course, the courtesy customarily extended to a president at the start of each new administration."

Like everyone else in the room, Colson was stunned by the brutality of this procedure. OK, Bob, everyone appointed by a president serves at his pleasure, he thought to himself, but why this, so soon and so crudely? As he walked out of the Roosevelt Room, Colson's immediate concerns were for the thirty members of his personal staff. One of his best qualities as a leader was that ever since his days as marine platoon commander he had given a high priority to down-the-line loyalty. During the previous three years he had been fiercely protective of his staffers, especially when they came under fire from other powerful figures in the administration. "Chuck was a terrific boss in personal terms," recalled his twenty-nine-year-old aide Steve Karalekas. "He demanded a lot but if you made a mistake or got into trouble with Haldeman or Ehrlichman he would fight for you like a lion. And when we all had to hand in our resignations on that day he immediately fought to find us good jobs elsewhere in the government—for me, for Balzano, for the girls. He was a fighter for all of us."

Whether or not Colson wanted to fight or needed to fight for himself was a complicated question. Ostensibly Nixon owed him a big debt and wished him to stay. On that same morning when everyone else's resignations were being demanded, Colson was summoned to the Oval Office, where the president reassured him that he was not in the same category as the rest of the staff and that he was not required to resign. However, as Colson rightly guessed from Nixon's ill-at-ease manner, this reassurance was not all that it seemed to be.

During the past few months, in secret discussions with Haldeman and Ehrlichman, Nixon had been planning a massive reorganization of the federal government at the start of his second term. The broad sweep of his plans was to shake up the big bureaucracies at the State Department, the Pentagon, the CIA, the Treasury, and the Department of Health, Education, and Welfare, putting them under the control of two or three "superaides" at the White House who would report directly to the president. Colson had no place in this ambitious restructuring scheme. Haldeman and Ehrlichman wanted him out of power for several reasons. First, they were

Colson (second row, middle) with his fraternity at Brown University. (Courtesy of the Colson family)

Nineteen-year-old Colson with his parents, Dizzy and Wendell Ball Colson. (Courtesy of the Colson family)

Colson in USMC fatigues at Quantico boot camp during the summer of 1952. (Courtesy of the Colson family)

(Left) Wendell, Emily, and Chris at the time of Senator Leverett Saltonstall's 1960 reelection campaign. (Courtesy of the Colson family)
(Right) Nancy Billings and Colson on their wedding day in June 1953.
(Courtesy of the Colson family)

Colson and Patty with Ed Brooke in 1967. In 1966 Colson was a key player in Brooke's election as a U.S. senator. (Courtesy of the Colson family)

Colson and his father, Wendell Sr., at the White House with President Nixon, 1970.
(Photo by Jack Knightlinger. Courtesy of the Nixon Presidential Materials Staff, NARA)

In the Oval Office, 1969. From left: Colson's assistant Henry Cashen, Colson, Nixon, and Post Office union leader Jim Rademacher. (Photo by Oliver Atkins. Courtesy of the Nixon Presidential Materials Staff, NARA)

Colson entering the Federal District Courthouse in Washington, D.C., for a Watergate trial hearing in 1974. (AP/Wide World Photos)

Colson shaking hands with inmates of a Pennsylvania prison during a Prison
Fellowship event, 1992. (Photo by David Singer. Courtesy of Prison Fellowship)

Colson with his former law partners Judge Joseph Mitchell Jr. and Charles
Morin Jr., at daughter Emily's wedding. (Courtesy of Charles Morin Jr.)

At work with former president Jimmy Carter on a Habitat for Humanity project in 1984. (Photo by David Singer. Courtesy of Prison Fellowship)

A 1988 Christmas photo with Patty.
(Courtesy of the Colson family)

Colson receiving the Templeton Prize from Prince Philip, Duke of Edinburgh, at Buckingham Palace in 1993. (Courtesy of Clifford Shirley)

Colson with his chosen successor, Mark Earley, the new president of Prison Fellowship, greeting the crowd at Angola Prison in April 2002. (Courtesy of Ray Dry)

Colson baptizing his autistic grandson, Max, in 2003.
(Courtesy of the Colson family)

Colson visiting a California women's state penitentiary, 2001.
(Photo by Charles Ledford. Courtesy of Prison Fellowship)

Christmas 2003. Chuck and Patty with George W. and Laura Bush at the White House. (Photo by Paul Morse. Courtesy of the White House)

Colson and author Jonathan Aitken (far left) at Parchman Prison in Mississippi, 2001. (Courtesy of Greg Jenson)

jealous of his close personal relationship with the president. Second, they thought of him as a loose cannon who pandered to Nixon's worst instincts. Third, and most important, they hoped they could set him up as the fall guy for Watergate. In the view of "the Germans," a Colson pushed out of the White House could easily be portrayed as a Colson taking the blame for Watergate. It was a convenient way of closing down the can of worms and scandals that was threatening to burst open. The thoughts of Haldeman and Ehrlichman had been infiltrated into the mind of the president as he set off for a weekend in the Florida sunshine at Key Biscayne. Colson was evidently on his conscience, for in a reference to him in his diary, Nixon wrote, "It is a very sad commentary that an individual can be bruised and battered and libeled and then expendable but in politics I fear it is the case." A franker version of the president's thinking is to be found in Bob Haldeman's diary for Wednesday, November 15, exactly a week after the election. "Later in the day, the P got into the Colson problem," recorded Haldeman.

> He said that he really should leave now for our interests and he doesn't really fit now, under the reorganization of the White House . . . we really need him out now and not later. The question was whether to have him as our RNC [Republican National Committee] counsel or instead have a member of his firm and not him. He said I should talk to Colson and say that I'm talking with the P's knowledge regarding Dean, E [Ehrlichman] and so forth, the inevitable problems with the Hunt trial, the P can't let you go into the fire, we can't be sure what will come out. On the positive side, you're needed outside now . . . you're going for a specific purpose and you will have a continual relation. . . . The problem is that your position inside will erode, you will have no great goal to pursue like the election. The P needs you on the outside where you are free to set up a campaign firm as well as a law firm. Now's the time to pick up the clients, law and PR, and we just don't have the job inside. The P is determined to get politics out of the White House so you become the man. You've got to go into the P and say that you thought it through, this is what he should do, you reached the conclusion. Be a big man.

It is not entirely clear from Haldeman's account of this conversation on Colson's future which big man was manipulating whom. Colson himself was understandably confused by these serpentine maneuverings. When he was summoned to Camp David as the first of a series of aides and cabinet officers to be told their fate, Haldeman briefed him on his own before meeting Nixon. According to Haldeman, Colson should, in the view of the president, leave the White House and play "the Clark Clifford role" as an outside lawyer closely tied to the president and as general counsel to the Republican National Committee. However when they joined Nixon for dinner, the president suddenly said to Colson, "No, I don't think you should leave. I think you should take over Clark McGregor's job as counsel for congressional relations." Faced with the choice of being a successor to the middle-ranking White House aide Clark McGregor or going into lucrative law practice in the style of Clark Clifford (the legendary Washington insider who had been legal adviser to several presidents), Colson unsurprisingly elected to take the second option. In political terms, it was a considerable disappointment to him. Some weeks earlier he had sent a memorandum to Nixon saying that in the second term he would like to be secretary of labor or chairman of the Republican National Committee. For various reasons neither appointment was offered, nor did Nixon make any attempt to create a powerful new place on the White House staff for him. Colson would almost certainly have accepted a post that kept him close to the president. However, Nixon was evidently not inclined to make a special gesture of gratitude or loyalty to the aide who had done most to win him the election.

When Colson told Haldeman he was thinking of returning to legal practice, the chief of staff urged him with alacrity to "go right now." Colson was immediately suspicious. "The way he said it made me really nervous," he recalled. "I got the clear impression that he and Ehrlichman were overeager to see me leave. I wasn't going to play their game." So Colson went back to Nixon on his own and said to him, "Mr. President, I don't think I should go immediately as it will look like I have been fired because of Watergate."

"Oh absolutely not," replied Nixon. "How long do you want to stay?"

"Maybe three or four months," said Colson.

"Fine, not a problem," was his immediate response. It was a less than generous ending to three tumultuous years of frontline political service to Richard Nixon, but Colson thought he could now look forward to a prosperous future as a top lawyer and Washington insider, with direct access to the president of the United States. He began to make his plans accordingly.

Last Weeks in the White House

In the month of December 1972, Colson became as close to Nixon as he had ever been. This was because he shared, at first hand, in the president's agonies over the Christmas bombing of Hanoi and over his subsequent rift with Henry Kissinger. Although he was not normally a presidential confidant on foreign policy issues, Colson was called into the inner circle of advisers in early December when Kissinger was reporting from Paris that the peace talks were floundering because of total North Vietnamese intransigence. Nixon, after long discussions with Colson and Haldeman, decided to take what he later called "the most difficult decision made during the entire war." This was to order a massive bombing campaign of military targets in North Vietnam during the period of December 18–30. It was Nixon's last, desperate gamble to bring the war to an end, and he told Colson that it had no better than a fifty-fifty chance of success.

Every day Colson met with Nixon during this period when the president's morale was being battered by fierce domestic criticism in the media and by heavy U.S. Air Force losses in the air. "Nixon was in pain," recalled Colson. "Each B-52 we lost hurt him personally, even though he tried not to show it. I remember him saying to me, 'That's what we have them for— to bomb and if necessary to get shot down. That's their job,' but it was pure rationalization. Nixon agonized all the time over our losses and over his media critics, who went wild, calling him insane and so on. Each day I spent with him he seemed to age visibly. He was not sleeping well. His speech was not clear. There wasn't the usual sparkle in his voice and mannerisms. The lonely ordeal was grinding him down."

Colson did his best to sustain his boss during this hour of trial. In addition to giving his personal support on a one-on-one basis, he organized four "new majority" parties in the White House just before Christmas. The guest lists—from labor, ethnics, and Democrats for Nixon—were drawn up by Colson to symbolize that a new coalition was supporting the president. Nixon spoke well at each party and was buoyed up by the strength of the backing these groups gave him in return, but behind the façade of these public performances Colson could see how much the president was suffering. On the morning of December 28 the mood changed. Colson was summoned to the president's EOB office, where an ebullient Nixon told him that the gamble had worked. The Christmas bombing, far from destroying the peace negotiations, had accelerated them. Hanoi's intransigence was ebbing in inverse proportion to the outrage that was rising in the liberal media. Following an exchange of secret messages to Washington, the North Vietnamese politburo sent its negotiating team back to the Paris peace talks with instructions to settle. This time, peace really was at hand.

Because both Haldeman and Kissinger were away from the White House, Colson handled all the press announcements and briefings on the peace breakthrough on December 30. Nixon called him eight times that day, anxious to gain his fair share of credit from the media for a policy that had succeeded. Unfortunately this expectation was ruined by the influential columnist James Reston. He reported in the *New York Times* on December 30 that Kissinger had opposed the Christmas bombing and had been dragged into supporting it by the president, who had capriciously sent the B-52s into action to try to get a better deal from Hanoi. Colson, who might have been wiser to pour a little oil on these journalistic waters, instead encouraged the president to believe that Kissinger himself was Reston's source. Nixon went ballistic. He ordered Colson to call Kissinger immediately. "I will not tolerate insubordination," barked Nixon. "You tell Henry he's to talk to no one, period! I mean no one. And tell him not to call me, I will accept no calls from him." As this rift deepened between the president and his national security adviser, Nixon not only refused to take Kissinger's calls; he ordered Colson to have the Secret Service tap Kissinger's telephone. When these taps, as reported by Colson, appeared to show that Kissinger was disobeying the president's orders by talking to newsmen such as Joe Kraft of the *Washington Post,* Nixon became incandescent. He told Colson: "Henry will be leaving within six or eight months."

These feuds were symptomatic of the unpleasant and unhappy atmosphere that prevailed in the White House as Nixon entered his second term. Much of the unhappiness was being created by the looming shadow of Watergate. It was certainly casting a pall of gloom over Colson, not only because of the continuing media attacks on him but also because of Howard Hunt.

Colson had a troubled conscience about his friend Hunt, whom he had originally admired for his loyalty, patriotism, and willingness to take risks in the service of the president. Now he had become an embarrassment and potentially something much worse. The realization that Hunt was going to become big trouble seems to have dawned on Colson when he spoke to him on the telephone some three weeks after the election, in late November. Colson taped the call. The conversation was an exercise in evasion on his part and an attempt at blackmail on Hunt's.

"Right now I don't know anything about the goddamn Watergate," said Colson uncomfortably as Hunt explained the reason for his call, which was, as he put it, that "commitments that were made to us all at the onset have not been kept . . . there's a great deal of financial expense that has not been covered."

"OK, don't tell me any more," replied Colson, changing the conversation to his future memoirs, which he claimed would say: "Watergate was brilliantly conceived as an escapade that would divert the Democrats from the real issues and therefore permit us to win in a landslide that we probably wouldn't have had otherwise."

"Whether you believe it or not" was the sarcastic riposte from Hunt, who demanded that the White House must give "creative thinking to the affair and some affirmative action." He continued to discomfit Colson by saying, "We're protecting the guys who are really responsible," and, "We think now is the time when a move should be made, and surely the cheapest commodity available is money."

"I'm reading you. You don't need to be more specific," answered Colson, signing off on the call by thanking God for the country and for the president who would be in charge of it for the next four years.

The president was feeling the pressure of Watergate too as the new year of 1973 opened. So was Haldeman, still trying hard to make Colson the scapegoat for the scandal. On January 3 Haldeman told the president that although Colson would be missed from the White House team, "there was more to his involvement in some of this stuff than I realized."

NIXON Really?

HALDEMAN Yes.

NIXON What part?

HALDEMAN Watergate.

NIXON Colson? Does he know?

HALDEMAN I think he knows.

NIXON Does he know you know?

HALDEMAN I don't think he knows I know.

NIXON What do you mean, through Hunt or what?

HALDEMAN Yes, through Hunt and Liddy. And if Liddy decides to pull the cord Colson could be in some real soup. Liddy can do it under oath and then Colson is in a position of having perjured

himself. See, Colson and Mitchell have both perjured themselves under oath already. . . .

NIXON You mean Colson was aware of the Watergate bugging?
That's hard for me to believe.

HALDEMAN Not only was he aware of it but was pushing very hard for results and very specifically that.

This extract from the White House tape transcripts illuminates not the
truth but Haldeman's determination to lie in order to tarnish his old adversary. The fact of the matter was that Colson never perjured himself at any
stage of the Watergate saga. He had not pushed for the break-in or bugging
of the Democratic National Committee offices. He had not been aware of
it. For better or worse he was always kept in the dark about this particular
CREEP enterprise.

By early February all the Watergate burglars plus Hunt and Liddy had
either been found guilty or had pleaded guilty. Colson had assured the president that Hunt and Liddy, who he called "good healthy right-wing exuber-
ants," could be trusted to keep silent. The president was not so sure. "The
cover-up is the main ingredient," he told Colson. "That's where we gotta
be at on the cover-up deal." With this kind of talk ringing in his ears, Colson was becoming scared. On a list of his engagements for February he
scribbled a revealing note alongside the date of February 6: "Watergate is
beginning to haunt me."

It went on haunting him during his last major public duty while on the
staff of the White House. This was an official mission to Moscow in February as the president's special envoy. The purpose of the visit was to persuade the Soviets to lift their contentious blockage on the emigration of
Jews. Arriving in the minus-twenty-degrees centigrade freeze of a Russian
winter, accompanied by Patty, Colson initially found his first venture in international diplomacy an equally chilly experience. However, his dialogues
with Assistant Secretary of State Vasily Kuznetsov gradually warmed up.
After Kuznetsov had been scornfully dismissive of the threats from Congress to nullify trade agreements over the emigration issue, Colson came
back strongly: "Mr. Minister, you don't understand the American people,"
he began. "We are all immigrants, a whole nation of them. One of my
grandfathers came from Sweden, the other from England . . . you see to us,
the right of a person, Jew or Gentile, white or black, to emigrate is a fundamental human right. We can't bargain it away; it's nonnegotiable. It's
God-given to everyone." Kuznestzov replied with a standard tirade straight

from the Kremlin scriptures, to which Colson riposted with a civics class
lecture on human freedom, heavily emphasizing the labor unions' concerns
for Soviet Jews. After much more of this stylized give and take, Kuznetsov
brought the meeting to a close by declaring with ponderous formality, "Mr.
Colson, we will do our part. You can tell the president." This turned out to
be the first signal, although it needed further diplomacy to confirm it, that
the Soviets were willing to increase their quotas for emigrating Jews by
thirty thousand a year.

On his last day in Moscow, Colson held a predeparture press conference
for Western newsmen. After giving a guarded account of his official meetings and answering reporters' queries on U.S.-Soviet relations, Colson was
flummoxed by a question out of left field: "Mr. Colson, here is a report
from Washington that you sent Howard Hunt to interview Dita Beard during the ITT affair. Is this true?" It was a brutal reminder that the tentacles
of Watergate were reaching even as far as Moscow.

Back in 1971 Colson had indeed dispatched Howard Hunt on a clandestine mission to investigate whether or not an embarrassing memorandum
that had been written by an ITT lobbyist, Dita Beard, was a forgery. Hunt,
equipped with a wig and disguise supplied to him by the CIA, botched the
investigation. Inside the White House, Colson was blamed for Hunt's farcical incompetence and was bawled out by Bob Haldeman. There the story
might have ended, but now journalists were digging up and turning over
any stone that had once had the name of Colson or Hunt upon it. Colson
tried to deflect the inquiry with a quip, but other uncomfortable Watergate
questions followed. The U.S. ambassador had to terminate the press conference ahead of schedule. Colson felt totally deflated. His pride over the
success of his mission evaporated. On his homeward journey, via Bucharest
and Vienna, he was troubled by sleeplessness and restlessness. "Watergate
had followed me round the world . . . I just couldn't shake off persistent
forebodings," he wrote later. Colson's forebodings increased when he returned home to be greeted by a hostile article in *Newsweek,* headlined
"Watergate Whispers." It blamed him for all manner of crimes and com-
plicities in the burgeoning scandal, mostly unfairly. This may have been the
first example of a phenomenon that was to distress Colson greatly in the
next few months—damaging leaks and briefings against him by the CIA.
Ironically this was the very offense that Colson was to be jailed for some
eighteen months later when he pleaded guilty to briefing journalists with
leaked material that was damaging to Daniel Ellsberg.

As a counterbalance to his troubles with the media, Colson was pleased

by the warmth of his valedictory farewells from his White House colleagues. After enjoying a festive farewell party on March 14 he savored the
many letters he received wishing him well for the future. The one he treasured the most came from the president:

Dear Chuck,

 *It is with deepest regret that I now officially accept your resigna-
tion as Special Counsel to the President.*

 *I shall not dwell on my reluctance at seeing you go for you know
how highly I value your remarkable record of achievements during
the past four years. Let me simply say that our administration has
been served by many outstanding men and women, but few can
match—and none exceed—the skill and dedication you brought to
the post of Special Counsel.*

 *Our association over the past few years has been marked by a
deep and abiding friendship. Even more gratifying however has
been knowledge that we share a common commitment—to make
these years the very best in our Nation's history. I shall always trea-
sure the superb work you did for our Party, our Administration, and
the people of this good land.*

 *It is good to know that we may continue to call upon you from
time to time as you may be certain that we will take advantage of
your generosity. As you return to private life, Pat and I extend to
your Pat and you our heartfelt good wishes for the success and happiness you both so richly deserve.*

Sincerely,

RN

The generosity of the valedictory sentiments in this letter from the president was in sharp contrast to the mean-spiritedness of the machinations
that brought about Colson's departure from the White House. It was almost as if two different Nixons were communicating with Colson at this
time. The emotional, at times paternal Nixon knew that he owed a tremendous debt to the aide who had come to understand him better than any
other member of his staff after working so intimately with him on the dark
side of delivering political power. That debt came close to being repaid by
a presidential decision to keep Colson on the team. On the other hand the
ruthless, calculating Nixon, pushed hard by Haldeman and Ehrlichman,
thought that Colson's high profile over Watergate required him to be jetti-

soned as a liability. After much agonizing, the ruthless Nixon triumphed over the emotional Nixon, and Colson departed. But the decision was a closer call than anyone other than Nixon realized at the time.

Colson's emotions were almost as mixed up as those of his boss. He had become strangely dependent on the president, whom he revered to the point of hero worship. If Nixon had offered Colson anything that meant staying closely in touch with him and keeping their complex political and emotional relationship alive, Colson would have taken it. But the politics of election winning, in which he was an asset, were over. The politics of survival, in which he was a liability, were about to begin. So Colson headed for the exit and for the amorphous "Clark Clifford role" as a future outside adviser to the president. It was a part he was to play with surprising vigor and loyalty, even when advised by his own lawyer that it was against his own best interests to be doing so.

One of the last formalities to be carried out before Colson left the White House was his appointment as an unpaid consultant to the president. This curious status was devised by John Dean, who thought that Colson would need the protection of executive privilege around him if, as expected, he was faced with legal demands to testify as a witness in Watergate litigation. Colson himself was interested in more profitable areas of litigation. The *New York Times* had predicted that he was "well on his way to becoming one of the busiest and best-paid lawyers in Washington." That legal road seemed to offer him exciting rewards as, with fourteen partners led from behind the scenes by his old friend Charlie Morin, he opened a law firm named Colson and Shapiro. With new clients and business opportunities soon pouring into his office, the future for Colson looked bright. Yet two unexpected factors changed that future beyond recognition. The first was the magnitude of the Watergate crisis. The second was the call of God.

CHAPTER TEN

Conversion

Conversion

Colson was not searching for Christ when he found him. The layman who led him to Christ had been praying that Colson would go away. From start to finish nothing typical or predictable happened on his Damascus road to conversion.

The detailed story of Colson's journey to God began with a fierce dispute about him in the world of mammon—the corporate headquarters of Raytheon, in Lexington, Massachusetts. The dispute arose in the spring of 1973 when Colson was trying to rebuild his law practice by bringing new business to his firm. One major corporation in his sights was the defense electronics manufacturer Raytheon, which Colson had previously represented as its Washington lawyer with considerable success in 1968–69, just before he entered the White House.

Raytheon's forceful executive vice president, Brainerd Holmes, wanted to direct all the company's legal business to Colson. Holmes was a great admirer of Colson's effectiveness as a Washington operator. He strongly believed this effectiveness would not be impaired by the hostile press coverage Colson was receiving for his alleged involvement in Watergate.

On the other side of the dispute inside Raytheon was Charles Adams, the company's chairman. Adams equally strongly believed that Colson was tainted by Watergate and that Raytheon should not be involved with anyone who had been mixed up in it. Caught in the crossfire between the arguments and counterarguments about Colson was the president of Raytheon, Tom Phillips. His position was further complicated by the knowledge that Brainerd Holmes was ambitious to succeed him as president.

"It was a very uncomfortable situation," recalled Phillips. "Holmes was adamant that Colson should get our legal work, Adams was equally adamant that he should not. It was a fight between Mr. Practical and Mr. Integrity, and it was creating a major breach within the company. I thought Colson could deliver the results we wanted but I was also nervous that by taking him on we might risk getting dragged into the Watergate affair. At that time I was a relatively new Christian. So this breach inside the company came into my prayers every day. Basically I prayed, 'Please, God, make Colson go away.' I said this many times until one night I thought I heard a voice saying, 'No, tell Chuck Colson about me.' "

At the time when Tom Phillips was praying for Colson's disappearance from the scene, Colson appeared at Raytheon's head office. In mid-March 1973, at the instigation of Brainerd Holmes, Colson had a series of meetings with senior company executives as a prelude to his anticipated appointment as Raytheon's legal adviser. Toward the end of the day he had a meeting with Tom Phillips. As Colson was heading toward the president of the company's office, Brainerd Holmes gave him a warning. "Chuck, maybe there's something I should tell you about Tom before you go in there. He's had quite a change—some kind of a religious experience," said Holmes, adding with an embarrassed smile, "He might come on—well— you know, maybe a little bit strong."

One subject that Tom Phillips did not come on strong about was directing Raytheon's legal business to Colson's law firm. So with this matter left in suspense, it was Colson who raised the subject of religion, toward the end of the twenty-minute conversation. "Tom—uh—Brainerd tells me you have become very involved in some religious activities," he said.

"Yes, that's true, Chuck," replied Phillips. "I have accepted Jesus Christ. I have committed my whole life to him and it has been the most marvelous experience."

For all his fine words, Phillips did not succeed in making his experience sound marvelous. His body language sent all the wrong signals to his guest. "Tom looked very embarrassed and uncomfortable," recalled Colson. "He didn't make eye contact with me. He looked away, gazing up at the clock on the wall. I wasn't impressed." In addition to feeling underwhelmed by Tom Phillips's declaration, Colson was baffled by it, for he had no idea what the words he had just heard really meant. He thought of Jesus Christ as a two-thousand-year-old historical figure, not as a living entity. Why would anyone "accept him" or "commit one's life to him" as if he were around today? Colson said to himself, his mind reeling. Struggling to find something polite to say to Tom Phillips, he responded, "Uh, maybe you and

I can discuss that sometime, Tom." Phillips nodded and the conversation moved on to other subjects.

When the talk turned to Watergate, Colson launched into a long and defensive explanation emphasizing that he had not been directly or indirectly involved in the break-in at the Democratic Party's offices. Phillips cut him short. "Don't explain," he said. "If you tell me you weren't responsible, that's all I need to hear."

As Colson was leaving, Phillips put his arm around Colson's shoulder and returned to the subject of religion. "I'd like to tell you the whole story someday about how I came to Christ," he said. "I had gotten to the point where I didn't think my life was worth anything. Now I have committed my life to him, everything has changed—attitude, values, the whole bit. If you'd like to hear more, give me a call."

Colson made his excuses and left. Initially, he did not intend to follow up this conversation. But the more he reflected on it, the more he became intrigued by what he had seen and heard. The biggest surprise had been the change he noticed in Tom Phillips. The harried, overworked chief executive he remembered from previous encounters had been replaced by a warmer, more radiant, and more serene human being. "There was a new compassion in his eyes and a gentleness in his voice," recalled Colson. At the same time he could not begin to understand how Phillips could possibly say his life wasn't worth anything when he was president of the biggest corporation in New England, enjoying a $250,000-a-year salary, big bonuses and stock options, a beautiful home, and a happy family life. Yet there was one point of contact that did touch a raw nerve with Colson. Phillips had spoken of the emptiness of his pre-Christian life. Colson was feeling the pangs of a similar emptiness. The comparison nagged away within him as he returned to Washington. For his part, Tom Phillips had a quiet certainty that his conversation with Colson about religion would soon be resumed. "I was pretty sure he would call," he said. "He may not have known it himself, but to me it was clear that he was both hurting and seeking. So yes, I thought he would get back in touch."

Bayonet Warfare over Watergate

Returning to Washington, Colson was beginning to endure a long hot summer of roasting torment. "On the griddle" was how he described it. In fact he was writhing in the heat from three separate yet connected griddles. The first roasting was taking place behind closed doors in his dialogues with his own lawyers and with the Watergate prosecutors. These ordeals are related in detail in the next chapter of this book, dealing with the nightmarish legal problems Colson had to face in the latter part of 1973.

Before the nightmares became serious, Colson had the sense to get himself a good lawyer. He needed one because the newspapers were full of stories suggesting that he was a prime target of the prosecutors. Unfortunately, however, Colson did not always have the good sense to take his lawyer's advice. This weakness, and the consequences that flowed from it, became a source of considerable frustration to the lawyer concerned, David Shapiro, who to this day believes that his client was never guilty of any previously known criminal statute in the United States legal code. Colson's lawyer was also his law partner in the new firm they founded together at the beginning of 1973, Colson and Shapiro. With Charlie Morin as the third man and linchpin of this partnership, they were instantly successful; big clients like the Teamsters union, Anheuser-Busch, and Raytheon started to switch all or part of their legal work to Colson and his team. So when the shadows and suspicions from early Watergate rumors started to fall upon Colson, his partners rallied round him with plenty of support and advice on how to handle the problems that he and they thought would be temporary. It was in this spirit that David Shapiro took on the task of becoming Colson's legal counsel.

David Shapiro was a legendary Brooklyn-born litigator with wide civil and criminal experience. His 250-pound physique, razor-sharp brain, abrasive tongue, and combative spirit had made him a much respected and much feared figure within his profession. His first move was to grill Colson on every aspect of his knowledge and actions over Watergate. His second move was to see Howard Hunt, who assured him that Colson had no prior knowledge of the Watergate or Ellsberg break-ins. His third move was to make his client take a lie detector test. When Colson came through these hurdles with flying colors, Shapiro told him he had nothing to fear from the criminal law. However, he also added: "Since nobody else believes you, keep your mouth shut, don't go near anyone in the White House, don't talk to reporters, and let's concentrate on the law and the evidence. That way you'll walk."

Colson, far more experienced in Washington power plays than at legal defense strategies, did not heed this advice with the rigor his lawyer had recommended. Instead, he became heavily involved in attempts to win friends and influence people by media manipulation and political string pulling. Why did he do it? "Because Colson worshiped Nixon and thought he could clear him," claimed Shapiro. If that was the Colson game plan, it was going horribly astray. For where both Colson and Nixon were suffering their worst roasting was in and around Senator Sam Ervin's Watergate investigation committee, whose televised hearings were holding America spellbound. Colson kept pressing to be called before the Ervin Committee as a witness. For political reasons, delaying tactics prevailed and he was not invited to appear before the committee until mid-September. However, that did not prevent Colson from being pejoratively mentioned and discussed at many sessions by the committee's witnesses and by the senators themselves.

The most painful, and largely unjustified, assault on Colson came from the junior Republican member of the Ervin Committee, Senator Lowell Weicker of Connecticut. One July afternoon Weicker angrily alleged, live on television, that Colson had planted a smear story about him in the press. "Efforts are being made to pressure this committee," he thundered as he read out various criminal statutes that he claimed had been violated by Colson in the planting of the hostile story. As the audience in the Senate caucus room burst into applause at the end of Weicker's furious harangue, Colson, watching the hearings on television in his law firm offices, professed total mystification. "I've never planted any stories about Weicker," he told his colleagues. "I've never met him. From all I know about him he's a reasonable fellow. . . . Let's call him, explain the misunderstanding, and I'm sure he'll retract this." This was to prove a vain hope.

Even though the next day's newspapers accurately reported that the smear story on Weicker had been planted by a Nixon aide other than Colson, these were not reports that the senator from Connecticut wanted to know about. For when Colson presented himself in the senator's office, saying, "I think there has been some mistake. I'm not the fellow who tried to stir up stories about you in the press," Weicker responded by exploding into an even worse rage than the one he had exhibited on television. "You guys in the White House make me sick," roared Weicker. "I don't know you—but I do know what you stand for, Mr. Colson, and we live in two different worlds. I deal in hard-nosed politics; you deal in ****. You make me so mad I'd like to break your ******* nose."

At that point in the dialogue David Shapiro thought his client's nose *was* going to get broken. For Weicker moved his three-hundred-pound frame from behind his desk and brought his flushed face within two or three inches of Colson's in an eyeball-to-eyeball confrontation of maximum menace. "You make me sick," bellowed Weicker. "Get your ass out of my office."

Exit Colson at speed, accompanied by his terrified lawyer. "I was scared shitless," recalled Shapiro. "I thought there was going to be a fistfight." The two men repaired to the Senate cafeteria. Both were in shock. Shapiro trembled so much that he spilled his first cup of coffee and stuck his finger in his second. Colson kept his cool for only slightly longer. For within the next hour Weicker's aides released a partisan version of the meeting. The result was a tempest of devastating headlines and anti-Colson press stories, even though in this episode he had been more sinned against than sinning.

Living in the media spotlight was Colson's third form of roasting. He made the heat far worse than it might have been by appointing himself Nixon's chief defender. When he was hesitating over whether or not to accept his first major interview request—from the ABC network—Nixon placed a timely call to him from the White House. Colson, who was attending the wedding of Charles Morin's son on the first Saturday afternoon in June, was summoned to the phone.

"Well, boy, how are you holding on? I hear you are considering some TV interviews," said the voice of the president of the United States. It was enough to transform Colson from reluctant interviewee into knight militant, ready to tilt his lance and charge at the enemies of the presidency.

"Howard Smith wants me to do a half-hour special," replied Colson. "I'll really give it to Dean."

"You'd be tremendous—no one better. Just be careful. Don't get caught in the line of fire yourself," said Nixon, who knew exactly how to psych up his warrior for battle. The two men talked for forty minutes. Colson sat cross-legged, Indian-style on the hotel bed as he listened to his coach's instructions. Patty, who watched the eager excitement with which her husband received his marching instructions, was troubled. In retrospect Colson was troubled too by his own obsequiousness. "I was thrilled that Nixon had called and needed my help," he remembers. "I needed a cause, and Nixon was my cause. There was the appeal to pride too. *I* could defend the president. *I* would turn the tide."

Pride came before the fall. Colson went out on a limb for his boss. "I know the president of the United States was not involved in the Watergate . . . I know the president of the United States was not involved in the cover-up," Colson told Howard Smith on ABC. Similar interviews followed on all the networks and across the entire news media. Colson, the president's staunchest defender, was on the national evening news programs two or three times a week during that obsessional summer of Watergate, usually making ferocious attacks on the president's principal accuser, John Dean.

The Colson style of giving interviews—robustly loyal in defense, ruthlessly pugilistic on the attack—made him a household name with the public, but it also made him many enemies in the media. The *Washington Post* and the *New York Times* were his principal tormentors, as some of their front-page headlines during June indicated:

COLSON SAID TO URGE BREAK-IN, ARSON (*Post,* June 9)

COLSON SAYS HE ORDERED HUNT TRIP (*Post,* June 15)

COLSON SAYS HE PUT HUNT ON ITT JOB (*Times,* June 15)

HUNT SAYS COLSON ORDERED BREAK-IN OF BREMER HOME (*Post,* June 20)

COLSON DENIES KNOWING OF HUNT'S CIA AID (*Times,* June 30)

Although some of these stories were untrue, the relentless drumbeat of hostility from these newspapers was disturbing to Colson.

Something else was disturbing him too. In early June another famous political voice made an important call to Colson. At first the caller to the law firm switchboard would not give his name. "Just tell him it's the vice president," he said.

The girl on the switchboard was puzzled. "The vice president of which company?" she asked.

"The vice president of the United States," was the reply.

Vice President Spiro Agnew was in trouble. The Justice Department had been investigating allegations of bribery, extortion, and tax fraud against him. While governor of Maryland, Agnew had regularly accepted kickbacks from contractors. Delayed payment of some of those kickbacks had been handed over in envelopes containing $1,000 or more in cash to Agnew at his office in the White House. There were over forty counts in the draft indictment against the vice president, all of them supported by solid evidence.

Agnew needed a defense lawyer. He approached Colson, who wisely turned the case over to other lawyers within his firm. Although Colson recused himself from the Agnew saga, he knew enough about its details and its implications to be deeply worried. "My mind grappled with the enormity of the crisis—a president and a vice president crippled," he recalled. "But the thoughts were so horrendous I quickly blotted them out."

Colson was also blotting out from his mind all thoughts that Richard Nixon might be guilty of criminal involvement in the Watergate affair. In his robust and ringing defenses of the president, Colson's support was unqualified. In one grueling, hour-long interview with NBC's crack Watergate reporter Carl Stern on the *Today* show, Colson got to the heart of the issues at stake when he said: "What happens to Charles Colson or Bob Haldeman or John Ehrlichman or John Mitchell or any of the others who served the president is really very secondary. There is a fundamental question that is before the American people and that is, was the president involved or wasn't he? I think it's imperative that the American people know immediately the truth about the president of the United States."

Colson, the ultimate Nixon loyalist, was supremely confident as he asserted the innocence of his boss, not only because he believed it but also because as a lawyer he believed that the president would survive Watergate so long as the only evidence against him came from the uncorroborated testimony of a sole accuser—John Dean. Although Dean's accusations in the Ervin Committee hearings had grievously wounded Nixon's credibility, as the dust began to settle on the evidence it seemed clear that the wounds from it were not mortal to the president. For this was a case of one man's word against another's. Dean had taken no notes of his conversations with the president and vice versa. The evidence on both sides was therefore entirely oral, with no corroboration available on either side. Whether it was thought to be a clash between a perjurer and a maligned president, or the case of an honest witness accurately pointing the finger at a crooked president, or a plague on both their houses, was a matter of opinion. There was no proof. Colson harbored a few fleeting worries as he admitted to himself that he had not been present at any of the meetings Dean testified about, yet these worries faded away with the realization that no corroborative evidence existed to support Dean's version of events.

Like almost everyone else in America, Colson was astounded when events took an explosively unexpected turn as a low-level White House aide, Alexander Butterfield, gave evidence to the Ervin Committee on July 16. Colson, aware of the rumors that a bombshell was coming, watched the committee hearings on TV with his lawyer, David Shapiro. The blood drained from Colson's face as Butterfield made the astounding revelation that all the president's conversations, both in meetings and on the telephone, had been recorded by a secret White House taping system known only to Nixon, Haldeman, two other aides, and a small group of technicians. "I didn't know it," Colson said shakily.

"Some friend you've got!" growled Shapiro, initially with contemptuous disbelief, which was replaced by sympathy as Colson's distress became plain.

In the next few hours Colson's emotions ran all the way from agony to ecstasy and back again. At first he was shocked and hurt that his friend the president had concealed the existence of the taping system from him. Then his umbrage turned to euphoria as he said to himself, The tapes will prove my noninvolvement in Watergate. The tapes will show that I'm right and Dean is lying.

This naive optimism was not shared by the president of the United States. As the media exploded in shock-horror headlines like NIXON BUGS HIMSELF, surreal discussions were taking place at the bedside of the president, who was in Bethesda Naval Hospital with viral pneumonia and a high fever. The tone of the discussions was "to burn or not to burn the tapes." The burners included Alexander Haig, Agnew, and Kissinger. Haldeman led the antiburners and various White House lawyers, including Len Garment, whose practical question "Who will fire the torch—Bebe Rebozo?" went unanswered. In the end, the president's indecision was final. The Ervin Committee issued a subpoena and a conflagration of the tapes was no longer an option. The slide toward resignation had begun. As Nixon later saw it, "From the time of the disclosure of the existence of the tapes and my decision not to destroy them, my Presidency had little chance of surviving to the end of its term."

Colson was more sanguine about his own chances of survival, but he had underestimated the force of the furies that the revelations about the secret taping system had unleashed. Like hounds scenting a fresh fox, Nixon's adversaries now had an exciting new quarry to pursue in the form of the tapes. The Senate Watergate committee duly set off in full cry, only to find themselves outrun and outgunned by a formidable new group of hunters in the Watergate jungle—the special prosecutor's office. Although Colson could not have known it as early as the summer of 1973, the appointment of Professor Archibald Cox as special prosecutor was to lead to his personal downfall. But that was all in the future. The present seemed almost worse. For not since the Civil War had the passions of politics been more tempestuous or the hatreds more divisive than they were in July 1973, the summer when Watergate boiled over. The atmosphere of Washington was poisonous. Fear paralyzed the White House and fury motivated the media. Colson was not alone in feeling under siege from what he called the forces of "recrimination reminiscent of McCarthy days." Those forces were violent as well as vicious. The FBI was called in three times to investigate bomb threats against the Colson home, which was in any case besieged by the daily stakeout of aggressive cameramen, reporters, and TV crews. As Colson himself put it, "Watergate was creating a madness I had never witnessed in twenty years in Washington, reducing political morality to the level of bayonet warfare."

Conversion Experience

In the middle of that midsummer madness, perhaps it was not surprising that Colson's thoughts should have turned toward Tom Phillips and the peaceful serenity he had conveyed in their conversation some four months earlier. "I thought often of Tom's words during this stormy time," recalled Colson. "Even more often I recalled the expression on his face, something radiant, peaceful, and very real." Eager to escape from the unreality of life in a hostile Washington, Colson decided to take an August vacation with Patty on the Maine coast they both loved. Their journey involved driving through Massachusetts and a stopover to see Colson's parents, Pop and Diz, who were living in retirement just outside Boston. From their home in Dover, Colson decided to call Tom Phillips. He was not entirely sure why he made that call, but Phillips was welcoming and hospitable. He invited Colson to come over to the Phillips family home in the nearby Boston suburb of Weston for a visit on the night of Saturday, August 12. It was an invitation that changed Charles Colson's life.

"It was an evening when we were both kinda confused but a lot happened," was Tom Phillips's recollection of the evening. The confusion started when Colson mistook the kitchen door of the Phillips' clapboard Colonial home for the front door, so was greeted by Tom's wife, Gert, in the middle of doing the dishes after supper. Tom thought his visitor would be arriving later, so he had gone out to play tennis with his teenage children. Formally dressed in suit, collar, and tie, Colson looked a tense and awkward figure as he waited. But he gradually unwound, took his jacket off, and settled down for a long one-on-one talk with Tom. It was a humid August night and the two men withdrew to sip glasses of iced tea on a screened porch at the far end of the house.

Their conversation began more or less at the point where it had ended in tantalizing mystery some five months earlier in the Raytheon office. Colson wanted to know more about why his highly successful friend had felt his life wasn't worth anything and why he had changed course.

"I felt a terrible emptiness," explained Phillips. "My life wasn't complete. I would go to the office each day and do my job, striving all the time to make the company succeed, but there was a big hole in my life. I began to read the scriptures, looking for answers. Something made me realize I needed a personal relationship with God, forced me to search."

Colson was gripped but still baffled. He was unable to comprehend how the forty-year-old president of one of America's greatest corporations could have become dissatisfied with his prosperous and powerful life.

"It may be hard to understand," said Phillips with a contented smile, "but I didn't seem to have anything that mattered. It was all on the surface. All the material things in life are meaningless if a man hasn't discovered what's underneath them." Phillips told Colson the story of how he had gone to a Billy Graham Crusade meeting in New York's Madison Square Garden. Graham's sermon that night had persuaded him what was missing in his life was a personal relationship with Jesus Christ. "So then and there I asked Christ to come into my life," Phillips continued. "I could feel his presence, his peace within me. I could sense his Spirit there with me. Then I went out alone on the streets of New York. I never liked New York before but this night it was beautiful. I walked for blocks and blocks I guess. Everything seemed different to me. It was raining softly and the city lights created a golden glow. Something had happened to me, and I knew it."

Colson was even more baffled by this mystical description. He had no idea what Phillips meant by a personal relationship with Jesus, or how to start one. "Do you mean you just have to ask to get Jesus Christ to come into your life?" asked Colson in a skeptical tone of voice.

"Simple as that," replied Tom Phillips. "Of course, you have to want Jesus in your life, really want him. That's the way it starts."

Colson could not swallow such simplicity. But as the conversation turned to Watergate, the contrasting complexity of his tortuous explanations for the excesses of his conduct in the Nixon White House made him feel ashamed. "Tom, one thing you don't understand. In politics it's dog-eat-dog," Colson floundered. "You simply can't survive otherwise. I've been in the political business for twenty years, including several campaigns right here in Massachusetts. I know how things are done. Politics is like war. If you don't keep the enemy on the defensive, you'll be on the defensive yourself. Tom, this man Nixon has been under constant attack all of his life. The only way he could make it was to fight back. Look at the criticism he took over Vietnam. Yet he was right. We would never have made it if we hadn't fought the way we did, hitting our critics, never letting them get the best of us. We didn't have any choice."

The more he talked in this vein, the more hollow his words sounded, even to himself. "Tired old lines" was his subsequent summary of this vacuous speech. Tom Phillips was equally underwhelmed by it as he moved with gentle yet piercing precision to puncture Colson's balloon of self-justification.

"Chuck, I hate to say this but you guys brought it on yourselves," said Phillips. "If you had put your faith in God, and if your cause were just, he would have guided you. And his help would have been a thousand times more powerful than all your phony ads and shady schemes put together."

His host's declaration of faith initially struck Colson as "pure Pollyanna." How on earth, he wondered, could the president of Raytheon possibly be so naive as to put his total trust in God's guidance? But another voice within Colson suggested that perhaps there could be something in the power of God if it had made Tom Phillips such a renowned corporate leader, presiding over soaring sales and rising profits. It's tough to argue with success, Colson said to himself.

Intuitively Tom Phillips seized the moment to get tough with his guest. "Chuck, I don't think you will understand what I'm saying about God until you are willing to face yourself honestly and squarely," he said, reaching for his paperback of *Mere Christianity* by C. S. Lewis. "This is the first step. Let me read you one chapter." Moving closer to the light of the table lamp on the screen porch, Phillips began to read aloud from Lewis's classic. He began at chapter eight, "The Great Sin": "The essential vice, the utmost evil is Pride. Unchastity, anger, greed, drunkenness and all that are mere fleabites in comparison: it was through Pride that the devil became the devil. Pride leads to every other vice. It is the complete anti-God state of mind."

As Phillips read on, Colson felt a hot flush burning into his face. Lewis's words were hitting him hard:

> It is Pride which has been the chief cause of misery in every nation and every family since the world began. Other vices may sometimes bring people together: you may find good fellowship and jokes and friendliness among drunken people or unchaste people. But Pride always means enmity—it *is* enmity. And not only enmity between man and man but enmity to God. . . .
>
> In God you come up against something which is in every respect immeasurably superior to yourself. Unless you know God as that—and therefore know yourself as nothing in comparison—you do not know God at all. As long as you are proud you cannot know God. A proud man is always looking down on things and people: and of course as long as you are looking down, you cannot see something that is above you.

Colson suddenly felt mercilessly exposed by the power of this passage. Lewis's words are describing me, he said to himself in anguish. Then as Tom Phillips continued, Colson was stunned by one particular sentence that seemed to summarize exactly what had gone wrong in his own life, and in the lives of so many who were working in the Nixon White House: "For Pride is spiritual cancer: it eats up the very possibility of love or contentment or even common sense."

For a few moments after hearing these words Colson entered a dream world of flashbacks, revisiting past episodes in his life when high-blown pride had puffed him up into excesses of arrogant behavior. Some of the images that whirled before his eyes went back to his prep school days at Browne & Nichols; to his first marriage, with Nancy; and to his early successes as a young Boston lawyer. However, most of the scenes that were suddenly tormenting his troubled mind involved incidents from his rise to power in the Nixon administration. These flashbacks were accompanied by echoing voices of the White House switchboard operators: "Mr. Colson, the president is calling . . . Mr. Colson, the president wants to see you right away." As he sat in silence on the dimly lit porch, shaken to the core of his being by these strange reveries, Colson was tortured by reminders of his godless life that kept flashing through his brain.

"My self-centered past was washing over me in waves. It was painful."

"Agony" is how he recalled those minutes. "Lewis's torpedo had hit me amidships. . . . In those brief moments while Tom read I saw myself as I never had before. And the picture was ugly."

Tom Phillips interrupted these portraits of ugliness by asking the question "How about it, Chuck?"

Colson was not ready for this evangelistic challenge. He backed away into a cloud of clichés in order to avoid the road well traveled by his host. "Tom, you've shaken me up, I'll admit that," he said, "but I can't tell you I'm ready to make the kind of commitment you did. I've got to be certain. I've got to learn a lot more, be sure all my reservations are satisfied. I've got a lot of intellectual hang-ups to get past."

Tom Phillips gave his guest a smile. "I understand," he said. The gentleness of his response caused Colson to pour out more of his hang-ups.

"You see," he continued, "I saw men turn to God in the marine corps; I did once myself. Then afterward it's just forgotten and everything is back to normal. Foxhole religion is just a way of using God. How can I make a commitment now? My whole world is crashing down around me. How can I be sure that I'm not just running for shelter and that when the crisis is over I'll forget it? I've got to answer all the intellectual arguments first, and if I can do that, I'll be sure."

Colson thought his host looked disappointed, but this was not the case.

"I didn't feel at all discouraged," recalled Tom Phillips, "because although Chuck turned my invitation down, he did so in a way that made it clear he was searching quite deeply. His attitude wasn't 'Thanks but no thanks.' It was 'Thanks but maybe.' So I felt I had planted a seed and I persevered with it then and there."

Phillips's perseverance took the immediate form of reading scripture to his guest. Reaching for his Bible he turned to Psalm 37, which contains some of the most beautiful and comforting verses in the Psalter. It has a calming message for everyone under stress from worries and pressures: "Do not fret. . . . Trust in the Lord and do good. . . . Delight in the Lord and he will give you the desires of your heart. Commit your life to the Lord, trust in him, and he will do this. . . . Be still before the Lord and wait patiently for him. . . . Refrain from anger and turn from wrath. Do not fret."

As Colson listened, the verses came alive to him. They seemed to bring him the healing balm of "a cold soothing ointment." He felt he desperately wanted to stop fretting and to start putting his trust in the Lord, but he had no idea how to do this. Tom Phillips read him the third chapter of John's gospel, which includes Jesus' explanation to Nicodemus of how to be Born Again of the Holy Spirit, and how to come into the light. This famous passage also leapt off the page to Colson, but again he had no clear idea of how to respond to it.

Tom Phillips closed his Bible and asked, "Would you like to pray together, Chuck?"

Colson was startled. He had never in his life prayed with anyone before. "Sure—I guess I would—fine," he replied nervously.

Phillips bowed his head, clasped his hands together, and leaned forward on the edge of his seat. "Lord," he began, "we pray for Chuck and his family that you might open his heart and show him the light and the way."

Colson's response to the prayer was a mixture of emotional engagement and personal embarrassment. "As Tom prayed, something began to flow into me—a kind of energy," is how he described his emotions. "Then came a wave of feeling which nearly brought tears. I fought them back. It sounded as if Tom were speaking directly and personally to God, almost as though he were sitting beside us." The embarrassment came in the long silence that followed Phillips's prayer. Colson realized that he was expected to pray too, but he felt far too inhibited to make the attempt. The only prayers he had heard in his life up to that moment were formal churchy supplications couched in ecclesiastical language, heavily sprinkled with "thee's" and "thou's."

Eventually Tom Phillips broke the silence. He handed Colson his paperback copy of C. S. Lewis's *Mere Christianity* and one or two Christian pam-

phlets. Then he told Colson that someone called Doug Coe would probably be getting in touch with him in Washington to offer further advice. After that there were exchanges of thanks and good nights. Tom walked
Colson to his car. "Take care of yourself, Chuck, and let me know what you
think of that book, will you?" he said, putting his arm round his guest's
shoulder. "I'll see you soon."

As he climbed into the seat of his car, the emotions Colson had been sup-
pressing during the prayer erupted inside him. His tears started to flow. Suddenly he felt a strong urge to return to the house and to pray with Tom
Phillips. So he switched off the motor and walked toward the front door. But
as he did so the kitchen light, the dining room light, and finally the hall light
were all switched off. The house was in darkness except for one light, which
came on in an upstairs bedroom. Realizing he had left too late, Colson began railing against himself. "Why hadn't I prayed when Tom gave me the
chance?" he sobbed. As he turned out of the driveway, Colson's tears became
so uncontrollable that he could see the cars coming toward him only with the
aqueous vision of an underwater swimmer. So he pulled onto the side of the
road that connects Wellesley and Weston, two of Boston's most affluent suburbs. Parked there with his head bent forward on the steering wheel and his
face cupped in his hands, the weeping Colson began to experience an extraordinary feeling summed up by Martin Luther some five centuries earlier: "It
can be our pain and our brokenness that releases us into the body of Christ."

Colson has described his emotions sitting in his car on that night of August 12, 1973:

> I had the strange sensation that water was not only running down
> my cheeks but surging through my whole body as well, cleansing and
> cooling as it went. They weren't tears of sadness and remorse, nor of
> joy—but somehow tears of relief.
>
> And then I prayed my first real prayer. "God I don't know how to
> find you, but I'm going to try! I'm not much the way I am now but
> somehow I want to give myself over to you." I didn't know how to
> say more so I repeated over and over the words *"Take me."*
>
> I had not "accepted" Christ—I still didn't know who He was. My
> mind told me it was important to find that out first, to be sure that I
> knew what I was doing, that I meant it and would stay with it. Only
> that night something inside me was urging me to surrender—to what
> or to whom I did not know.
>
> I stayed there in the car, wet-eyed, praying, thinking for perhaps

half an hour, perhaps longer, alone in the dark of the quiet night. Yet for the first time in my life I was not alone at all.

The only person Colson initially told about his experiences on the night of August 12 was his wife, Patty. She was far more knowledgeable than her husband on spiritual matters, having been a regular, churchgoing Catholic for more than thirty years. However, Patty was unschooled in the terminology of evangelical Protestantism, to which Tom Phillips had introduced Colson that evening. She was also unclear on the nature of their discussion since it had been described to her in advance as a business meeting.

The first intimation to Patty of the real business that had taken place came from Chuck when he returned after midnight to his parents' home in Dover. After climbing into bed with his sleepy spouse, he asked her, "Do you know what a conversion experience is?"

"No," yawned Patty.

"Well, I've had one," said Chuck.

Patty opened her eyes in surprise. She noticed that her husband, for the first time in months, looked contented and at peace. This is great, she thought to herself, he's had a conversion without knowing what it was. Rousing herself still further, she studied Chuck's face more carefully and was amazed by its serenity. "Well, I don't know exactly what the term means but I guess you're saying that you've turned to the Lord," said Patty, "and if it makes you happy, then I'm all for it."

On that note of spiritual happiness Charles and Patty Colson, at one with the Lord for the first time in their nine years of marriage, fell into a deep and peaceful sleep.

Glimmerings of Understanding

"Our souls are not made over to God by one act of conversion but by the long unremitting and courageous effort that conversion begins," wrote the twentieth-century English mystic Evelyn Underhill. Charles Colson was to discover the truth of these words in the days immediately following his conversion experience on the roadside near Tom Phillips's house. The first phase of his "unremitting and courageous effort" took the form of an intellectual wrestling match with himself at a vacation cottage overlooking the sea on a beautiful stretch of the Maine coast.

Colson is one of those men who have enjoyed a lifelong love affair with the sea. Being on or near the water calms him, centers him, uplifts him, and can sometimes bring out the romantic and spiritual sides of his nature. All these forces of change were at work when he and Patty checked into a coastal inn near the small Maine fishing village of Boothbay Harbor on the night of August 13, 1973—just twenty-four hours after his meeting with Tom Phillips.

Arriving in picturesque Boothbay Harbor without reservations at the peak of the tourist season meant that the Colsons were nearly faced with a "no room at the inn" situation. Eventually they found an unfashionable hotel twelve miles out of town that did have one last accommodation available. This was a cottage whose TV set was broken and whose isolated position, perched on a narrow spit of headland, would not have appealed to every type of visitor. It was, however, exactly what the Colsons were looking for. Amazed to discover from the laconic innkeeper that the cottage was free for a week, they moved in with enthusiasm, relishing the view of the blue-green ocean that crashed onto the rocks beneath their windows. "What a great place to relax," Chuck told Patty, although the stronger but silent agenda in his mind was "What a great place to think about God."

Colson's early thought processes about God were remarkably similar to those of a lawyer preparing for a court case. He unpacked C. S. Lewis's *Mere Christianity* and alongside it placed a yellow legal pad. On the top of the pad he wrote, "Is there a God?" He then divided the page under the headings "pros" and "cons." Although this technique of legal analysis is far from ideal when applied to matters of faith, Colson diligently scribbled away and quickly covered two pages on the "pros" side of the yellow paper. He filled up an equal quantity of space in the "cons" column.

Then he got stuck, more or less at the point where he had ended on Tom Phillips's porch, in the area of pride and ego. C. S. Lewis is tough on this subject, and not only in the "Great Sin" chapter. "Is my reluctance to knock at this door due to my pride?" is one of the key questions Lewis suggests his readers should ask themselves, ramming home the point that the supreme obstacle to faith comes when "the searcher reaches the moment you have a self at all, and there is a possibility of putting yourself first— wanting to be the center—wanting to be God." Having played God all too often in his White House days of power, Colson had many egotistical problems to resolve. After being left alone with Lewis and the yellow legal pads for three days, he reckoned he had sorted out all but one: how did Jesus

Christ fit into the new picture of God he was formulating? After all, many religions believe in a supreme deity. "Hindus believe in God and say that he can be worshiped in almost any way anyone pleases," reflected Colson. "All my analyzing so far had only gotten me to Hinduism."

Colson's great leap forward from Hinduism, or other forms of theism, to accepting Christ was not an easy process. The first obstacle was his chosen methodology of legalistic debate. This led Colson off on trails of analyzing legal principles such as the Supreme Court's power of judicial review as established by the landmark case of *Marbury v. Madison*. Although Colson felt those complex jurisprudential arguments were helpful to him in his search for the truth about the Christian God, his published account of them suggests that anyone other than a lawyer would have found this part of his intellectual searchings far more confusing than enlightening.

A second source of confusion was his early attempt to communicate with Patty about the spiritual revolution that was turning his heart and mind upside down. Apart from telling her on the night he came back from Tom Phillips's house that he thought he'd had a conversion experience, even though he didn't know what it was, Colson did not raise the topic with his wife again until they were two days into their vacation at the Maine cottage. He then broached the subject with disconcerting lack of subtlety: "You believe in God, don't you, honey?" he suddenly asked when they were sitting out on the sundeck.

Patty bridled. "You know I do," she replied with a touch of asperity in her voice, wondering if her spouse was suffering from self-induced amnesia about her lifelong commitment to her Catholic faith.

"But have you ever really thought about it—deeply I mean?" persisted Colson. "Like who is God and how does he watch over each of us and why did he create us, things like that?"

Patty was puzzled. "What's in that book you're reading?" she asked, pointing to the green-and-white cover of Macmillan's paperback edition of *Mere Christianity*. Colson launched into a long account of his evening with Tom Phillips. He told her of the searchings Phillips's readings had triggered in him but left out the tears, the emotional upheavals, and the "Take me" prayer he had said alone in the car. Even with these excisions, Patty realized from his story that Chuck was deeply troubled. "Maybe you should talk to a priest," she suggested. In the absence of an ordained minister on this lonely Maine peninsula, Patty took over the role of confidante and confessor. She listened intently while Chuck unburdened his soul. The couple talked long into the night as a fog swirled around their cottage, and out to sea a sonorous bell buoy clanged to guide the lobster fishermen away from the rocks and reefs.

Patty was no theological navigator for her husband's voyage of discovery, but far more important, she gave him her loving support in these early days of turmoil. As Colson described her role: "Patty is the gentlest, most caring person I've ever known, taking others' problems as her own, feeling the full weight of every burden I ever had to bear. She hadn't expected this one—a search for God—but I sensed she was ready to share it with me. . . . It was a relief to have Patty know of my search to find new peace within myself and to acquire an antidote for the disease which had been sucking life out of me, vampire-like. . . . We ended by deciding to get out the family Bible when we returned home, and begin reading it."

With no Bible in the cottage, Colson had to rely on just two sources in his quest for Jesus Christ—his recollections of the discussion with Tom Phillips and his readings from the writings of C. S. Lewis. What nagged away most strongly in Colson's mind was a couple of sentences that resonated from his first spiritual conversation in the Raytheon office when Tom Phillips told him, "Chuck, I have accepted Jesus Christ. I have committed my life to him and it has been the most marvelous experience of my whole life." For a long time Colson could not get his head round these concepts. To him, Jesus Christ was an impressive historical personage and a great moral leader. However, he had lived two thousand years ago, so a contemporary human being could not possibly "accept" him or "commit one's life" to him as if he were around today. These thoughts were shattered when Colson, with the help of Lewis, grasped the central part of the Christian faith: Jesus is God.

The passage in *Mere Christianity* that shattered Colson's blinkered view of Jesus as merely a historical figure and moral teacher was Lewis's final paragraph of the fourth chapter, "The Shocking Alternative." "I am trying here to prevent anyone saying the really foolish thing that people often say about Him: 'I'm ready to accept Jesus as a great moral teacher but I don't accept his claim to be God.' That is the one thing we must not say," wrote Lewis.

A man who was really a man and said the sort of thing Jesus said would not be a great moral teacher. He would either be a lunatic—on a level with a man who says he is a poached egg—or else he would be the Devil of Hell. You must make your choice. Either this man was and is the Son of God: or else a madman or something worse. You can shut Him up for a fool, or you can spit at Him and kill Him as a demon; or you can fall at His feet and call Him Lord and God. But let us not come with any patronizing nonsense about His being a great human teacher. He has not left that open to us. He did not intend to.

Colson picked up the gauntlet Lewis's words had thrown down before him. He immediately recognized the dramatic immensity of the challenge he was facing. "There was my choice as simple, stark and frightening as that. No fine shadings, no gradations, no compromises. No one had ever thrust this truth at me in such a direct and unsetting way," was how he described his reaction.

By now it was the fifth day of the week in the Maine cottage. For a change of scene Chuck and Patty took time out to visit Boothbay Harbor. Wandering around the town they came across a band concert being performed from the steps of the library. Colson so much enjoyed the picturesque appearances of the local musicians, who ranged from a tot with a trumpet to an octogenarian trombonist in denim dungarees, that he compared the scene to "a Norman Rockwell *Saturday Evening Post* cover come to life." Yet for all the pleasure he took from the band's energetic repertoire, Colson was listening to the beat of a different drum. Jesus Christ, lunatic or God? was the question that kept pounding away in his head. On Friday morning he answered it.

After a near sleepless night wrestling with more doubts about his motives for turning toward Christ ("Was I seeking a safe port in a storm, a temporary hiding place?"), Colson eventually returned to the state of surrender he had entered six days earlier, when he said the "Take me" prayer in his car on the country road close to the Phillips's home. He felt as though he had been on a spiritual journey of a thousand miles in the intervening period but now he had come back to the same point of departure. Putting aside his yellow pads and the pros and cons of the intellectual debate he now realized was far less important than the act of faith he was about to make, Colson said a prayer taken from one of the pamphlets Tom Phillips had given him. Sitting alone, staring out across the rocks to the Atlantic Ocean he loved, Charles Colson said these words: "Lord Jesus, I believe you. I accept you. Please come into my life. I commit it to you."

As he said this prayer of acceptance, Colson felt an immediate inner surge of strength and serenity. Old fears, tensions, and animosities were draining away. They were replaced by a new sense of peace and assurance. His conversion experience was complete. "The long unremitting and courageous effort that conversion begins" was about to open as a new chapter in his life.

CHAPTER ELEVEN

Prayers and Pleadings

Falling Apart

Charles Colson's spiritual journey from conversion to repentance was accompanied by a legal journey from fighting to prove his innocence to entering a plea of guilty. These concurrent journeys, which dominated his life from August 1973 to June 1974, converged into an inner struggle between his old instincts and his new beliefs. The fact that he barely understood what these new beliefs meant was less important than his willingness to make a leap of faith in the company of four newfound Christian "brothers." Alongside his spiritual searchings with these brothers, Colson had to deal with a plethora of personal problems. They included high stress levels, heavy drinking, money worries, anxieties over the fate of his innocent subordinates, public legal battles, and private anxieties for his wife and children. These pressures developed into a desperate desire to escape from what he called "the drip-by-drip Chinese water torture" of interminable court proceedings and seemingly endless defeats. Yet in the midst of all this turmoil, Colson was being changed into a different man.

The change was neither a quick nor easy process. When Colson returned from New England to Washington in mid-August, his first instinct was "business as usual." By this he meant getting new clients for his law firm, fighting old battles with the press, and extricating himself from the legal quagmire of Watergate. However, he did make one important move in his spiritual journey, which was to write a letter of thanks to Tom Phillips:

20th August, 1973
Dear Tom,
    I appreciate more than I can tell you the evening that you gave

*me while I was in Boston. It was a very rare experience and I hope
I am not overstating it when I say that it was one of the most inspiring few hours that I have ever spent. You opened my eyes to a
great many things. As a matter of fact, I can say I thought of little
else of a serious nature while I was in Maine. I read the Lewis
book which is superb and I am ready at any time that it can be
conveniently arranged to meet with Mr. Coe. In fact, I am anxious
to do so.*

A day or two later, Doug Coe showed up unannounced at the offices of
Colson and Shapiro. Holly Holm, Colson's secretary, initially tried to turn
away the unknown visitor, whose reluctance to identify himself caused suspicions that he was yet another reporter pursuing the Watergate story.
When this misunderstanding was sorted out, Colson found himself in conversation with a six-foot-one-inch handsome bear of a man with dark curly
hair, sparkling black eyes, a contagious smile, and the warmest of personalities.

"This is just great, just great, what Tom has told me about you," began
Coe. "I hope you don't mind. He read me your letter."

Colson did mind. He felt the disclosure of his correspondence to a
stranger was an invasion of his privacy. But the disarming Doug Coe soon
managed to convince him that he was talking to no ordinary stranger. In
fact, Coe was an established Washington insider, organizer of the National
Prayer Breakfast, head of a politico-Christian network called the Fellowship, and a close friend of several senators and congressmen well known
to Colson. Within minutes, a good rapport was established. At Coe's
prompting, Colson gave a short account of his conversion experience. This
was difficult for him because it was the first time he had articulated his
commitment out loud to another person. But after a hesitant start, Colson
told his story, ending up with the words "And so, Doug, I've asked Christ
into my life."

"That's so exciting, just tremendous," enthused Coe, adding unexpectedly, "You'll want to meet Senator Hughes. Harold is a tremendous Christian."

Colson did not want to do any such thing. He knew too much about the
track record of this ultraliberal Democratic senator from Iowa. "Harold
Hughes won't want to meet me," he demurred. "From what I've heard, he
considers me the number-one menace to America. He's antiwar, anti-
Nixon, anti-Colson, and we couldn't be farther apart politically."

"That doesn't matter now," retorted Coe.

"Are you telling me that because I've accepted Christ, Harold Hughes, just like that, wants to be my friend?" asked the skeptical Colson, shaking his head in disbelief.

"Wait and see, Chuck, wait and see," said Coe. "You will have brothers all over this city, hundreds of them; men and women you don't even know, who will want nothing more than to help you. Some of them know we are meeting and are praying for you right now."

Colson was amazed. The pressures he had been subjected to since leaving the White House had been steadily driving him into a defensive and often depressed mood. He had become a prime Watergate target for investigators of one sort and another—from the special prosecutor's office, from several congressional committees, including Senator Sam Ervin's, and from the news media. It was a lonely and largely friendless period in his life. Yet here was Doug Coe telling him that hundreds of strangers cared enough about him to hold him in their prayers. "The idea almost paralyzed my mind," was how Colson described this moment afterward.

Colson's mind was transported into another new experience when Doug Coe suggested they pray together. When it became clear that he meant they should pray *aloud* together, Colson had a second moment of paralysis. He had never done anything like it before, not even with Tom Phillips. He started to worry that one of his law partners might come into his office and think he had gone mad. But the experienced pastor, Doug Coe, prayed with him in such a gentle and relaxed way that Colson shed his reticence and managed to stumble through a few words of oral prayer on his own. Another breakthrough had been made. Another barrier had come down.

Before departing with a cheery "Bye, brother!" Doug Coe gave Colson a copy of the New Testament. It was the J. B. Phillips translation, which Coe inscribed with the words "To Charles—it is better to fail in a cause that will ultimately succeed than to succeed in a cause that will ultimately fail—Matthew 6:33."

The cause that was weighing most heavily on Colson's mind at the end of August was how to escape from the clutches of the Watergate special prosecutor's office. When he learned that the grand jury investigating the break-in at the office of Daniel Ellsberg's psychiatrist was hearing evidence about his role in the affair, Colson opted for a high-risk strategy. He volunteered to testify. That was how it came about that on August 30, Colson entered the U.S. courthouse in Washington, D.C., took the oath, and heard the assistant special prosecutor, William Merrill, open with these ominous words:

"You are here before this grand jury which is inquiring into the possibility of violations of federal law relating to the break-in of Doctor Fielding's office in Los Angeles. . . . I think I should tell you also that from evidence the grand jury has heard, you are a prospective defendant in the violation of certain criminal statutes relating to that matter."

After listening to this prologue, which made him break out into a cold sweat, Colson was expecting to be grilled about the Fielding office break-in. Not so. Prosecutor Merrill played shamelessly to the largely black D.C. jury by asking Colson loaded political questions: Had he organized anti-Kennedy dirty tricks in the New Hampshire primary? Had he ever written a memo saying that it would be a good tactic to "paint Ellsberg black"? These attempts to portray Colson as a Kennedy-hating homophobe who wrote racist memos seemed to be making the intended negative impact on the grand jury. After enduring two days of these interrogations, Colson concluded that he should stop his voluntary testimony. It had been a disaster. A week later, Prosecutor Merrill contacted Colson's lawyer, David Shapiro, with the dreaded news: "We are going to indict your client, probably next week."

This projected indictment hung like the sword of Damocles over Colson's head. In fact, it dangled in midair for several months, sometimes looking menacing and immediate while at other times it seemed vague and unlikely. But whatever form it took, it had a devastating impact on Colson.

The first episode of devastation came in mid-September with the arrival of a summons to appear before the Ervin Committee. For the past five months, Colson had been eager to take the stand at these nationally televised Senate hearings on Watergate. Time and again, his appearance had been postponed, probably because Senator Ervin was reluctant to let such an articulate defender of the president have his say before 80 million viewers until the case against Nixon had been fully presented. Now the committee's invitation put Colson on the horns of a painful dilemma. He had been advised by the special prosecutor's office that his indictment as a criminal defendant in the Fielding break-in case was "imminent." His legal team simultaneously advised him that he must not jeopardize his rights in court by testifying before the Senate. The only way of complying with his lawyer's recommended course of action was for Colson to take the Fifth. This he initially refused to do.

"The Fifth Amendment to me is the scarlet letter of American politics," was how he expressed his aversion to the proposal. "Nothing creates the aura of guilt and the stench of cowardice more than refusing to testify." His law partner David Shapiro refused to countenance such stupidity. "Chuck, you stick your neck out now and you're dead," he bellowed in his most belligerent Brooklynese. "Do you want to commit suicide? Have you got a death wish? The only place you testify now is in court. You can say nothing. We don't know what those guys in Cox's office will use against you, and we avoid giving them more ammunition."

Colson gave no ground in this angry shouting match. But he was swayed by the unanimity of the advice he received, not only from Shapiro but from all his partners, including Charlie Morin. Even so, right up to the moment when he took the oath before the Ervin Committee, Colson was in a whirlwind of indecision about what he should do. As the committee's counsel, Sam Dash, began asking the first question—"Mr. Colson, are you acquainted with E. Howard Hunt?"—Shapiro whispered, "You have to do it or you can get yourself another set of lawyers. If you open your mouth, then I'm outta here."

Colson felt his world was falling apart. Biting his lip and stammering, he addressed the chairman: "Senator, I wanted more than I can tell you to appear before this committee and to be able to testify. I never thought I would be in this position where I felt that my own legal rights were being prejudiced and I had to avail myself of my constitutional privilege. I do not like doing this. I very much dislike it. I hate it. I am going, Mr. Chairman, to follow the instructions of my counsel, which I have to say are not the instructions of my conscience."

After that, it was all over except for the reporting—which was savage. The TV networks, no doubt reveling in the ruin of their former pressurizer, led their evening news bulletins with scathing political obituaries of the former hatchet man. The next day's newspapers buried Colson with equal relish. COLSON WON'T REPLY TO WATERGATE QUIZ, screamed the front-page headline of his old enemy the *Washington Post*. Even his old friends in journalism wrote him off with scorn. What friend and foe alike agreed on was that Colson was guilty and that Colson was finished. By taking the Fifth, he had destroyed himself in the arena of political success, which had been his be-all and end-all. Yet worse was to come.

Brothers and Pressures

As a new believer who had accepted Jesus Christ into his life just over a month earlier, Colson might have been expected at this time of deepening crisis to be praying on a regular basis. That was not what happened. He changed nothing in his routine to create a daily quiet time or a disciplined prayer life. However, in the middle of the storms and disasters that were crashing over him, Colson suddenly found himself calling out to God in prayers of desperation. "I remember one such moment of desperate prayer on a day when I was suddenly accused in the media of misusing funds from the Milk Producers," he has recalled. "To answer the charges, I had to try and reconstruct what had happened by looking at the files of an old White House colleague, Murray Chotiner. I arrived in his office before he got there. So I took out a pocket edition of the Bible and tried to read a psalm. I got something from it but not much because I could only concentrate for a minute or so at a time before my mind kept swinging back to whatever had gone on with the Milk Producers. Then I tried to pray, saying something like, 'Lord, you've got to help me. I just don't know what to do with this thing. Please help me.' I remember it well because it was such an improbable thing for me to be doing in Murray's office. My prayer was sincere but it was a self-centered prayer of fear born out of my anguish and powerlessness. I really didn't know what I was doing. All I knew was that I believed."

Looking back at this period of high drama over thirty years after the events of 1973, Colson now feels he understands what God was doing in his life. What had happened to him in Tom Phillips's driveway was the start of his journey into faith, a gift from God of the ability to believe. "Once I had accepted that gift by making a commitment which I did not then understand, a process began," explains Colson. "It was driven by a conviction of sin and wanting to change into a better person, just as Tom had changed. In that process, which was very painful in those early months of losing everything, I now realize that God was stripping me of my worldly pride and values in order to raise me up again as his servant. It made no sense to me at the time, but now it makes total sense. All I could do when the blows were raining down on me was to hang on to my faith and to trust God. It was extremely difficult but I did hang on, thanks to that nebulous concept called 'Christian fellowship' which gave me my only sense of security in all the turmoil."

The first manifestation of Christian fellowship was the number of supportive calls Colson received in the days after Doug Coe's visit to his office. These were from people he had known in the government, although he had not realized any of them were Christians. They included Mel Laird, the former congressman and defense secretary; Curtis Tarr, the former president of Lawrence University, now undersecretary of state; and Ken BeLieu, a retired army colonel who had worked with Colson in the White House. These well-wishers and several others were men Colson respected and liked. "I was really impressed and touched that such people were calling me at a time when most of my former associates wanted to have nothing more to do with me," he has recalled. "They said things to me like, 'I'm with you all the way'; 'Call me if there's anything I can do for you'; 'You are my brother in Christ'; 'You are in my prayers.' I hardly knew how to respond to these extraordinary words of kindness but they sure strengthened me at a bad time."

The greatest source of strength to Colson at this time was the fellowship group that was formed around him by Doug Coe. Recruiting members for it had been a hard task. For almost everyone Coe called with a personal invitation to "come take part in a prayer group to support our new Christian brother Chuck Colson" had refused to join. At a time when Watergate hysteria was at its zenith, Colson's reputation was at its nadir. He was such a disgraced, villfied, and hated figure that not even the most forgiving of Christian members in the Fellowship wanted to be in the same room with him.

Anyone other than Doug Coe might have been discouraged by the number of rebuffs and refusals he received in response to his trawl for supporters of Colson in prayer. But Coe was an eternal optimist with a long track record of success as a consummate Washington networker. So eventually he did assemble a group of four friends (including himself) who were both sufficiently Christian and sufficiently politically knowledgeable to be potentially useful participants in fellowship with Colson.

The three men who joined Coe in this enterprise were Al Quie, a nine-term Republican congressman from Minnesota; Graham Purcell, a former Democratic congressman from Texas who had lost his seat in the House of Representatives in 1972, largely as a result of the blue-collar vote swing to the Colson-Nixon new majority; and Harold Hughes, an abrasive ex–truck driver, ex-alcoholic, ex-governor of Iowa who, since 1968, had been the Corn State's liberal Democratic senator. (Hughes was high on the Nixon White House enemies list on account of his anti–Vietnam War views.)

Initially, Harold Hughes had delivered just about the most virulent of refusals to Doug Coe's invitation to join a Colson-supporting prayer group. "There isn't anyone I dislike more than Chuck Colson. I hate everything he stands for. No, no, no!" shouted the volatile Iowa senator as he slammed down the phone. Next day, Doug Coe called back to suggest that such an attitude was far removed from Jesus' commandment to love your neighbor. After a heated discussion, Hughes relented. However, he insisted on strict conditions for the meeting with Colson, which he said must take place outside the Beltway, after dark, and in conditions of total privacy. And so the first meeting of the proposed Colson-supporting fellowship group (plus wives on this introductory occasion) was arranged at the Colonial-style home of Al and Gretchen Quie, in the Maryland countryside, at eight-thirty in the evening.

During the early part of the evening, Hughes and Colson circled each other warily, more in the manner of mutually suspicious sharks than mutually supportive followers of the Lord. As soon as dessert was finished, Hughes addressed Colson with impatient bluntness: "Chuck, they tell me you have had an encounter with Jesus Christ," he said. "Would you tell us about it?"

Colson felt uncomfortable about being put on the spot in this way. Patty looked even more embarrassed than her husband, as he began a stumbling account of what had happened between himself and Tom Phillips. As he shared his intimate spiritual experiences with this group of strangers, Colson nearly lost his nerve. Are they going to think I'm some kind of nut? Do people really go around talking about their personal encounters with God? he wondered to himself. He need not have worried. As he finished his story, choking back the tears and saying, "As a new Christian, I have everything to learn. I know that. I'm grateful for any help you can give me," Harold Hughes came over and gave him an enormous bear hug.

"That's all I need to know, Chuck," said Hughes, embracing his former political adversary. "You have accepted Jesus and he has forgiven you. I do the same. I love you now as my brother in Christ. I will stand with you, defend you anywhere, and trust you with anything I have."

Such instant enthusiasm would have seemed extraordinary from anyone other than Harold Hughes, but he was a man of instant emotions. One moment he could explode into the undeleted expletives learned in his former occupation as a truck driver, the next he could be pouring out his heart with gentle Christian love. Behind this volatility lay a combination of idiosyncrasy and humanity. Colson met the idiosyncratic side of his new brother early in their relationship when Hughes told him, "Don't pray with your arms folded or your legs crossed because the Holy Spirit can't get into your body." That sounded bizarre, even to as trusting a neophyte believer as Colson was at that moment. Over the ensuing months, he developed a number of concerns about Hughes's New Age nostrums, such as his belief in "signs" derived from experiences as mundane as breaking a plate while washing the dishes. Yet Colson's doubts were assuaged by the avalanche of

warmth that swept over him from Hughes and from the other four brothers who resolved to meet regularly every Monday morning for breakfast in
Fellowship House, the headquarters of Doug Coe's ministry.

By the standards of the evangelical theology Colson later adopted, the
fellowship of his new brethren was not a spiritually challenging experience.
However, at the time, it provided just the right warm glow of mutual support that Colson needed. The leader of the group was its convener, Doug
Coe. He specialized in therapeutic Christianity. His concept of fellowship
was to read out a verse of scripture, to give a five-minute homily on it, and
then to declare that among five trusting brothers, anything could be
brought before the Lord—for confession, guidance, or prayer. After that,
most of the next hour was spent analyzing Colson's latest dramas or Harold
Hughes's past sins. The confessional nature of these discussions was not
entirely to the taste of all the brothers at first. After one of the early sessions, Al Quie said to Graham Purcell, "We're kinda out of our league here
with no problems like drinking, womanizing, or going to prison to share."

The sharing format suited Colson because the brothers were so warm
and loving in their prayers for him. However, he had no real idea of where
he was heading spiritually, nor did he receive any meaningful Christian instruction from the group. At that stage his journey was fueled by a fuzzy
mixture of crumbling egotism and easy believism. The crumbling was real
enough because back in the Watergate arena, his life was fast becoming the
personification of that Irish adage known as Murphy's Law: "If something
can go wrong, it will."

There were three disaster areas in Colson's life at this time—his relationship with the media, his relationship with the president, and his relationship with the special prosecutor. The first was infuriating to him, the
second seemed tragic, and the third brought about his downfall. The combination of these pressures took him to the brink of a breakdown. "I was
about as stressed out as a guy can possibly be," he has recalled. "Every
night I would have at least three or four large scotch and sodas in the hope
of drowning it all out. I was waking up in the morning as tired as when I
had gone to bed the night before. In the middle of the night I was waking
up, sometimes to think about prison but more often to get angry about the
things being said about me that were untrue . . . my greatest agony in this
period was hearing something or seeing something written about me that
was completely wrong. So I'd try and correct it by testifying or by writing
a letter, only to find out that nobody would believe me. It was excruciating
torture. Time and again I wanted to scream, 'But it's true! It's true!' "

The files of Colson's correspondence in 1973–74 are full of letters equivalent to such screams. Frequently he wrote to editors such as Abe Rosenthal of the *New York Times,* or to columnists like Mary McGrory of the *Washington Star,* Clark Mollenhoff of UPI, or George Frazier of the *Boston Globe,* complaining about their inaccurate reporting of his Watergate involvement. Sometimes these letters go into voluminous points of detail rebutting a false allegation. In other letters, Colson resorted to vituperation ("McCarthyism is evidently alive and well in the *Boston Globe* in 1973") or to raging furiously about a wild headline such as "Colson Okayed Watergate." These angry attempts to set the record straight consumed large quantities of Colson's time and energy but the end result was total failure. His activities in combat against his media tormentors bring to mind the despairing cry of Shakespeare's *Macbeth:*

They have tied me to the stake, I cannot fly
But Bear-like I must fight the course.

One unexpected course that opened up during Colson's rough ride in the media began when the Washington press corps discovered that the former hatchet man had turned holy man. This discovery was made on December 6, when Senator Harold Hughes accepted an invitation to speak at a small private prayer group in the White House. Unknown to Colson, during his years of presidential service a handful of members of the White House staff had been meeting regularly for Christian fellowship over breakfast in a basement office in the West Wing. Soon after Hughes announced he was leaving the Senate to enter full-time Christian lay ministry, this group invited him to share his testimony. Hughes brought Colson along as his guest. In such a setting it was naive of them to imagine that their double act as prayer partners would remain a private matter. Sure enough, some three hours later, at the 11 A.M. White House press briefing, deputy press secretary Jerry Warren found himself engulfed in an unusual exchange with Dan Rather of CBS.

> RATHER Jerry, what is the president doing, continuing to
> see Charles Colson?
> WARREN I don't think he is.
> RATHER What was Mr. Colson doing at the White House
> today?
> WARREN *[pause]* Well *[pause]* . . . he was attending a meet-

ing in the dining room downstairs, which is held
every other Thursday. A group of White House
staff members get together for a prayer breakfast
and Mr. Colson was attending that . . .

UNIDENTIFIED VOICE 1 Prayer!
UNIDENTIFIED VOICE 2 Is he going to be a preacher?

The room erupted in laughter, followed by a flood of cynical questions
and more ribald merriment. It was quite a story. COLSON HAS FOUND RELI-
GION was the *New York Times* headline. The news media across the country followed suit. Columnists, editorial writers, and cartoonists had a field
day of mockery. Syndicated columnist Harriet Van Horne caught the general mood when she wrote, "I cannot accept the sudden coming to Christ
of Charles Colson. If he isn't embarrassed by this sudden excess of piety,
then surely the Lord must be."

Someone else who did feel seriously embarrassed by Colson putting
his head above the religious parapet was his partner and defense lawyer,
David Shapiro. Storming into Colson's office on the morning when the
White House prayer breakfast story was in all the papers, Shapiro raged:
"You've done it this time, Colson, you've really done it. I hope he"—Colson
thought this was a reference to Jesus Christ—"can save your butt now because I can't."

"Calm yourself, Dave," said Colson.

"Calm myself!" bellowed Shapiro, pounding his fist on the desk. "Just
when we thought we had the Ellsberg thing licked, just when you've been
out of the press for a month, now this! It looks like the biggest dirty trick
you've ever pulled, the final big play for sympathy. It probably is. As far as
I'm concerned they ought to indict you for this one."

Caught in this maelstrom of negative reactions, balanced later by some
more positive comments, Colson remained uncharacteristically calm. This
was because he had been deeply moved by his encounter at the White House
prayer group with the chairman of the Federal Reserve, Arthur Burns.
There was a history of enmity between Colson and Burns arising from a
Nixon-Colson dirty trick some two years earlier. At a time when the Fed
had been pressing for wage restraint (an unpopular demand for the president
with his eye on winning reelection) Nixon suggested that Colson should try
and damage the Fed by leaking a story that Burns was pressing for a personal
wage hike. The story of the Fed chairman's alleged double standards was duly

planted by Colson. It was untrue. Burns was hurt and mortified. He was also angry with Colson, who was identified as the leaker of the story.

Against this background, it was hardly surprising that when Colson arrived at the White House prayer group on December 6, he received the chilliest of formal nods from Arthur Burns. However, after Harold Hughes came to the end of his testimony talk with the words "I've learned how wrong it is to hate. . . . One of the men I hated most was Chuck Colson, but now that we share a commitment together in Christ, I love him as my brother," the effect on Burns was dramatic. He closed the meeting by saying that Hughes's comments on Colson were "one of the most beautiful things I have ever heard from any man." Then he prayed with Colson, accepted an apology from him, and the two former adversaries parted in loving reconciliation. Colson was amazed by the change in the cantankerous and hostile character that he had previously thought Burns to be. Observing such change was beginning to become part of a pattern. In the weeks following the media coverage of Colson's newfound faith, all sorts of people wrote to tell him of the transformation in their own lives since coming to Christ. The letter that moved him the most came from a staff sergeant in the U.S. Air Force.

Dear Sir,

This may seem to you as an unusual letter, however, after reading an article in the Charleston Evening Post on you I gathered that you were (in the past) an unusual person. I'm a S/Sgt. in the USAF. For 19 years I've been trying to find myself. I've went to church on several occasions but they (the pastors) didn't reach me. After reading your article it has helped me more than anything in my entire life. It is Christmas morning. I'm usually drunk or trying to get drunk by now, but here I am watching the children open up their presents and thinking about going to church somewhere, instead of the club or someone's house and get drunk. I didn't even buy any "booze" this year. It's people in positions like you who confess their past (maybe not so good life—wrongs) or whatever it may be called. Sure do help people in a position like me. I truly feel free within my inner self this morning and I pray that God may help both of us in all of our trying efforts.

I am going to try and find that book "Mere Christianity" down here and read it myself.

> *God Blessing You,*
> *S/Sgt. Nathaniel Green*

Colson wept as he read and reread Sergeant Green's letter. "It's all worth it, Holly," he said to his bemused secretary. Equally worthwhile were Colson's Christian contacts in and around Washington with former opponents and adversaries, among them another antiwar senator, Mark Hatfield of Oregon. Recognizing in the characters of these targets for his previous hostility the changes that had come into their lives, and beginning to notice changes within himself, Colson saw a sequence of events recurring again and again. "Even though I didn't fully understand what it meant to follow Christ, I could see that those who did follow Christ really had changed," he has recalled. "The big contrast in me that appeared in this period was between the old man who had gone out of his way to have broken or hostile relationships and the new man who wanted to heal those relationships."

Such thoughts led Colson to make an attempt to heal and minister to the beleaguered occupant of the Oval Office—Richard M. Nixon.

Advising Nixon

Colson and Nixon maintained a surprisingly close relationship throughout 1973 and 1974. Both were deeply troubled and beleaguered, but Nixon was far lonelier, with fewer friends and no "brothers" to sustain him. These were good reasons why both men reached out to each other at visible times of crisis in their respective journeys toward catastrophe.

On the night when Colson took the Fifth rather than testify before the Ervin Committee, the president called him at home to say, "Well, at least you've got one friend left in this town." The rest of the conversation consisted largely of Nixon giving his former special counsel a series of pep talks on how to build up his law practice, how to stay ahead of the prosecutors, and how to advise Vice President Agnew. One of Colson's partners was Agnew's legal counsel in the plea bargaining deal that was about to end in his resignation with a nolo contendere response to a charge of tax evasion. The president, via Colson, was clearly trying to edge his vice president out quietly, rather than having an impeachment fight. "We have made the best possible deal for him," said Nixon. "It's right for both Ted and the country."

Losing a vice president on criminal charges was by no means the most damaging problem facing Nixon in this period. Rocked by worse and worse revelations over Watergate, the president had to find a new chief of staff to replace the dismissed Haldeman, and to appoint a new lawyer for his own defense in the legal battle over the White House tapes. Colson's recommendations of General Alexander Haig for the first role and James St. Clair for the second were both accepted. These were not the only personnel matters in which Colson became involved. He sorted out an earthshaking row between Haig and press secretary Ron Ziegler, which might otherwise have ended in Haig's resignation. He was on the phone and in correspondence with the president on many other matters. But even Colson did not realize quite how desperate life had become for Nixon until he was summoned to the White House on December 18, 1973, for a very strange meeting.

Instead of going straight to the Oval Office or to the president's EOB hideaway, Colson was taken on a detour to the second floor of the White House by Nixon's military aide, Steve Bull, who said to him: "No one knows you're seeing the boss. He's upstairs in the Lincoln sitting room. Safer that way. Can't even trust the staff in the West Wing anymore."

The mood of paranoia deepened when Colson, who was meeting the president for the first time since the disclosure of the secret White House taping system, tried to introduce a note of humor into the opening pleasantries by saying that he hoped their conversation wasn't being recorded. Nixon sat bolt upright in his chair, looking frightened. "What do you mean, recorded?" he asked. "Who would do that to us?"

Colson tried to explain that he had only been joking, but Nixon kept interrupting. "Can I trust the Secret Service, Chuck? I don't know that I can. You don't suppose Jaworski would bug *this* room, do you?" Colson, no admirer of the new special prosecutor, Leon Jaworski, nevertheless did his best to reassure the president that this was impossible. Nixon was not satisfied. "The problem, Chuck, is that I don't think I can trust anybody, not even the secretaries," he muttered.

As if to demonstrate his mistrust, Nixon then asked Colson for his recollection of various conversations they had held together in the Oval Office. His responses were checked carefully by the president against sheets of paper piled high on his lap. They were evidently the tape transcripts, although Nixon did not say so. Time and again he interrupted Colson's memories to ask, "You're sure of that, are you?" Eventually, when the president's inquiring seemed to be finished, he asked a final question: "Are you sure you never asked me to grant clemency to Hunt, Chuck?"

"Positive," replied Colson. "I started to once and you cut me off. I remember it well."

"Good, good, so long as you are positive. Well, let's talk about more pleasant subjects," said the president. It was not at all clear what he meant by this. The only clue was that Nixon seemed intrigued by the recent press reports about Colson's religious conversion. Although this subject was now of paramount importance to him, Colson felt too inhibited to talk about it. Instead of emulating Tom Phillips with an attempt to evangelize his companion in the Lincoln sitting room, Colson came over all shy. "The papers will print anything nowadays," he said weakly. "Crazy times, Mr. President."

For months and years afterward, Colson reproached himself for having missed his opportunity to give Christian witness to the president. However, it seems unlikely that Nixon would ever have responded favorably to such overtures. A few weeks earlier Colson had suggested, through Nixon's personal secretary, Rose Mary Woods, that Harold Hughes should be invited into the White House to pray with the president.

"You've got to be kidding, Chuck," retorted the fiery Rose. "After the terrible things that man has said about the president, I never want to see them in the same room." There is little doubt that Miss Woods was echoing her master's voice. Nixon's overdeveloped sense of personal privacy made him hate the idea of sharing his spiritual feelings with strangers. Colson may well have got closer to him in this area than anyone else, particularly on the night before the National Prayer Breakfast in January 1974 when the two men had a long and deeply personal telephone call. Nixon gave an address of high quality to the prayer breakfast the following morning using several of Colson's ideas. However, since Nixon said soon after the event, "I'd rather go to the dentist without an anesthetic than to go to another of those darn prayer breakfasts," it would appear that he was still a long way from being converted by anything Colson had said to him.

Nixon was sinking both personally and politically at this time. He was also taking a lot of people down with him. One of the saddest, yet finest, of those going down was thirty-one-year-old Egil "Bud" Krogh, who had pleaded guilty to charges relating to his role in the Fielding break-in as head of the Plumbers. A week before Krogh began his sentence at the Allenwood prison, in Pennsylvania, Colson invited him to join him and his four brothers for a prayer session at Fellowship House. The encounter turned out to be an inspirational experience, but more for Colson than for Krogh, who was the one who did most of the inspiring.

Colson was expecting his former White House colleague to look gaunt and haggard, weighed down by the fear of going to prison. Instead, Bud Krogh seemed to be suffused with physical vigor and emotional vitality. He explained that he and his wife, Suzanne, were spending several hours a day in prayer and Bible study. "It may seem a bit strange," said Krogh, "but we really thank God for what has happened to us." The depth of his faith stunned the normally voluble Doug Coe and Harold Hughes into silence, making a great impact on all the brothers, especially Colson. Colson, in his heart of hearts, was scared of going to prison. He had heard too many stories of violence behind bars and how it was sometimes used as a tool of revenge against former government officials who fell foul of the law. There was a real risk that bitter prisoners might take it out on officials of the Nixon administration who joined them in jail. Yet Bud Krogh's faith obviously gave him real serenity in the face of his coming adversity. Colson was awed by Krogh's courage, which contrasted so favorably with his own and Richard Nixon's fearfulness. In a moment of premonition, Colson asked himself, Could the Lord be using Bud to help me prepare for the path ahead?

Feeling the Heat

Colson was a prime target for the Watergate special prosecutor's office, whose activities seemed to him to be just as much influenced by the galleries of politics and the media as they were by the courts of law. In the play to the first two galleries, Colson, after the president, was the great white whale whom the prosecutors longed to harpoon. This was partly Colson's own fault. His robust, some might say reckless, support for Nixon on numerous TV shows in 1973 had given him the highest and most pugnacious of profiles. His new Christian profile had not helped him either. His lawyer, David Shapiro, longed for a breathing space, with Colson out of the headlines, so that purely legal considerations could be quietly applied to his case. For courts of law require evidence. The problem for even the most partisan of prosecutors was that the factual evidence against Colson was nonexistent in the Watergate break-in case and weak in the Ellsberg case.

The first federal prosecutor who investigated the case against Colson, Seymour Glanzer, concluded that there was no evidence to support an indictment. When he reported his findings to the newly appointed special prosecutor, Archibald Cox, the reaction was unexpected. "Where's Colson? Why isn't he in this? We've got to get Colson," demanded Cox, apparently exhibiting more political bias than prosecutorial balance. With those instructions in mind, the assistant special prosecutor who replaced

Glanzer, William Merrill, went after Colson with renewed zeal. But all the zeal available produced nothing whatever to link Colson with the Watergate burglary.

As for the Ellsberg break-in, there was evidence that Colson had been a conduit, via CREEP to John Ehrlichman, for passing along the $5,000 that was used to fund the Plumbers' expenses for their raid on Dr. Fielding's office. But Colson said when he asked Ehrlichman what the money was for, he received the answer: "Don't ask. It's a national security matter." Ehrlichman subsequently confirmed this to David Shapiro. So Colson's guilty knowledge, or *mens rea,* in the Ellsberg break-in was likely to be impossible to prove.

In spite of these fundamental weaknesses in the prosecution's case against Colson, five days after his August 30 appearance before the grand jury, assistant special prosecutor William Merrill formally warned David Shapiro that his client's indictment was "imminent." This was bluff. The wiser heads in the special prosecutor's office continued to advise their boss, Professor Cox, that there was no evidence on which Colson could be indicted. After the firing of Archibald Cox in the Saturday night massacre of October 20 (an episode in which Colson played no part), it looked for a while as though the new special prosecutor, Leon Jaworski, might be accepting the difficulties of proving a case against the president's hatchet man. High-pressure interrogations by Jaworski's team of all Colson's White House staffers failed to yield any incriminating testimony. Meanwhile, Shapiro's team was jubilant as their client passed three lie detector tests in which he was grilled with charges on Watergate, Ellsberg, and the alleged offer of clemency to Hunt. If Colson had been a low-level suspect on the prosecutors' hit list, it is unlikely from this point on in the saga that much more would have been heard about his case. But as the big fish the special prosecutor longed to catch, Colson needed to be hauled in with unusual angling methods. This became apparent during a meeting between Jaworski, Colson, and their two legal teams at a meeting held on January 11, 1974.

"Mr. Colson, unless my staff can show me a lot more evidence, I would not include you in the Watergate cover-up indictment," said Jaworski, with a smile as cold as the silver plate on a casket, when he came to the end of a grueling two-hour session of questions and legal arguments. The discussion had started with a threat of two indictments. Jaworski was clearly inclined to drop one of them. But after a long pause, he continued, "Of course, even if you are not indicted, there is still this Ellsberg thing." To

Colson's ears, the last six words sounded like harbingers of yet another round of bluffing and pressurizing. That impression was confirmed a few moments later when Jaworski said to Shapiro, "Why don't you, Dave, get together with Bill here"—the special prosecutor pointed to his assistant William Merrill—"and see if you can't work it out. I think Mr. Colson really wants to wipe the slate clean and look forward to a useful career as a citizen and as *a lawyer.*"

In the coded language of plea bargaining, Jaworski's words spoke volumes to all the lawyers present in the room. Colson was being offered a deal. What Jaworski appeared to be saying, without spelling it out specifically, was: Plead guilty to a misdemeanor, cooperate with the prosecutors, and you will receive, at the maximum, a one-year prison sentence, but more probably a term of probation. A plea to a misdemeanor will allow you to continue to practice law. If, on the other hand, you are tried on charges of felony and are found guilty, you can expect a prison term of up to five years and disbarment from your profession as a lawyer.

As Jaworski left the room, Colson might have been expected to feel gratitude and relief at the offer of avoiding a trial on two counts of felony. However, as the discussion between Merrill and Shapiro got under way, the small print of the deal became clear. To keep his side of the bargain Colson would need to swear under oath that he had been guilty of conspiring to break into the office of Daniel Ellsberg's psychiatrist, Dr. Fielding. In addition, the special prosecutor's staff wanted Colson's testimony, in advance, against other Watergate figures, including Nixon.

The more he pondered Jaworski's proposals, the more uneasy Colson became about them. Over the next few days, Shapiro intensified his negotiations with the special prosecutor's office. Sometimes he came back sunk in gloom, saying, "They're out to get your butt, no matter what." On other days he was upbeat after bargaining keenly with Merrill over the vital details that would preserve Colson's license to practice law. "We're making progress," reported Shapiro, dancing a little jig as he delivered what he thought was good news to his worried client. "C'mon, smile! I'm going to walk you out of this a free man."

Colson was not in the mood to share his partner's festive spirits. "Dave, I just don't know that I can do this," he said.

"Chuck, you gotta be off your rocker," replied Shapiro, aghast. "You'll do it or I'll have you committed to the funny farm."

Colson's commitment to his newfound Christian conscience was the source of his anxiety. Once it was established that the first part of the plea bargain deal required him to swear on oath that he had known and approved the break-in to the psychiatrist's office, he was greatly troubled. He was also concerned about the second part of the deal—cooperating with the prosecutors in other cases—because he had so greatly admired Bud Krogh's refusal to plea bargain on the very same grounds. Trading testimony against others in return for leniency to himself went against the grain. On the other hand, Colson longed for an end to his legal nightmares. He felt he owed it to his family—particularly to his father, Wendell Sr., whose health was visibly deteriorating under the strain of sharing in his son's pressures—to make a clean break and to start life again. So once more Colson found himself impaled on the horns of a difficult dilemma. In search of an answer to it he went to see Harold Hughes.

In the months since the five brothers had been meeting together for their Monday morning fellowship breakfasts, Hughes was the one who had become Colson's closest confidant. For all his idiosyncrasies, Hughes, with his salty language, political realism, yet overpowering Christian love, was the most practical bridge builder between the old and new Colson. The two men met frequently on a one-on-one basis between the weekly breakfasts. So it was no great surprise when Colson dropped in to Hughes's home the Saturday after Jaworski's offer, with the opening line "Brother, I need help."

Colson explained his dilemma in precise detail, emphasizing his extreme reluctance at the prospect of testifying against Nixon and his extreme disquiet at the prospect of pleading guilty to actions he had not actually taken. "Are you guilty of what you'd have to plead to, Chuck?" asked Hughes. "Legally no," replied Colson. "I didn't order the burglary at the psychiatrist's. I didn't know about it until it was over. But I'm not sure there's much moral difference. I'd have done anything to stop Ellsberg, anything the president ordered."

"That's not the point, Chuck," said Hughes. "Is what you would have to say in court true in your own heart? I mean between you and God."

"No," replied Colson. "The misdemeanor plea would require me to say I knew and approved the break-in. This would not be true."

Having extracted the answer to the crucial question, Hughes backed off from giving advice on it. "Well, you are going to have to ask Christ to give you the answer, brother," he said. "If it were me with my family involved and all the rest, I don't know if I could turn it down. . . . I can tell you the correct answer, but I'm not sure I'd follow it myself, so how can I advise you?"

Colson's next stop on the advice-taking trail was his own family. His son Wendell Jr., responding to a father-to-son phone call at his student lodgings

at Princeton, said, "Do what is right, Dad." Patty agreed that the plea bargain deal was wrong but her body language seemed to be saying "Take it,"
all the same. Colson flew to Boston to see his two youngest children,
seventeen-year-old Chris and fifteen-year-old Emily. He gave them a long
explanation of the various legal options that had been offered to him. Then
he asked if they understood the difference between a felony and a misdemeanor.

"Sure," said Emily. "A misdemeanor means only a one-year prison sentence."

"Most of my friends already think you're in jail," chipped in Chris, "so
that doesn't matter."

The Colson kids were growing up fast. Yet the family's participation in
the extended discussion on the pros and cons of the plea bargain deal with
the prosecutors did not yield a decisive result until Emily spoke out. "Did
you do what they want you to say you did?" she demanded.

"No, I didn't," replied Colson.

"Well then, don't say you did it," she said firmly.

"Out of the mouths of babes and sucklings has thou ordained strength,"
says the psalmist. Fifteen-year-old Emily, by the moral clarity of her answer,
gave her father the strength he needed to reject the plea bargain deal.

David Shapiro was furious, and so were the prosecutors. They now had
to face the choice of dropping Colson from their planned list of indictments or of proceeding with felony charges, which on the available evidence would be very hard to make stick. Perhaps unsurprisingly, given the
climate of hysteria that continued to surround the Watergate saga, they
opted for the high road of felony charges.

At 9:30 A.M. on Friday, March 1, David Shapiro walked into Colson's
office. His woebegone face told the whole story before he articulated
the bad news. "The prosecutor just called," he began. Then, after a sorrowful pause, he gave Colson the thumbs-down sign, saying, "I'm sorry. I'm
sorry." It was a time for tears and embraces—from Patty, who had come
into the office to hear the news; from Holly Holm, his secretary; and from
Colson's two senior law partners, Shapiro and Morin.

Eight days later, on March 8, Colson walked up the steps of the federal
courthouse in Washington, D.C., to enter his plea to the charges against
him. The scene around him was one of media mayhem. The indictments
that had been handed down included Bob Haldeman, John Ehrlichman,
John Mitchell, Charles Colson, plus three much less important figures
in the Nixon administration—Gordon Strachan, Kenneth Parkinson, and

Robert Mardian. In the courtroom of journalism, all had already been judged guilty. Indictment and conviction had become blurred into a single entity in many of the front pages and news bulletins. Outside the court, the surging crowd of reporters and cameramen had the mood of a lynch mob.

Inside Judge John Sirica's courtroom, Colson was wondering how to conduct himself toward his fellow defendants. For all their past tensions and enmities, this was a time for the former hatchet man to be burying his hatchet. Conscious that he was now "Christ's man," Colson made all the right moves toward reconciliation. He exchanged warm handshakes and kind words with Haldeman, Ehrlichman, and Mitchell. The harsh expression on the face of the ex–attorney general relaxed and turned into a smile as Colson wished him well. There was a moment of Christian encouragement to the youngest of the defendants, twenty-seven-year-old Gordon Strachan. "Hang in there, Gordon," said Colson, knowing that this junior Haldeman aide was now a regular Bible reader. "God will give you the strength if you ask."

Judge Sirica ordered all seven defendants to stand at the bar of the court below his bench as the arraignments were read out. The surreal words "The United States of America charges Charles W. Colson . . ." rang out sonorously, followed by the counts of the indictment and the question "How do you plead?" Through a parched mouth and pinched lips, Colson managed to get out the words "Not guilty to all counts." It was the right legal answer to those specific charges. But other considerations soon began to lead Colson in a different direction.

Liberation

"It would be nice to be able to say that my reasons for entering a plea of guilty were all down to my Christian conscience, but in fact they were a mixture of the practical as well as the spiritual," said Charles Colson in a retrospective analysis of his actions and motives in the period from March to June 1974. The ninety-four days between his indictment and his change of plea to one of guilty were at first the most difficult but eventually the most liberating time of his life. How he sorted out his priorities into a coherent course of action is a revealing story.

On Monday, March 3, forty-eight hours after his arraignment in Judge Gerhard Gesell's courtroom, Colson attended the regular weekly breakfast meeting with his four prayer partners at Fellowship House. All of them were shaken by the tidal wave of media coverage of the indictments over the weekend.

"Brother, look at it this way. It's good. We've got a Christian in the news," was Doug Coe's Pollyannaish opening comment. Colson had a more somber reaction. "In view of the indictments, shouldn't I withdraw from this fellowship?" he asked. "Two of you are in public office and this thing could hurt you."

The brothers wouldn't hear of it. Congressman Al Quie set the tone with his instant response to Colson's question. "If you're indicted, Chuck, we all are. We're together. That's the way it is." Al Quie was the quietest man but in some ways the strongest man in the group. He had taken to Colson more slowly than the others because he was more uncertain about the genuineness of his conversion. Quie was a good judge of such matters. He had been deeply rooted in his faith since accepting Christ into his life as a child. Known among his fellow congressmen as "the straightest of straight arrows," he had evidently walked his talk through the minefields of politics. He was serious about scripture and knowledgeable in biblical theology. Away from Capitol Hill, his passion was training horses, but he also had a good eye for the training of men.

Back in his White House days, Colson had been dismissive of Quie, referring to him as "the milk drinker." This was a put-down acquired from Nixon, who never got over the Minnesota congressman's request at a presidential reception to be served a glass of milk instead of wine or spirits. In the weeks after his indictment, Colson became closer to Quie, seeing him not as "the milk drinker" but as his Bible mentor. "He was the solid rock of the brothers," recalled Colson. "Al had the biggest influence on me. He was my role model."

For his part, Quie no longer had any doubts about Colson's religious sincerity. However, after being told all the facts of the Ellsberg case, he had doubts over the wisdom of a not guilty plea. Nevertheless he kept these doubts to himself, committing them to daily prayer. He was encouraged that Colson's spiritual journey seemed to be taking him to deeper levels of faith that were more challenging than the superficial affirmations of "feel-good Christianity" that so often characterized the brothers' conversations at their fellowship breakfasts. "I could see that Chuck was moving into a more profound relationship with the Lord," recalled Quie. "I think this started when we went away to a house on the eastern shore of Maryland for a weekend retreat on the scriptures, conducted by Richard Lovelace. He really got Chuck focusing on the Word. Afterward I could see there was a step change in Colson's concept of Christian accountability. In fact, I've never seen anyone who became so committed to his brothers as Chuck did. He would never do something we didn't agree with."

At first, some of the brothers seemed to agree that Colson should fight to the death to prove his innocence. One of the first moves in this strategy was to persuade the judge to accept a delay motion on the grounds that a fair trial had been prejudiced by the massive pretrial publicity accusing Colson of every Watergate crime under the sun. In support of the delay motion, Colson's defense lawyers wanted to exhibit all the derogatory articles on their client that had been published in the last two years. "You've got to be kidding," said Colson. "There must be thousands of articles. We'd need fifty people full-time. It's impossible."

Doug Coe had other ideas. He and his aide John Bishop recruited over eighty volunteers to cut out and collate the mountains of anti-Colson stories that had appeared across the country in newspapers and magazines. Calling themselves "Christians for Colson," these volunteers worked around the clock in shifts at the law firm for the next three weeks. Under Coe's leadership, a wonderful spirit was created by these toiling Christians, who achieved their gargantuan task with hours to spare. On the eve of the hearing of the delay motion, thirty-nine volumes of press clippings had been neatly color-coded and cataloged for presentation to Judge Gesell. Alas, it was a labor in vain. On May 1, the judge dismissed the motion for delay and with it a motion to have the case transferred to a city less suffused with Watergate fever than Washington. So on the legal battlefield, Colson was back to square one.

The defeat over the pretrial motions was only one of the blows raining in on Colson in the spring of 1974. He had to resign from his law partnership, which led to worries about his future financial security. He was devastated by the release of the first set of White House tapes, which showed Nixon in the worst of lights—profane, devious, vacillating, and hurtfully mendacious to and about Colson. The discovery that his hero, the president of the United States, had feet of clay and a lying tongue caused Colson great grief, not least because he became full of remorse for his own contribution to the moral decay of the Nixon administration. The worst blow of all arrived when his loyal White House aide Dick Howard called to say that he had been questioned by the prosecutors about an allegation that Colson had hired a group of thugs to beat up Ellsberg. Howard insisted the allegation was untrue. The prosecutors did not believe him. "They've told me I'm going to be indicted for perjury," he said, his voice breaking as he described the pressures that were being applied to him.

Colson was outraged. He knew that the proposed charges against Howard were utterly untrue and unfair. He also knew that an indictment would have a catastrophic effect on Howard's finances and family life. Colson went round to discuss the Howard crisis with Doug Coe.

"Doug, I can't let this happen to Dick and his family," said Colson. "He has no money. His new job will fall through. If it will get Dick off the hook, I'll plead guilty. I'll say whatever they want me to say."

Coe did his best to calm the distraught Colson, saying firmly, "No, you can't do that. We must get the Lord's answer to this." The Lord's answer eventually arrived through CBS television—the network Colson had loved to hate in his White House years. At this time, there was growing tension among Colson's advisers. In one camp were his lawyers, who wanted their client to shut up in order to keep his legal testimony for his trial. In the other were the evangelistic members of his fellowship group, who wanted their brother to open up with more of his Christian testimony on the media. The leaders of the second group were Doug Coe and Harold Hughes. They persuaded Colson to give an interview about his faith to the CBS current affairs program *60 Minutes* on May 19.

Before an audience of more than 20 million viewers, Mike Wallace put Colson on the spot with tough questions:

WALLACE Have you done more than pray? . . . Have you tried to make it
        up to those you've hurt?
COLSON In my own heart . . .
WALLACE But have you tried to make it up? . . . Have you apologized?
COLSON There are a couple of instances . . .

With Colson's answers coming over as slow and faltering, Wallace attacked with a quick-fire burst of examples of people who deserved apologies. They included Arthur Burns, for the pay rise smear; CBS, for being intimidated; and various journalists whom Colson had attacked. Then came the most uncomfortable part of the interview, which Colson was sharing with Harold Hughes:

WALLACE Let's turn, then, to the White House tapes. Do they show a
        morality in the Oval Office?
HUGHES Not the standards that I would hope to see in the Oval Office,
        no.
WALLACE Do they to you, Mr. Colson?
COLSON I'm not going to try to characterize how I look at those tran-
        scripts, because I don't think you can—
WALLACE Well, wait—
COLSON I've sat in many, many meetings in the Oval Office, Mike, and I
        did not know there was a recording system. I suppose—

WALLACE Is that moral?

COLSON I'm not going to try to draw a moral judgment on it . . .

WALLACE Wait a minute. Let me understand something about this new
Christianity, then. You say that you are a new man in Jesus
Christ. It seems as though your *prior faith* takes precedence
over your *new faith.*

Mike Wallace had hit the bull's-eye. For as Colson knew in his heart, and
as millions of viewers could see with their eyes, there was indeed a conflict
between his old life and his new life. On-screen, Hughes did his best to rescue his floundering brother by describing Colson as "a baby in Christ . . .
not full maturity, not full understanding." Off-screen, Colson was far
harder on himself.

His appearance on *60 Minutes* was a turning point on his journey because it made him face the realization that he could not be a criminal defendant and a faithful witness for Christ at the same time. Another, more
private turning point came a few days later, when Colson visited his ailing
father in the hospital. Wendell was struggling to recover from a heart attack. He asked his son, "Are you innocent of the charges?" Colson assured
him that he had not known in advance of the Ellsberg break-in. Then he
added the less convincing prediction "Don't worry, Dad, we're going to lick
these indictments. The prosecutors won't get a conviction." Almost as he
said those words, the hollow unreality of them troubled his heart. For because of the Watergate fever in Washington, he knew that his chances of
being found not guilty by a D.C. jury were extremely slim. According to his
lawyers, he had excellent chances of winning his freedom on appeal. However, that process could take another three years and the erosion of his life
savings. Could he and his family bear the drip, drip, drip of legal and media water tortures for that length of time? And could he bear the burden
of watching his innocent aide Dick Howard go through the devastating
agony of a perjury trial all because of him? These were the practical pressures weighing on Colson in the third week of May 1974. He shared his
agony over them in prayer with his brothers.

"In my fumbling way I was calling out for help in the fellowship as never
before," he recalled. "I knew that I could not go on living in two worlds that
were colliding. In the battles I was fighting in my old world, I was losing
every time. I hadn't had a single break in the courts, in the media, or anywhere. Not one! Yet as I thought about it, I realized that God was at work,
stripping away the ugliness of my old world, piece by piece. And simultane-

ously he was showing me the beauty of a new way to live in his world. But I could only see that beauty through the pain of the stripping away process. If it hadn't been for all the negatives of my defeats and reverses, I suppose I would have had a pain-free conversion experience that would not have been authentic. I'd have started going to a good church. I expect I'd have done quite a few good things with my life. But without being stripped and broken, I could not have gone out and served Christ in the way that happened."

A text that spoke to Colson and his brothers as they prayed together at this time was Philippians 3:8: "I consider everything as loss compared to the surpassing greatness of knowing Christ Jesus my Lord, for whose sake I have lost all things." Yet Colson, for all his many defects and losses, had not quite given up all things. He and his lawyers were still fighting to win some new and crucially important pretrial motions, including one that would have allowed him to plead a defense of having been motivated in his actions toward Ellsberg by national security considerations. He was still pleading not guilty. His two worlds were still in conflict.

A further sign of how much this conflict was troubling Colson came on May 22, when he addressed a Christian prayer breakfast meeting in Owosso, Michigan. Toward the end of his extempore talk, he heard himself deliver the sentence "I know in my own heart that I am innocent of many of the charges against me." The good folk of Owosso would probably not have noticed anything out of the ordinary about this part of the speech had Colson not stopped in his tracks. With a hot flush spreading over his face, his mind and conscience went into rewind. Then he froze over the words he had just spoken: "*many* of the charges." Did that mean he was admitting he was not innocent of *all* the charges?

After an embarrassing pause, Colson corrected himself: "Er . . . I am innocent of all the charges I stand accused of." Nobody in the audience seemed to have spotted his slip. But as he flew back to Washington to resume his meetings with his lawyers, the words that highlighted his dilemma came back to haunt him over and over again. Many, but not *all* the charges?

Although he would not have recognized the term at that time, Colson was engaging in that most agonizing of spiritual disciplines—the examination of conscience. Out of the depths of depression he cried to God for help. What God helped him to see was that his lack of direct involvement in the break-in at the offices of Ellsberg's psychiatrist was pure happenstance. He had obtained the money to pay for a covert operation against Ellsberg. He had tried to smear Ellsberg in the press in much the same way as the CIA and the staff of the Ervin Committee had been smearing him. Now that he could see how wrong and how prejudicial to a defendant's legal rights that kind of conduct could be, in all conscience before God he could not fight against his criminally culpable involvement. He must give up the conflict of fighting on two fronts. If surrendering on the battlefields of his old world meant going to prison, he knew he had to accept it as God's will.

These agonizings and the surrender to God that came at the end of them marked an important turning point in Colson's spiritual journey. Until this time he had never thought of himself as a bad person. Although in the arena of politics he had done many a dirty trick playing hardball against opponents, in his self-justifying eyes these games seemed no worse than those played by the Democrats. So by his own standards Colson regarded himself as a good person. He thought God would agree and would eventually give him A grades, in the manner of a celestial college professor at the end of the life examination class. These certainties crumbled to dust as Colson's spiritual conscience convicted him of sin. As he went through many dark nights of the soul, his conviction took him on a downward spiral into an abyss of shame and remorse.

"In the months that followed the night in Tom Phillips's driveway I felt really unclean, unworthy, and in despair," Colson has recalled. "My despair was at its deepest when I realized what a sinful person I was. I remember reading Paul's words about being the worst of sinners and I knew that they applied to me too. I thought a lot about all the people I had hurt. I didn't fully understand it at the time, but now I do. It is exactly what God has to do when he gives us his redeeming love. He strips us bare, breaks us down, and exposes us as we really are—not as we think we are. Then as a continuing process of his redemption, having convicted us of our sin, he leads us to repentance and to a change of our hearts and minds."

The next manifestation of the change of heart and mind in Colson was that he decided to plead guilty. Patty was the first person to be told of the decision. She did not understand and at first she fought against it. "Why? Why do you have to do it?" she kept asking. "Dave says you'll be acquitted. Then our lives will be normal again. You'll be practicing law. We can travel."

Colson had to work hard to persuade his wife to share his vision. "Trust me that this is the way things will get better," he told her. "I just have to do it." Eventually, with an aching heart, Patty agreed.

The next stop was Harold Hughes—the nearest available brother on that fateful weekend. After hearing Colson's explanation for his new decision, Hughes asked, "How much time will you get?"

"Five years is maximum," replied Colson, mysteriously feeling far less fearful than he ever had before at the prospect of prison.

"That's tough. I don't think I could do it," said the grim-faced Hughes.

"I'm going to," said Colson, "unless you and the other brothers disagree. I'm convinced I must."

Hughes suddenly broke into unexpected rejoicing. "Hallelujah!" he shouted, his face beaming with happiness. "I could never have advised you to do it, but I've been waiting for this day. It kills me, it hurts me, but I'm swelling up with joy!"

The next confidant to react to the news was the opposite of joyful. David Shapiro exploded into obscenities. Almost his only printable comment was "You are nuts, crazy, you've gone *meshuga*." Colson, who was used to shouting matches with his partner, had to hold the telephone away from his ear for some minutes as Shapiro's tirade continued, eventually ending with the announcement "I'm taking you to a shrink on Monday morning!"

"Dave, calm down. It's a decision I've reached and I know what I am doing," said Colson. "I want you to talk to the prosecutors Monday. See Bill Merrill. Tell him we want no deal, no strings. Just say I'm ready to plead guilty."

As Shapiro gradually simmered down, Colson, sitting at his kitchen table in Virginia, suggested that one charge he could plead guilty to with a clear conscience would be that of disseminating derogatory information to the press about Daniel Ellsberg while he was a criminal defendant.

"It's not a crime," retorted Shapiro. "How can I plead that for you? No one has ever been charged with that."

Colson said he thought the prosecutor might accept it as an obstruction of justice charge.

"You're an idiot," shouted Shapiro. "You are going to end up in the slammer."

"I know," was the soft answer. When Colson finally put down the telephone having instructed his lawyer to offer his plea of guilty, for the first time in many months he felt a great sense of peace. Colson's worlds were no longer in conflict. He was liberated from his past, even though prison was his immediate future.

CHAPTER TWELVE

Prison

Final Preparations

Colson had anticipated that the acceptance of his plea would be easy and that his sentence would be light. Neither expectation was fulfilled. Although the prosecutors were initially positive when they received Shapiro's call on Monday, May 27, difficulties soon emerged with the judge. Gerhard Gesell, who was on vacation at his summer home in Maine, needed to be convinced that what Colson was pleading to was a crime. As Shapiro had pointed out during his Saturday morning shouting match with Colson, no one had ever before pleaded guilty to an offense of "disseminating information" prejudicial to another party's legal rights. What had Colson actually done? What law had he broken?

Ironically, it fell to Shapiro to prepare the argument that would persuade the judge of his client's criminality. The facts were that back in the summer of 1971, when Pentagon Papers fever was at its height, Colson had set out, in the words of his own memorandum, "to paint Ellsberg black." As part of that exercise, Colson had acquired a two-page FBI report on Ellsberg's lawyer, Leonard Boudin. This report was so tabloid in its tone and so flawed in its facts that even a scandal sheet like the *National Enquirer* would have hesitated before publishing it. Colson gave the report to a highly reputable journalist, Jerald ter Horst of the *Detroit News* (later to become President Gerald Ford's press secretary). Ter Horst took one look at the report's tawdry rumors about Ellsberg's alleged sexual practices and communist affiliations, then he spiked it.

Precisely how Colson's failed leaking effort to Jerry ter Horst actually prejudiced Daniel Ellsberg's legal rights is a question that remains unanswered. Shapiro, laboring on his client's behalf to come up with an answer, had a meeting with Judge Gesell and the prosecutors and offered a solution. "Colson is willing to plead guilty to obstruction of justice," said Shapiro, "but the problem is that he didn't do what he has been indicted for because he didn't know a damn thing about the plan to break in to Fielding's office and get Ellsberg's records. But what he did do was to instigate a process to attempt to blacken a criminal defendant's name."

"Yeah, he sure did that," said Gesell.

"Well, I can't find that's a crime," said Shapiro, "but that's what we're pleading to."

"I'll take the plea," said Judge Gesell.

With Shapiro still playing the highly unusual role for a defense lawyer of drafting the charges, he produced the proposition that Colson's activities might have violated 18 USC section 1503, which deals with obstruction of justice. The actual words of the charge under this statute were these: "In July and August 1971, the defendant Charles W. Colson endeavored to and did release defamatory and derogatory allegations concerning one of the attorneys engaged in the legal defense of Daniel Ellsberg for the purpose of publicly disseminating the said allegations the known and probable consequences of which would be to influence, obstruct and impede the conduct and outcome of the criminal prosecution of Daniel Ellsberg."

In any other jurisdiction or period of history the validity of a defendant's plea of guilty to such a unique charge would surely have been hotly argued over. In Washington, at the height of the Watergate drama, it was gratefully accepted. Judge Gesell not only went along with it; he warned Shapiro that Colson should expect a tough prison sentence for his crime.

"You understand, Mr. Shapiro, *if* I accept this plea, that my policy with high government officials is to impose a prison sentence," said Gesell.

"I understand, Your Honor, and Mr. Colson does too," replied Shapiro.

"There can be no deal here," continued the judge. "There is no understanding in advance about sentence. You and Mr. Colson are coming before me voluntarily with no limits on what I may do."

When the judge's ominous words were reported to him, Colson became extremely pessimistic about his chances of receiving a noncustodial penalty such as a suspended sentence or probation. However, he did believe that his jail term would be a short one. The logical benchmark he had in mind was Bud Krogh's six-month sentence for his plea of guilty to the more serious offense of masterminding the Ellsberg break-in. On the other hand, Colson well knew that in several Watergate cases, judicial severity had superseded judicial logic. So he prepared himself for the worst—which could be a five-year sentence.

By contrast, Patty prepared herself only for the best. She was in denial as the date for the guilty plea before the court, June 3, drew nearer. "I'm scared, Chuck, I don't know if I can go through with it," she told her husband. In truth, they were both scared. Colson had been worried by press reports on the frequency of homosexual rape in the D.C. jail. Patty was fearful about living on her own. Over many years she had developed an aversion to spending a night alone. Colson was an exceptionally considerate husband toward her anxieties. He made great efforts never to leave his wife by herself in their house, which was surrounded by woodlands and isolated from neighbors. So when he could not get back from an out-of-town trip, he invariably asked his secretary, Holly Holm, to sleep over at the Colson residence to keep Patty company. Such marital protectiveness was now in jeopardy and at the mercy of the court.

Patty could not bring herself to face these realities. She started the habit of ending every conversation about the coming court appearance with the surreal words "Well, it's just not going to happen, that's all."

Another new and better habit that started at this time was husband-and-wife prayer. This was a big breakthrough. Ever since Colson's conversion experience Patty had kept a somewhat awkward distance from her spouse's journey into faith. She supported it, but she preferred her own, more private, Catholic spirituality. Whenever Chuck came home with enthusiastic reports from his meetings with the brothers of shared prayers and confessions, Patty's attitude had been "If it makes you happy, it's fine with me." Although she liked the brothers and their wives she did not want to imitate them in their religious ways.

Under the pressures of adversity, Patty changed. One evening during this intense period of waiting and worrying Colson said to her, "Honey, let's pray about it. Let's ask God to protect us both and help us face what we must." At that moment, for the first time in their lives, Mr. and Mrs. Colson began praying together. Their first prayers were silent ones, but in time, Colson used spontaneous oral interventions. At this most crucial moment in his life he had found a new prayer partner.

On Sunday, June 2, Colson convened a special meeting of his more usual prayer partners. His purpose was to ask his brothers' blessing on his proposed plea of guilty the following morning. The discussions did not go entirely according to plan. Al Quie, who Colson had come to regard as his mentor and role model, was grounded in Minnesota by a thunderstorm. Graham Purcell, normally the quietest and most easygoing member of the group, entered a surprisingly strong objection. It was all the more powerful because he had been a district judge in Texas prior to his election to Congress.

"But what you are pleading to isn't any crime, nor do they have a case against you in either indictment," said Purcell. "You can't just up and decide to go to prison. I don't think being a Christian requires you to do that."

Doug Coe and Harold Hughes supported Colson's plan. They started praying for Judge Gesell to accept the guilty plea on Monday morning. "You guys can't expect me to pray for the judge to do this," interrupted Purcell, pacing up and down the room in high dudgeon. At that moment Al Quie finally came through on the phone. His opinion was swift and decisive: "I think it's tremendous. I have been expecting you to do this and I'm with you all the way. God bless you, brother."

Quie's strength weakened Purcell's objection. Eventually, after much further pacing and agonizing, the former judge and Texas congressman said to Colson: "If this is what it takes to give you freedom of the spirit, then I'm with you. But it hurts, man it hurts." After that the brothers prayed in unity until after midnight.

The following morning, just before setting off to court, Colson had an important call to make—to the president of the United States. Nixon was tied up with visitors in the Oval Office so he could not come to the line immediately. Colson asked to be put through to the president's in-house lawyer, Fred Buzhardt. "Fred, please tell the president right now so he gets it from me first," said Colson. "I'm pleading guilty this morning," he said.

"Oh no," gasped Buzhardt. "But why?"

"Just the truth, Fred. I have to. I'll explain later," replied Colson, "but I'm not turning against the president. Only telling the truth." Like the men in the White House, the men in the courthouse were flabbergasted by Colson's plea of guilty. No one, except for Shapiro and the prosecutors, was expecting it. As Colson arrived in court he came face-to-face with the former leader of the Plumbers, G. Gordon Liddy, who had been brought out of jail for a subpoena hearing. Liddy was the weirdest of the Watergaters. A crazy brave of iron will and unhinged judgment, he was stoically enduring the twenty-year sentence passed on him by Judge "Maximum John" Sirica, rather than cooperate with the prosecutors. At the sight of Colson,

Liddy leapt to his feet and gave him a smart military salute. Little did Liddy know that his revered icon Colson was about to break the hard man's code of silence and enter, because he had become God's man, a plea of guilty.

The judge announced that before Liddy's subpoena issue was argued there would be "a deposition." Experienced court reporters sat up with surprise, knowing that this meant a plea of guilty. Who could it be from? There was amazement a few moments later when Colson stepped forward to the bar of the court to hear the charges against him read out. Judge Gesell then asked him if he understood that by pleading guilty he waived his constitutional rights to a trial.

"Yes sir," said Colson. Then in a shaky voice he read out a fifty-three-word prepared statement: "I have come to believe in the very depths of my being that official threats to the right of fair trial for defendants such as those charged in this information must be stopped; and by this plea, Your Honor, I am prepared to take whatever consequences I must to help in stopping them."

"Do you still wish to plead guilty?" asked the judge.

"Yes I do, Your Honor," replied Colson. It was his final step in this courtroom ritual. All that was left to happen was for the reporters to sprint to the telephones and for Gesell to fix the sentencing date for June 21, 1974.

Sentenced

To Colson skeptics, of whom there were still a great many, his plea of guilty was seen as a move of expediency rather than a change of heart. *Newsweek* captured this mood in a four-page article headlined BEAT THE DEVIL. Its presumption was that the onetime hatchet man had traded damaging secrets against others in return for leniency to himself. As one source for the article put it, "I'm convinced he's going to lash out in spite of his so-called conversion. He is going to say, 'I am the avenging angel of the Lord.' "

The prosecutors who had struck the deal with Shapiro were similar believers in the vengeance theory. They were sure that Colson would now incriminate his former colleagues. They expected a rich harvest of testimony from their contrite defendant. When Colson was called in for an interview he was assured that he had been granted immunity for any perjury he might have committed in his previous interviews. Would he now testify truthfully? For a start, how about telling the true story of how he and

Nixon ordered the firebombing of the Brookings Institution? "I told you the truth about Brookings," replied Colson. "I never ordered it to be bombed or set fire to."

"Now you *are* committing perjury," warned prosecutor Henry Ruth. Colson stuck to his guns on this and a whole range of other issues on which he remained wholly truthful.

Over on Capitol Hill, the House Judiciary Committee, chaired by Congressman Rodino, assumed that Colson would help them in their impeachment proceedings against the president. They were disappointed. At an informal session of questioning by committee staffers on June 17, Colson gave them nothing new. Eventually he was asked: "When have you last heard from the president?"

"Last week. He called me," replied Colson, going on to describe his most recent and entirely amicable conversation with Nixon. "He also wrote me a letter," added Colson.

The committee staffers asked to see the letter that the president had written a few hours after learning of Colson's plea of guilty. It read:

June 3rd 1974
Dear Chuck,

  I know what a terribly sad and difficult day this must be for you and your fine family. I want you to know that in a very personal way it is an equally sad day for me. You must however keep your faith in the fact that as time goes on, your dedicated service to the nation will be remembered long after this incident has become only a footnote in history.

                                        Always—your friend,
                                        RN

The Judiciary Committee's interrogators were dumbfounded. "But—but how can you still be friendly?" one of them stuttered.

Colson had many friendly correspondents at this difficult time. Over 150 of them wrote directly to Judge Gesell pleading for leniency. Among the most effective of these unsolicited letters were those from Ricky Austin, the alleged young burglar Colson had successfully defended pro bono in 1966, and from Judge Joseph Mitchell, the black lawyer whose appointment as the first associate at Colson and Morin in 1962 had broken the color bar in Boston's legal establishment. On the other hand, Colson's lawyers were disappointed by a handful of correspondents who wrote unhelpful letters to the judge. The most notable of these was the retired senator from Massachusetts Leverett Saltonstall.

In his religious life, Colson was buoyed up by the prayers of his brothers, who were meeting him almost daily. Their help was practical as well as spiritual. A great weight was lifted from Colson's shoulders when Paula Coe, Doug Coe's twenty-three-year-old daughter, volunteered to move into the Colson home to keep Patty company for the duration of whatever sentence the court imposed. This was one of the many great kindnesses that poured in on Colson as he prepared for his high noon in Judge Gesell's courtroom. Mike Balzano, a former Colson aide in the White House, tried to give his life savings to his former boss. Columnist Jack Anderson, a fierce critic of Colson in recent years, offered money to help the family. So did several others.

The family itself was a mixed bag of emotions. Twenty-year-old Wendell, a star oarsman in the Princeton VIII, passed up the university crew's tour of Europe in order to be at home for the summer in support of Patty. Fifteen-year-old Emily shed tears but told her dad how proud she was of him. Chris, a seventeen-year-old high school senior, bottled up his emotions in subdued silence—a warning sign that was missed. Patty remained in denial, insisting that the sentence would be suspended altogether. Even Colson himself was becoming cautiously optimistic as a result of the flow of letters (the negative ones were never shown to him) and favorable opinions. On balance, he agreed with David Shapiro, whose view was "The maximum as I see it is six months. It could go to nine but my money is on six."

The odds changed once the case arrived in court, on July 21, 1974. David Shapiro later claimed that he and his client were "double-crossed" by Judge Gesell. For according to Shapiro, Gesell had promised at their previous meeting to listen carefully to his speech of mitigation and then to withdraw for a recess to reflect on it before passing sentence. Instead of such a measured approach, Judge Gesell was openly dismissive to Shapiro's arguments of mitigation on Colson's behalf. "You are barking up the wrong tree," was the judge's first interruption. "You are beating a dead horse," was his second. Collapse of stout attorney. Al Quie and Graham Purcell were equally shaken by these signs of impending judicial severity. Colson's heart sank into his boots as he realized that his flickering hopes of a noncustodial sentence had been snuffed out.

Without bothering to take a recess at the conclusion of Shapiro's speech, Judge Gesell passed the sentence with a strange carelessness about the facts before him. "The defendant's deliberate misconduct affected the conduct of a pending federal prosecution," he began. Colson wanted to jump out of his skin when he heard this judicial exaggeration. Neither the prosecutors nor the charge sheet had made that claim. Whatever Colson had "endeavored" in the way of "probable consequences" (as the indictment put it) to do to Ellsberg's legal rights, those rights had remained unaffected. An attempt to obstruct justice is a lesser charge than an actual obstruction of justice. Colson was arraigned for the first. The judge seemed to be punishing him for the second.

The judge's final words were "The court will impose a sentence of one to three years and a fine of five thousand dollars." The crack of his gavel on the hardwood bench was accompanied by a muffled scream from the well of the court and a woman's high-pitched shriek, "Oh, no!"

Colson rocked on his feet. He felt a sharp pain in his body like a needle jabbing into his flesh. For a moment he thought he was going to vomit. As Shapiro steadied his client with a firm grip on the shoulder, Colson bit his lip, praying that the high-pitched shriek had not come from Patty. It had.

She was not the only person in the room to feel shattered by the harshness of the sentence. "I can't believe it. I can't believe it," said Shapiro over and over again, shaking his head in sorrowful bemusement. Al Quie was one of the worst affected. "I was in total shock and so was the whole courtroom," he recalled. "I just couldn't accept Chuck should be going to jail for a term of between one and three years. I was so upset I just couldn't bear to be in that atmosphere for a moment longer. So I took off. When I got outside I started to run. Unfortunately, a reporter from *Time* magazine ran after me. 'Are you going to visit him in prison?' he asked when he caught up with me. 'Sure,' I said. Then the reporter said something extraordinary I'll never forget. He said in a very slow and thoughtful voice, 'My, he's a lucky man to have friends like you.' "

Colson was fortunate in his friendships. His three prayer partners who stayed in court—Doug Coe, Harold Hughes, and Graham Purcell—prayed with him and Patty in a side room as the court officials fixed the date—July 8—on which he would surrender to the U.S. marshals and enter prison. Hughes, in his prayer, asked God to take all bitterness away from Colson, who responded saying, "For some strange reason I even feel a sense of understanding toward Judge Gesell." The next prayer of the brothers was for Colson to be given wisdom and discernment by the Holy Spirit when he faced the media on the courtroom steps. It was a prayer well answered. Although he had prepared nothing in advance, when he reached the massed

ranks of reporters, microphones, and cameras, Colson heard himself saying: "What happened in court today was the court's will and the Lord's
will. I have committed my life to Jesus Christ and I can work for him in
prison as well as out." This dignified statement turned out to be an accurate prophecy of Colson's future life and work.

Going In

Colson's final days of freedom where hectic in their practical arrangements
and cathartic in their spiritual release. A mass of administrative details had
to be attended to but he set aside plenty of time for prayer with his brothers. He also found time for laughter. On the day before his incarceration
he was guest of honor at a bittersweet but at times hilarious social event
known as the Going-In Party. There was a deepening of Colson's prayer life
at this time, based on his fresh understanding of 2 Corinthians 5:17:
"Therefore, if anyone is in Christ he is a new creation: the old has gone, the
new has come!" The old Colson had been too busy fighting legal and media battles to find space in his day for regular quiet time and Bible study.
The new Colson took on both disciplines with the zeal of a true convert.
They were to serve him well during his time in prison.

At this time an amusing cartoon by Pat Oliphant was published in the
Los Angeles Times. It depicted Colson clad in a monk's habit, painting the
word REPENT in big black letters on the gates of the White House. Colson
enjoyed the joke as much as anyone. Yet he was serious about his repentance, not with the connotations of sackcloth and ashes that some might
imagine, but more with appreciation of its richer meaning in the original
Greek term *metanoia,* which translates as "a change of heart and mind."

Everyone who watched Colson closely at this time noticed how much he
was changing. His old friend Fred Rhodes perceptively observed, "I saw
him resolving an inner struggle day by day. Of course he didn't achieve
overnight spiritual transformation. There were occasional flashes of the old
Colson egotism, impatience, and arrogance. But I emphasize the word 'occasional,' for he was in visible transformation from old man to new man.
He knew when he was going wrong. 'I die daily,' was his cry, just as it had
once been Saint Paul's. And as he died to his old life you could see the new
life of peace and purposefulness that was rising in him. I began to feel certain that he was on a journey to do some remarkable service for the Lord."

Colson's more worldly friends wanted to give him a remarkable send-off. Under the leadership of Charlie Morin a party was organized at the Palm Restaurant on Nineteenth Street in downtown Washington. One of those who attended, Colson's former White House aide Steve Karalekas, described it as "the most extraordinary social occasion you can possibly imagine. There were senators, congressmen, White House stalwarts, big names from corporate America, top lawyers, and old buddies, all packing into one of the smallest restaurants in town to celebrate what? . . . A friend going to jail the next day!"

It was inevitable that the mood at such a party should be mixed. Charlie Morin did his best to lighten his guests' hearts with some well-scripted humorous remarks that came to a climax with an announcement of the famous grandmother's demise. "She passed away many years ago," he intoned solemnly. Enter on cue, evidently resurrected for the party, an elderly gray-haired woman in an old-fashioned floor-length brown dress. Adjusting her pince-nez she peered sternly about the room. Then she spied Colson. "There's my grandson," she cackled. Striding over to the guest of honor, she began whomping him over the head with her purse. "Run over me, will you! This will teach you to respect your old granny!" she shouted as the blows rained down on Colson's broad shoulders. With the guests cheering and laughing, "Granny" pulled off her gray wig and gave her victim a kiss. She was Pat Owens, Charlie Morin's long-serving secretary.

As a counterbalance to the humor, Bryce Harlow, a veteran White House aide of the Eisenhower and Nixon administrations, made a speech saying: "I don't feel like cracking jokes at a time like this. Chuck is my friend. I helped him get the job as Nixon's special counsel and I'm hurting for him as I see him going off to prison . . . there's something wrong in our country when a loyal dedicated man like Chuck has to serve time in a federal penitentiary for carrying out the orders of the president of the United States."

Then it was the guest of honor's turn at the microphone. Colson began with a W. C. Fields line about traveling from the White House to the big house, then he switched to a more somber vein. He said he was proud to have served a president who had ended America's involvement in Vietnam. "I have two sons, eighteen and twenty," he said. "Because of what this administration achieved, I thank God they won't have to go fight a war." He ended his remarks with a tribute to his friends. "I've been blessed to know what real friendship is," he said. "I've become a rich man in the kind of wealth most millionaires never achieve. To know love and friendship and to know in this cold and impersonal world there are people who care for each other as human beings, whether they're in the White House, a fellow-ship group, or a penitentiary, is a gift from God. . . . I know I've made mis-takes, but they were mistakes of passion, not greed. I have some regrets but I am also very much at peace."

Colson slept peacefully on his final night of freedom. The next morning, July 8, was anything but peaceful thanks to the dawn arrival of TV crews outside the house and a media car chase all the way to the gates of Fort Ho-labird, the federal detention center near Baltimore where Colson had agreed to surrender to U.S. marshals. One of the last of the reporters' ques-tions he answered was a shout of "What books are you taking with you?"

"Just two editions of the Bible," was the reply.

Arriving at Fort Holabird, Colson felt a chill of fear as his car drew up to a green building surrounded by a nine-foot-high chain-link fence topped with heavy coils of barbed wire. Two burly guards with .38 revolvers on their hips came out of a booth to unlock the main gate. They slammed it aggressively as soon as the new arrival had entered the facility. Colson re-membered that David Shapiro had often used the term "the slammer." Now he knew why.

Holabird

Colson's first experiences of prison were disorienting and demeaning. He spent several hours going through the tedious bureaucratic and physical processes that all new prisoners have to endure—fingerprinting, strip-searching for drugs, inspection of every nook and cranny in the contents of his luggage, mug shot photographs for criminal records, and endless forms to be filled out. These procedures seemed even more oppressive than usual because of the hundred-degree temperature. Baltimore was in the grip of a heat wave, which caused walls as well as humans to sweat. As Colson watched drips of water trickling down the cracked plaster and peeling paint of the center's reception rooms, he felt deeply depressed even though he was not yet experiencing the full misery of a real prison.

Fort Holabird, an almost deserted onetime army barracks, was by 1974 a secretive penal establishment. It was used mainly as a holding center for underworld turncoats who had agreed to give evidence against their former criminal associates. These despised and isolated inmates of the prison system were known as "snitches." Colson was no snitch, but he had agreed to testify in several ongoing Watergate trials and hearings. This was why he had been ordered to spend the first few weeks of his sentence at Holabird.

Colson made one mistake in the early hours of his incarceration—he asked a question. "Can you tell me something about this place?" he inquired to one of the deputies in the control room.

"No! The important thing for you to remember is that you remember nothing," snapped the deputy. "No one knows this place exists. You will meet some very unusual men here. Don't discuss business with them and don't ask them about theirs. When you leave here, forget you ever met them. You will only know them by their first names anyway. Obey the rules and mind your own business."

Although Colson did mind his own business, many of Holabird's inmates were ready to talk about theirs, or at least to gossip freely about the bad deeds of others. So in no time Colson's social circle was expanding. He met "Mike," a hit man from Boston who had killed twenty-eight victims; "Pete," a narcotics boss from New York; "Pat and Andy," two big-time crime syndicate bosses; "Eddie and Jimmy," two corrupt Baltimore policemen; and "Frank," a dwarf who scowled and muttered menacingly whenever he saw Colson reading his Bible. The explanation for Frank's hostility was that he blamed Christian conversions for his incarceration. The dwarf had devised a scheme to relieve the Brink's Company of a large amount of currency by concealing himself in a container full of banknotes. In the final stages of this operation, one partner in crime attended a Southern religious festival, was converted by a Holy Spirit experience, and immediately snitched on the dwarf and the rest of the gang.

Despite the occasional glowerings and threatening gestures from the anti-Christian dwarf, Colson's faith continued to strengthen. His brothers continued to make frequent trips to Holabird throughout July and August. So did Patty. Colson was thrilled when she sent him a letter after one of these visits: "I prayed most of the way home for both of us," wrote Patty, "and I think it might be nice if from now on we prayed together before leaving each other in the evening." Colson was overjoyed when he read these words. Patty was lifting the barriers of her spiritual reticence. From that time onward the two Colsons held hands and prayed aloud together in both public and private settings every time Patty visited. One unexpected visit by Patty brought sad news. Colson knew something was seriously wrong as soon as he saw his wife's woebegone face in the visitors' room at the unusual time of a Monday morning.

"It's Dad, isn't it?" Colson asked immediately.

"Yes, Chuck, but he went very peacefully this morning."

Colson was devastated, his pain made greater by the knowledge that his father had passed away while packing for a trip (against doctors' orders) to visit Holabird. Blaming himself for bringing on the death of his dad, Colson suffered deeply. After much bureaucratic wrangling, he was allowed to go to the funeral under the armed escort of two U.S. marshals. In the hours after the service, Colson spent some time sorting out his father's papers. He was amazed to discover that back in the 1940s and 1950s, Wendell had done a great deal of pro bono legal work and prison visiting for the United Prison Association of New England. It was an early signpost toward Colson's own future commitment to prison ministry.

As the only son of a just-widowed mother, Colson was in anguish for the pangs of bereavement that Diz was having to bear alone. She wrote her son a brave letter soon after his return to prison from the funeral: "I can't say it's been easy going into the empty house without Pop. . . . I just wish you weren't so far away. I know it's been hard on you too but you are no sissy and you've always done well what you've had to do in life. . . . Just remember you are no criminal. You served your country in the Marines and in the service of the Pres and we are all proud of you. Good will come out of it yet."

The immediate good that Colson was hoping would come to him was a presidential pardon. Nixon had hinted in recent months that he would eventually find a way to exercise clemency for the leading Watergate defendants. With the president's own resignation becoming inevitable by early August, Colson hoped and prayed that a pardon would be granted to him before Nixon left office. His hopes were dashed when Nixon resigned without saying a word about clemency for his aides, but they rose again when the new president, Gerald R. Ford, pardoned his predecessor. For the next few weeks, Colson expended great energy in trying to secure a similar pardon for himself. In addition to badgering his four Christian brothers for help in this exercise, Colson wrote several impassioned letters to Charlie Morin urging him to organize approaches to a list of influential contacts believed to have the ear of the new president. Colson's list included Billy Graham, Ed Brooke, Elliot Richardson, Leverett Saltonstall, Bryce Harlow, Frank Fitzsimmons, Strom Thurmond, and Barry Goldwater. Some of these were very long shots indeed. The notion that they would all be willing to intercede with President Ford on his behalf for a pardon suggests that Colson may have been suffering from a resurgence of his "old man" pride, or that he had lost touch with his sense of reality. These impressions were fortified by the peremptory tone of his instructions to his old friend and partner.

"Old Pal, as you can see, I believe we should be pounding on the table and kicking the doors in," he wrote to Morin. "We need a steady drumbeat of pressure. The idea is to keep Ford constantly aware of the interest on my behalf. It's got to bother him and work on his conscience. He knows me too well to be callous about it." Ford may not have been callous, but after the public's massively hostile reaction to his pardon of Nixon, it was politically impossible for him to repeat the favor for Nixon's hatchet man. Even so, a trial balloon suggesting that clemency for the remaining Watergaters was under consideration by the president did get sent up by the White House press office in early September. It was swiftly shot down by press and public opinion. After that even the old Colson abandoned hope of a pardon. As he put it in a round-robin letter to the brothers dated September 12, "I made the very foolish mistake of putting my faith in the President to release me. It is God's plan and not Jerry Ford's that will decide. I know that. I believe it with every fiber of my being yet I still err, as we all do, and foolishly, for a few days, I allowed myself to become expectant and hopeful. It was a cruel thing for the wives and families to be encouraged by the Trial Balloon . . . but I can remember sending up Trial Balloons myself when I was in the White House and I only cared about how the public would react. That the story might be false made no difference. I am learning." The letter ended with a news item. Colson had just been told that he was leaving Holabird for the Maxwell federal penitentiary, in Alabama.

"I will be 'transported' Monday or Tuesday," he wrote, adding gloomily, "The first few days will be trying, getting adjusted to a new environment, one that is nowhere near as free as this one." It was an accurate prediction, for a time of trial lay ahead of him.

Maxwell

The Maxwell prison was a far more restrictive and disagreeable institution than Fort Holabird. Even though it was categorized as "low security," its claustrophobic atmosphere and pettifogging rules soon put its inmates under high pressure. In the hours after his arrival, Charles Colson tasted the bitter flavor of Maxwell through his earliest contacts with surly guards and hostile inmates.

It was standard practice for any new prisoner entering Maxwell to be deloused under an antiseptic shower; to have his body searched for drugs; to be stripped of all "disallowed" personal possessions (in Colson's case this meant handing in his Brown University signet ring); to be photographed, fingerprinted, and issued the standard and usually ill-fitting drab brown uniform. After going through these humiliating rituals in the entry control area, Colson exchanged his name for a prison number—23226—and was assigned to Dormitory G. He was sent on his way by a hulking guard who barked, "Take my advice. Keep your mind where your butt is. The time will go fast if you do; if you think of home and outside things, this place will be hell."

Dormitory G turned out to be a passable imitation of hell, and some of its natives were far from friendly. Colson described his impressions in a letter to Charlie Morin: "At first I was a little nervous here. I've had one threat and some of the Blacks gave me concern. Looked to me like they were getting the sticks and the big black pot ready. The rats eat anything left in the locker beside the bed, anything, that is, that the roaches don't get first. That gave me a little sleeplessness at first but I've adjusted." Adjusting took patience and courage. The first threat came via a well-meaning prisoner who asked Colson if he realized he had enemies at Maxwell. He continued: "I overheard this dude say to his friend that he wants to kill you. Guys talk like this sometimes, but this one sounded like he really meant it."

Colson was shaken by this warning but decided not to repeat the threat to the guards on the grounds that it would most likely result in his being shipped out to a maximum-security prison for his own protection. But he kept a wary eye over his shoulder for quite some time, although his priorities were directed more on how to get accepted than on how not to get attacked.

Because Maxwell was a small jail with only 250 inmates, no secrets could be hidden for long in the community. Colson was under constant scrutiny. Every move he made, every conversation he had, every real or imaginary favor or mistreatment he received from the guards was the focus of intense attention, for such is the lot of the high-profile prisoner. In a calculated move to get rid of his celebrity status, Colson deliberately took more than his fair share of the menial chores. While he was mopping the floor area around the showers a young black prisoner taunted him, saying, "How d'ya like living with the scum after having all those servants in the White House?" Colson described his reaction to the challenge in a letter to his brothers: "He was kind of young. So I simply told him I had done this for years before he was born and I'd lived in the Marines while he was in diapers. That apparently did it. Today I've had nothing but friendly greetings from all of the inmates."

There were other such episodes that won Colson respect. More important, by keeping his head down and going with the flow of the prison, he demonstrated that he had no airs or graces, nor was he receiving any special treatment from the "hacks," or guards. His prison job also helped to establish him as a "regular guy." He was assigned to work in the laundry. It was not too privileged a post, like becoming the office orderly, and not too demeaning a job, like cleaning out the latrines. Just right.

As he established increasing contact with his fellow inmates Colson received plenty of advice from them. "Don't practice law." "Don't complain." "Don't get involved." "Never leave your watch out." "Keep anything valuable locked in your locker." In only one way did Colson deviate from these recommendations during his early days at Maxwell. He always left his Bible on top of his locker in the hope that someone would want to talk to him about it. No one did. The only comment on his exhibit came when one prisoner pointed to the Bible and chuckled, "Ain't nobody here gonna steal that from you!"

The Bible had become much more important to Colson. In all his spiritual searchings before he went to prison he had never applied himself to any serious Bible study. Now it was his highest priority. Doug Coe had given him the Design for Discipleship Bible reading course, published by the Navigators, which Colson studied every day. This discipline gave him his first real grounding in scripture.

One passage that gripped Colson was in chapter 2 of Hebrews, which the course recommended under the heading "Valuable information about the humanity of Christ." Understanding from the early verses that Jesus had come down temporarily to be lower than his heavenly angels in order to suffer and die for men on earth, Colson was stirred by the eleventh verse: "For the one who makes men holy and the men who are made holy share a common humanity. So Jesus is not ashamed to call them brothers."

Reading this verse over and over again, Colson felt that God was speaking directly to him. Suddenly he recognized that he was in prison for a purpose. He was being chastened as a prisoner so that he could shed his old life and start a new life with an understanding of suffering. Once he knew suffering he could reach out in common humanity to help the suffering, knowing God as a *brother* through the person of Jesus Christ.

It is impossible to recapture on the printed page the high-voltage emotions that struck Colson as he recognized that his outwardly ruined life now had a God-given purpose. Just where this would take him he did not know. He simply believed and was willing to obey. Obedience took him into deeper prayer. Some of it was personal, but he also had a strong urge to share prayers with others. Missing the prayerful fellowship of the four brothers who had sustained him so well in the world of freedom, Colson tried to create a similar mutual support operation in the world of Maxwell. He approached a twenty-seven-year-old prisoner, Paul Kramer, who wore a cross around his neck. Kramer had told Colson in an earlier conversation that he had regretted his drug-dealing past and that he had accepted the Lord.

"Paul, couldn't we get a couple of other Christians and meet a few times a week just to share our problems and pray together?" asked Colson.

"I don't know, Chuck, they laugh at 'Jesus freaks' here," replied Kramer. "You can't carry a Bible around without people ribbing you."

Colson was upset by the rebuff. He could not persuade Paul Kramer to help him start a fellowship group. He made other approaches but they failed too. So Colson prayed on alone until he met a prisoner he described as "a red-necked, red-headed edition of Popeye with short bulging biceps and a jutting chin." He was an enthusiastic Christian called Tex. Colson overheard Tex describing the agonies of another inmate, Bob Ferguson, who was up for a hearing before the parole board examiners the following day. "Bob is in terrible shape," Tex was saying. "We gotta help him. Poor devil, wife and five kids and no money. If he doesn't get paroled they ain't gonna survive. Praise God, we gotta help him. Maybe pray with him." Colson walked over to Tex and his group of listeners, which included Paul Kramer. "Sorry, but I couldn't help hearing about this fellow Ferguson," said Colson. "I'd like to pray with him too."

Tex needed no second bidding. He grabbed Colson's arm. "Come along, brother. Come along. Praise the Lord," he said as he went off in search of Bob Ferguson. Parole paranoia was raging through Maxwell that Monday evening as though it was an epidemic of Asian flu. The parole board examiners had completed the first of two days of hearings, rejecting over 80 percent of the applications. Ferguson's was the first case to be heard the next day. Paul Kramer was on the list too. Both men's prospects looked bleak because their applications did not fully comply with the board's guidelines. Tex laid his hands on Ferguson and prayed for him with the vehemence of a celestial Popeye at full throttle. Colson was not far behind in the eloquence of his supplications. "Lord, strip away the calluses on the hearts of those parole judges," intoned the voice of Nixon's former strongman on law and order. "Let them not be hardened by their years of dealing so impersonally with criminals. Please give them wisdom, love, and compassion."

Colson's prayer made a great impact on the small group of prisoners that Tex had recruited to gather round and support Ferguson. Perhaps it impacted the parole board too. For at the following day's hearings 70 percent of the applications were granted, including Bob Ferguson's and Paul Kramer's. Old-timers said it was the best day's parole results in living memory. Word of the prayer meeting whistled round the prison. When Colson again suggested starting up a fellowship group, he had four or five new brothers willing to join him.

Colson's first steps in prison ministry were a success. He had a gift for prayer leading and Bible teaching. He gave his testimony in the prison chapel under the auspices of a local Southern Baptist preacher, the Reverend Edmond Blow, who conducted weekly services in the prison. Brother Blow was so carried away by prisoner 23226's story that he almost blew the roof off with his revivalist interjections of "Praise the Lord's," hallelujahs, and amens into the testimony. Although there were snide comments from some prisoners along the lines of "There go the Jesus freaks," as the fellowship group's activities became more visible, among others there were signs of growing respect and even admiration for what Colson was doing.

What exactly was Colson doing? He was not entirely clear that he knew the answer to this question himself, for he was still the newest of new Christians, with no experience of ministry. Nevertheless he had seized on two or three key ideas and biblical texts, which were guiding him at this time. The first was the power of the Holy Spirit to change lives. At the time of his own acceptance of Christ he had felt the movement of the Spirit within his heart. Yet in the old-man-versus-new-man conflicts of Colson's life before prison, he had not been free enough to welcome the Holy Spirit. It was a strange paradox, but once Colson had lost his own freedom, he became free to let the Holy Spirit change him.

Colson recognized the Holy Spirit's transforming power partly in his own life and partly through the changes he saw in the lives of the men to whom he ministered. The individual stories of the Maxwell prisoners whose lives were changed through Colson's evangelism are well told in his memoir, *Born Again*. They included Paul Kramer, the young drug dealer; Lee Corbin, a middle-aged forger; Homer Welsh, an old Tennessee moonshiner; and several others. One of the reasons why Colson was so effective with them was that he lived by another biblical text that became important to him. "Faith without works is dead." (James 2:26)

All his life Colson had been a man of action. A journey of faith limited to prayer, study, and contemplation would never have fulfilled him. Yet up to now that was what his spiritual journey had largely consisted of. At Maxwell he found his vocation. It was to work for, as well as minister to, prisoners.

All the advice Colson had been given on entering prison was contrary to the idea of "works." He had been told, "Don't get involved," and, "Don't become a lawyer," with many variations on that theme. Gradually he broke away from these self-denying ordinances. It was Homer Welsh, the silver-haired moonshiner, who started Colson down the path of faith *with* works. They were discussing some passages in the Bible together when Homer hesitantly asked Colson, "Do you suppose you could help me with a letter to my judge?" Bending slightly from his "Don't get involved" rule, Colson told the moonshiner to go away and prepare a draft. He would look it over and make suggestions. "Yes sir. I'll write it. I'll go right to work on it today. Thank you, Mr. Colson," said Homer.

For several days afterward Colson saw Homer writing busily on pads of lined paper. When the draft was eventually produced it consisted of half a page of illegible hieroglyphics. Homer was illiterate, as are approximately a quarter of all prisoners in U.S. federal and state jails. Colson's heart went out to the old man, who was long overdue for the parole the judge had promised him. From that moment on Colson had a new role in the prison. He resolved to help anyone who wanted his assistance in writing parole applications, furlough requests, and family letters. "I could not refuse those who needed help," he said afterward. "These were my brothers. The Lord had shown the way and now I was following."

Around the time when Colson became so active in ministering to his fellow prisoners, an old friend came down to visit him from Washington. This was Fred "Dusty" Rhodes, a dedicated Christian who had tried to interest Colson in the gospel as early as 1962. Thanks to Colson's patronage from the White House, Rhodes had been appointed chairman of the U.S. Postal Rate Commission; he was now close to retirement from this post. A stalwart Colson supporter in correspondence and prayer, Rhodes was Colson's closest friend and adviser on matters spiritual, apart from the four original fellowship group brothers.

On his weekend visit to Alabama, Rhodes met Colson's new prayer partners at Maxwell prison. He was deeply impressed by their stories and by

the role Colson had played in bringing them to faith. When the other prisoners had gone, Rhodes and Colson were alone together in a reflective
mood. Colson picked up his Bible and turned to Hebrews 2.

"Dusty, I had an amazing experience the other day during free time
when I was reading my Bible," he began. "I read something that set me off
thinking that the Lord has a purpose for my being here in prison." Colson
then expounded Hebrews 2:11, ending by reading out the words "Jesus is
not ashamed to call them brothers."

"If God chose to come to earth to suffer and know us as brothers," continued Colson, "maybe God's plan for me was to be in prison and to know
men in here as a brother. Then out of that startling thought came the beginning of a revelation that I was being given a prison ministry, both inside
while serving as a prisoner, and then someday later on the outside."

Rhodes stood up as though he'd been given a sudden jolt. "Wow, Chuck.
That blows my mind. Is the Lord saying to you that he wants you to help
him with prison work?"

Colson responded cautiously. "This needs a lot of prayer. I have no idea
how it will work out once I'm outside." Then, sounding as though the idea
had already taken root in him, he added, "But whatever I get into in the
way of a prison program, I'm going to need help."

Fred Rhodes, who enjoyed describing himself as "a quiet, colorless,
sixty-year-old lawyer on the verge of retirement," felt another powerful jolt,
or perhaps a call. For without a second's hesitation he replied, "If the Lord
can use me in any prison work you start, Chuck, count me in. Full-time if
necessary."

It was the first commitment to a Colson prison ministry.

Emotional Turmoil

Although Colson's ministry to other prisoners was going well, there were
times when he must have longed to be able to follow the Biblical exhortation "Physician, heal thyself." About a month after his arrival at Maxwell
he entered a phase of depression and dramatic mood swings. These tensions, often accompanied by cries to God for help, were recorded in his private diary.

October 16, 1974, was Colson's forty-third birthday. Charles Morin and
another of his former law partners, Arthur Mason, came down to Alabama
for it. They might have succeeded in their objective of cheering up their old

friend had it not been for their discovery of a microphone planted in the desk all three men were sitting at in the visiting cubicle. "Room was bugged! I am getting scared to death what to say. No matter what I do, the prison paranoia is closing in on me," wrote Colson in his diary. "Mason spotted it. Desk immovable. Tape reel in the next room." Although his law partners were smart enough to outwit the eavesdropping by scribbling notes to one another, the episode left its scars on Colson. "I'm beginning to feel like I did in the USSR in 1973. I don't know that I can take the Big Brother aspects," he confided to his notebook. "It is truly wearing on me and I can't get a handle on what's happening to my case outside. Mason and Morin were crushed and couldn't hide it. I couldn't relax. . . . All in all a tough birthday. Will pray tonight for the Lord to give me strength."

This prayer for strength was emotionally repeated in the next day's diary entry: "Felt myself slipping badly . . . I so badly want to be home with my loved ones . . . I feel the tenseness and pressure of confinement . . . it comes right down to the simple truth: I'm flesh and I'm homesick. Morale has been low for two days—what can I look forward to—eight to nine more months? God give me the strength."

Homesickness was only one of Colson's problems. His anxieties swung to and fro like a gyrating compass, sometimes leading him to bursts of weakness and self-pity, sometimes to panic attacks over ongoing Watergate litigation, and most often to agonizing over the plight of his wife and family. Yet even in the darkest of the bouts of despair Colson never forgot that he was now navigating with the help of God. "Today was tough, the camp really closed in on me," he wrote in his diary for October 21. "Just seemed so empty, so hopeless and frustrating. There are days like that—oppression of the human spirit—I collapsed on my bed and slept from 2:15 to 3:15. In the rest of the afternoon I was just so ready to give up. It was all too much for me . . . I'm weak. Father, give me strength. Fill me with the spirit. Help me remove all doubts."

In early November Colson was moved back to Holabird. Returning to an easier prison regime brought temporary relief to his jagged nerves but it did not last long. "One week here at Holabird and I've done little else but sleep. I can't describe the total exhaustion," he recorded on November 14.

I can now fully appreciate why some men ask for solitary confinement. Just to escape from the constant pressure of people closing in all the time . . . I was wearing myself out and I couldn't understand why. It was the pressure of so many people who asked for my help and my complete refusal to become part of the system. It was a real struggle. I could do it for eight weeks but I wonder if I could for a year or more. The decision today that I will spend a few more weeks at Holabird is God's blessing.

God's blessing also brought with it the prosecutors' curse. Colson had been transferred back to Holabird so that he could be subpoenaed to give damaging evidence against other Watergate defendants. He nonetheless insisted he had no such evidence. "Another round with Prosecutors today," he wrote on November 20.

> They seem to be picking the carcass apart. . . . Shapiro fears anything I say could create enough conflict in the testimony to at least permit Andy Miller (a red haired Hitler) to slap a perjury indictment on me. I would only tell the truth but that's not the issue. . . . Is there no justice? I can't even defend myself. When will this damnable persecution end? Why do men want to hurt and harm one another, not to prevent offenses but to punish, to revenge—to what end? Why? Who really benefits? The agonizing truth is that I'm on the receiving end. . . . I want to fight, I want to defend myself. Theology is so much simpler. If one is square with God it is clean, open, uncluttered and terribly easy. The law is filled with horrendous twists and turns, games, deceits. God, what a dilemma!

The dilemma troubling Colson was that the prosecutors wanted him to testify in the trials of Haldeman, Ehrlichman, and Mitchell. If he refused to do so his chances of early parole could be ended. Also he would lose any chance of retaining his license to practice law, which he badly wanted to do, as it seemed to be his only hope for earning a living.

To make his dilemma even more painful, the prosecutors expected Colson to testify in detail about an Oval Office discussion on January 8, 1973, in which he had taken part. The substance of the discussion was not damaging to him but it could be interpreted as highly damaging to other Watergate defendants and to Nixon. Colson's problem was that even after listening to the tape, he had absolutely no recollection of the conversation. This was a genuine memory blank. He had told Charles Morin and David Shapiro that the January 8 tape meant nothing to him, long before the prosecutors took an interest in it. The convenient route for Colson to follow would be to help the prosecutors by pretending to remember the substance of the taped conversation and giving them the interpretation of it they wanted. But his conscience would not allow him to do that. Colson wrote in his diary on December 11: "The real dilemma is ahead this week. The Watergate trial! It would be so easy to take the easy way out, say what the prosecutors want and get it over with. I'd be able to look forward to getting home but I couldn't live with myself."

In order to live with himself, Colson, to quote his own words, "told the truth and looked like an idiot." When he got into the courtroom he put on the headset and listened to the January 8 tape with knotted brows. After it had been played over he agreed that he recognized the voices, including his own, but he still did not recall taking part in any such discussion in the Oval Office. The tape had not refreshed his memory. This unlikely explanation drove the lawyers wild, particularly John Mitchell's attorney, William Hundley, who was advocating the equally unlikely explanation that Colson rather than his client was the architect of Watergate. Hundley asked what Colson meant by his remarks on the January 8 tape. Colson responded that he couldn't answer that question because he didn't remember having made any such remarks. Hundley went ballistic at his answer.

"But you heard yourself on the tape, didn't you?" he thundered.

"I heard my voice, yes," agreed Colson.

"Well what did 'the Colson voice' mean here?" demanded Mitchell's counsel, in tones dripping with vitriol. Colson couldn't or wouldn't answer that one either. For the next hour or so in the witness box he was taunted and pounded for his amnesia over "the Colson voice," but he stuck to his guns.

Writing that night in his diary, Colson explained why he had made himself look an idiot—or worse. "Had I been able to say I remembered it [the January 8 tape] I would have wiped away any charges of perjury . . . but in my own heart I would have had to commit perjury to say I remembered it. Oh well, the Christian way isn't always the easiest!"

At least once his uncomfortable time on the witness stand had finished, Colson was given no more pain from the Watergate prosecutors. But he continued to suffer great pain over the plight of Patty. Her agonies had been his prime concern since the day he went into prison. One of his first letters from Maxwell, to Doug Coe, set out his fear with poignant anxiety.

Only one real burden, brother, is my concern for Patty, which you have detected, at least I gather so from your letter. Our problem is quite simple. We are, after eleven years of marriage, very much in

*love and very dependent on one another. Maybe we have been too
close. I have not been one to chase the gals or to enjoy going off
with the boys—or take the business trip "flings" that so many men
I know do. My first marriage was a mistake. I was much too young,
in too much of a hurry, too eager to get out of college and find the
security and acceptability I had not known in my life by marrying a
nice upper-middle-class girl whose parents had a big house in the
suburbs. Because the last five years of my first marriage were so unhappy (mostly my fault) I suppose I have treasured my relationship
with Patty all the more. What hurts me now is not what I am going
through but what I see her going through. She is fighting so hard to
get me out, she is flying, which she detests, just to be here with me
and I can tell that it is wearing her down.*

In fact, Patty did a wonderful job lifting up Colson's spirits. Her frequent visits to Maxwell and to Holabird were a boost to prisoner 23226's
morale, both gastronomically and spiritually. During the months they were
parted, Patty became something of a gourmet cook, bringing in Colson's favorite dishes, such as deviled eggs and crab cakes. She was even better at
nourishing her husband with the bread of life. "I thank God every night for
Patty's faith," Colson told his brothers in a letter. "She is really walking in
the Spirit. She has come a long, long way and it is a source of great
strength and comfort to me. Patty is not discouraged and certainly not bitter that her prayers are not being answered. But it is hard to see my problems causing so much anguish for someone I love so much."

Colson's prison diaries were filled with many more annotations chroni-
cling the sufferings of Patty and the rest of the family: "Patty is really feeling the strain. . . . Last night I called and Patty had been crying
hysterically. . . . Diz is in very bad condition. . . . Patty today really hurting. . . . Why should she have to suffer so?"

To steady his own nerves, Colson enlarged his spiritual reading list, not
always with good results. He was dismissive of books like *Prison to Praise*
("shallow") and *Sunday* ("vapid"), but he loved Dietrich Bonhoeffer's *Letters and Papers from Prison* ("magnificent"). His staple diet of reading continued to be the Bible, and he also continued his ministry to other
prisoners. One of them was Herb Kalmbach, Nixon's former lawyer, serving a one-year sentence for obstruction of justice. Colson prayed regularly
with Kalmbach, read him the chapter on pride from C. S. Lewis's *Mere
Christianity,* and persuaded him to accept Christ into his life.

Kalmbach was one of four Watergate-related prisoners who had been brought back to Holabird to testify in the trials of Haldeman, Ehrlichman, and Mitchell. The other three were John Dean, Jeb Magruder, and Colson himself. Colson had a reconciliation of sorts with Dean. He found it much harder to reconcile himself to Magruder, even though he too had become a Born Again Christian. Colson had always disliked Magruder. This enmity intensified with the revelations from the courtroom that some of the worst and stupidest excesses of Watergate, including the break-in at the Democratic National Committee office, had been initiated by Magruder when he was Mitchell's number two at the Committee to Re-elect the President. Struggling with his conscience and his desire, at least in theory, to obey the Christian teachings on forgiveness, Colson did manage to make one small gesture of reconciliation to his bête noire. On Christmas Eve 1974, the four Watergaters at Holabird met in Dean's cell for a makeshift midnight service of prayer and scripture. The gospel passages from Luke and Matthew on the nativity of Christ were read to the group by Jeb Magruder, with whom Colson managed to exchange a handshake of peace.

Christmas is the low point of the year in the life of many a prisoner, but Colson was to sink far lower during the month of January. As 1975 dawned, there was widespread expectation that the Holabird Four would be paroled. They had all served a reasonable percentage of their sentences, their crimes were relatively minor, and they had all cooperated with the prosecutors. It was also expected that they would be paroled together. It did not work out that way. On January 8 Judge Sirica ordered the release of John Dean, Jeb Magruder, and Herb Kalmbach. Colson received the news of his exclusion from the parole order in a phone call from Dean's lawyer, who made the obvious point that his release could be authorized only by Judge Gesell. Colson's misery was compounded by a junior associate from the special prosecutor's office who, on arriving at Holabird, congratulated him on his freedom, saying: "This is one day you'll never forget." Unfortunately the associate had got her Watergate prisoners mixed up and had mistaken Colson for Dean.

In the next forty-eight hours, Colson hit rock bottom. He was devastated by reports that Judge Gesell was not inclined to follow Judge Sirica. "This is the hardest day of my whole time. I'm in more agony than I've ever been in since my confinement began," Colson wrote in his diary on January 10. "I am trying to pray but I feel so depressed, lonely and lost. Maybe this suffering is a penance for my un-Christian attitude toward Magruder. If so I guess it is deserved. I just pray that the Holy Spirit takes over. . . . I don't believe God has forsaken me and my faith is not shaken but the pain in my heart is the worst it has ever been."

Three more blows arrived to increase Colson's pain in the next couple of weeks. The first came when he was told he would be transferred to Maxwell at the end of the month because Holabird was to close down. Although he was miserable at the prospect of going back to the harsher regime of the Alabama prison, Colson's emotions were mild compared to the terror felt by the snitches of Holabird at being compelled to reenter the federal prison system. "Sat up on Friday night as they explained all the ways to kill a man in prison," recorded Colson. "Poison, attacks in the showers, pay-offs to guards, etc. I'm worried about going back to Maxwell because of commuting, etc., for Patty but these guys are truly scared for their lives."

Colson did, however, become scared for his own livelihood when the second blow hit him. This was the news that he was going to be disbarred from practicing law in Virginia. "Disbarred for my part in Ellsberg's psychiatrist's break-in, the radio just announced," wrote Colson. "How much punishment is a man supposed to take? The only one left in jail, and now disbarred for defaming Ellsberg! Who's ever been more defamed than me and more unjustly?"

A few lines further on in his diary, Colson's thoughts changed gear almost in the manner of an author of one of the lament psalms, ending up with a doxology. "God opens new doors as He closes old ones. It is obvious I wasn't meant to practice law. I may have a future career as a writer—infinitely more interesting and challenging. So we praise God for all things. God is certainly shaping my future for me."

This mood of optimism did not last. On January 23 Colson was devastated by his third, and worst, blow. He was summoned to the Holabird telephone to take a call from his attorney. He picked up the receiver hoping that he would get the news of his release. On the line was an associate from his law firm, Ken Adams. "Chuck, are you ready for a tough one?" he asked.

How many tough ones are left? wondered Colson as he replied calmly, "Go ahead, Ken."

"Your son Christian has been arrested for narcotics possession."

It was almost more than Colson could bear. "Two Colsons in jail today," he wrote sorrowfully in his diary. "When will it end? Jan 8th, Holabird closing, disbarment, and now poor Chris."

It was his darkest hour in prison.

CHAPTER THIRTEEN

Released and Born Again

Last Days at Holabird

The last three weeks of January 1975 were the lowest point of Charles Colson's imprisonment. Outwardly bereft of the companionship he had derived from his fellow Watergaters, who had been released by Judge Sirica, and inwardly railing against Judge Gesell for not treating him equally, Colson's morale plummeted. He slept badly at night and found it difficult to concentrate by day. Although he persisted with his prayers and his daily reading of scripture, he found his mind wandering. Occasionally he gained temporary comfort from biblical texts such as Psalms 37:7: "Be still before the Lord and wait patiently for him. Do not fret." However, for most of the time Colson could not stop himself from sinking into precisely the opposite frame of mind recommended by the psalm. He became restless, impatient, fretful, and deeply pessimistic.

There were several causes for Colson's descent into gloom. One was the emotional collapse of Patty, who found it unbearable to watch the televised homecomings of Dean, Kalmbach, and Magruder, as they rejoiced with their families while her husband languished in jail. Another was a pessimistic report from David Shapiro on the chances of early release. "The scuttlebutt from the courthouse ain't good," he told his client in a phone call to Holabird. "Gesell doesn't like anyone to think he is being forced to follow Sirica's lead. Hang tough, my boy." A third source of dismay was the news that Fort Holabird would be closing down as a federal penitentiary in February. Colson was notified that he would be transferred back to Maxwell, where the tougher regime and stricter visiting arrangements would be far harder to endure. A fourth blow came from the Virginia Supreme Court, which on January 20 handed down a judgment disbarring

Colson from practicing law. His old friend Charles Morin, who acted as his advocate in the hearing, had been optimistic that the majority of the justices would vote against disbarment. So this unexpected decision, which in practical terms appeared to put an end to his prospects for earning a living as a lawyer, hit Colson badly.

The fifth and by far the unkindest cut of all was the news of his son Christian's arrest for possession of narcotics. As he heard the details of the charge from Ken Adams, Colson reeled as if he had been kicked hard in his solar plexus. His eighteen-year-old son, a freshman at the University of South Carolina, was the quietest and gentlest of his children. In his father's eyes, Chris was a most improbable candidate for experimenting with drugs. But the facts of the case were damning. Chris had taken $150 of school board money advanced to him during the Christmas vacation and had used it to buy fifteen ounces of marijuana. His plan was to sell it for a good profit and to invest the proceeds in a secondhand car. Inevitably Colson blamed his own troubles for creating the psychological instability that might have caused his son to go astray. Chris's poignant comment to the police officer who arrested him, "Now you've got both of us," made front-page headlines and pierced his father's heart. Colson's agony was all the more acute because he was unable to fly down to the Columbia campus to be with his younger son in his hour of need.

The intensity of his pain was matched by an intensity of prayer. Back at Fellowship House, the brothers went into intercessionary overdrive. Congressman Al Quie discovered from a researcher in the Library of Congress that an obscure statute could be used to secure the release of a federal prisoner if a congressman was willing to take his place. Al Quie decided to ask the president for permission to resurrect this ancient loophole for freeing prisoners so that his brother and prayer partner could be released from Holabird immediately.

When Quie called Colson to explain his bizarre but totally genuine act of sacrifice, the proposed beneficiary could not believe his ears. "Al, I just won't let you do this," said Colson.

"I mean it, Chuck. I haven't come to this decision lightly," said Quie. "Your family needs you and I can't sleep while you're in prison. I think I'd be a lot happier being inside myself."

Although deeply moved by his friend's offer, Colson turned it down, so the idea was dropped. The prayers of the visiting brothers, however, went on. They climaxed one afternoon with Harold Hughes making an impassioned plea for Colson to hand all his troubles over to God. This was not an easy suggestion to follow. Colson now felt certain he would have to serve the remaining two years and five months of his sentence; he was distraught at the arrest of Chris; and he was shattered by the loss of his license to practice law. His fortunes had never been at a lower ebb. Yet that same evening, January 29, in the loneliness of the prison night, he offered his prayer of surrender: "Lord, if this is what it is all about, then I thank you. I praise you for leaving me in prison, for letting them take away my license to practice law—yes, even for my son being arrested. I praise you for giving me your love through these men, for being God, for just letting me walk with Jesus."

These brave words of faith, with echoes in their anguish of Jesus' prayer at Gethsemane, brought their reward. Soon after saying them aloud to the empty walls of his room at Holabird, Colson felt his spirits soaring to strange heights of spiritual ecstasy. "In the hours that followed I discovered more strength than I had ever known before," he recalled. "This was the real mountaintop experience. Above and around me the world was filled with love and beauty. For the first time I felt truly free."

Physical liberation was soon to follow. David Shapiro placed a call to Judge Gesell to ask if Colson could be released for a ten-day furlough from prison to visit Chris. "I took Gesell over the story and I could tell he was really affected by those newspaper reports of the boy saying, 'Now you've got two Colsons in jail.' Then, outta the blue, Gesell says, 'I'll release Colson for good today.' I was blown away by that. Why did Gesell do it? I think it was because he had a son of the same age himself and he knew how much he needed his father."

At the time of this Gesell-Shapiro telephone conversation, Colson was in Shapiro's office in Washington, preparing for yet more legal formalities related to the cases of other Watergate defendants. Shapiro barreled down the corridor to tell his client, "Chuck, you're free! Gesell's freed you! You're free!"

"Don't kid me, Dave, I can't take it," was Colson's downbeat response. After weeks of frustration and disappointment his emotions were too frozen to explode into outpourings of instant joy. "You're free, I tell you, you're free," bellowed Shapiro. Colson broke down in tears of relief. His prison ordeal was over.

It took some hours for the paperwork to be issued by Gesell's office, and for the signed judicial release to be driven over to the jail. So Colson had time to get back to Holabird and to exchange farewell hugs, handshakes, and prayers with its remaining eighteen inmates. After these emotional leave-takings, the final exit formalities were processed by the duty marshal, a believer named Jack, who said with a warm smile, "The Lord really takes care of his own men. I kind of knew he would set you free today."

Outside the barbed-wire entrance of Holabird, Patty Colson was sitting at the wheel of the family station wagon. Having shared none of the marshal's certainties about her husband's release date, she was weeping from shock and relief. As the couple embraced before driving back to their home along Interstate 95 toward Washington, Colson made what proved to be an accurate prophecy. "From now on, life will be different."

First Weeks of Freedom

The immediate problems Colson had to face in the hours after his release were media intrusion, disorientation, and sleeplessness. When he arrived home after the thirty-mile drive from Holabird, he was mobbed by over a hundred reporters and cameramen, crammed into the driveway of his house. The pre-prison Colson had faced many such media stakeouts during Watergate and knew how to handle them. The post-prison Colson could not cope. As he blinked nervously into the TV lights, his once-confident voice sounded strangled, almost shell-shocked, as he managed to stumble through a few words of thanks to God for changing his life and to Judge Gesell for releasing him. This faltering statement produced the headline GESELL FREES COLSON. COLSON THANKS THE LORD in the next morning's *Washington Post.*

The stumbling and the faltering continued even after Colson was safely inside the front door. There were moments when he did not seem to know his way around his own house. His conversation was disjointed, with odd pauses in the middle of his sentences. The welcome-home party consisted of Patty and the Coe family. "Hiya, brother," said Doug, embracing the ex-prisoner in a warm bear hug with exactly the same words of greeting he had used at their first encounter in Colson's law firm offices eighteen months earlier. Coe's daughter Paula, who had been living in the house for the past seven months to keep Patty company, had prepared flowers, snacks, and a blazing fire in the hearth with the help of her mother, Jan. Colson's disorientation soon faded as he was enfolded in the laughter and the love of friends that flowed through his living room on that first evening.

The first night was more difficult. Colson tossed and turned in the unfamiliar softness of his bed. Unable to sleep, he found himself staring at the ceiling as he kept up a drowsy dialogue, first with God and then with him-self. "Lord, I did my time . . . I paid my debt . . . Now I'm free, ready to build a new life . . . a more simple life . . . No more politics . . . maybe a good job in business . . . perhaps some writing . . . more time with my family."

When he finally drifted off into sleep, Colson had nightmares. He dreamt he was back in Dormitory G at Maxwell. Reliving the familiar sounds, smells, and sweaty air of his incarceration, he found himself sur-rounded by the sallow faces of the inmates he had known. Some of them were playing a boisterous card game. Suddenly one of the players, a six-foot-six-inch prison veteran called Archie, broke away from the game to strike up an aggressive conversation. "Hey, Colson," said Archie, towering over him, putting out his heavily tattooed chest with the menace of a tank turret preparing to open fire. "You'll be out of here soon. What are you go-ing to do for us?"

Suddenly the whole room fell silent. All ears were straining to hear the answer. "I'll help in some way," replied Colson. "I'll never forget you guys or this stinking place."

"Bull!" roared Archie, slamming down the pack of cards on the table. "You all say that. I've seen big shots like you come and go. They all say the same things while they're inside. Then they get out and forget us fast. There ain't nobody cares about us. Nobody!"

"I'll care. I'll remember," said Colson.

"Bull!" bellowed Archie again, making an obscene gesture.

Colson woke from his dream with a start. He was shivering and sweat-ing. Patty sat up and put her arm round him to calm him down. The scene faded from his eyes but not from his memory in the way that nightmares usually do. There was good reason for this. For Archie's angry confronta-tion was not a fantasy from the world of dreams. It had actually happened. Colson remembered the words and the atmosphere as if he were right back in Dormitory G with the aggressive eyes of Archie glowering into his face. What could it mean? Was it some sort of message? With these disturbing questions pounding through his brain, Colson eventually dozed off into a few more hours of fitful sleep.

Next morning was not much easier. The media stakeout, though smaller, continued. Colson felt he was a prisoner in his own home. This was a psy-chological as much as a physical condition. "I was scared to go out. I was scared to get into the car and drive over to the store," recalled Colson. "I just couldn't adjust. I kept thinking to myself: What are people going to think? What are they going to say to me? I felt I was carrying a stigma with a lot of shame attached to it. So I was feeling very uncomfortable and very nervous."

Colson's nervousness was increased by the large number of press calls that continually interrupted his early days of settling in. Reporters followed him on his first trip away from home. Four days after his release he traveled to South Carolina with Patty to visit Chris. On the flight down to Columbia, Colson resolved to give his son a strict warning about the dangers of taking drugs. This resolve evaporated as soon as father and son were reunited at the airport. Colson's heart melted when he caught his first glimpse of Chris, looking pale and woebegone as he waited at the terminal gate. So instead of a lecture, the prodigal father clasped the prodigal son in a warm embrace. "You'll be all right," he said through hugs and tears.

Chris had been expecting a stern father and was moved at encountering a loving one. "As I saw him get off the plane I said to myself, Now here comes my dad to yell at me, but not at all. He was really kind and good. I told him exactly what had happened and he said, 'Chris, we all make our mistakes in life. One time is understandable, but to make the same mistake twice would be stupid.' "

Colson himself was getting into the business of not repeating mistakes. He was overcome with remorse as he talked to Chris for hours over that weekend and came to realize how deeply his own problems had affected his son. It was not just the past seven months of his imprisonment that had caused pain to Chris. Colson had been a distant and neglectful father during most of his three and a half years of service in the White House and during the ensuing two years of his embroilment in Watergate-related legal battles. So their father-and-son relationship needed a great deal of fence mending and bridge building. Colson, deeply chastened as he took all this on board, was determined to change himself into a much more involved and caring parent.

After this visit to Chris, Colson flew the short distance to Montgomery, Alabama, in order to visit the friends he had left behind in the Maxwell penitentiary. Going back into the jail was a strange experience a mere seven days after his release. Despite the unwelcome presence of TV crews, Colson managed to have a joyful reunion with his old prison prayer partners, particularly with twenty-seven-year-old Paul Kramer. Although neither of them knew it, they were destined to be partners again within a year—in prison ministry.

Soon after returning to Washington, Colson traveled to Spain for a getting-away-from-it-all vacation. He and Patty stayed for two and a half weeks in a beautiful villa overlooking the Mediterranean on the Costa del Sol. The house was lent to him by Paul Temple, a wealthy associate of Doug Coe's in the Fellowship. "It was a time of real decompression," recalled Colson. "Patty and I were on our own and we just went for walks, drank the local wine, ate great paella, and relaxed. I wasn't doing any serious thinking, any planning, any studying—nothing."

Colson, who was normally not much good at doing nothing, soon swung back into hyperactivity when he returned to the United States. One of his first moves was to accept an invitation to be interviewed by Barbara Walters on the *Today* show. It was a near disaster. Little or nothing of the new Colson came across on the screen. Instead there was plenty of the old Colson on view. In the absence of his legendary grandmother, he walked all over Henry Kissinger, savaging the secretary of state with heavy-footed criticism of his alleged media manipulations. According to Colson these transgressions included disloyalty to the president and the planting of stories in the *New York Times* that were to Kissinger's advantage and Nixon's detriment.

A great many Colson watchers were disappointed with this interview. His Christian friends chided him for his negativity, lack of love, and lack of references to his newfound faith. Under headlines like SAME OLD HATCHET MAN, his adversaries in the press gave him harsh reviews. Perhaps his most surprising critic was Richard Nixon. Calling from San Clemente, his Saint Helena–like place of exile on the coast of southern California, the former president gave his former special counsel a gentle but unmistakable rebuke.

"I, uh, caught some excerpts of your interview on the *Today* show and, uh, well, Henry called me," said Nixon. "You know, we only have one president now. One secretary of state. So we need to support them, you know, Chuck. . . . I mean, you and I know Henry's faults but as Americans we support our leaders and our country, right?"

Colson accepted the implied reprimand. He knew his ex-boss was right. Never again did Colson indulge in political combat with old adversaries. He apologized to Henry Kissinger. He told his Christian friends that he had learned an important lesson from the episode. "When I let my old political nature emerge, my witness for Jesus Christ gets hurt."

At this time Colson received many different streams of advice about how, or indeed whether at all, he should be putting himself forward as a

Christian witness. One of those advising restraint was Richard Nixon. Soon after the ex-president's phone call about the *Today* show he invited Colson to come and visit him in California. At that meeting Nixon told him bluntly: "Don't give up everything for religious work. You have great abilities, great imagination, and great drive. You will succeed in whatever you do. Go out now and make some money for your family. There are plenty of things outside the law."

Contrary to Nixon's assumptions about the impossibility of Colson going back to his old profession, in fact a return to the law was looking hopeful. Although Virginia had disbarred him, Colson's prospects of regaining a license to practice in Massachusetts were good, according to Charles Morin, who was tireless in fighting battles to get his partner reinstated as a member of the state bar. These battles were outwardly about Colson's status in the legal profession but inwardly they were about the future direction of his life. Financially, Colson was not under pressure, since his old law firm had agreed to pay him $60,000 a year for the next three years for past services. Moreover, several of his former partners believed that Colson could once again bring in substantial earnings for himself and the firm if he was willing to travel down the road toward reestablishing himself as an attorney-at-law in Boston. One of the most enthusiastic of these partners was Myron Mintz, who recalled driving Colson along Boston's State Street (the prime location for the city's leading law firms) just after the Massachusetts Supreme Court had voted against disbarring him. "I was excited. I thought Colson could be a big business getter for the firm all over again and I told him so," said Mintz, "but my enthusiasm was not matched by his. I remember him turning his head away and saying in a dreamy sort of voice, 'But I may have other plans.' "

What were those other plans? Colson himself did not know. He listened to some lucrative offers, including invitations to take senior executive positions from a West Coast industrialist and from an East Coast communications corporation. Something inside him made him turn them down just as he turned down the overtures from his old law firm. These rejections puzzled his friends and baffled his wife. His relationship with Patty went through a period of strain. Similar tensions surfaced in Colson's relationship with his prayer partners at Fellowship House. Doug Coe, Al Quie, Harold Hughes, and Graham Purcell kept prodding their celebrated brother to commit himself to various speaking engagements and projects endorsed by the Fellowship. Colson's reluctance to go along with their plans started to cause friction among the brothers. "There was a time when we were frustrated with Chuck because he just didn't seem able to decide what he wanted to do," recalled Doug Coe.

The indecision was ended by a vision. One sunny morning in April 1975, Colson had an extraordinary experience when peering into his bathroom mirror. "As I stared at my reflection, a startling series of images flashed across my mind. I saw men in prison gray moving about. Classes. Discussions. Prayers," he has recalled. "The pictures became more sharply focused—of smiling men and women streaming out of prisons, of Bibles, and study groups around tables. These mental images lasted but a few seconds, then they were gone. I had never experienced anything like it before or since."

Colson's vision unsettled him at first. Was it of God? Or was it just a flash of secular inspiration? A bright idea that had suddenly popped into his consciousness? As he was pondering these alternative explanations, a voice seemed to be speaking within him, issuing clear commands: "Take the prisoners out, teach them, return them to prisons to build Christian fellowships. Spread these fellowships through every penitentiary in America."

Excited and energized by the clarity of the message he thought he had received, Colson raced to the telephone and called Harold Hughes. Twenty minutes later the Iowa senator was sipping coffee in the makeshift basement office Patty had created for her husband. Colson began, "Brother, you may think I'm crazy, but I've had a new idea . . ." Colson's enthusiasm carried him away into making detailed plans on the hoof as he outlined his new idea. He spoke of furloughing inmates out of prisons for two- or three-week periods; of teaching them the principles of discipleship in classes at Fellowship House; of quartering them in nearby accommodations in the surrounding residential areas of Washington; and of sending them back into their prisons to build their own Christian fellowships.

Harold Hughes listened intently to these radical schemes, although his expression suggested he was wondering if Colson had eaten something too rich the night before. Eventually, when the vision had been fully explained, Hughes leaned back in his chair, folding his arms across his chest. "It's of God, no doubt about it," he said. Then he heard a sigh and added: "But of course, it's also impossible. We couldn't get inside prisons, much less take men out."

Colson was not in the mood to take no for an answer. "With God all things are possible," replied Colson, quoting Mark 10:27, one of Hughes's favorite texts from scripture.

"But where would we begin?" demanded Hughes. "There are hundreds of prisons; wardens are a hard-nosed bunch." He added that during his terms as governor of Iowa and as a United States senator he had found both the public and the politicians highly resistant to ideas for prison reform.

Harold Hughes's initial pessimism seemed to be well rooted in political reality. He took Colson to a meeting on Capitol Hill with his fellow senator James Eastland, chairman of the Judiciary Committee, which handles all federal laws relating to prisons and criminal justice. Eastland listened courteously to Colson's plan but had no grasp of what it was really about. Perhaps that was not surprising, for Colson's questions elicited the remarkable revelation that the chairman of the Judiciary Committee had never visited a single prison. Eastland concluded the meeting in a cloud of genialities and generalities, promising to look into the "mighty interesting" scheme and get back to his visitors on it. He never did, despite persistent calls from Colson to the senator's staff. It was the first of many disappointments.

Although the politicians' doors on Capitol Hill remained stubbornly closed to Colson's vision of a Christian discipleship program for prisoners, the bureaucracy of prison administration was unexpectedly open to it. This breakthrough came on a sunny Washington morning in June 1975 when Colson and Harold Hughes met with the head of the Federal Bureau of Prisons, Norman Carlson. As Colson outlined his plans for an experimental training scheme at Fellowship House for furloughed prisoners, Carlson remained impassive. Hughes thought the chemistry between the two men was going badly wrong, particularly when Colson hammered away at a number of negative features in the system where Carlson had spent his career, such as the failure of the existing rehabilitation schemes and the high reoffending rate—80 percent in some states. After listing these negatives, Colson declared that the one and only person who could make a difference in changing the system was Jesus Christ. So could Mr. Carlson please issue an order that would allow the Fellowship House team to go into any federal prison in the United States and bring out selected prisoners for training as disciples of Jesus Christ?

In the silence that followed this proposition, Colson realized it must sound utterly preposterous to a professional prison administrator. He almost started to laugh out loud at the absurdity of what he had asked for until Carlson asked him sharply: "Is that it?"

"Yes sir," replied Colson.

Another enigmatic silence followed. It was broken by a surprising inquiry from the head of the prison bureau: "Let me ask you a question. A few weeks ago my wife and I were at the Terminal Island prison, in southern California. On Sunday we went to chapel. At one point in the service the chaplain asked the inmates to join in with spontaneous prayers. In the back—I couldn't see him—a man prayed for my wife and me. I was surprised that he did that. Why did he do it?"

Colson was caught off guard by this story. He paused to assess it. "Well, Mr. Carlson, he's a Christian," Colson eventually replied. "We're taught to pray for those in authority. I did for the warden at Maxwell."

"But I'm the one keeping him in prison," objected Carlson in an emotional voice, jabbing his fingers into his own chest.

"Mr. Carlson," said Colson, seizing this electrifying moment with some high-voltage emotion of his own, "that man prayed for you because he loves you."

Norman Carlson shook his head in bewilderment. Then he asked several administrative questions about the obvious difficulties the proposal might create. His audience of two felt certain that he was leading up to a rejection of the scheme. But Carlson continued to be a man of surprises. He concluded the meeting with an abrupt, three-sentence answer. "Go ahead with your plans, Mr. Colson, Senator Hughes," said the head of the prison bureau. "I'll issue the order. Get together with my staff and work out the details."

Hughes and Colson walked back into the Washington sunlight dazed and astonished by the result of their meeting. Getting into their waiting car, driven by Fred Rhodes, they gave thanks to God for the unknown inmate at the back of the Terminal Island prison chapel who had prayed aloud for Mr. and Mrs. Norman Carlson.

This meeting was a turning point in Colson's life in more ways than one. With a new sense of purpose for his vision, he threw himself into the work of implementing the discipleship scheme with all his old drive and energy. On the home front his relationship with Patty moved back onto its familiar track of loving partnership. Their happiness increased when the news came through that all charges against Chris would be dropped. With Wendell doing exceptionally well at Princeton and Emily at high school, family life was back on track too.

Colson's relationships at Fellowship House were equally revitalized as he and his fraternal prayer partners began to immerse themselves in the planning of the prisoner training scheme. Because this was not yet a twenty-four-hour-a-day occupation, Colson had time for his writing and for taking on a growing program of Christian speaking engagements. To help him with these tasks, Colson teamed up with Fred Rhodes, who became his voluntary but full-time assistant. As these new threads in his post-prison life of writing, speaking, and prison discipleship started to come together, Colson, for the first time since his release, began to feel a deep sense of vocation.

Christian Public Speaker

Colson had been reluctant in his first six months of freedom to embark on any program of public speaking. He was still a bruised pilgrim, uncertain of what direction his life would take. The first major request he considered seriously was an invitation from the annual Southern Baptist Convention. This massive event, attended by over twenty thousand pastors from America's largest Protestant denomination, was to be held in Miami Beach in June 1975. Colson accepted the invitation partly because he was strongly urged to do so by Fred Rhodes, an ardent Southern Baptist. Another key factor was that Colson would be introduced at the convention by his former prison chaplain at the Maxwell federal penitentiary, the Reverend Edmond Blow.

As soon as it was reported that Colson would be addressing the convention, much un-Christian controversy erupted among the Christian attendees. The chairman, James L. Pleitz, pastor of the First Baptist Church of Pensacola, came under pressure to withdraw the invitation. This was resisted, but Pleitz had to yield to demands that Colson's billing at the conference be downgraded in order to avoid the impression that he was being given special treatment. As a result of these grumblings, Colson arrived in Miami Beach to be told that the time allocated to his address had been reduced from thirty-five minutes to twenty-three minutes. His appearance on the podium was put back to a later hour, 8 P.M. He was also instructed to keep strictly to his time limit.

Cutting twelve minutes from a carefully structured speech of thirty-five minutes at the last moment was a tall order, but Colson had to agree to it. To ensure that his remarks ran to time, he and Fred Rhodes worked out a signaling plan. Rhodes was to sit in the front row equipped with a stop-

watch and a text of the abbreviated talk. If Colson were in danger of over-
running, Rhodes would take off his glasses as a signal that additional para-
graphs should be deleted.

With the antennae of an experienced public speaker, Colson detected, as
soon as he arrived on the platform, that the convention was in an unrecep-
tive mood. A pastor who delivered a keynote speech immediately before
him was given scant attention and only perfunctory applause. With delegates milling around in the aisles, Brother Blow's warm introduction was
heard in chilly silence. Yet at least Blow quieted the restless audience into
a tense hush. As Colson rose to deliver his opening text from scripture,
"That which we have seen and heard, declare we unto you" (1 John 1:3),
an electrifying atmosphere of expectancy filled the hall.

Speaking in the auditorium he had last entered three years earlier, alongside the president of the United States, for the 1972 Republican National
Convention, Colson told his story of how pride had caused him to fall from
power to prison, and of how on that most painful of descents he had discovered the incomparable joy and fulfillment of a faithful relationship with
Jesus Christ. Nervous and stumbling over his words at the beginning of his
speech, Colson, in the words of Fred Rhodes, resembled "a rabbit caught
in the glare of headlights." This was not Rhodes's only worry. He quickly
realized that Colson had mixed up his notes and was delivering the uncut
version of the speech. As a result he was running long over time. So
Rhodes removed and replaced his glasses. Colson, whose delivery was
growing in confidence, took no notice of this prearranged signal. With increasing desperation Rhodes waved his spectacles in the air.

These frantic warnings made not the slightest impression on Colson. He
was completely blinded by the TV lights and could not see Rhodes or anyone else in the audience. So his speech ran for the full thirty-five minutes
of its original length, ending with these words: "Paul made an eloquent
statement when he said in his letter to the Philippians, 'I count everything
a loss compared to the surpassing greatness of knowing Christ Jesus my
Lord.' Well, here tonight I too count it all as loss—the White House, the
limousines, the yachts, the hundred-thousand-dollar-a-year law practice,
all those temples of wealth and power, are loss compared to the overwhelming gain of being able to walk through this life with Christ Jesus."

As Colson returned to his seat, for a few seconds the vast assembly of
pastors seemed to suspend its judgment in eerie silence. Then there came
a low rumble like an advancing posse of horses' hooves. It magnified into

the thunder of a mighty charge of cavalry pounding over an iron bridge. On and on rolled the enthusiastic applause as twenty thousand clergymen rose to their feet, letting their seats slam into their chair backs as they cheered, clapped their hands, and stamped their feet with wild appreciation. As these waves of sound crested over him for several minutes Colson was dazed, bewildered, even a little frightened. He said afterward to Rhodes, "Dusty, I've felt the presence of the Holy Spirit before, but I've never felt his power flowing through a great audience."

The Miami Beach address to the Southern Baptist Convention marked a watershed in Colson's career as a Christian public speaker. It made him understand how his words could be empowered by the Holy Spirit. It opened the floodgates to a torrent of speaking invitations from churches and religious organizations all across America. It also dangled before his eyes the temptation to turn himself into that most caricaturable of religious stereotypes, the "celebrity Christian." The first friend to warn him of this temptation was the Reverend Edward Blow. Before the applause had died away in the Miami Beach auditorium, Brother Blow embraced Colson and whispered, "Careful, boy! The devil is on your back now."

Colson was quick to heed his former prison chaplain's words of wisdom. As he flew back to Washington with Fred Rhodes, Colson was in a mood of humility mingled with caution. "Dusty, before I go out and do more speaking engagements I want to learn a lot more about the Christian faith," he confided to his old friend. "I don't just mean knowing the Bible better or learning the history of popes and Protestant leaders. I want to understand how God works in the lives of his servants. John Wesley fascinates me. So does George Whitefield, and William Wilberforce perhaps most of all. Because of my interest in prison work, Christian social causes interest me deeply. But I want to educate myself before I start making commitments to this or that group."

Although he did start his self-devised regime of Christian education by reading voraciously in the fields of biography and apologetics, Colson could not escape from the changes that the speech to the Southern Baptist Convention created in his life. By the fall of 1975 over a thousand speaking invitations had piled up on his desk. When he tried to decide which of them should be accepted, he turned to his brothers at Fellowship House for advice. They did not always give him encouragement, as in the case of the invitation from the student body of George Washington University. "The audience of GW will be mostly Jews, atheists, and intellectuals, three groups that hate everything you and Nixon stand for," said Harold Hughes. "They'll probably tar and feather you," joked Doug Coe, "but at least you'll be joining a long line of Christian martyrs."

There was still enough of the combative spirit in Colson to fire him up with a readiness, if not a relish, for meeting challenges from difficult audiences. So he accepted the students' invitation. On the night of November 12, 1975, he walked into a crowded auditorium on the George Washington campus surrounded with posters announcing, "Charles Colson Speaks on Watergate, Prison, and Spiritual Rebirth." It turned out to be the toughest assignment of his early years as a Christian speaker. The evening began badly. With over eight hundred students crushed into a hall seating five hundred, Colson tried to ease the physical pressure by saying, "Those of you standing at the back, feel free to come to the front and sit on the floor. There's plenty of room. And don't worry, I'm not going to preach to you."

A bearded young man in a bright red coat jumped to his feet and began walking down the aisle. "We've had enough of your preaching from the White House over the last four years, Colson," he shouted, turning back to the audience to ask, "Right?"

"That's right," came a chorus of voices.

Another youth stood up, his face contorted with anger. "You belong back in jail, Colson." Hoots and jeers filled the hall. A slow handclap started. Then other voices chipped in with cries of "Let him speak! Let him speak!" As the cacophony of demonstration and counterdemonstration grew, the place became bedlam. One or two students came to blows. Someone yelled, "Call the police!" Gradually the shouts of "Let him speak" seemed to climb into the ascendant.

Colson stood calmly at the podium. When there was a lull in the fracas he addressed the original red-coated heckler, who was still attacking him. "We'll have a question-and-answer time after I've spoken. Come up to the microphone then and we'll talk." It was a skillful deflection of the crisis. The red-coat stroked his beard, shook his head, and sat down.

Colson then announced: "I'd like to begin this meeting with a prayer." Disbelief, embarrassment, and in some cases suppressed fury spread over the faces of the young audience. Opening a student meeting with a prayer on this liberal campus, which had been in the vanguard of the antiwar protest movement, was an unheard-of innovation. But despite some rumblings of protest Colson was able to pray that the Holy Spirit would speak through him to the hearts of his hearers. Then he began his story, in which he traveled from the Oval Office to Tom Phillips's porch, to the cottage on the Maine coast, to Fellowship House, to Judge Gesell's courtroom, to Holabird and Maxwell prisons, ending up with love, joy, and peace in the Lord Jesus Christ.

Colson was listened to by the students in tense silence. Then for over an hour they fired questions at him. Some were skeptical, a few were hostile, all were difficult. A sample of the exchanges:

"Why do you think Jesus is so superior to Allah or Muhammad or Buddha?"

"Because he came to this earth to teach us about love, then died on the cross for our sins. He rose again. He lives. I am convinced he is the only one who can save us from our messed-up selves."

"What have you done about the sins you committed while in the White House?"

"I've confessed them to God and asked his forgiveness. I've made restitution to certain people when it was possible to do so."

"Like who?"

"Arthur Burns, chairman of the Federal Reserve Board. I leaked an untrue story about him which was hurtful. I apologized to Arthur a year ago and we are now good friends."

"It doesn't seem like you've been punished very much for your sins."

Colson drew a deep breath, fighting for composure. "During the past year I've spent seven months in prison, I lost my father, I've been disbarred from practicing law, and my life has been turned upside down."

There were murmurs of sympathy at this answer, but the audience tensed up again when the subject turned to the thirty-seventh president of the United States. With boos and jeers breaking out at the mention of Nixon's name, Colson's companion Fred Rhodes whispered to a friend, "Thank God the campus police have arrived. Chuck may need protection if this gets violent."

"You say you've seen the light, Mr. Colson, but Nixon still doesn't think he's done anything wrong. How do you feel about him?" asked a young coed, her voice screeching with scorn. Colson was under pressure on this one. He still admired Nixon but he felt betrayed by many disclosures on the White House tapes, particularly by the ex-president's lies to his aides and to the American people. Yet he could not bear to go down the road traveled by Haldeman, Ehrlichman, and others by expressing condemnation of his former boss. Before the meeting Colson had prayed with Rhodes to be given wisdom and discernment in his answers if an anti-Nixon question was asked. Now he was on the spot.

"Like every man the former president has his weaknesses and strengths. We all know his weaknesses. They've been hashed over for many months. He has his good side too. In all fairness we need to remember this," replied Colson. He hesitated a moment before continuing, "But Richard Nixon has been my friend and I'm not going to turn away from a friend."

The last sentence was spoken with real passion. For a moment there was stunned silence. Colson expected the hall to explode with anger. Instead it erupted with spontaneous and sustained applause. Afterward several students came up to say that the courage of the reply had touched the need in their own lives for loyal friendship.

Soon after the totally unexpected reaction to the Nixon answer, the campus chaplain who was chairing the meeting, the Reverend David Schreier, brought the proceedings to a close. Schreier added that if any of the students wanted to continue the discussion, he would like to invite them back to his home for coffee. About seventy students turned up, among them the red-coated heckler who had been so aggressive at the start of the meeting. When he approached Colson the boy's face was as red as his jacket. His opening words seemed to presage a further confrontation. "I was in the courtroom when they sentenced you," he began, "and I wanted them to give you life imprisonment." Then the boy smiled and put out his hand. "Now I want to apologize to you. I'm Jewish so I don't share your faith but I liked what you said tonight and I respect you."

It was the first of many warm encounters between Colson and individual students that evening, which ended with an extended session of prayer. With blue-jeaned bodies jammed into every inch of space on the floor of David Schreier's living room, the focus of the final half hour was praying to Jesus Christ. As the clock ticked toward midnight a familiar voice, now close to tears, was heard to say, "God help me to find what these people have. I want it, I need it. Amen." The voice belonged to the bearded boy in the red coat.

Not all of Colson's public speaking engagements went as well as the evenings at George Washington University or at the Miami Beach convention of Southern Baptists. He had his failures and his downers. Even in Christian churches, Colson's account of his conversion produced its disbelievers. A measure of skepticism, cynicism, and sometimes outright hostility followed him wherever he traveled. One of the first denominational leaders to invite Colson to his home church, in Leesburg, Virginia, was C. P. Bryant, the editor of *Baptist World* magazine. A leading deacon in that church, a former official of the Internal Revenue Service, promptly declared, "If Colson ever darkens these doors I will walk out of them and never come back." In similar vein, a Presbyterian minister rose at the beginning of a prayer breakfast in New York to attack the guest speaker with the denunciation "Mr. Colson, I think you're a fraud who's trying to rip off Jesus Christ."

Back in the secular world, where passions still ran high over Watergate, the going could be even rougher. There was an episode at Chicago's O'Hare airport in October 1975 when an angry man chased Colson up and down an escalator shouting personal abuse at him. In all such encounters Colson displayed grace under pressure. "Well, blessings on you," he kept saying gently to his O'Hare tormentor. The ex-IRS deacon was disarmed after being persuaded to stay and listen to Colson's testimony. And the Presbyterian minister came round too after Colson had said, "Don't judge me by my words after one speech. Judge me by life and work for Christ ten years from now."

Fred Rhodes, the chronicler of these episodes, thought that Colson was showing the signs of being "a new creation." But in his role as a candid friend Rhodes also worried that the new creation was getting overtired and overstressed. One of his concerns was that in those early months after his release, Colson liked to relax from stress by drinking and smoking—two minor vices that in the eyes of some evangelical Christians are major sins.

The issue of Colson's smoking came to a head after he had delivered a testimony talk at a church in Illionis. The evening ended with intense irritation for Colson when the local pastor interrupted the quiet time immediately after the talk for a fund-raising appeal linked to the enrolling of new members in his church. As enrollment forms were being handed out by stewards, Colson's distaste for this blatant form of religious hucksterism caused him to slip out of the church and into the parking lot, where he cooled down by lighting up a cigarette. An elderly member of the congregation spotted him and increased his irritation. "You gave us a fine testimony tonight, Mr. Colson. I hate to see you spoil it by smoking a cigarette here on church property," said this religious vigilante.

Colson sighed, inhaled one more time, and stubbed out the cigarette. "You're right," he said mildly. "I still have many victories to win in my Christian life. But I consider smoking more dangerous to my health than to my Christianity."

Instead of accepting this partial act of repentance by a smoking sinner, the elderly man wanted to start an argument. "Tobacco is as obnoxious to the Lord as any other sin," he asserted. "I've seen the demon of nicotine ruin marriages, destroy careers, and bring fine people to an early grave. Like alcohol, it's a powerful tool for Satan."

Colson bristled and entered into a dispute about the scriptural authority
for the view that smoking is a sin. Although the argument ended in tetchy
disagreement, Colson let his hair down later when alone with Fred Rhodes.
"I've had enough of these people and all this stuff," he complained bitterly.
"Satan's not the problem behind my smoking. The problem is my lousy
tobacco-stained weakness of will, which got weaker because of the cigarettes
I smoked in prison. But there's no connection between my faith and my will."

Rhodes begged to differ. The two friends had a no-holds-barred argument in which Colson said he'd prefer to quit shoddy church fund-raising
events rather than quit smoking. Suddenly all his frustration and his despondency at being exploited as a celebrity Christian poured out of him.
He did not mean all the angry words he said, but Rhodes was in no doubt
that Colson was close to the breaking point.

The two men were an odd couple to be brothers in Christ. Fred Rhodes
was a pedantic, precise, slightly overfussy lawyer-turned-bureaucrat. Colson was a highly strung, high-voltage, combative crusader, always at the
ready to charge over the top for the causes in which he believed. Although
he was still at an early and perhaps immature stage in his Christian journey, the great cause that now united him with Rhodes was their love of Jesus. It was a love that had a calming, bonding, and growing effect on both
of them. Within hours the two friends had exchanged mutual apologies,
mutual embraces, and were working out a new strategy for speaking engagements that would be pleasing to the Lord.

Rhodes went so far as to put his thoughts down on paper. In a personal
handwritten memo to Colson he wrote: "You are at a crossroads . . . there are
some very real dangers in allowing the acumen, the brilliance and the leadership abilities of the old Chuck Colson take over in doing the Lord's work. Using your manifold talents in the way you are used to harnessing them will
cause you to give way to your natural feelings of frustration, disappointment
and disillusionment when things and people do not work out as planned."

After pointing out that Jesus had said that *people will know you are
mine by the way you love one another*, and adding tartly, "He knew full
well how unlovely the Christian community can be at times," Rhodes
moved to practical suggestions: "Future platform appearances should be
accepted only as they relate specifically to what God is calling you to do.
Beyond what is presently scheduled the platform should not be used to
raise money as a primary goal or to entertain the curious. You do not have
the time or the health for this. Therefore beginning now you must discipline yourself to take time off regularly."

In his old-fashioned but perceptive way, Fred Rhodes had hit the nail on the head. Colson was in danger of confusing movement with action on his spiritual journey. He was rushing around too much, taking on too many speaking engagements, and not setting aside enough time for reading, reflection, prayer, and writing.

Another factor in Colson's overpressured life at this time was that his relationship with Patty was coming under strain. Not only was the hectic nature of her husband's schedule causing tension because of his absences from home; Patty also found it difficult to come to terms with the "open prayer—open heart" aspects of evangelical Christianity, when she herself preferred the quieter, more private, and more contemplative practices of her Catholic spirituality.

Fred Rhodes knew about these strains and stresses on the home front. In another personal memorandum to Colson he urged him to carve out "more personal time which has to include time for family. Last but not least, time must be budgeted for study, prayer and meditation." This memo ended with the suggestion (unexpected because of Rhodes's previous aversion to Colson's nautical activities) that Chuck should "join a restricted and hopefully remote yacht club which itself might provide some restricted privacy for you and Patty . . . you should buy a boat which will sleep two people only . . . you two need to go out, drop anchor and do nothing but read, think and pray."

Although Colson did not follow Fred Rhodes's advice to the letter by joining an isolated yacht club and sailing away into the wide blue yonder with Patty, he followed it in spirit. He dropped anchor to the extent of cutting back his schedule and staying at home to do much more reading, thinking, and praying. However, action man does not become contemplative man quite so easily. Colson needed to be busy with a project so he threw himself into finishing an endeavor he had started in prison and to which he devoted much prayer, thought, and energy. The project was finalizing the book that was to make him world famous as a Christian author. Its title was *Born Again*.

Born Again

The idea of writing a book had been suggested to Colson many times since he left the White House. In the early days the approaches came from secular publishers, with offers of advances in the $150,000–$250,000 range.

This was big money for an author in the mid-1970s and Colson was attracted by it. He was also attracted by the opportunity to set the record straight on his years of service as a presidential aide. In the frenzy of Watergate a great many inaccuracies, falsehoods, and calumnies had been published about Nixon's grandmother-trampling hatchet man. Colson liked the idea of writing a memoir that would settle a few old scores and justify many of his actions. So in 1973 he drafted some twenty-six chapters of a book along these lines. This unpublished manuscript survives in his archives at Wheaton College, Illinois. Like many political autobiographies of the Watergate era, it makes fascinating reading but it is a self-serving composition, occasionally economical with the truth. Writing it was not a happy experience for the author because the old Colson was so clearly in conflict with the new Colson who was starting to emerge as a committed Christian believer at this time.

When Colson was serving his sentence at the Maxwell prison he began to receive invitations from other publishers, asking him to write a book about his conversion. In October 1974 Colson sent a letter to Doug Coe telling him about these approaches. "I'm not interested in getting out a book just to make money," wrote Colson. "I want it to be a Christian book and I would prefer to do it with Christians if this is possible. Do you have any contacts here at Fellowship House who could advise me about publishers?"

The ubiquitous Doug Coe made contact with Leonard LeSourd. He had recently retired from a twenty-eight-year stint as editor of the Christian magazine *Guideposts*. With his wife, Catherine Marshall, best-selling author of *A Man Called Peter* and *Christy*, LeSourd had become the leading partner in a small but fast-expanding Christian publishing firm, Chosen Books. Doug Coe's suggestion of signing up Colson as an author in the Maxwell prison seemed to LeSourd the longest of long shots, particularly as he knew that Chosen Books could not compete financially with the advances likely to be offered by larger publishers. LeSourd was open about this weakness. "We give our authors maximum shepherding, generous contracts, low advances," he explained in his letter to Colson, advising against a "quickie book" on his conversion, recommending instead an in-depth story focusing on the struggles of a new Christian. Convinced that his frankness about the low advances would be a showstopper, LeSourd mailed the letter and forgot about it for several weeks. Then out of the blue came a call from Doug Coe setting up a meeting with Colson in an office adjacent to the Washington courtroom where he had to testify in the trial of John Mitchell and other Watergate defendants during the last weeks of 1974.

The first meeting between Colson and LeSourd lasted less than an hour. What impressed the publisher was that Colson wanted to pray about the project before discussing it. What impressed the author was that LeSourd had a clear vision of the proposed book. He wanted it to be written not as an exposition, but as a human story with plenty of colorful details, confrontation scenes, and personal touches. "Show, don't tell" was one of the publisher's strongest recommendations. Colson took copious notes of the conversation and promised to send in an outline and a couple of sample chapters within the next ten days. He delivered ahead of schedule. Writing with great energy each day as he sat in a courtroom office waiting to testify in the Watergate trials, Colson in one week produced 125 pages of longhand manuscript, which Patty typed up each night and delivered to Chosen Books.

LeSourd and his team of editors were ecstatic. One of the sample chapters that convinced them Colson had real talent as a writer described the scene in which he went to take a lie detector test in the seedy New York offices of Scientific Detection Services. The colorful details, the rising tensions, the high-pressure atmosphere, and the outpourings of emotional relief when Colson was told by his lawyer, David Shapiro, that he had passed the polygraph test were all brilliantly captured. "I cannot believe a lawyer could write so vividly," said LeSourd's partner John Sherrill after the passage was read aloud at an editorial meeting. From that moment, Chosen Books was mustard-keen to sign up Colson as its latest author. After much prayer on both sides the deal went through despite the low advance of $25,000.

As all authors and publishers know, it can be a long journey between an outline supported by one or two sample chapters and a finished manuscript. Colson's book was no exception. When the first draft was nearing completion he suffered a major crisis of confidence. In an anguished memorandum to LeSourd, he wrote: "I am worried that the tone of the whole manuscript is overly emotional. There are too many instances of tears, tearful prayers, etc. I am afraid that read in its entirety it will appear soapy. I am worried that I am not showing enough of my own weaknesses and that the material will appear self justifying . . . another problem is that I have over written and have, in the process, lost my objectivity."

These were just a few of the author's self-doubts expressed in his memo, which included a fusillade of agonized questions: "Do I come across as bitter . . . am I unfair with the treatment of Magruder, who remains one of my own personal Christian hang-ups? . . . Does Patty come across as a real person?" Colson even seemed to be plagued with sudden concerns that he could not write English, for he put this plea to LeSourd: "I know your reservations about picking up the blue pencil but as we go along someone is going to have to take out some of the harshness, substitute better phrases, better adjectives, correct grammar, etc."

None of these problems troubled LeSourd, who took the view that Colson had written a remarkable testimony with a compelling narrative. However, the first draft, coming in at over two hundred thousand words, was too long and had to be cut by about a quarter. While this not inconsiderable editing job was in progress, the project was put in jeopardy when another Christian publisher announced the imminent release of a totally unexpected paperback, entitled *The Colson Story*. Although most of the rival book was culled from old press cuttings, some parts of it consisted of new material taken from a long interview Colson had given to the writer during the early part of his prison sentence.

Colson was furious. He said the author had never mentioned his intention of writing a book and had requested the interview solely for a magazine article. Reverting to his former persona of pugnacious lawyer, Colson decided to sue the rival publishing house for invasion of his privacy. Len LeSourd opposed this plan. "We're faced with a spiritual dilemma here. The Bible says one Christian should not sue another Christian," he told his author. "After nearly thirty years in Christian publishing I've come to believe that when we violate this principle the Lord will not bless the work we are doing."

Colson was astonished by this argument and demanded to know the scriptural basis for it. Publisher and author got out their Bibles and looked at 1 Corinthians 6:7, "To have lawsuits against each other is a defect for you. Why not rather suffer wrong?"

Colson was underwhelmed. "This text doesn't say that Christians can't *threaten* to sue, does it?" he argued.

"That's pretty shaky theology," replied LeSourd. "Let's try persuasion and prayer."

"I'll agree to that with the addition of one word—pressure," said Colson. "The threat of a lawsuit can sometimes be as effective as the suit itself."

Whatever the theological merits or demerits of the proposed legal threats, they worked. Overruling LeSourd's objections, Colson got heavy.

He instructed an attorney from his old firm to call the rival publishing house and threaten it with a lawsuit. The rival publisher was so alarmed that he canceled the print order for *The Colson Story*. The rival author was more combative. Calling Colson "a phony . . . the same old hatchet man," he announced his intention of suing Chosen Books for loss of profits. For a time the situation looked as though it would explode into nasty publicity. However, after spending many hours in phone conversations with LeSourd, the aggrieved writer eventually backed off. Months later this author wrote to Colson admitting he had been in the wrong and apologizing for the trouble he had caused.

Choosing the title was the final hurdle, and it proved a difficult one. Scores of suggestions were put forward by those close to the project. Eventually *A Mountain Yet to Climb* was selected, but somehow it did not seem to be right. Two days after reluctantly giving his approval to this choice, Colson accompanied his wife to mass in her local parish church. The service was so crowded that the congregation had to share hymnals. As they started to sing a hymn together, Patty nudged her husband and pointed to the title at the top of the page—"Born Again." "That's you. That's your book," she whispered. "A chill went through me," Colson recalled later. "I immediately knew that we had found our title."

Others were less certain. "Not bad," said Len LeSourd. "Over your name it might be provocative. But it is a very overworked Protestant cliché."

"It came from the Catholic hymnbook!" replied Colson.

"Well, let's try it out on others," was the publisher's doubtful response.

Most of the others who were asked for their reactions seemed even more doubtful. Harold Hughes and Doug Coe thought it sounded trite. Marketing experts told Colson he would be throwing away secular sales and inter-denominational sales if he stuck to a title with such narrow Bible Belt connotations. In 1975 the words "Born Again" were known in religious circles to those familiar with the story of Nicodemus in John's gospel, but even inside those circles, they had not become well known, except perhaps to the Protestant charismatic groups, which emphasized them heavily. When warned of these downsides to the title *Born Again,* Colson refused to budge. "I think it comes from the Lord," he told the team at Chosen Books, who eventually accepted it.

When the first copies of *Born Again* rolled off the presses in January 1976, initial reactions within the book trade were lukewarm. "So far *Reader's Digest* and all the other big magazines have rejected the opportunity to serialize extracts from it," reported LeSourd at a meeting with his author, "and we're not getting good responses from the book clubs either. Right now it seems to fall between the secular and the religious markets. The secular group sees it as too religious, while the Christian media considers it too political."

These worries were committed to prayer. Fred Rhodes, who was present at this meeting, remembered the publisher praying for *Born Again* to be anointed by the Lord for his glory and the author asking forgiveness for anything he had done that might have displeased the Lord, particularly his threats of a lawsuit against the rival Christian publishing house. "I am absolutely convinced, looking back on it, that those prayers were a turning point," recalled Rhodes.

Something turned in the fortunes of *Born Again,* for by its publication date of February 18, orders from bookshops were gathering momentum. The first print run of forty thousand copies sold out within a week. Colson's appearances on the *Today* show for a fourteen-minute interview with Barbara Walters and on *The Mike Douglas Show* helped to get the book on the national best-seller lists, with recorded sales of 175,000 by the end of March. But this was only the beginning of its roll. The two words of the title assumed a national political significance. This happened when Jimmy Carter, contesting the New Hampshire primary as an obscure ex-governor of Georgia, was asked by an enterprising reporter who had read the book whether he was "Born Again"? "Yes, I am Born Again," was the reply.

When Carter emerged from the early primaries as the Democratic front-runner, his strange-sounding answer began to feature in political columns and cover stories across the country. By the fall of 1976, as the Carter bandwagon rolled toward the White House, Colson's hardback sales topped five hundred thousand copies, and a print run of 2 million paperback copies arrived in the bookshops. "Born Again" had entered the secular and spiritual vocabularies as the catchphrase of the year.

The reviews of *Born Again* were surprising. Sometimes they were surprisingly hostile. In the *Washington Post,* Nicholas von Hoffman ridiculed Colson's conversion as "a socially approved way of having a nervous breakdown." But in the *New York Times,* Garry Wills, the author of a scathingly adversarial biography, *Nixon Agonistes,* hailed Colson as "the truest American Christian since Andrew Carnegie—the man Mark Twain took as the perfect specimen." The syndicated columnist Jack Anderson was equally complimentary. Across the country most newspapers gave the book extensive coverage, reporting favorably on Colson's self-deprecating humor, his honest assessment of the moral failings in the Nixon White House, and his harrowing descriptions of life in prison. As for his Born Again Christianity, the prevailing view was that its sincerity should be given the benefit of the doubt. Writing in the *Wall Street Journal,* columnist Edmund Fuller captured this mood when he wrote, "This reviewer approached it [the conversion] with deep skepticism, struggling too with skepticism against Mr. Colson. Now he must say forthrightly, even though he is not at home in the evangelical style, that he believes Mr. Colson's conversion, that he does not find rebirth an exaggerated term, and hopes that Mr. Colson never experiences in that metaphor a 'redeath.' "

That same hope was being prayerfully expressed by America's evangelical Christians, whose word-of-mouth recommendations were the biggest single factor in the runaway success of *Born Again.* Their endorsement was vital to making the book a best seller not only in the United States but also around the world. The international evangelical community lionized Colson on his book tour of Germany, Belgium, Holland, France, Switzerland, Sweden, Finland, and Britain in the early summer of 1976. Before the year was out *Born Again* had been translated into eleven foreign languages. Three decades after its first publication it is still in the bookshops as a Christian classic, having now sold over 3 million copies in its hardback, paperback, and international editions.

The impact of *Born Again* was far greater than the making of a best seller. The phrase passed into the common currency of English and other languages, although its coinage became somewhat debased in the process. For the words "Born Again" started to collect the pejorative connotations associated with over-the-top and overly simplistic religious conversions. Colson himself was always uneasy with the promises of instant salvation that were being offered in too many evangelical and charismatic churches. At the start of his spiritual journey in the mid-1970s he was not a member of any particular church or denomination. He had no idea what terms like "evangelical" or "charismatic" meant. In those early days he sometimes referred to himself as "a baby Christian." But he was a baby with brains and character, so it did not take him long to work out his own theological and spiritual identity, which was far removed from that of any caricature Born-Againer.

What Colson personified as an individual and as an author was bringing the age-old Christian message on repentance, redemption, and spiritual rebirth into the spotlight of the twentieth-century media. Colson the messenger was now in the same spotlight. Would he stay there for the long haul

as an authentic Christian witness? Would he self-destruct into another tarnished televangelist or religious snake oil salesman in the mold of Sinclair
Lewis's Elmer Gantry? The answer was to be found in his soon-to-be-made
commitment to prison ministry.

Discipling Prisoners

Colson's early plans for bringing prisoners out of jail, on furlough, for
Christian discipleship training took more time and caused more trouble
than he had expected. Even though a pilot program for his scheme had
been given the green light by the head of the Federal Bureau of Prisons,
Norman Carlson, objections and obstacles were put in its way by others.

The first to object were a group of affluent residents from the neighborhood around Fellowship House in Washington. They were up in arms after reading an anodyne report in the *Washington Post* that Colson and
Harold Hughes would soon be bringing a small group of federal prisoners
to stay at Fellowship House for a religious retreat. The spokesman for the
residents was the legendary Tommy Corcoran, the political architect of the
New Deal who had been a senior White House aide to President Franklin
Roosevelt in the 1930s.

"Chuck, you've gone too far," said Corcoran in an angry phone call to
Colson. "Have you considered what this will do to our property values?
What about the women and children who will be afraid to go outside their
homes if you turn these criminals loose? . . . We'll see you in court."

Although that threat never materialized, in the prison system Colson
was having problems with the chief of federal chaplains, who insisted that
his men should select the inmates who would attend the prison seminars.
Colson argued that the prisoners would distrust the program if the
government-employed chaplains did the selecting. Thanks to Norman Carlson, Colson won this argument, but it was the first of much more serious
clashes between his radical ideas and the conservatism of old-fashioned
prison chaplains who preferred to keep doing things their way.

By the time the first group of twelve furloughed prisoners arrived in
Washington for their two-week course of discipleship training, in November 1975, Colson realized that he had underestimated the anxieties, the
practical difficulties, the shortage of funds, and a host of other problems
that fell on his shoulders in the drive to make the program succeed. He had

to lead from the front, teaching the first seminar. "What Is Fellowship?" Doug Coe followed him with a talk: "Who Is Jesus?" Harold Hughes led the group in prayer, and Fred Rhodes acted as the inmates' chauffeur. One way or another all the Colson prayer partners were at full stretch.

The first program came to an end with an emotional communion service and a prisoner named Peter declaring, "I've learned a lot in these two weeks about prayer, fellowship, and what a disciple of Jesus is supposed to be. For the first time in years I believe I can give love to others and receive it." Colson, deeply moved, felt his experiment had broken new ground and was on its way. But he did not yet realize how difficult the way ahead was going to be.

Before the second group of furloughed prisoners arrived for their two-week course, in February 1976, dissension had broken out in the ranks of the disciples' teachers. Colson's grandiose master plan for implementing his vision of a nationwide seminar program for prisoners had irritated some of his colleagues. In particular he upset a hardworking prison ministry leader on the team, John Staggers, who wanted Colson to think smaller and to model his plans on a local program that was working well at the Lorton penitentiary, in Virginia. Colson went out to Lorton and gave a talk to the prisoners. As he recounted his personal experiences in Maxwell he told the story of a young black prisoner he met there who did not know why he had been sentenced. "As I looked into this black boy's eyes," declared Colson, "I realized how the system penalized those without education or money. This boy and I became good friends." John Staggers was shocked as Colson went on to use the racially offensive term "boy" eleven times in his address. After the talk was over Staggers expressed himself forcefully. "You call a black in here 'boy' and he will slit your throat," he said. Amazingly the black prisoners in the audience did not appear to have taken umbrage. But Colson was full of remorse at his own insensitivity, saying afterward, "Maybe I'm just not cut out for this work. I've sure got a lot to learn."

Colson's learning curve produced other difficulties. The second group of furloughed prisoners did not measure up to the quality of the first class. There were several setbacks on the course, culminating in the escape of one of the newly trained disciples just after he returned from Washington to his jail in Atlanta. Within the federal prison service, resistance to the Colson program seemed to be growing among a number of wardens and chaplains. The success of *Born Again* caused its own jealousies and tensions. As Colson traveled across America and Europe on book tours he was seen as an absentee from the hard grind of face-to-face counseling and ministering to prisoners. His relationship with John Staggers deteriorated.

For his part, Colson became worried that Fellowship House might not be the right parent organization for his activities. At a meeting with Doug Coe and Harold Hughes in April, Colson effectively offered his resignation. "Brothers, I think there is only one answer," he said at the end of a discussion on the program's problems. "Let's ask John Staggers to take over this ministry. It's only been a part-time project for me. I'll continue to help, raise money, and do anything I can."

This was not a tactical maneuver by Colson. He was uncertain about his future plans and felt unwilling to commit himself to a permanent role in the Fellowship. Doug Coe's administrative aversion to the publication of financial statements began to disturb Colson. He wanted to publish all his financial earnings from speaking honoraria, in order to prepare for the media scrutiny that he knew would come his way. Coe preferred the Fellowship to be run in an opaque if not secretive style of financial management. These opposite views became a divisive issue between the two men.

At the time of these divisions, other career opportunities opened up for Colson in business and in law following an offer from the Massachusetts Bar Counsel to restore his license to practice. His belief that Patty wanted him to return to a legal career made him decide to resign from the Fellowship. But at the meeting when he put his resignation on the table, Harold Hughes asked the question that was also uppermost in Colson's mind: "What does God want you to do, Chuck?"

God made his will clear through the mouth of Patty. Toward the end of a summer in which the rising sales of *Born Again* had been quietly matched by the rising morale of the prison discipleship classes, the Colsons took a short vacation in Oregon at the seaside home of Senator Mark Hatfield. It was a break with uncanny echoes of the days the couple had spent in a cottage on the Maine coast at the time of Colson's conversion experience, almost exactly three years earlier, in August 1973. During his Oregon coastal sojourn of August 1976, Colson was again in spiritual turmoil, seeking inspiration from the waves of an ocean and the pages of a Christian classic. As he immersed himself in *The Cost of Discipleship* by Dietrich Bonhoeffer, Colson was uplifted by the Lutheran martyr's words: "Only he who believes is obedient: only he who is obedient believes." As he came to recognize that obedience to God's will must be the guiding principle of his life, Colson struggled to understand what exactly God was calling him to do.

His most recent visits to a series of federal penitentiaries, coupled with a growing sense of fulfillment at the end of the third and most successful of the inmate discipleship courses in Washington earlier that summer, had given Colson a renewed enthusiasm for prison ministry. But his work with prisoners had been taking up no more than a quarter of his time. Could it be that God was calling him into full-time prison ministry? A passage of scripture that seemed to be speaking to him at this time was Matthew 25:31–46—the parable of the sheep and the goats, which could well be interpreted as such a call.

Just as he had done in the cottage by the sea in Maine, Colson took out a yellow legal pad and began to summarize the pros and cons of the arguments—this time about making a commitment to full-time prison ministry. At the top of the pros column he wrote OBEDIENCE in large capital letters. On the opposite side of the page he scribbled a disconcertingly long list of negatives: "hard to raise money"; "no one cares"; "tough to get in"; "painful memories"; "staying in the public eye"; "Patty's fears." But when he returned to the points-in-favor column, he wrote at the bottom of it: "Obedient discipleship offers me no other path."

It was not, however, a path on which he wanted to travel alone. Would Patty be his companion and partner in prison ministry? The question had not been resolved between husband and wife in their earlier discussions. There were times in the last few months when Patty had seemed uncomfortable with the culture of evangelicalism and equivocal about prison ministry. So Colson was right to be anxious about her fears and hesitations. As he recalled later, "I knew I couldn't go into ministry unless she was with me."

Far from wanting to exercise a veto over Colson's calling, Patty had already decided that she would give him her full support. She waited for the right moment to tell him this good news. The moment came on the evening of August 28, 1976, when the couple were relaxing after dinner in Mark Hatfield's home. Sipping coffee as the Pacific waves pounded the nearby Oregon shoreline, Colson noticed that Patty was gazing into the fireplace of blazing driftwood logs with an unusually pensive expression. "Any thoughts you want to share?" he asked her.

"I think so, since they're about you," she replied. "I've watched you these past couple of months and I've realized what's happening. Before I wasn't so sure, but I am now."

"Sure of what?" asked Colson with impatience.

"You know full well, Chuck Colson. You can't fool me. Six months ago you were all caught up in the glamour of your book, television appearances, public speaking. But you weren't really into it. Now it's different. You're serious. Prison work is your life, isn't it?"

Colson avoided a direct answer. "I don't know. What do you think?"

"I've been thinking about it a lot," said Patty, furrowing her brow as if to emphasize the seriousness of her statement. "First, we've always had a good marriage even when things were so rough. But lately it's been even better and I've been thinking about why this is so. I've come to a conclusion that may surprise you. I think it is so much better because Christ is in it. He really does make all the difference." She paused for a moment. Colson's heart was leaping with such joy that he had to suppress an urge to hug her.

"Second," continued Patty, "I see now that God wants you to be in full-time ministry. We can't deny that and we shouldn't, no matter what our preferences might be." Then she paused again, this time to break into a big smile. "Well, I just want you to know that if that's what you want, I'm with you all the way."

Colson was beside himself with excitement and gratitude. He leapt out of his chair and pulled Patty into his arms. His love for her was all the more overwhelming because he knew his wife was making a great sacrifice. Patty's real wish was to have a quiet and comfortable life of privacy, yet she was committing herself to a difficult and demanding road of public ministry.

"So where do we go next, Chuck Colson?" she asked, looking deep into her husband's eyes.

"Into the prisons, honey—into every prison in this country," he replied.

CHAPTER FOURTEEN

Starting the Ministry

First Steps

The first months of Colson's full-time prison ministry were packed with excitement. The start-up was a hectic operation, largely because of Colson's energetic drive on matters like logistics, recruitment, and new activities. There were also strains and tensions caused by Colson's decision to have an amicable separation from Doug Coe's organization at Fellowship House. Then followed a period of extraordinary growth as the fledgling ministry took off into an unknown and hitherto unheard of activity—holding in-prison seminars for inmates around the country. While these and other new projects were gathering momentum, Colson was developing as a public speaker, as a student of theology, and as an emerging leader in the Christian community. Yet at the same time his steps were dogged by skepticism and controversy. Some of the controversies were self-inflicted, such as Colson's clashes with the federal prison chaplaincy. At other times he found himself, through circumstances beyond his control, at the center of colorful episodes, some of which threatened and some of which enhanced the standing of the ministry. Yet seen in the round, the opening years of Colson's full-time work in prisons were remarkably innovative and successful.

Colson launched his ministry full of confidence but short on competence. He soon ran into problems with old partners, new personnel, and established professionals within the prison service. Yet within three years of starting out, he had built an organization operating in over one hundred prisons, supported by thirty thousand donors and six thousand trained volunteers. Both the problems and the progress in this period make for a fascinating historical record.

The first problem was Colson's relationship with his prayer partners and other supporters at Fellowship House. From this base, Doug Coe's loosely structured team of "brothers" (no other title was allowed) had been running the initial wave of prison discipleship courses. This arrangement had worked—but only just. There had been personality clashes and other underlying tensions. Some of them were exacerbated by Colson's ego. "We all loved Chuck but there were times when he neglected us," recalls Coe. "He had to struggle to stay faithful to our concept of small group ministry. The acclaim of those big crowds he was addressing rather went to his head."

It was a complaint more forcefully expressed by some long-serving specialists in prison ministry who resented Colson's high profile and high-handed ways. The "not invented here" mind-set of the old hands inevitably clashed with the "I'll do it my way" attitude of the newcomer. Caught in the crossfire of such conflicts, Colson had to fight against his old demon of pride. But he was also confident enough to fight for his vision of a ministry that was utterly different from Coe's. Part of the difference was that Coe had created an intimate network of prayer groups for the well-connected of Washington. Elitist in its membership, cloudy in its theology, and low-profile in its operations, the Fellowship was almost the polar opposite of what Colson dreamed of building. He wanted a nationwide ministry to the least well connected people in America, run with maximum visibility, clear theology, and a high level of publicity. Although the Fellowship hoped to keep Colson as one of its key players, in his heart Colson himself knew that he had to run his own show. After much discussion the brothers had an amicable parting and their organizations went their separate ways. However, they signaled that they would continue to remain mutually supportive by agreeing to name the new ministry Prison Fellowship—an elegant blend of Colsonism and Coeism.

Without the day-to-day financial backing of Coe's network of wealthy Washingtonians, Prison Fellowship had to operate on the proverbial wing and a prayer. Since it could not afford to pay the salaries of more than one or two part-time staffers, it was, by necessity, an association of volunteers. In the beginning most of them were Colson's friends or relatives. So Fred Rhodes became the new organization's first president. Its first legal counsel was Myron Mintz, who incorporated the name Prison Fellowship on August 10, 1976, with what he later described as "the most inauspicious legal formalities you can imagine for an organization that was to make such a national and international impact." Al Hagen, a friendly accountant, secured the organization's nonprofit status from the Internal Revenue

Service. Twenty-four-year-old Wendell Colson, recently graduated from Princeton, used his skills as an amateur carpenter to make desks and doors for the first Prison Fellowship office—a three-room suite in Arlington, Virginia, rented for $350 a week. Two other young volunteers came in to man telephones, set up office systems, and organize files. It was a far cry from the trappings of a top Washington law firm, let alone the Executive Office Building of the White House, but the spirit was willing even if the finances were weak.

The finances were so fragile in those early years that the ministry would never have got off the ground at all without the support it received from Colson's own pocket. In 1976 the Prison Fellowship budget was $85,000, of which he donated $77,000. By 1977 the organization's income had grown to $440,000, but $240,000 of it came from Colson. It was a generosity he could barely afford. His only source of regular income was his share of the historic profits of his law firm, which, under an agreement with his former partners, brought in $60,000 a year for three years. To maintain the comfortable lifestyle he had enjoyed in his good times, Colson needed the earnings that were now coming in from his book royalties and speaking fees. However, he decided to donate 90 percent of these earnings to Prison Fellowship and to live frugally. Patty supported him wholeheartedly in the cutbacks in their lifestyle that this frugality required. First to go was the family Mercedes, traded in for a compact. Later on came a move to a much smaller home. Other economy measures included a family rule that the Colsons would, in future, buy new clothes only during sales, and a travel rule that they would never again buy a first or business class ticket.

Some of Colson's friends thought he was too hard on himself financially. He himself believed that the leader of a Christian ministry to prisoners must live inexpensively and donate generously. Colson has lived up to those ideals, long after those early years in which Prison Fellowship's hand-to-mouth finances kept the ministry dependent on his book royalties from *Born Again*. After the $60,000-a-year payout arrangement with his law partners ended in 1979, Colson began taking a $59,000-a-year salary from Prison Fellowship. After allowances for inflation, this figure has remained virtually static during the past twenty-five years, despite numerous exhortations from his board to accept a proper level of remuneration. In 2005, Colson's annual salary from Prison Fellowship is only $78,000, while his donations from his book royalties have continued to run at the level of $100,000–$200,000. He has never kept a speaking fee for himself, nor any book royalties since 1980. The skeptical voices that in the post-Watergate era suggested that Colson must be starting up a Christian ministry in order to feather his own nest have long ago been silenced by his impeccable track record of personal generosity and financial probity.

Those skeptical voices were noisy with their suspicions of Colson's ministry in the mid-1970s. The first management executive recruited to Prison Fellowship was thirty-eight-year-old Gordon Loux, who was director of public relations at the Moody Bible Institute of Chicago. When Loux told friends and colleagues that he was leaving to join Colson's ministry, he was warned against the move by a doom-laden chorus of disbelievers:

"You're crazy. Colson's just going to be a flash in the pan before he goes back to his dirty tricks."

"Colson's just making a play in prison work to clean up his hatchet man image."

These were just two of the pejorative comments made to Loux. They were typical of a large swath of public opinion at that time. Fortunately Loux was unshaken, replying that he was convinced of Colson's sincerity. He felt certain that Colson would make a big contribution to the Christian world in the years ahead.

For all this perceptiveness Gordon Loux was in some ways an odd choice to be appointed as Colson's number two in Prison Fellowship (a role he filled for eleven years), because he knew nothing at all about prison ministry. Son of a Mennonite butcher-turned-pastor, Loux held robustly conservative views about criminals deserving long sentences that were totally out of tune with the liberal views of most Prison Fellowship volunteers. Loux had heard Colson speak at a Christian booksellers' conference in Anaheim, California, in 1975 and had instantly formed a great admiration for him. The feeling was mutual. Colson admired Loux's energetic drive and expert knowledge of the Christian community, so he offered him the post of executive vice president of the new ministry. Loux accepted, but when he arrived at Prison Fellowship in August 1976, he discovered that his corporate title had been withdrawn at the request of Fred Rhodes and two ex-offenders working in the office, Paul Kramer and Jackie Buttner, on the grounds that they wanted everyone in the team to be on the same level. When Loux protested at this egalitarianism, his title was reinstated but Colson warned him, "For me, an executive vice president is what a fire hydrant is to a dog."

Although Loux was concerned about the lack of fraternal warmth from his boss (when he complained about it, Colson's response was usually "Oh come on, Gordon, you're just having your bad time of the month"), such tensions were usually smoothed over because of the two men's common goals and shared sense of mission. Prison Fellowship expanded fast. Loux was good at public relations initiatives and mail shots that brought in both donors and volunteers in their thousands. Thanks to his high profile Colson was creating a momentum for nationwide prison ministry that had never existed before.

The Washington seminars, which brought inmates with leadership qualities out of their prisons on furlough for two-week programs in discipleship training, continued to be the main activity of Prison Fellowship in the early months of its existence. But there were tensions and great surprises at the fourth discipleship seminar when the top explosives expert of the Ku Klux Klan came face-to-face with the leader of the Black Panthers. How these two ex-terrorists bonded together with Colson as brothers in Christ is one of the most colorful stories from the early days of Prison Fellowship.

The Bombers Who Became Brothers

The Ku Klux Klansman was Tommy Tarrants, a skilled marksman and bomb maker with the White Knights, the terrorist wing of the Klan. In 1976 he was in the Parchman penitentiary, in Mississippi, halfway through his thirty-year sentence for attempting to blow up a Jewish businessman's home. Colson heard from Billy Graham that Tarrants, a strong personality of considerable intellectual ability, had become a Christian convert and a leader of Bible studies in Parchman. After further inquiries, Colson persuaded Mississippi's governor, Cliff Finch, to release Tarrants on furlough for two weeks so that he could attend Prison Fellowship's fourth discipleship seminar in Washington.

The Black Panther was Eldridge Cleaver. He too had been a bomber and a gunman. After a notorious 1968 shoot-out with police and FBI agents in Oakland, California, Cleaver fled into exile. For seven years he lived the life of an international fugitive, but in 1975 he voluntarily returned to the United States. He too became a committed Christian, while awaiting trial in a California jail. There he was befriended by Art DeMoss, an evangelistic businessman who had founded the Liberty Life group of insurance companies. DeMoss was so convinced of Eldridge Cleaver's sincerity that he put up a $50,000 bond to secure his release on bail.

Art DeMoss had been one of Prison Fellowship's earliest and most generous supporters. He had given a dinner in honor of Colson in January 1976 at the DeMoss family home in Bryn Mawr, Pennsylvania. The evening had not been an unequivocal success. As Art's wife, Nancy, recalled, "When our guests came through the receiving line it came as quite a shock to see how many people, country club types who were normally so proper, backed off physically from Chuck. When he put out his hand these people refused to shake it. Apparently they just didn't believe he was genuine." The country club set had even more difficulty in accepting the bona fides of the next convict club guest for whom Art DeMoss gave a dinner. This was Eldridge Cleaver. Nancy DeMoss has recalled the shocked hostility of her Bryn Mawr neighbors: "We had Eldridge staying in our home for a week and some of the people in our neighborhood behaved as though we'd done something criminal. All conversation stopped when I walked into the hairdresser's or places I'd been going to for the last twenty years. People were showing their disapproval."

In search of someone who would warmly approve of Eldridge Cleaver's Christian conversion, Art DeMoss thought of his second-most-controversial friend, Chuck Colson. So it was arranged that Nancy DeMoss should take Eldridge and his wife, Kathleen, down by train from Pennsylvania to Washington in order to meet Colson, who, at the time, was leading the fourth prisoners' discipleship seminar at Fellowship House. Colson was more uneasy about extending a warm welcome to Eldridge Cleaver than he had admitted to Art and Nancy DeMoss. Bad memories of the Black Panther chief's obscene excesses, such as a notorious telecast of him chanting, "Kill the pigs—rape the white women," were deeply burned into Colson's memory. "Though the Lord had moved strongly in my life it would take more than a few extra doses of his grace for me to stomach Cleaver, conversion or no conversion," he recalled.

After Nancy DeMoss had arrived and made the introductions, Colson and Cleaver withdrew to an upstairs library and talked alone for over two hours. Cleaver described his years on the run in countries like Cuba, North Vietnam, and the Soviet Union. Although he was welcomed by his communist hosts, his intelligent mind soon saw through their Marxist propaganda. He became homesick. One night his emotions exploded and he found himself reciting the Lord's Prayer and the Twenty-third Psalm, which he had learned at his mother's knee. He decided he must return to the United States even if it resulted in a long spell in prison. So he came back without any sort of deal with the prosecuting authorities. While in jail awaiting trial he began reading the Bible. Later on, a Christian visitor gave him a

copy of *Born Again*. Some of Colson's inner turmoils at the time of Watergate struck Cleaver as remarkably similar to his own experiences. "That's
what happened to me!" he found himself shouting as he turned over the
pages of the book in his cell. As their conversation in the library deepened,
Colson became more and more impressed. He believed that what he
was hearing was "another of Christ's miracles working in the unlikeliest of
people."

Fred Rhodes came in and interrupted the dialogue with the announcement that supper was ready. Colson had almost forgotten about the seminar and its participants. "I hope you don't mind eating with eleven
convicts, brother," he joked. "Hey, man, you'll make me feel right at
home," replied Cleaver. Colson then remembered that among the eleven
furloughed prisoners in the seminar was Tommy Tarrants.

"I guess it was one of the strangest introductions I have ever heard in
my life when Chuck started to say, 'Hey, Eldridge, say hello to Tommy Tarrants, whose background is a little different from yours,' " recalled Fred
Rhodes, "and he didn't gild the lily one bit. He ran through all Tommy's
history as a bomb thrower and Ku Klux Klan leader in Mississippi, but Eldridge didn't back off. He looked Tarrants straight in the eye, shook his
hand, and said, 'We both have a lot to live down, don't we?' "

The rest of the evening, according to Rhodes, was "almost surreal."
Over the meal, Cleaver and Tarrants gave their testimonies. So did several
of the furloughed prisoners. Harold Hughes arrived and gave Cleaver what
Nancy DeMoss called "the biggest hug I've ever seen in my life." Colson
delivered a talk on the transforming power of God's love and ended with
the words "Let's welcome Eldridge as our new brother in Christ!" More
hugs all round. Then everyone present held hands and said prayers for one
another, their families, their personal hopes, fears, and needs, and for their
relationship with the Lord.

"I have never seen anything like it before or since," recalled Fred
Rhodes. "Who else could have assembled such a diverse cast of characters
and got them to pray for one another? I mean, there was Nancy DeMoss,
a lady of strong Republican opinions and great wealth. There was Harold
Hughes, the ex–truck driver, about as liberal and hate-the-rich Democratic
senator as you could find. There was Tommy Tarrants, who had spent years
of his life trying to kill blacks, and Eldridge Cleaver, who had spent his life
trying to kill whites. Both of them had tried to destabilize the government
of the United States while Chuck Colson had been helping to run the government of the United States. And don't forget the other ten convicts still

serving their sentences, or me, who once upon a time had been a boring old lawyer and bureaucrat. It was quite a party."

In one sense the party lasted longer than any cynical observer might have expected. The eleven prisoners on furlough went back to their jails and remained committed disciples of Christ. Tommy Tarrants, the outstanding intellect among them, was paroled halfway through his sentence. After his release he became a renowned Christian public speaker and is now director of the C. S. Lewis Institute in Washington, D.C. Eldridge Cleaver became a Mormon and, toward the end of his life, enrolled in a Christian seminary. The fourth Washington discipleship class was undoubtedly one to remember. It made a deep impact on Colson, who later described it as "a very decisive moment in the ministry. I had seen the reconciling power of Christ's love in action."

Over the next three years, over thirty more classes were held; around 330 furloughed prisoners graduated from these seminars. So the program was a success story although its achievements were somewhat eclipsed by the new and unexpected development in Prison Fellowship's ministry—the in-prison seminars.

In-Prison Seminars

The most exciting development in the early years of Colson's ministry, the program of in-prison seminars, was unplanned, unforeseen, and unexpected. In this regard it set a pattern for most of the important initiatives in Prison Fellowship during the next quarter of a century. Colson now likes to say that these programs all happened without him. This is too modest a disclaimer, for he was always the leader of the ministry's projects even if he did not initiate them himself. However, in the case of the in-prison seminars, they started by accident in a moment of rejection that had nothing to do with Colson.

The rejection came from George Ralston, the tough, abrasive warden of the Oxford federal prison, in Wisconsin. He was refusing to allow any of his inmates to attend Prison Fellowship's discipleship seminars in Washington. In a heated telephone call with Paul Kramer, Colson's prayer partner at Maxwell who had joined the Prison Fellowship staff, Ralston rejected all requests for furlough leave for his prisoners, adding testily: "If you guys are so good, why don't you bring your teaching team into our prison and run your course here?"

When he heard about this off-the-cuff remark, Colson regarded it as a bluff by Warden Ralston. So he promptly accepted the invitation as a counterbluff, feeling certain that Ralston would withdraw the offer. Colson thought that this would give him the leverage for an appeal to Norman Carlson, the head of the Federal Bureau of Prisons, for Ralston to be overruled on grounds of unreasonable behavior. To Colson's amazement Ralston called the counterbluff. Prison Fellowship was invited to conduct an in-prison course of Christian teaching at Oxford penitentiary starting in three weeks' time. Colson and his team then had to scramble furiously not only to devise the curriculum but also to find teachers for it and to recruit a team of local volunteers willing to participate in the program.

Colson's insistence on the involvement of Christians from the local community was a crucial ingredient in this and all subsequent in-prison seminars. He knew that teaching Christianity in a prison for a week and then departing would leave a vacuum, and a feeling of "mission unaccomplished," unless it was followed up by a continuing program of Bible studies and counseling from local church volunteers in the months after. So, despite the considerable difficulties in recruiting such volunteers in rural Wisconsin, Colson insisted on it and was delighted when thirty of them turned up as participants. He was even more delighted when some ninety-five of Oxford's 450 inmates filed into the chapel to listen to lectures from Fred Rhodes, George Soltau, John Jolliffe, and Paul Kramer. Colson joined the team toward the end of the week, giving his own testimony, ending with altar call, or an invitation to commit to Christ. With twenty-five men coming forward in the chapel to make this commitment and more committing themselves in a private room after the service, it was clear that the first ever in-prison seminar had made a real impact on the hearts and minds of the inmates.

One other heart that was touched belonged to the warden. George Ralston was a tough prison boss of the old school, but possibly because he had a son of his own serving a jail sentence, behind his crusty façade he was deeply interested in the power of the gospel to change lives. As the seminar progressed Ralston became increasingly positive about the effect of the teaching on some of his worst inmates. By the end of the program he was completely won over. "This has been a tremendous week," he told Colson. "You should do this in every prison. I'll recommend it if you want."

George Ralston was as good as his word. Thanks to his recommendations to other wardens, Prison Fellowship's in-prison seminars began spreading across state and federal penitentiaries throughout the Midwest.

A year after they began in Oxford, over a thousand prisoners had been discipled through the new program, and some two hundred of them had come forward at the end of the seminars to commit their lives to Jesus Christ. One other person who made that commitment was George Ralston. Two years later, when he was warden at the Terre Haute federal penitentiary, in Indiana, he attended a businessman's prayer breakfast in the city addressed by Colson. At the end of it Ralston filled in a commitment card, saying that he wanted to become involved in Christian ministry. Ralston subsequently became a stalwart supporter of Prison Fellowship and was active in its work for many years.

The first in-prison seminar, at the Oxford penitentiary, was a turning point in the history of Colson's ministry because it changed the direction and the dynamics of Prison Fellowship. The Washington discipleship seminars, which prior to Oxford were the core activity of the ministry, would always involve small numbers. The best forecast was that seventy to a hundred furloughed prisoners a year could be taken out of their jails and offered training. These constraints on Prison Fellowship's reach and effectiveness were lifted by the in-prison seminars. Instead of training a maximum of a hundred inmates a year, the in-prison seminars were discipling ten times that number. To this day, twenty-nine years after the Oxford experiment, twenty thousand inmates a year across the country are being discipled by the same Prison Fellowship program of in-prison seminars, with follow-up provided by a volunteer army of thirty thousand trained Christian counselors. So George Ralston's initial intransigence was the trigger for a quantum leap in Prison Fellowship's size and effectiveness.

Clashing with the Chaplains

The success of the in-prison seminars brought progress to the ministry but also a resurgence of pride in its founder. Colson's old demon of hubris surfaced when he provoked a wholly unnecessary and avoidable clash with the chaplains of the Federal Bureau of Prisons. Ironically, the trouble was started by a glowing report on Prison Fellowship to the head of the service. In late 1976, Norman Carlson had commissioned an assessment of the Washington discipleship seminars. Written by a psychiatrist, Dr. Daniel R. Peterson, who had visited seven of the jails from which inmates had been furloughed, the assessment was so laudatory that Norman Carlson called Colson into his office to congratulate him. When he read the concluding paragraph of the report Colson was exhilarated. For in Dr. Peterson's judgment, "Inmates who have participated in the experience have almost universally been instrumental in turning the institutional religious programs around or revitalizing existing programs. This appears to be a valuable and dynamic ministry . . . every chaplain we have talked with is totally sold on the Prison Fellowship program."

The federal chaplains' enthusiasm for Colson and his programs was short-lived. In early 1977 Norman Carlson offered Prison Fellowship the opportunity to recruit two of its own chaplains for a new penitentiary that was under construction in Memphis, Tennessee. Colson impulsively accepted the offer without having the slightest idea how it would work. Nor did he have any idea where the chaplains, or the funds to pay their salaries, were coming from. Nevertheless he made a premature announcement of the initiative at the Washington National Prayer Breakfast in February 1977. So enthusiastic was the response from the audience that Colson made the announcement again a few days later, this time at a civic luncheon in Memphis. In his exuberance over what he called the historic decision to allow a nongovernmental Christian ministry to appoint its own chaplains in a federal prison, Colson moved into dangerous territory as he began criticizing existing chaplains: "I know what it can mean to those men inside to have someone they can trust. In the prison I was in the visiting chaplain was a military officer stationed at Maxwell Air Force Base. He was a fine, decent man but a friend of the warden, and no inmate would confide in him. Government-paid chaplains are a part of the system, and the system is the 'enemy' to most inmates."

To make matters worse, Colson then repeated a story he had been told by Eldridge Cleaver. According to Cleaver, an inmate in San Quentin prison in the 1950s went to confession and told the chaplain of his complicity in a celebrated murder case. The chaplain allegedly broke the seal of the confessional and turned in the prisoner, who was later executed for this crime. The story may have been apocryphal and Colson had no means of checking the accuracy of what Cleaver had told him. So it was reckless to use the story in a public speech to an audience that included several prison chaplains.

Colson immediately found himself in a firestorm of controversy. The chaplains were rightly furious. In an angry meeting following the lunch they attacked him with passion. "You have maligned my professional and personal integrity," snapped one of the chaplains. It was a mild reaction compared to some of the fiercer criticisms. Although Colson admitted his remarks had been too partisan, he underestimated the strength of the ill feeling he had generated. As he left Memphis, Paul Kramer warned him,

"Those chaplains are really mad." Colson nonchalantly replied, "It will pass. When they see how much good can be done they will be with us."

In fact the chaplains stayed mad. Some of them worked hard to undermine the appointments Colson made to the new prison in Memphis. One of these chaplains was a white pastor, the other black. This second appointment doubled the number of black pastors in the entire federal prison service. This fact was itself an indictment of the existing system of chaplaincy appointments. Norman Carlson, who had long been dissatisfied with the conservatism of many of his chaplains, was delighted at the controversy Colson had stirred up. Prison Fellowship's executive vice president, Gordon Loux, saw the battle in positive terms. "We were being used as Norman Carlson's tool for challenging the chaplains," he recalled. "It raised our profile and gave us access to more and more federal prisons. Suddenly we were news."

It was not always the news that Colson wanted to read about himself, for some of the chaplains were surprisingly adept at the media art of negative spin-doctoring. COLSON'S PRISON EVANGELIZING PROVES IRKSOME TO CHAPLAINS was one headline above a long and critical *New York Times* article about the dispute. Within the federal prison system the row simmered on for a year or so. In the end both sides backed off, with Colson ending up the bigger loser. The Memphis experiment failed, for his appointments there were judged to have been unsuccessful. The two Prison Fellowship chaplains were withdrawn and never replaced. No more such appointments were made in any other federal penitentiary.

For his part Colson came to realize he had made a bad mistake and that he must in future work with the grain of the prison service professionals and not against them. The episode revealed that he still had an impulsive streak in him that, if not checked, could result in arrogant words with unfortunate consequences. Yet he learned a good lesson from the episode, saying afterward, "I deserved a real black eye. I was stupid in some of the things I said about the chaplains, who I looked at simply as an extension of the prison system. I was dead wrong and I probably set back the advance of the ministry."

Negative Forces

Although there were no other major setbacks in the early years of Prison Fellowship, Colson himself had one or two near disasters with public relations problems. These arose mostly from the baggage he carried over from Watergate and the Nixon White House.

The first and potentially most damaging of these problems surfaced on Sunday, November 18, 1976, when Colson, relaxing at home with Patty, picked up a copy of *Parade* magazine (circulation 27 million) and read an article that purported to describe a dinner the Colsons had enjoyed some months earlier with fellow Watergater John Dean and his wife, Mo. The offending passage began:

"One night the Colsons, Chuck and Patty, were in Los Angeles promoting his book. They came up for dinner and Colson got very drunk." As his eyes reeled with horror at the last four words, Colson thought he might be reading his obituary notice. In the teetotal world of evangelical Christians, from whom he was drawing his greatest support, taking one glass of alcohol was severely frowned upon, and drunkenness was equated with adultery as a mortal sin. Colson feared that his credibility as a Christian speaker and leader of a ministry would be put in jeopardy and perhaps ruined as a result of this damaging article.

The *Parade* story not only reported that Colson had been drunk. It implied that Patty thought he was a hypocrite. The article quoted Taylor Branch, a friend of John Dean's who had been present at the dinner, as saying, "His wife kept making these jokes. She'd say, 'I know Chuck's very sincere about this religious business, but he was also very sincere about the marines. And of course he was very, very sincere about Nixon.' "

Patty broke down in tears when she read the words attributed to her. "But it is so unfair—it is not true," she cried. "This hurts . . . more than anything they said about us during the Watergate years. Because now it involves the Lord."

Colson nodded in agreement. He had been through many a bad bout of pain caused by unfair stories during his White House years, but he could remember no previous journalistic calumny that inflicted such deep misery. The unmistakable message of the *Parade* piece was that he was a religious phony. It hurt.

Colson's next move was to invite his two closest confidants, Fred Rhodes and Gordon Loux, to come over to discuss the crisis. Rhodes was even more depressed than Colson. "It's bad, very bad," he reported. "Everyone in my church this morning was talking about it. They gave me a hard time." Rhodes imitated two high-pitched ladies' voices saying, "Oh dear, does your friend Mr. Colson have a drinking problem? And Mrs. Colson—is she a loyal wife? Is their marriage in trouble?" Rhodes pointedly reminded Colson that he had strongly advised him not to accept John Dean's dinner invitation when it had arrived back in January.

"You were right, Fred," said Colson. "You warned us not to go to the Deans' that night. I should have listened but I wanted John and Mo to know that we are their friends."

"*Were,*" snapped Loux, adding that he was sure John Dean was out to destroy his old White House adversary, Colson. While her husband tried to refute this conspiracy theory Patty Colson intervened with the announcement "I'm going to call Mo and find out what this is all about." Patty's call produced some interesting results. The Deans had not seen the *Parade* article but after they read it they were almost as outraged as the Colsons. When John Dean came on the line he sounded angry and upset. "Chuck, I don't know what to say. It's untrue. I'll issue a statement. Anything you want," he said, also confirming that Colson had consumed only one glass of wine all evening and had gone home sober.

In due course both John Dean and his friend Taylor Branch issued denials of the *Parade* story. These denials were reported with heavy solemnity in the Christian press, and with wry amusement in the secular media, under headlines like "Colson Not Drunk." Seen in retrospect, the episode was nothing more than a storm in a wineglass. The letters that came in to Prison Fellowship about it were mostly sympathetic. One or two of the correspondents erred rather too much on the side of sympathy by offering Colson opportunities to join Alcoholics Anonymous. But apart from these, most Colson supporters wanted to disbelieve the *Parade* article. There was no perceptible falling away in volunteer or donor support for the ministry. Gordon Loux took the view that Colson had overreacted. "He was personally hurt by the article and terribly frightened that it would destroy his integrity. But that just did not happen. No one thought he was another Elmer Gantry. Life went on exactly as before and the ministry went on growing."

There was, however, one part of Colson's life that did not go on exactly as before. The *Parade* episode scared him so badly that he immediately stopped drinking in public, even among friends. Within two years he renounced alcohol completely and became a teetotaler. This was not a spiritual decision. To this day Colson believes that there is nothing in scripture that requires abstinence and that prohibitions against alcohol are nonbiblical. He gave up drinking because of the risk of losing his reputation in the eyes of the evangelical churches. It was a tough, practical discipline but Colson took the decision and has stuck with it ever since.

Another media scare that greatly troubled Colson started with a *Time* magazine story reporting that in 1973 he had received $500,000 in cash as a payoff from the Teamsters to Richard Nixon for freeing Jimmy Hoffa from prison. This allegation had been made in 1976 by a man serving a life sentence for a long list of crimes, including murder and perjury. Two FBI agents had interviewed Colson as part of their investigation of the allegation, but by the end of their questioning, they appeared to be satisfied that the charges were false. The senior FBI agent apologized to Colson, saying that the allegations had come from an unreliable and unbelievable source and that they were sorry to have wasted his time.

Despite this reassurance, the *Time* magazine story that broke in April 1977 contained the damaging sentence "The FBI believes that Colson, after getting President Nixon's approval on the evening of January 3, 1973, either himself or through an associate received the money in Las Vegas on January 6, 1973." The old saying that a lie can get halfway round the world before truth has got its boots on proved painfully accurate in the case of this calumny. All across America, newspapers, radio news bulletins, and TV programs repeated *Time*'s claims as if they were facts. Colson was plunged into an abyss of despair, which he later described as "the lowest point since my release from prison." He seriously considered suing *Time* for libel, abandoning the idea only because of the huge financial costs he knew he would have to incur to prove his innocence.

As a result of the nationwide publicity given to the *Time* story, the FBI renewed its investigation. Colson's bank records were subpoenaed and dozens of his former associates were interviewed. The only "suspicious" item of evidence that was turned up by the investigators was Colson's diary for January 6, 1973—the day he was supposed to have been in Las Vegas receiving the payoff of $500,000 in cash. In his diary, that page was blank. This was hardly surprising since January 6, 1973, was a Saturday— often an engagement-free day in his calendar. Colson said he had spent it quietly at home with Patty and had not been anywhere near Las Vegas. But could he prove it? demanded the investigators. For several agonizing weeks the answer was no, so a cloud of suspicion lingered over him. As Colson later described this miserable period of his life, "God seemed far away. Doubts were assailing me. My old nemesis self-pity was besieging me again. The same old questions arose to haunt me: Why take all this nonsense? Why put your family through it again? I'll always be a target for some crusading reporter or trigger-happy government investigator. Wouldn't Prison Fellowship be better off without me?"

The worst of the misery came to an end when Patty turned up some old hospitality records, which showed that on January 6, 1973, the Colsons had hosted a lunch in their McLean home for several members of his White

House staff. These individuals were contacted and quickly corroborated their presence at the lunch. Their evidence meant that Colson could not possibly have been in Las Vegas on the date of the alleged handover of the Teamsters payoff. Collapse of false charges.

Although this should have been the end of the story, Colson remained plagued by self-doubt. He again felt "convicted of sin," an experience shared by Christian converts down the ages from Augustine on. In Colson's case it meant a renewed despondency about his past sinfulness. As he said afterward, "Perhaps it took the *Time* story to sink me so far into the pit of despair that I could really see deep within myself. No, I hadn't been a bagman for the Teamsters. But yes, I was a man still filled with pride and vanity and ego and insensitivity."

These wallowings in self-recrimination had at least one ring of truth to them. His pride and ego problems, though greatly diminished since his days of political power, remained a negative force within him. Although Colson had done great service for the Lord since coming out of prison, he had also achieved great publicity for himself. This was not always through his own design. Nevertheless, there was an element in him of "backing away into the limelight." It was not always clear where the boundary lay between publicizing Prison Fellowship and publicizing its founder. Perhaps such a delineation was impossible anyway, given the personalized reporting of the media and the runaway success of *Born Again.* Whatever the explanations for it, by the end of the 1970s Colson was well and truly established as a "celebrity Christian."

However much he enjoyed the favorable side of his coverage in the media, Colson was sufficiently steeped in his faith to know that the term "celebrity Christian" is an obnoxious oxymoron, a complete contradiction of the humility that should lie at the heart of every Christian life. So he was totally turned off by the label and by the synthetic religious hucksterism that so often goes with it.

Colson's revulsion against celebrity Christians came to a head when an evangelical organization held a conference in Washington at around the time of his conviction-of-sin worries triggered by the *Time* magazine article. The flashpoint came when he found himself sharing a press conference with a new and extremely doubtful Born Again celebrity, Larry Flynt, a notorious publisher of pornographic magazines. Flynt had been brought to the conference through the well-meaning but misguided encouragement of Ruth Stapleton, President Jimmy Carter's sister. Colson was horrified to find himself a central figure in such a circus. For some time he had been worried that he was becoming the prisoner of one particular section of the Christian community. Evangelicals were his greatest admirers and supporters but he wanted to reach out beyond some of their simplistic slogans and promotional propaganda. Several of the strongest and most personal influences around him, from his wife, Patty, to his old political mentor Bryce Harlow, were worried that he had embraced the thinking and practices of the evangelical churches far too uncritically. His unqualified acceptance of their "Born Again" label, together with his unthinking repetition of some charismatic clichés, exposed Colson to the criticism that he was becoming an overpublicized caricature of the new Christian convert who is all heart but no head.

Discovering Theology

The first employee of Prison Fellowship who had the temerity to suggest that Colson might be vulnerable to such criticisms was Michael Cromartie, then a twenty-five-year-old graduate of Covenant College in Georgia, who sported a beard and who had been a conscientious objector to the Vietnam War (qualifications that would never have appealed to the old Colson). Cromartie was a superbright researcher and part-time aide with a far deeper knowledge of theology than his boss. "As I traveled round the country to prisons and speaking engagements with Chuck I saw that his conversion was genuine and that he was tremendously gifted. But he was new to the faith and there were huge gaps in his understanding, which could make his speeches sound hollow," recalled Cromartie. "He had somehow acquired a narrow persona of pietism. I recall how he often used to say that the only thing that mattered was winning hearts for the Lord and that he wished he'd never wasted all those years in politics. There were parts of fundamentalism and evangelicalism, like withdrawing from civics and politics, which he was close to swallowing whole. He came close to going off in completely the wrong direction with that baggage. I think it was providential that God kept him on the right track just when he might have got caught up in crazy stuff with the extreme right-wing fundamentalists."

Colson was saved from the clutches of the religious right by Cromartie's insistence that he must meet and study with some of the finest minds among America's Christian intellectuals. This process started on a trip to Grand Rapids, Michigan, in the autumn of 1977 when Cromartie arranged a three-hour meeting at Calvin College between Colson and a remarkable group of professors: Nicholas Wolterstorff, a world-famous philosopher; Richard Mouw, an eminent theologian; Paul Henry, a professor of politics; and Stephen Monsma, another distinguished philosopher, who hosted the gathering. Colson had prepared for the meeting by sending his interlocutors a list of questions he wanted to discuss. They included

—What should be the relationship between Christianity and the state?

—What should be the relationship between Christianity and social concern?

—What was Augustine's view of these questions?

—What was Luther's view?

—What was Calvin's view?

—What was the Anabaptists' view?

The Calvin College professors may have been surprised by the ignorance of their visiting celebrity but they were soon impressed by the sharpness of his intellect. For his part, Colson was fascinated by the dialogue that afternoon and asked Cromartie to arrange more encounters with the academic community. So meetings took place over the next few months with theological luminaries such as R. C. Sproul of the Ligonier Study Center in Pennsylvania; Dr. Carl Henry of Arlington, Virginia; Francis Schaeffer of L'Abri Fellowship; Os Guinness of the Trinity Forum; Martin Marty of Chicago University; and Richard Lovelace of Gordon-Conwell Theological Seminary. There were moments on these visits when Colson could appear naive. When he arrived at the Gordon-Conwell campus in Massachusetts, Professor Richard Lovelace assembled the entire senior faculty for a question-and-answer session. Colson's opening gambit was, "I've just written a book called *Born Again*. What do you think is the meaning of 'Born Again'?" An embarrassed silence spread across the room. It was broken by Michael Cromartie. Suspecting that the academics felt they were being kidded, he sought to reassure them by saying, "Gentlemen, Mr. Colson is serious! He really wants to understand the doctrinal explanation of divine regeneration."

That first meeting was enough to open the floodgates of Gordon-Conwell scholarship, whose waters continued to flow over Colson for several months. Professor Richard Lovelace was persuaded to come down to Washington to give a series of lectures and teaching sessions at Fellowship House every Monday morning from eight to twelve on the history of revivals and spiritual awakenings. Colson, who organized the weekly lecture audience, said of these programs: "It was the next best thing to the seminary training I was beginning to yearn for. I was drinking in the teachings like a thirsty man in a desert, rearranging my schedule to be in Washington whenever Lovelace was there."

This was one of many signs that Colson was becoming riveted by the study of theology, church history, Christian ethics, and Christian spirituality. He became a voracious reader in these fields, constantly annotating books like Francis Schaeffer's classic *How Should We Then Live?* and listening to tapes of academic teaching. One January morning when snow was falling in Washington, Cromartie got a call from his boss. "Come on over, Mike. We can't make it to the office so let's spend the day watching all six hours of R. C. Sproul's lectures on 'The Holiness of God.' " And they did, both ending on their knees in prayer at the power of the teaching.

Under the influence of such theological tutors, Colson's spiritual horizons soon broadened. Narrow evangelicalism, he discovered, was not enough. He quietly abandoned the restrictive pietist view that the only worthwhile Christian activity is to win hearts for the Lord. He did his share of one-on-one ministry, particularly in the prisons, but he knew he must also share in the public arena of action and debate. His readings of Luther, Calvin, Zwingli, and other sixteenth-century Protestant leaders made him increasingly sympathetic to the Reformed perspective of key doctrines and theological concepts. As a result, he began a systematic study of the writings of R. C. Sproul, the eminent Reformed theologian whom Colson regarded as the greatest intellectual influence on his spiritual development. His passionate study of the life of William Wilberforce made him eager to engage in the cultural, social, and political controversies of the day. What gradually emerged from these searchings was Colson's conviction that he must strive to understand and implement a comprehensive Christian worldview regarding life and society.

In his quest for the Christian worldview, two of Colson's key attributes were his realism and his populism. He had an intelligent mind that lived *off* ideas, not an intellectual's mind that lived *for* ideas. For all his curiosity about academic theology he was far more interested in applying its concepts to the marketplace of life. His strategy was to combine the authenticity given to him by his prison ministry with the authority he derived from his biblical and theological studies.

If Colson had been less impatient to start his own ministry, he might have gained strength and credibility from a period of full-time study in a seminary. Instead he used his celebrity to gain access to eminent seminary professors. These men and women of learning seemed delighted to have America's most famous Christian convert knocking on their doors. For his part, Colson was delighted when those doors opened and supplied him with crash courses in Christian scholarship. So the relationship was mutually beneficial at the time and brought far wider benefits later. For Colson's part-time studies in the 1970s became the fuel that expanded his ministry. His field became the world and his vision became making a change in the culture and nature of society.

The Changing Colson

In August 1979 Prison Fellowship reached its third anniversary. Although Colson did not see this milestone as a significant turning point at the time, in fact it more or less coincided with the start of a new era for both the man and his ministry. For Colson was on the move spiritually and this made a big impact on his leadership of Prison Fellowship practically. So the fall of 1979 is an appropriate moment at which to make an assessment of the past progress and future direction of Colson as a Christian leader.

Colson had started his ministry in faith but also in naivete. He had received no formal religious education of the kind that most Christians in leadership roles acquire in seminaries or colleges. He had no grounding in theology, doctrine, church history, or even biblical knowledge. Although he had done considerable Bible study in prison and at Fellowship House under Doug Coe, Colson was rather like someone who had picked up a language, spoke it quite fluently, yet had never mastered its grammar and syntax. So he was on a steep learning curve as he launched out on his journey into do-it-yourself theology with the help of various professors and learned tutors.

Another problem was that Colson had no experience of working in, let alone leading, a Christian ministry of volunteers. This did not deter him any more than his complete lack of legal experience had deterred him from setting up his own law firm back in 1961. But his get-up-and-go enthusiasm could lead him into brashness, insensitivity, and consequent mistakes in his handling of people. The clash with the federal prison chaplains was one such mistake but by no means the only one. As Gordon Loux put it,

"Under Colson's fatherhood Prison Fellowship in its early years was rather like a baby. It made lots of messes but it also grew fast."

The growth was spectacular. By 1979 Prison Fellowship had a professional staff of one hundred, operating in twenty-three states. The staff was supported by 30,000 donors and 6,880 trained volunteers who did the follow-up work after the in-prison seminars, from which over 9,000 inmates had graduated in 600 penitentiaries. In a neglected area of Christian mission, Prison Fellowship had become a powerful force for unity, ministry, and evangelism.

None of this would have happened without Colson's leadership, although he himself was always scrupulous in giving the glory to God for it. But if there was one human element in the ministry's success to be singled out above all others, it was the power of Colson as a public speaker.

In the earliest days after his release from prison, Colson was not a natural orator. Experience on Christian platforms and the narrative of the fascinating story he had to tell made him a better speaker. "But he could still stumble around and overdo things in his speeches until he started talking in prisons," recalled Gordon Loux. "That was when he really began to be empowered." Colson, thanks to the in-prison seminars, became an extraordinarily effective communicator when addressing prisoners. To inmates, he had a special credibility as "the big shot who comes back." Capitalizing on this unique status, Colson pulled out all the stops, reminding his listeners of the mystical bond between offenders and ex-offenders. One of his regular opening lines to a jail audience was, "Brothers, I have been where you now are." Another was, "Fellow sinners—those that have been caught and those who have not been caught. I am here because I am called to be here by the man to whom I have given my life."

Colson was good at leavening his evangelistic message with touches of humor. He always won plenty of laughs from lines such as "I changed my voter registration from Republican to Democrat before I went to prison— I just couldn't stand the idea of a Republican going to jail."

The serious theme of his addresses, always illustrated by rapport-building personal anecdotes from his time as an inmate, was that Jesus Christ reaches out with love to prisoners. "They say church people don't understand what it is like being in a prison. Maybe they don't. But Jesus knew. Jesus understood," Colson would thunder in his compelling countertenor. "Jesus Christ never owned anything in his life. He was born in a borrowed manger. He rode into Jerusalem on a borrowed donkey. He was buried in a borrowed tomb. In his life he was the prophet of losers. You and I are losers. Anyone who's been behind bars in any stinking jail knows what it feels like to be a loser . . . but if you ever have that feeling, if you ever feel lost or hopeless, or useless, or powerless, don't give up hope. Because if you open your heart to Jesus and pray, you will have the love and the power of God with you."

The most important ingredient of all in Colson's oratory, according to many of the Christian believers who heard him speak in prisons, was the power of the Holy Spirit. Belief in this divine empowerment was a key article of faith to his evangelical supporters. They saw Colson's leadership, sense of mission, speaking ability, and success in bringing prisoners to Christ as such a powerful combination of forces that they could only be the signs of an "anointment" by the Holy Spirit.

There were spiritual dangers as well as spiritual blessings in this growing perception by evangelicals. Apart from the effect it might have on Colson's ego, a greater fear was that it might constrict the transdenominational appeal of Prison Fellowship into a narrow, sectarian approach. Colson was always too intelligent a believer to accept many of the instant "I'm saved, now you're saved" nostrums beloved by some of his followers. But his limited knowledge of Christian teachings, together with his lack of exposure to the wider and deeper doctrines of faith, left him vulnerable to the pressures of sectarianism.

One thoughtful observer of Colson who worried about these pressures was Gordon Loux. For all his insecurities about his relationship with his boss, he was Colson's closest and most perceptive adviser on how to rise above the factionalism of the evangelical subculture in the 1970s. "I liked the reality of who Colson was," recalled Loux. "I saw the value in him of a flawed person who smoked, lost his temper occasionally, and had all sorts of weaknesses. But he was such a wonderful servant of the Lord, so brilliant at communicating the gospel on a visceral as well as on an intellectual level, that in my own heart I did believe he was anointed. At the same time I worried a lot about his growing status as an evangelical celebrity. I thought he was bound to get disillusioned by what I called the Noah's ark atmosphere he was living in. He had survived the storms on the outside but pretty soon he was going to get killed by the overpowering stench of evangelical bullshit on the inside. So it was part of my job to keep him looking out for trouble and to give him a broader understanding of the community he was working in."

Gordon Loux was helpful in steering Colson through some of the minefields of rival denominations and groupings in American Christianity of the 1970s. One of Loux's earliest achievements was to constrain Colson's range of highly expressive gestures so that they did not include hands raised above the head when singing a hymn or making a point in a sermon. That move, if photographed, warned Loux, would electrify the charismatic and Pentecostal supporters of Prison Fellowship but switch off the conservative evangelicals, Lutherans, Episcopalians, and Catholics. When he first received this advice Colson had only the dimmest of perceptions of what the differences were between these religious groups. But by 1979 he was learning fast. Although some of Colson's learning came from contact with his theological tutors, more of it came from his voracious reading of the books they recommended. These ranged from the great classics, such as Thomas à Kempis's *Imitation of Christ* and Augustine's *Confessions,* to the writings of Reformation leaders like Luther, Calvin, and Zwingli, and to books by nineteenth- and twentieth-century authors such as Abraham Kuyper, William Wilberforce, Dietrich Bonhoeffer, Alexander Solzhenitsyn, and Paul Johnson. For there was an intellectual side to Colson that preferred the inward swing of solitary study to the outward swing of evangelizing and leading a ministry. Although Colson always regarded the evangelization of prisoners as central to his ministry he was becoming restless at the prospect of just being a preacher working his way through the jails of America like an itinerant, if high-profile, chaplain. His reading and his reform theology were opening his eyes to new horizons. Gradually, the idea began forming in his mind of an expanded ministry. He wanted to do even more for the inmates than bring them the gospel. His vision was to improve their conditions, reform their prisons, change the attitudes of the outside world toward prisoners, and to engage with the leaders of American society in first understanding and then tackling the causes of crime. This was the agenda of Colson's dreams, which soared far above denominational or even purely religious concerns. The chance to start turning those dreams into realities first came his way in a place called Walla Walla.

CHAPTER FIFTEEN

Expanding the Ministry

Walla Walla and Justice Fellowship

A major turning point in Colson's life and ministry was his visit to "the worst prison in the United States." This widely quoted label had been applied to the Washington State Penitentiary, in Walla Walla. Prison Fellowship's plan to hold an in-prison seminar there in late 1979 was known to involve an element of risk because the inmates had such a history of violence. As it turned out, the risks were far more dangerous and the results were far more important than Colson or anyone else had anticipated.

The assistant warden at Walla Walla, Walter "Kip" Kautzky, had the job of welcoming Colson to the jail on his first visit. "It became quite a scary experience," recalled Kautzky, "especially when Mr. Colson insisted on going into our worst segregation unit, which was called Big Red. I had to warn Mr. Colson of the dangers. I told him we couldn't provide him with an escort of guards. I also told him he was very likely to have urine and excrement thrown over him, so I offered to lend him a raincoat."

Colson declined the raincoat and went in. Unaccompanied by guards, he toured Big Red, appalled by the filth, the overcrowding, the anarchy, and the anger of the inmates. He had many one-on-one conversations with leaders of the various power groups, such as bikers, lifers, Hispanics, and Native Americans. "I'm here to help you," was his opening to each encounter. "May I pray for you?" was his closing question, followed by a prayer for the inmate's personal needs. No one threw anything at him.

In the early afternoon Colson gave a talk in a cavernous auditorium with seats for a thousand prisoners. Only 150 of them turned up. However, that was many more than would have come to the only other available meeting place, the chapel, because it had become such a notorious enclave for homosexual activities. Colson's talk was a failure. None of his usual laugh lines, punch lines, or evangelistic appeals appeared to make an impact. He was heard in stony silence. However, two older inmates did approach him after the event to say, "We've been talking and we believe you." Colson grabbed their hands and responded, "I'll do everything I can to help you guys."

Watching these scenes, Assistant Warden Kip Kautzky was moved and impressed. "It was clear that Colson's caring was very real and very personal," he recalled. "He got through to the inmates and convinced them that he wasn't on a wham-bam-thank-you-ma'am tour like so many outside visitors. He was there to begin a process. He promised that he would take the concerns he'd seen and heard about for himself to the movers and shakers outside. He promised he'd come back. The guys believed him. Later that day we learned they'd called off a riot they'd been planning."

How Colson stopped Walla Walla from rioting is quite a story. Tension had been rising in the jail for some weeks prior to his arrival. In the highly charged atmosphere that had built up, a number of prisoners began planning a riot to draw attention to their living conditions. Specific instructions were passed round by the inmates' leaders on where to assemble the rioters, where to start wrecking or attacking, where to set fire to prison property, and which prison officers to kill or take hostage. These very serious riot plans were going to be implemented on the afternoon of the Prison Fellowship visit.

So tense was the atmosphere in Big Red on the morning of the day chosen for the riot that Colson's unexpected arrival in the segregation unit could easily have precipitated the planned mayhem. However, unlike any previous VIP visitor to the jail, he seemed to have plenty of time to sit down with the inmates and listen to their grievances. He was also willing to tour the worst of the facilities and to witness at first hand the appalling conditions: faucets running with raw sewage, cells crawling with cockroaches, the smell of excrement everywhere. Colson was shocked by what he saw. His willingness to agree that the conditions were subhuman and his firmness in promising that he would get something done about them defused some of the tension. Colson's sincerity won grudging respect for himself and some breathing space for the prison. The planned riot, which was scheduled to erupt when Colson was speaking in the auditorium, was called off, or at least postponed. Why? "The only explanation was that the inmates thought Colson was real and that he was going to try and help them," said Assistant Warden Kautzky.

Making promises of action inside the prison was one thing. Delivering them on the outside was another. Colson had a fight on his hands. His first port of call was Olympia, the state capital. There he addressed both the Republican and Democratic caucuses of state legislators, gripping them with his detailed descriptions of the squalor in the prison and with his alarmist predictions of the violence that could occur if the problems went unaddressed. Then Colson traveled to Seattle, the commercial center of Washington State. He talked to audiences of politicians, judges, and businessmen about the horrors of Walla Walla. Later he took his case to the media, giving interviews about the jail on TV and radio.

At first, tangible progress within the walls of Walla Walla was slow in coming. The situation inside the jail remained potentially explosive. However, Prison Fellowship did its best to reduce the emotional temperature by leaving a ministry team there. One of Colson's assistants, Al Elliott, virtually camped out in the prison and on at least one occasion narrowly prevented another possible riot by leaping up on a table in the dining room and pleading with the assembled rioters to cool it. Another Prison Fellowship hero of the Walla Walla saga was an outstanding Presbyterian minister, George Soltau, who preached and counseled the inmates at numerous events, seminars, and one-on-one sessions. Colson himself stayed closely involved and went back to the prison. On his third visit he had an encounter that left him in the unusual condition of being utterly speechless.

Because the jail was once again on the verge of hysteria, Colson asked to meet with the inmate council. This was a power group, completely beyond the control of the prison staff, whose authority when it came to stopping or starting an uprising was absolute. Colson met them in a large cell, which they had converted into something resembling a conference room. The "councillors" stood up when Colson came in and he went down the line shaking hands. "As I walked along the row of them greeting them one by one I made it a point to look with a steely gaze into their eyes. I wanted them to know that I meant business and I was serious. All of a sudden I came across this inmate who had lipstick, rouge, and fully developed breasts. Had I seen her in any other context I would have completely believed she was a woman—but he was a transvestite. I was stunned. My assistant, Al Elliott, said afterward it was the only time he had ever seen me at a loss for words!"

Colson needed to recover his speaking voice quickly because he had to sit down with the hard men of the inmates' council and talk with them about their detailed litany of woes. "They were a tough crowd," he recalled. "We sat there for two hours. They questioned me closely about what I was doing to get their voices heard."

After preaching in the big prison auditorium at a service where many inmates came forward to give their lives for Christ, Colson asked for permission to go and pray with the prisoners on death row. The warden at Walla Walla strongly advised him not to do this, adding that the filth in some of the condemned men's cells was so disgusting, and the chance of having that filth thrown at visitors was so high, that he himself would not dare go on death row. Colson nevertheless insisted on visiting the inmates facing execution. As he came out of the warden's office he said to a newly recruited aide, Dan Van Ness, "This is unbelievable—a warden who is afraid to go into parts of his own prison."

Dan Van Ness, a young Chicago lawyer who had joined Prison Fellowship in order to help with the legal and legislative issues raised by the conditions at Walla Walla, was impressed by Colson's courage that afternoon. "The death row conditions were awful and some of the inmates were initially very hostile," he recalled, "but Chuck went right up to the bars of every cell and just stood there quietly in his business suit talking and praying with every prisoner there. I'll never forget how he got through to an angry young Native American who was desperate because his brother had hanged himself in Walla Walla a few days earlier. The way Chuck calmed him down, read him some verses from the Bible, and prayed with him was just magnificent."

Colson was far from calm within himself as he left death row. He was furious about the deteriorating conditions at Walla Walla. He decided to express his anger to the reporters and TV crews waiting for him outside the prison gates. Dan Van Ness, who could see that Colson was steamed up, tried to restrain his boss. "Be careful, Chuck, be a little cautious," he advised. The recommendation fell on deaf ears. Colson threw caution to the winds, saying he owed it to the men inside to tell the media how bad things were. So in front of the cameras he called Walla Walla "just about the worst prison in the world." Colson said it was far worse than the Maze prison in Northern Ireland, where he had seen dirty protests with excrement smeared on walls, "but at least in Northern Ireland the prison officers are in control and get it cleaned up. Here the staff have lost control."

Inevitably, Colson's comments caused a furor. The next day he went back to the politicians at Olympia and increased the pressure on them to deliver a program of reforms. This time they responded and the wheels of government began to turn. In 1981 the Washington State legislature passed a package of reforms that transferred prisoners to other jails and allocated several million dollars to clean up and refurbish Walla Walla.

Six years after his first visit, Colson returned to "the worst prison in the United States," on Easter Day 1985. Going back into Big Red, he found freshly painted cells, well-scrubbed floors, and recreation areas that had been built as a result of his lobbying efforts. He met several of the inmates who had been surly and aggressive at their previous encounters with him. Now they were friendly and even enthusiastic in their greetings. Some of them had become committed Christians as a result of the Prison Fellowship seminars. Colson came away from the Easter services in the packed prison chapel saying that Walla Walla had been "miraculously transformed." Was he exaggerating? Kip Kautzky, by now promoted to the post of state director of prisons, did not think so. "I wouldn't disagree with the view that Walla Walla was miraculously transformed," he said. "It was a terrible place with a terrible history. I tried to change it but the people in the administration effectively said to me, 'Go play in the traffic.' But they listened to Colson. He changed their perception of what had to be done and he got it done."

Walla Walla was a seminal episode in Colson's ministry because it changed him from being a prison preacher into a prison reformer. He did not abandon the former role but complemented it with a new emphasis on campaigning for better conditions and a fairer dispension of justice within prisons. He set up a task force and then a new department within Prison Fellowship called Justice Fellowship. The focus of Justice Fellowship, which was headed by Dan Van Ness, was matters like overcrowding, poor living conditions, and work programs within prisons. It offered administrative and legislative advice for dealing with these justice issues. The work of Justice Fellowship made its first big impact in Washington State, where, thanks to Colson's campaign to improve Walla Walla, the legislature enacted many of its proposals. Soon, Justice Fellowship was advising other state legislatures on prison justice issues. This advice reached Capitol Hill, where Senator Sam Nunn and other federal legislators started to use Justice Fellowship's recommendations as the basis of new clauses in criminal justice statutes.

Senator Nunn was particularly interested in Colson's and Justice Fellowship's advocacy of concepts originally called "intermediate justice" and "victims' rights." The former meant sentencing nonviolent offenders to community service and other noncustodial sanctions involving restitution. The latter meant giving victims certain rights in the criminal justice process, such as the right to restitution and reconciliation. Both ideas were later merged into a concept called "restorative justice." Colson became an early champion of restorative justice, later writing an important book on it, *Justice That Restores,* which became essential reading in countries and in governments (among them Britain, Norway, and New Zealand) that pioneered restorative justice programs as alternatives to custody. This international influence was part of a wider dimension to Colson's ministry, which began in the late 1970s as he started to launch Prison Fellowship in countries outside America.

The Start of Prison Fellowship International

Colson displayed an uncharacteristic hesitancy when he was first asked to consider expanding Prison Fellowship beyond the United States of America. Throughout the 1970s he was so busy building up his ministry domestically that the idea of developing it internationally seemed an unnecessary diversion. He was weaned away from his isolationism by a combination of events and people, of whom the most influential was Sylvia Mary Alison. Alison was the wife of Michael Alison, a British member of Parliament with strong Christian connections. One of them was with Doug Coe, who had introduced both Alisons to Colson during the earliest stages of his post-conversion experiences in the period when his closest associates were his brothers at Fellowship House.

At Coe's suggestion, Sylvia Mary invited Chuck, Patty, and Emily Colson to stay in the Alisons' London apartment in the summer of 1976, during the European promotion tour for *Born Again*. The visit was not without its difficulties. "I think back about the length of time we were with you and the way in which we disrupted your lives and I shudder," wrote Colson in his thank-you letter. Those shudders were not just a figure of speech, because for many hostesses the disruptions of the visit could have turned the Colson family's sojourn into a burden rather than a blessing. Colson was stretched to exhaustion by his whistle-stop tour of dawn-to-midnight appearances in TV studios, pulpits, and bookstores across the United Kingdom, France, and Germany. Emily became "decidedly bolshie" about her father's frenetic activities. Patty was equivocal about them too, for she was still in the stage of pressing her husband to stop evangelizing and start practicing law again. In the middle of these frank family discussions the demands of the book tour intensified. Colson's schedule—and his stay at the

Alisons'—had to be extended by two weeks. Yet despite these pressures, the Colsons and the Alisons bonded together in a friendship that was to have profound ramifications on an overseas prison ministry, which was then unborn but which today, as Prison Fellowship International, operates in 105 countries across the world.

The first fruits of the Colson-Alison friendship were more visits to each other's houses on both sides of the Atlantic; extensive theological discussions between Chuck and Michael; and a visionary commitment to prison ministry by Sylvia Mary. The discussions on theology were important because they reflected the enormous changes that were taking place in Colson's deepening understanding of his Christian faith during the late 1970s. Colson was benefiting from his tutorial-style relationships with learned American theologians, but within his intimate circle there were very few personal friends, and no international friends at all, who were sufficiently up to speed on theology to be able to engage with him intellectually about the scriptural and doctrinal questions that were becoming increasingly important to his fertile mind. Michael Alison filled this gap. After doing his military service in the British army he had studied for ordination in the Church of England at Ridley Hall, Cambridge, until deciding that his true vocation lay in politics. His career choices had given Alison a useful grounding in scripture and theology as well as a practical knowledge of the life of politics. So it was no surprise that these threads quickly became woven into a growing tapestry of friendship between the two complementary characters as they talked long into the night.

"My early conversations with Chuck revealed a huge hunger in him for biblical teaching," recalls Michael Alison. "I saw that his theological searchings were very much issue-based. We would scour the scriptures to find answers which Chuck could then convert into the currency of contemporary culture for use in his speeches."

One answer that did not initially surface in Alison and Colson's conversations on theology was the concept of Prison Fellowship going international. The inspiration for this move came from the prayers and visions of Sylvia Mary. After a visit she made, at Colson's instigation, to a Prison Fellowship seminar at the Pleasanton women's penitentiary, near San Francisco, in March 1978, Sylvia Mary became convinced that she was being called by God to some form of prison ministry in Britain. Attending a Christian conference at Saint George's House, Windsor, a few weeks later, she confided in Lord Longford, the leading advocate of lay Christian ministry and prison visiting in the U.K. Their conversation culminated in

Sylvia Mary asking Longford if he would be willing to head up a British organization similar to Prison Fellowship. The following morning Longford said that during his prayers, he had received clear guidance that Sylvia Mary, rather than he, should be the leader of any such initiative. However, they both agreed to jointly convene a Christian conference on prison ministry. A date was set for November 1978 and Colson was invited to deliver the keynote address.

Colson's reactions to Sylvia Mary Alison's initiative ranged from being underwhelmed by it to becoming overdomineering toward it. Initially he did not want to go to the London conference at all, and tried to send Gordon Loux to London as his substitute. Gentle persuasion from the Alisons changed his mind, so much so that Colson was transformed into an ardent enthusiast for the project. Not only would he come and give a speech to the conference, he wanted to be welcomed with a major media launch announcing the inauguration of Prison Fellowship U.K. From Washington he issued detailed instructions on the composition of the new organization's board of trustees, which was to be controlled by a majority of board members from Prison Fellowship in the United States. Under this proposed structure, Colson would be firmly in charge of Prison Fellowship U.K. as its executive chairman.

These plans were fiercely resisted in London and at first Colson had some difficulty in understanding the resentment they created. For the control issue was not something he felt strongly about. The pressure to keep an American majority on the British board came not from him but from George Wilson, the executive vice president of the Billy Graham Evangelistic Association, who was also a director of Prison Fellowship. Wilson advised Colson to follow Billy Graham's practice of keeping control of all foreign boards with which his name was associated. At first Colson went along with this advice. But Gordon Loux, who in turn was influenced by Sylvia Mary Alison, suggested that a better blueprint for Prison Fellowship's expansion overseas would be to set up individual national ministries under indigenous national control. Colson accepted this. Nevertheless the new blueprint did not curb his personal tendency to be a control freak and to micromanage every corner of Prison Fellowship, including the new corner opening up on the other side of the Atlantic. This style of leadership was not always appreciated in Britain, even by Colson's greatest admirers. "I simply had to slow Chuck down and stop him giving orders—especially irrelevant and inappropriate orders," recalled Sylvia Mary Alison. "At one point I had to say to him, 'Please stop being a tornado even though you are a very nice tomado.' It took him quite some time before he understood that we simply couldn't be under American control and that we had to move slowly and carefully to win the cooperation of the U.K. prison chaplaincy service."

The first reactions from the U.K. prison chaplaincy service to Colson's concept of Prison Fellowship were decidedly negative. A month before the conference started, the chaplain of HMP Albany, on the Isle of Wight, wrote to Sylvia Mary Alison asking for the event to be canceled on the grounds that the mere idea of allowing Christian volunteers to enter British prisons was totally unacceptable. This hostility to Prison Fellowship's methods of operation appeared to be shared by the entire prison establishment in the U.K., from senior Home Office officials to the chaplain general of the Prison Service, right through the ranks of individual prison chaplains. Colson did not break down this wall of prejudice on his first visit. He and Gordon Loux were startled to be told at a meeting in Church House by the chaplain general, "Your kind of Christianity is dangerous. We will never allow it in our prisons here." Even in the face of such opposition Colson did not take no for an answer. Although some British chaplains gradually softened their attitudes after the first conference and then a second one six months later, it was some years before the pioneers of Prison Fellowship U.K. (which they initially insisted on calling Prison Christian Fellowship against Colson's wishes) were allowed to do anything more than pray together for prisoners at a safe distance outside the jails of Britain.

The innovations that had been so successful in America, such as in-prison seminars and furloughs for the training of selected prisoners, were not put on the British agenda for a long time. Colson found this terribly frustrating. He made various interventions of his own in Britain that were not always sensitive or productive. One example of Colson rushing in where angels fear to tread was an imperious memo he circulated giving the impression that the board of Prison Fellowship in Washington thought both Ireland and Northern Ireland were component parts of the United Kingdom. "I guess I'll have to be a little more careful in sorting out my countries," said a chastened Colson after that mistake had been pointed out to him.

Worse chastenings were to come. Colson fought and lost a running battle with Sylvia Mary Alison over the upbeat media announcements he loved to make about progress in Britain. "Insensitive publicity has the effect of destroying tenuous relationships and making our work of building far more difficult," she told him sternly in a letter demanding his silence on Prison

Fellowship's first moves into the jails of Northern Ireland. "On the whole I am against publicity except of a very specific and judicious kind." In the same letter Sylvia May Alison warned Colson of the dangers of "usurping each other's roles and functions and treading on each other's toes." She made it clear that Prison Fellowship U.K. could work as a Christian cell alongside Prison Fellowship in America, "but not under it."

Colson was not good at working under anyone at this stage of his ministry, so he took a surprisingly long time to understand the British sensitivities on these issues. Perhaps the steepest moment of his learning curve came when he attended a 1982 board meeting of Prison Fellowship U.K. The last item on the agenda was the formal affiliation with Prison Fellowship International (PFI), the new umbrella organization Colson had formed to link together the amorphous Prison Fellowship groups that were springing up in England, Scotland, Canada, France, and New Zealand. Colson assumed the affiliation would go through on the nod as a welcome formality. Instead, the British directors spent over an hour discussing in painful detail the reasons why they might not want to be associated with PFI at all. In the end, they voted in favor of affiliation, but the call was a close and distressing one to Prison Fellowship's founder.

"Poor Chuck had to sit there like a wounded animal hearing us talk about past mistakes in the relationship and nearly rejecting the PFI connection," recalled Sylvia Mary Alison. "But at the same time we really loved him for his larger than life qualities of energy, dynamism, compassion, love for prisoners, and electrifying speaking ability. We realized that it was his work in America that had triggered our work in Britain. We couldn't possibly have done it without him. But we wanted to develop along different lines even though it sometimes made him impatient with us. To his great credit, he very humbly accepted that different methods were needed for different countries."

Colson had fewer of the problems he experienced in London when dealing with the other new international ministries that came into existence in the early 1980s with PFI's encouragement. This was partly because the American control issue had been strategically defused, and partly because the rest of the newcomers did not share the British establishment's hostility toward Colson's penchant for publicity and media initiatives. Indeed, several of PFI's earliest offspring were conceived in the excitement of media interest generated by the international premieres of the film *Born Again*. The story of that film could well be subtitled "How Not to Create a Movie." Correctly believing that no Hollywood studio would ever produce a sympathetic movie about a senior member of the Nixon administration making a spiritual journey from power to prison to peace, a group of Christian investors raised the $2.6 million to finance their own film. They insisted that the script and the direction must be faithful to the letter of Colson's best seller.

Fidelity to the book resulted in tedium on the screen. Most of the actors, including Dean Jones as Colson, gave stilted performances. As a result, the film achieved the improbable result of being far more boring than the real life story, missing much of the drama, passion, and even humor of the Colson saga. It got bad notices from the secular reviewers for being too religious and critical reviews in the Christian press for being too secular. Yet although *Born Again* as a movie was a flop, as a motivator for people around the world to support Prison Fellowship it was a success.

This was all the more surprising because Colson himself was so negative about the film. In one tongue-in-cheek reaction he told its producers that he would demonstrate outside any movie theater where it was being shown, holding up a protestor's placard with the words "This is *not* the story of my life." Yet in a contradictory stance he was positive about the film's potential for fund-raising. So he attended thirty-two premieres of *Born Again* in cities across the United States, starting with a glitzy gala at the Kennedy Center in Washington. Then he took it across the English-speaking world with another round of premieres in Canadian, British, Australian, and New Zealand cities. "For the backers the movie was a financial disaster," recalled Gordon Loux. "But for Prison Fellowship it built a new financial base. In many of those U.S. cities the *Born Again* premiere became the social event of the year for evangelicals, and large numbers of new donors signed on for us. In foreign countries the premieres gave us a completely new network of overseas supporters who became the national ministries of Prison Fellowship International."

A young Canadian who heard Colson speak at this time was Ron Nikkel, later to become PFI's president. "Good grief, that guy is arrogant," was Nikkel's first reaction to Colson's oratory, but he reversed his opinion a few hours later when he met Colson privately and was captivated by his humility and grace. This meeting led to Ron Nikkel joining the Colson team as executive director of the new Prison Fellowship International in 1982. "In my perspective, PFI was very much Gordon Loux's baby in those days," recalls Nikkel. "Chuck didn't seem to have much interest in an international ministry. He thought it was very difficult and that nothing much would ever come of it."

In fact, Ron Nikkel misjudged Colson's growing commitment to PFI. For as a result of several moving experiences he had on vision trips to prisons in Africa, Asia, South America, and Europe during the early 1980s, Colson became convinced of the need for a global prison ministry. For example, in the Trivandrum prison, in India, Colson addressed over a thousand inmates condemned as untouchables by the caste system. After the speech the prisoners surged round him, stretching their hands upward. Colson's Indian companions explained that these gestures were the inmates' way of trying to discover whether their American speaker was real enough in his Christian compassion to touch untouchables. Colson passed this test by not leaving the prison courtyard until he had physical contact with every man in the jail. He was emotionally exhausted but spiritually inspired to do more international ministry.

Another milestone in Colson's overseas work was his leadership of the first ever PFI Convocation in Northern Ireland in 1980. This event was originally called a symposium until the word was looked up in an Ulster dictionary, which defined it as "a drunken orgy with intellectual conversation." Changing the name was not the only peculiarity on the part of the stern Orangemen who organized the convocation. Some of them expressed grave misgivings about Colson's participation, on the grounds that he was a smoker and his wife was a Catholic.

Colson himself was determined that his international ministry should not be tainted by sectarianism. So he chose as the theme for the convocation "Reconciliation Between Catholics and Protestants." The topic was provocative at a time when Northern Ireland's troubles were at their height, but Colson delivered a brilliant keynote speech on the importance of denominational unity in prison ministry. He also recruited several outstanding speakers who gave addresses on reconciliation. They included IRA and UDF terrorists who had reconciled themselves to each other by coming to Christ, and a mother who publicly forgave the killer who had gunned down her daughter while she was walking home after choir practice. Such acts and speeches of reconciliation made a considerable impact on the people of Northern Ireland, as well as on the 125 delegates attending the convocation.

Colson's visits to several prisons in the province, including the Maze, also excited much spiritual and even political excitement because of his willingness to go into the cells of IRA, UDF, and UDA terrorists to pray with them. As one of the organization's organizers, William Fitch, has recalled, "This convocation far exceeded expectations. We had to move it to the largest auditorium in the University of Belfast to cope with the numbers. Only Chuck Colson could have brought so many people to Belfast from over thirty countries, as well as attracting large numbers of supporters in the province to discuss reconciliation and prison ministry. Only Chuck Colson could have got access to so many prisons and broken all the sectarian taboos by going into the cells of Catholic and Protestant prisoners. It was a great breakthrough, and revolutionary in the context of Northern Ireland."

Colson also regarded the 1980 Belfast convocation as a major breakthrough for both himself and PFI. From then on he made reconciliation a major plank of Prison Fellowship's programs. He also started searching for ways of minimizing the divisions between Catholics and Protestants, a cause that he later formally espoused as cofounder of ECT—Evangelicals and Catholics Together. Above all, the Belfast convocation deepened Colson's commitment to Prison Fellowship International's ministry. As the next chapter will tell, this commitment was to bear remarkable fruit in many different ways.

Black Ministry

As Prison Fellowship grew in the United States its ministry inevitably reached out to more and more African-Americans, who make up 30 to 40 percent of the prison population. Colson had become virtually color blind as a result of his own incarceration. He seemed to have a natural empathy with black inmates, several of whom he recruited, after their release, to the staff of Prison Fellowship. Some of these appointments may have been too impulsive, owing more to Colson's heart than his head, for a worrying percentage of them failed. This was partly because of moral and human weaknesses in the individuals concerned, but also because they were sometimes pushed too quickly into the limelight, giving their testimonies and taking on leadership roles. "One of our greatest mistakes was that we gave high-profile visibility to African-American ex-cons far too soon," recalled Gordon Loux, who also worried about Prison Fellowship's lack of support from black churches. "The truth is that we did not do a good job in getting the minority church involved with us," said Loux. "We tried hard but for many reasons we failed."

What were those reasons? One was that the suspicious cynicism directed toward Colson by many Americans in the aftermath of Watergate went deeper and lasted longer among black Americans. He was politically identified with conservative Republicanism, and his notorious alleged comment "I would walk over my grandmother for Richard Nixon" resonated more offensively in black culture, which reveres matriarchy. Moreover, in the early days of his ministry Colson had unintentionally given the impression of being insensitive toward black churchmen. In particular, his clashes with John Staggers, the revered black leader of prison ministry at the Lorton penitentiary, near Washington, had harmed Colson's reputation in the African-American Christian community.

These perceptions gradually changed as Prison Fellowship grew and gathered momentum. The visits Colson made to jail after jail all over the country left an increasingly positive impression in the black community. Even so, his touch was not always sure in the wider community outside the prisons. "Chuck had a tremendous emotional connection with black offenders and ex-offenders," recalled Ralph Veerman, who in 1978 became Prison Fellowship's vice president for prison ministry. "But at first he couldn't make the same connection with black community leaders because he just didn't have a historical or intellectual understanding of black issues."

The gaps in Colson's understanding were slowly filled as he won the confidence of black pastors and community leaders. One of the first to endorse him was John Perkins, the Mississippi civil rights hero, who became a close friend. With guidance from Perkins and others, Colson's recruitment of black staffers grew more discerning. One of his early successes was John Peyton, a pastor who gave exceptional service to the ministry. Another was the Reverend George "Huggy Bear" Taylor, who created a culture of hugging in Prison Fellowship and converted its founder into a far more tactile human being. Another black staffer was Al Lawrence, a former inmate of Maxwell, who in 1985 witnessed what he describes as "a supernatural experience" between Colson and a prisoner named Bessie Shipp. When the story of this encounter became widely known it did wonders for Colson's image in the African-American community.

The story began on Christmas Day 1985, when Colson was visiting a women's prison in North Carolina. Al Lawrence, Prison Fellowship's newly appointed field director for the state, had been accompanying his boss throughout an arduous day of preaching and one-on-one ministry in various cell blocks. At the end of the afternoon the prison chaplain, the Reverend Jenny Lancaster, said there was one last prisoner she would like Colson to visit. This was Bessie Shipp, a notorious shoplifter from

Winston-Salem, who was being held in an isolation cell. "The reason she's there," explained the chaplain, "is that she's got AIDS."

In 1985, ignorant rumors were rife about AIDS and how it could be spread by sharing toilet facilities, going to the dentist, or even shaking hands with an HIV-positive person. Al Lawrence vividly recalled the shock that he and just about everyone else in Colson's entourage felt when the chaplain suggested this visit to a prisoner with AIDS. "Now, when Jenny Lancaster said we should go visit Bessie Shipp because she was dying of AIDS, everyone fell back in horror. No one in Chuck's crew wanted to do that. But Jenny challenged us and said, 'Come on, you men of God, go down and see this poor woman with AIDS.' Then Chuck turned to me and said, 'Come on, Al, we've got to go.'

"So Chuck and I and Jenny, the chaplain, walked on alone until we got to that cell, which was quite isolated from the rest of the prison. It was the cell that was built for Velma Barfield, the only woman ever to be executed in the state of North Carolina. When we got there the cell door was not locked, because Bessie Shipp was in there for medical reasons, not because she was dangerous. So we came in through this rusty door and there she was, sitting on the bed. And Chuck walked in and stood there for a moment, saying, 'Where is she?'

"Now, I really thought he was being funny when he said, 'Where is she?' because she was right there a few feet away from him, a black girl with real dark ebony skin and bright shining eyes. And then, after a pause, Chuck walked over to her, hugged her, and held her hands as he talked to her."

Colson's perspective on this encounter was rather different. "What was going through my mind as I met Bessie Shipp was absolute terror," he has recalled. "I was far too afraid to touch her. But then a supernatural moment took over. I remembered that the night before, when I arrived at the hotel, I had flipped on the TV before going to bed, and there was Mother Teresa in New York with her arms around two AIDS victims. I went to bed thinking that I, a big tough ex-marine, couldn't possibly do what that little ninety-pound Albanian nun had been doing. I was too full of fear. But then the very next day I was confronted with my fear, and in that supernatural moment in Bessie Shipp's cell, I conquered it. Out of that overcoming of my fear came a renewed confidence in me about the ministry."

Colson's first sign of renewed confidence was displayed in the way he talked to Bessie Shipp. "It was something very special and very powerful," said Al Lawrence. "Chuck witnessed to her, he embraced her, and he made beautiful promises to her that changed her life when they were fulfilled."

Two promises emerged from Colson's talk with Bessie Shipp. The first was a spiritual promise of the Lord's love, forgiveness, and salvation, which Bessie accepted. The second was a practical promise of clemency representations about her parole application, which Colson said he would make to the governor of North Carolina. As they came out of the isolation cell, Colson and Lawrence had a private word together. "Al, you know, I didn't see her at first," said Colson. "I saw something but I thought it was an angel."

Al Lawrence was astonished. "I was bowled right over for two reasons," he recalled. "The first thing that hits me is that Chuck isn't surprised if he walks into a room and sees an angel in there. And then he isn't surprised when the angel he sees has dark skin. So I said to myself, Wow! I mean, I am black but I have never envisaged seeing a black angel. In my mind angels are always white. But there's Chuck who's telling me he's seen a black angel, and it touched my heart so deep that from that day on I was fighting mad if ever anyone said Chuck Colson was insensitive to black folks."

Immediately after these experiences, Colson went back to his hotel and wrote to Governor James Martin of North Carolina requesting Christmas parole for Bessie Shipp. Al Lawrence delivered the letter to the governor's mansion later in the evening of December 25, and it fell on receptive ears. A campaign to grant Bessie clemency on compassionate grounds had been building for some time. Colson's intervention seems to have been the tipping point. On December 29 the governor issued an executive order for the release of Bessie Shipp.

So Bessie walked free and returned to her hometown of Winston-Salem, where she was known as Lil Bessie the Booster, partly for her heroin addiction and partly for her habit of boosting her shopping bag and those of her accomplices with stolen goods. But her habits had changed. For the first time in her life, Bessie avoided the temptations of the local heroin dealers and the shopping malls. Instead, she headed for Mars Hill Baptist Church on Cherry Street in Winston-Salem, and there she "set the whole congregation on fire," as she proclaimed her new faith in Jesus Christ and told the story of Colson's witness to her.

Within two weeks of coming out of prison, Bessie's AIDS infection reached a critical stage and she had to be rushed to intensive care. Al Lawrence went to visit her and recalled the scene. "So I came here to say a prayer for Bessie in the intensive care and she opened her eyes and said to me, 'Reverend, don't pray for heaven because heaven is already mine. I have confessed Christ before my brothers and sisters. I am at peace. But there is just one more thing I would like to do on this earth, and that is, I would like to get baptized.' "

Bessie Shipp was having difficulty in speaking as she said these words. Al Lawrence wondered what he could do in response to her request, given the obstacles of the drips, tubes, breathing apparatus, and other medical equipment around the bed. Then a nurse came up and asked, "What was Bessie just saying?"

"She said she wants to be baptized," replied Lawrence.

"Hallelujah! Let's do it right now," said the nurse.

So space was cleared around the bedside, and shortly before midnight, Bessie Shipp was baptized by the Reverend Al Lawrence. He then had an eight-hour drive back to his home. When he arrived, just after 8:30 A.M., the phone rang and the same nurse told him, "Bessie passed away in the night while you were driving on the highway."

Al Lawrence sums up the story in these words: "Now all this happened just over two weeks since Chuck Colson went into that isolation cell and witnessed to Bessie and encouraged the governor to pardon her. And anyone who heard Bessie giving her testimony in the days after she came out of the jail knew that she had come to know and love the Lord. Who brought her here? It was Chuck, the Lord's man, who hugged her when she was dying of AIDS, showed her compassion, and brought her to Christ. Now do you see why I am ready to fight anyone who says that Charles W. Colson is insensitive to blacks?!"

The Planting of Angel Tree

Colson's reputation as a Christian leader whose words to prisoners were matched by his deeds on their behalf grew steadily during the 1980s. But the program that became the largest, most compassionate, most generous, and most successful of all his ministry's activities began as a purely local initiative without Colson's knowledge or involvement. It was called Angel Tree.

Angel Tree was the brainchild of an ex-prisoner known in her criminal days as "the Bonnie Parker of Alabama," a nickname derived from the infamous bank robbers Bonnie and Clyde. The real-life Bonnie who devised Angel Tree was Mary Kay Beard. After a colorful career in safecracking and bank holdups she began serving a twenty-one-year sentence, until unexpectedly she was paroled after only six years. During her time as an inmate in the Julia Tutwiler Prison for Women, in Alabama, Beard became a committed Christian. She also started attending academic classes, getting exceptional grades, which eventually brought her a master's degree in education.

Colson met Mary Kay Beard in 1982. He had heard about her story from a Southern pastor. Immediately impressed by her energy and abilities, he offered her a job on the staff of Prison Fellowship. His initial thinking was that he needed her to help with the ministry's outreach to the women inmates, who made up 6 percent of America's prison population. Mary Kay Beard continued to impress Colson, who promoted her to the post of PF's state director in her native Alabama. In that role Beard addressed many organizations and groups. At one luncheon for a ladies' group, a woman present vented the common "Lock 'em up and throw away the key" sentiment. In reply, Beard took up a theme that she had heard Colson speaking on—the tragedies that can happen in the lives of prisoners' children when their fathers or mothers are incarcerated for long sentences.

The woman who had seemed so hostile to Beard's presentation suddenly softened. "I haven't even thought about them having kids," she said. A dialogue started. The woman explained how a mall in her hometown had urged shoppers to buy Christmas gifts for poor children. Could something similar be done for prisoners' kids? Mary Kay Beard responded with a recollection from her own years behind bars. When she had been in solitary confinement, a local church had sent her a Christmas gift—a box containing dozens of miniature tubes of toothpaste. Realizing that she had been well enough supplied to clean her own teeth for at least a year, Beard gave away many of the toothpaste tubes to her fellow inmates. To her astonishment these inmates lovingly wrapped up the tubes and sent them out as Christmas presents to their children.

"Can you imagine wrapping up a miniature tube of toothpaste to give to your child for Christmas?" said Mary Kay Beard. "But several of those mothers told me how much it meant to them to be able to send something to their kids with the label 'Love from Mama' on it, as they had nothing else to give them."

With these memories in mind, Beard went back into the jail where she had served her sentence and collected names and addresses of prisoners' children. Then she and a handful of Prison Fellowship volunteers put up Christmas trees in Birmingham and Montgomery, calling them "Angel Trees" and advertising for the public "to come by and purchase a Christmas gift for an angel."

The response was amazing. Beard had thought she might perhaps get one gift each for two hundred children. In fact, 556 children received four gifts each, all labeled "With Love from Mama," from their imprisoned mothers. The joy that was given by this first ever Angel Tree initiative was enormous among prisoners' families in Alabama.

At first Beard did not spread the good tidings of her initiative to her bosses at Prison Fellowship's headquarters in Washington. "I thought that if I told you about it, you'd stop me," she told Gordon Loux. But then a new dimension to Angel Tree opened up. "Around January or February 1984, the Bible study groups and the in-prison seminars Prison Fellowship was running across the state increased their attendance dramatically," recalled Beard. "Inmates were asking, 'Is that the same group that got those Christmas presents for my kids? I think I'll go to this seminar.' " Mary Kay Beard's Angel Tree scheme continued to grow for the next couple of years in Alabama. It was imitated by three or four other Prison Fellowship state directors in other parts of the country. However, it remained a small, localized cottage industry until Colson focused on Angel Tree. He immediately embraced the scheme with characteristic energy and enthusiasm. "I cannot claim the slightest credit for Angel Tree but I saw its potential and believed that it came from God," said Colson. A skillful popularizer as always, he persuaded the Prison Fellowship board to mandate it as a nationwide program in 1986. That Christmas, Angel Tree really took off, with massive support from churches across the country.

In January 1987 Gordon Loux reported to Colson on the results and numbers. "I went to see him when he was hospitalized in January 1987 and I said to him, 'I've got some good news that will really make you feel better,' " recalled Loux. " 'Angel Tree gave presents over Christmas to ninety thousand prisoners' kids. Isn't that an amazing figure?' " Colson was indeed amazed. Giving thanks for Angel Tree in prayer, he saw an even greater potential for it in the years ahead and commissioned an internal report on its expansion. Where that report led is the second part of the Angel Tree story, covered in the next chapter.

Ten Years of Change

The tenth anniversary of Prison Fellowship, in 1986, was a good time to take stock of what had been achieved by the ministry and its founder. It is also a good moment to make an interim assessment of the personal and spiritual journey of Charles Colson. Never one to rest on his laurels, he was more interested in the challenges of the future rather than the history of the past. However, he was rightly proud of his ministry's record, even though his greatest hopes and challenges lay ahead of him. After ten years of continuous expansion, Prison Fellowship's core activity was bringing the gospel to inmates through its in-prison seminars. These were running at the rate of four hundred a year, discipling some fifty thousand prisoners, with the help of twenty-five thousand trained volunteers. Although the original program of discipleship training for furloughed prisoners in Washington, D.C., was winding down, Colson was energetically expanding into new projects. In addition to the activities of Prison Fellowship International, Justice Fellowship, and Angel Tree, several important new programs were created. These included the community service projects, which took nonviolent offenders out of jail and into the community to work on schemes such as providing repairs and insulation to low-income homes. There was also a big expansion of the scope of the seminar program into areas such as the marriage seminars, which offered Christian counseling to couples separated by one partner's incarceration; the life plan seminars, which prepared inmates for life after their release; the financial seminars, which taught prisoners how to deal with money matters; and the death row seminars, which prepared condemned men and women for their execution and death.

Away from the five hundred or so prisons in which Prison Fellowship was operating, Colson launched a program to support victims of crime, called Neighbors Who Care. He was also continually trying to get his ministry's message across to a wider audience through a new subsidiary of Prison Fellowship named Fellowship Communications, which published books, tapes, videos, Bible study guides, and *Jubilee*—a monthly magazine with a circulation of twenty-five thousand. All this activity needed staff, organization, and money. Although Prison Fellowship was always a lean machine, relying heavily on volunteers, by 1986 it had over two hundred employees, of whom over half were working in the field, under twenty-one state or regional directors. The annual budget of Prison Fellowship at this time was $12 million, a figure that required an energetic program of fundraising from a wide base of donors, large and small.

A key aide to Colson on both the organizational and the fund-raising sides of the ministry was Ralph Veerman. Recruited from the Youth for Christ ministry to Prison Fellowship in 1978 with the title of vice president for prison ministry, Veerman was initially given the job of recruiting the first state and regional directors and creating a structure for operations in the field. In 1983 he was promoted to senior vice president for public ministry, with responsibility for communications and fund-raising. In both roles Veerman worked closely with Colson, and he took away many interesting insights into his boss.

"Chuck was a real hands-on manager, at times a micromanager," recalled Veerman, "but he never lost the touch of a politician when running the ministry. For example, he worked tremendously hard at fund-raising, but in an original and sensitive way, which I realized owed much to his experiences at building bloc politics in his White House years. He saw everything in terms of segmentation, and was forever crafting special messages and letters to each segment or bloc of potential PF supporters. This proactive approach worked wonders, especially with our major donors. He used the same segmentation technique when it came to communications. He would design different ways of telling the PF story to opinion formers, breaking them down into blocs such as political leaders, key pastors of big churches, academics, print journalists, TV people, and so on. This was tremendously effective."

As he had been in his legal and political years, Colson was a driven leader with extraordinary energy and a gargantuan appetite for hard work. His number two, Gordon Loux, who in 1984 had been promoted to the post of president of Prison Fellowship, was awed by Colson's industry. "I believe he worked as hard as, if not harder than, any corporate executive in America," said Loux. "Every night we used to give him huge batches of letters to sign—thank-you letters, appeal letters, ministry letters, and personal correspondence he'd dictated to his secretaries. Every morning back they'd come, all signed, many with personal handwritten notes on the bottom, plus tape after tape of fresh dictation. It was an amazing output of work."

On top of the heavy load he carried in correspondence, administration, and public speaking, Colson found time for theological reading and daily Bible study. One strong influence on Colson's devotional life throughout the first ten years of his ministry was the Reverend Neal Jones, who was pastor of Columbia Baptist Church in Falls Church, Virginia, from 1969 to 1995, and later a board member of Prison Fellowship. Jones had baptized Colson in 1976 when he changed denominations from Episcopalian to Baptist. A few years after joining the Baptists, Colson asked Jones, "What do you ministers do to stop from burning out when you are working so hard preaching the gospel?"

"Build yourself a strong devotional discipline," replied Jones, "with Bible reading at the heart of it."

Colson took this advice to heart. His personal Bible reflects his discipline, for he wrote a stream of notes and comments in its margins. Some of these annotations are fascinating, for they provide insights into Colson's spiritual development. For example, alongside Matthew 4:8, where the devil tempts Jesus by taking him up a mountain and offering the kingdoms of the world, Colson wrote, "Same today. Same issue. Devil offers us world's kingdoms."

Opposite Matthew 12:31, which warns against blasphemy against the Spirit, Colson wrote in block capitals: "UNFORGIVABLE SIN."

Beneath the parable of the Good Samaritan, in Luke 10:30–37, Colson commented: "Practical, overt act of charity in name of Christ—act of God's love—what world needs today."

There are also heavy double underlinings of key phrases and verses that Colson evidently felt should be guiding his life and ministry. These included:

> "Preach the Word in season and out of season." 2 Timothy 4:2
> "My brothers are those who hear God's word and put it into practice." Luke 8:21
> "He who is generous will be blessed." Proverbs 22:9
> "May they be one just as we are one. I in them and you in me. May they be brought to complete unity." John 17:22–23

Although it is possible to read too much into these extrapolations from a heavily annotated Bible, the picture that emerges is that of a searcher linking up the Word to the world.

Among those close to Colson who observed the path he was climbing was Ralph Veerman. "I was stunned by Chuck's intellectual growth and how it translated into spiritual growth," he has recalled. "That growth was fueled by his very systematic studies of the Bible and by his study of theology. I remember him saying to me in the context of some book he'd been reading by R. C. Sproul, 'My calling is to be a prophetic voice to change the culture, and my prison ministry is the illumination of that change.' "

Colson was also in the business of changing himself. After ten years of full-time ministry, all sorts of personal softenings in him were becoming manifest. His brashness and bullheadedness were gradually being replaced by a gentler and more patient attitude to those who worked with him.

There were behavioral changes too. His drinking had stopped completely after the episode of the John Dean dinner in 1976. Smoking was next to go. Even his enthusiasm for practical joking was slowing, reined in from its wilder excesses.

Colson's struggle to give up smoking was a tough one. He battled with his craving for nicotine for at least seven of the first ten years of his public ministry. In his heyday of power he had been a fifty-cigarettes-a-day man—and more. He cut down to fifteen a day by the late 1970s, and these he smoked in the privacy of his home or office. It was deference to the evangelical code of conduct on tobacco that drove Colson into becoming a secret smoker. The hypocrisy of this bothered him and even one day gave him a warning in flames—although not from the fires of hell but from the pocket of his aide Mike Cromartie.

Colson was enjoying a clandestine smoke after giving an address in 1979 when his hosts unexpectedly rejoined him in the room. Anxious not to be caught in the sinful act of inhaling tobacco, Colson whispered to his faithful aide, "Hey, Mike, take care of this for me," and passed over the cigarette. So far as the shortsighted Cromartie could see, the cigarette had not yet been lit. So to help his boss he concealed the offending object by putting it in his own pocket. As the general conversation went on nothing untoward happened for some minutes, but unfortunately the cigarette, on which Colson *had* taken a couple of puffs, kept smoldering away. Quietly it burned through the lining of the pocket and set light to Cromartie's suit. As the flames were extinguished with much slapping and dowsing with water, Colson thought it uproariously funny.

Soon after this episode Colson threw away his cigarettes completely. This decision was taken on a plane flight to Europe in early 1980, when Colson finally admitted to himself that he was in thrall to nicotine addiction, or at least to nicotine-induced compulsive behavior. Despite this realization, his conversion from smoking was initially limited in its scope. He gave up cigarettes but turned to a pipe. Some encouragement to this alternative form of nicotine consumption was given to him on a visit to the museum and former home of C. S. Lewis in Oxford. The curator of the museum presented Colson with one of Lewis's favorite pipes. It became a talking point and an excuse for Colson's continuation of the habit for three more years. But when he found he had ruined a number of pipes by chewing their stems off, Colson finally faced up to his compulsive weakness and eventually stopped smoking completely in 1983. The only trace of his old vice today is that he likes to joke, "When I get to heaven my first words will be, 'Could I please have a cigarette?' "

Colson's joking habits were not quite as compulsive as his smoking habits, but they too had to be toned down. In the early days of Prison Fellowship the founder's penchant for pranks became a legend. Some of the worthy Christians in Colson's new life were a little surprised by what he considered funny. In addition to a regular stream of hoax telephone calls and spoof memos, Colson enjoyed tricks such as putting red ink in the showerhead of a colleague's bathroom; inserting a carefully concealed layer of Saran wrap in a toilet bowl with what might delicately be called "reverse flow consequences"; or even tricking visitors into shaking hands with an outstretched elastic hand that, in turn, came apart as a bloodstained artificial limb, amputated at the shoulder. Age rather than repentance seems to have cooled Colson's ardor for such juvenile japes, for they were diminishing if not entirely vanishing from his repertoire by the late 1980s.

For all his joviality Colson was a deeper and more private man than many around him recognized. His greatest strengths lay not in his public speeches and appearances, effective though they were, but in his reflective journeys of the mind and spirit. These journeys would not have been possible had it not been for the blissful married life he enjoyed with Patty. She gave him a rock solid base of support and contentment without which his dreams and visions would never have turned into reality. As Doug Coe observed, "Most people consider Patty only as the wife of Chuck Colson, but that's too simple. They're a team, and if it wasn't for her and her vision, her heart and commitment, I would say there wouldn't be a Prison Fellowship."

Those who knew Prison Fellowship from the inside, as staff members, came to similar conclusions about the role of Patty. "There was no more supportive person of Chuck's vision and passion for Christian service than Patty," recalled Ralph Veerman, "but I think her greatest contribution was that she kept him centered and balanced. She didn't take Chuck quite as seriously as, at times, he took himself. She lightened him up with loving humor. She knew what would wear him out or hurt his calling, so she very quietly and skillfully reined him in and kept him focused."

Colson's focus was changing after ten years of ministry. His theological travels were taking him further and further down the road toward his goal of changing the culture. He wrote two important books in the 1980s that were both aimed at reaching a wider cultural audience. These were *Loving*

God (1983), a storytelling presentation of the power of God's love; and *Kingdoms in Conflict* (1987), a treatise on the roles of the church and the state. Ellen Vaughn, who worked closely with Colson on *Loving God,* said, "Chuck's great strength as a popular writer is that he combines a storyteller's heart with a lawyer's head."

Colson's heart and head were both captivated by an important academic study, *Crime and Human Nature,* published in 1985 by two Harvard professors, James Q. Wilson and Richard J. Herrnstein. Wilson and Herrnstein's thesis made a huge impact on Colson. Their central argument was that the basic cause of crime is not poverty or social environment but the lack of moral training in a young person's formative years. In simplified form, the message was: Crime is a moral problem.

"It was soon after I read this study, and other findings on the same theme by eminent social scientists, that I realized we weren't going to do anything about the criminal justice problem and the exploding prison population until we did something about the breakdown of moral values in our culture," recalled Colson. "So this was a major maturing point in our ministry, when I began to see that we couldn't just preach in the prisons, we couldn't even just be concerned with the systematic problems in the criminal justice system. We had also to deal with the moral collapse of the culture."

When Colson first started to speak about this culture change, which he called a "worldview," he remembers "drawing all kinds of blank stares." Many people had no idea what he was talking about. Even among those who did, there were some voices, not least among senior staffers in Prison Fellowship, who thought Colson's new interest in worldview was diluting his commitment to basic prison ministry. These tensions were even ventilated at board level, but Colson calmed them easily by insisting that all he was trying to do was to strike the right balance between his fundamental calling to prison work and his new calling to changing America's moral and cultural climate. "You are my accountability group," he told the board members of Prison Fellowship. "You will help me to get the balance right." Finding this balance was to be the big challenge for Colson's second decade of ministry as he looked toward new developments.

CHAPTER SIXTEEN

New Developments

At Death's Door

There were nearly no new horizons at all. In January 1987, Colson had a close call with death in a Washington hospital following major surgery for stomach cancer. The postoperative complications caused him horrendous pain and required long nights of bedside vigil by his family. Yet there were silver linings to these clouds. For the fruits of his spiritual journey during his hospitalization included a strengthening of his faith and that of his newly converted daughter, Emily. In addition, Colson had a profound prayer experience at the deathbed of a fellow patient in the same hospital—CIA director William J. Casey. At the time, this was an entirely private encounter between Colson, Casey, and Casey's wife, Sophia. However, the episode later developed into a public controversy when Colson challenged author Bob Woodward's account of Casey's alleged deathbed confessions.

Colson's medical dramas began in November 1986 when he was touring the Philippines on behalf of Prison Fellowship International. Returning to his hotel in Manila from a prison visit, he saw blood in his stools. A local doctor (inappropriately a urologist) summoned by the national PFI chairman, Menardo Jiminez, advised an endoscopy and immediate hospitalization if the bleeding continued. However, the bleeding stopped for long enough to allow Colson to deliver the keynote speech to a conference of businessmen. Immediately afterward he flew back to Florida, announcing somewhat melodramatically that he would prefer to die on a Northwest Airlines flight than in a Manila hospital.

Colson's imminent demise seemed improbable to the doctors at his hospital in Naples, Florida, the city to which he and Patty had moved in 1980. After extensive tests, these doctors reassured their patient that he was suffering from a bleeding ulcer—a problem that had troubled him intermittently since the early 1960s. However, Colson's general practitioner, Dr. Joseph Spano, did not accept this diagnosis. After further tests it was established that the bleeding had been caused by a tumor that had penetrated the wall of the stomach. The radiologist analyzing the X rays reported that the tumor was unattached to the stomach, which meant that it was likely to be nonmalignant. Buoyed up with false optimism by this opinion, Colson declared that he was prepared to have the necessary surgery to remove the benign growth, but only after he had completed all the speaking engagements on his current schedule. This meant no operation for over a year.

Wiser counsels altered this timetable after an eminent stomach specialist from Texas, Dr. Joseph Bailey, bluntly advised, "Have it out immediately—it could easily be cancerous." So on January 2, 1987, Colson was flown on the private plane of Nancy DeMoss to Washington, where he was admitted to the Georgetown University Hospital, a nationally renowned center for cancer surgery.

Colson entered the hospital feeling certain that he was in good health. He doubted whether he really needed a major operation. When he had his first meeting with his surgeon, Dr. John Dillon, Colson expressed these doubts forcefully. Liking as always to be in complete control, he explained that he wanted only minor surgery to remove the benign tumor. He did not require the major operation, known as a stomach resection, that had been scheduled for him.

Unaccustomed to receiving such instructions from a patient, Dr. Dillon took umbrage. "Are you telling me what to do?" he demanded.

Colson backtracked, though not perhaps with sufficient medical humility to smooth the ruffled feathers of his eminent surgeon. Dr. Dillon listened with ill-concealed impatience to his patient's detailed ideas on how the operation should be performed. As he left the room he said gruffly, "I won't compromise on surgery."

The surgery that took place the following morning was not minor. Colson was on the operating table for over four hours and had 60 percent of his stomach removed. When he came round from the anesthetic he saw the anxious faces of Patty and Emily peering down at him on his bed in the intensive care unit.

"Two questions," he asked groggily. "Was it cancer? Did they get it all?"

"Yes" was the reply to both questions.

Colson professed not to be unduly concerned by this news. He recalled saying, "If it's all out, at least I can avoid chemotherapy." Unfortunately, however, there were other complications he could not avoid. Within forty-eight hours it became clear that his condition was deteriorating. He had a rising fever, and efforts to bring his temperature down proved unsuccessful. The drugs to control his acute postoperative pain were not working well either. He was slipping in and out of delirium. His breathing was shallow and the tubes into his nose repeatedly became blocked. Tests revealed that his wound had been infected by a virulent strain of staphylococcus—a cross-infection that occasionally surfaces in hospitals as a result of hygiene failures.

A staph infection is one of the most feared complications following major surgery. Colson had it with a vengeance. An emergency drainage tube had to be inserted in his wound without an anesthetic, an experience he later described as "total torture." But this did not work either. Late at night on January 7, the nursing staff was sufficiently concerned about Colson's chances of survival to call Patty and Emily to his bedside. "Two or three times in that period I really did think I was dying," recalled Colson. "I was often delirious, so I just couldn't concentrate. I couldn't even pray; I simply couldn't get the words out. So what I did was to meditate silently on the Lord's Prayer, phrase after phrase. As I began to realize that I might not make it through to the morning, I remember thinking how awful it would be to lie here on the brink of death and feel that you were coming to the end of everything. I knew that if I was going to slip over the line, I was going to meet Christ. So I was deeply grateful for my faith."

The next morning Colson was on the right side of the line but still dangerously ill. A decision was taken to reopen his wound surgically and to have it swabbed with alcohol every few hours. "This was the most excruciating pain imaginable," he recalled. "The only way I could bear it was to grip the bedposts and hang in there until the agony was over."

During the worst part of this three-week ordeal, most visitors apart from family were discouraged. Even these restrictions were not always enough to give the patient peace. One afternoon Colson's mother, Diz, came to his bedside accompanied by a friend, to whom she chatted with her customary high-decibel effervescence. Eventually her son shouted, "Get out of here—please! I just can't bear noise." A more sensitive and more permanent family visitor was Emily. Wanting to give the strongest possible filial support, she moved into the hospital, sleeping there overnight for ten days in a reclining orange armchair alongside her father's bed. "This was the first time I had ever seen Dad so vulnerable, so still, and so obviously in need of help," she recalled. "He had dreadful pain from the constant dressings of his wound and he was given a lot of morphine, which made him have terrible nightmares. He saw monkeys climbing up the wall and things like that. So I tried to help him both physically by cooling his body down and mentally by guided-imagery techniques such as talking him through imaginary cruises on his sailboat. It was a difficult experience but a great one too because I had always wanted to have a close relationship with Dad and now suddenly I had it."

The closest relationship of all at this perilous time in Colson's life was, of course, with Patty. She too slept many nights in the hospital, prayed with her husband, brought him home-cooked meals, and gave him that special support only a wife can give. Patty also carried the load of passing on the (sometimes carefully edited) news of Colson's condition to his many friends. In the case of family members the news bulletins were not edited, which added to Patty's pressures at the time when Colson was in a critical condition. As Chris Colson remembers, "Patty was always a great stepmother and she was at her greatest in this crisis. She called us every few hours, told me and Wendell when to fly in to see Dad, had us to stay, cooked all those meals, and held us together as a family."

Gradually Colson pulled through the crisis and began to strengthen. There is no doubt in his mind that the love and prayers from Patty and his three children were a key factor in his recovery. As he improved, although still weak from the knock-on effects of the staph infection, another relationship in Colson's life unexpectedly blossomed. This was with the legendary William J. Casey, with whom he had enjoyed a good friendship since their days together in the Nixon administration in the late 1960s.

Colson had no knowledge that Casey was his fellow patient until just before the end of his hospitalization, when the chief administrator of the hospital mentioned it in the course of telling the story of how a well-known journalist's attempted break-in had been foiled. "Mr. Colson, I have started to appreciate today what you went through from the news media at the time of Watergate," began the chief administrator as he dropped in during his daily rounds. "I have just prevented Bob Woodward from getting into a VIP patient's room upstairs. I had to throw him out physically."

"Who on earth was the VIP patient?" asked Colson.

"Bill Casey—he's in the room immediately above yours."

Colson's feelings of indignation at the behavior of the *Washington Post*'s celebrated investigative reporter were surpassed by his feelings of compassion for his old friend. For Bill Casey, the legendary old warrior of the U.S. intelligence community who had been appointed by President Reagan to be director of the CIA, was terminally ill after undergoing major brain surgery.

After a phone call to Casey's wife, Sophia, Colson went up to the next floor of the hospital. Clutching his intravenous drip, he was checked out by the two CIA guards in the corridor and admitted to Casey's room, where he was registered under the alias Lacey.

"Bill was in a very bad way," recalled Colson. "His head was caved in from the surgery and he was sagging sideways on the pillow. But his face lit up with a wonderful smile as he recognized me. He couldn't speak. His words were unintelligible. Yet he managed to communicate quite well, with me doing all the talking and him making facial expressions and giving nods. I know I really got through to him. At one moment when I was holding his hand I pointed to a statuette of Christ on his cross and asked him, 'Bill, you see that crucifix hanging on the wall there—do you know what it means?'"

Casey grunted, signifying that he did know.

"Then you know it means that Christ died for your sins," continued Colson. "It's important for you to know him personally at this time. Would you like to pray?"

Casey immediately grabbed Colson's hand, smiled, and nodded vigorously. With Sophia Casey joining in, the three of them had what Colson described as "one of the greatest, deepest, and most marvelous prayer sessions I have ever known," in which the dying CIA director was fully participating and comprehending, despite his inability to speak. "If there was ever any doubt about it, I just know that those prayers guaranteed the certainty of Casey's salvation," said Colson, "and afterward, I figured it out that being able to pray with Bill on that day shortly before he passed away was the real reason I was in that hospital."

Meanwhile, back at the *Washington Post,* Bob Woodward was writing a dramatic account of his alleged conversation with the CIA director on that same day in the same room of the Georgetown hospital. According to Woodward, Casey gave him a deathbed interview in which, despite the pain from his cranial surgery, he acknowledged his wrongdoing over the Iran-Contra scandal and admitted he had known about it all along.

"Why?" asked Woodward.

"I believed," replied Casey.

This interview is reported in the final pages of Bob Woodward's 1987 book, *Veil: The Secret Wars of the CIA 1981–1987.*

Colson said at the time of the book's publication, "I would stake my life on Woodward's account being untrue." In support of his position, Colson emphasized that he was told by the chief administrator of the hospital, by the CIA guards, and by Sophia Casey that Woodward never entered the

room. Even if he had entered it, Colson was certain that Casey was incapable of speaking the words he is quoted in *Veil* as saying. Despite this disagreement between them in 1987, Colson and Woodward are now on good
terms, exchanging occasional phone calls. "Because of this episode, I don't
have the respect I would like to have for Bob Woodward," says Colson,
"but I am at peace with him and feel no ill will."

In addition to praying with Bill Casey, Colson was deepening his own
prayer life as his convalescence continued, particularly with his daughter,
Emily. Away from the hospital vigils at her father's bedside, she was having
to bear some heavy burdens in her personal life. A few weeks earlier she had
been emotionally drained by another cancer drama in the family when her
much loved maternal grandmother, Emily Billings, after whom she was
named, passed away. During her father's convalescence Emily suffered a
third major trauma when her marriage broke up. The blow of this betrayal
hit Emily hard. Colson gave her his full support, both practically (she came
to work at Prison Fellowship as a graphic artist) and spiritually. Their father-
daughter relationship, which had not always been an easy one during Emily's
teenage years, ripened into a deeper intimacy as a result of the nurturing and
mentoring Colson was able to give his daughter in her newfound Christian
faith. For Emily had not understood for most of her adult life what being a
Christian really meant. During the years after her father's conversion she had
often been asked whether she was Born Again. For several years she did not
know what the phrase signified. But in 1987 Emily Colson was guided into a
real and committed relationship with the Lord. It was a commitment that
strengthened as a result of the deep prayer experiences she shared with her
father during and after his medical crises in the Georgetown hospital.

By the beginning of February 1987 Colson was out of the hospital. As his
energy slowly returned to him, he spent the early weeks of his convalescence answering the mountain of mail sent to him by well-wishers. One of
these letters was to Billy Graham, in which Colson described his narrow escape from death: "I had a close call. The cancer had just turned malignant.
So it was gotten in time. The prognosis is now one hundred percent. It is
amazing how God works. I had wanted to put the operation off six months
but one dear brother insisted I do it at once; that probably saved my life."

Richard Nixon was another of Colson's correspondents, sending an exceptionally gracious handwritten letter to the hospital. When Colson came to
reply to his old boss he struck a religious note that had never been recorded
in their many conversations together in the Oval Office: "I can't say that I've
enjoyed the sense of absolute helplessness and dependence on others; on the

other hand, difficult though that has been, it has been a spiritual experience of real depth because I have felt the presence of God holding me, and the Body of Christ supporting me. When I am weak, then I am strong." Then in a scribbled postscript that recalled the jauntier can-do spirit of their relationship in the White House years, Colson told Nixon, "It takes more than Watergate or a little cancer to hold me down. I'll be back stronger than ever."

Coming Back and Changing Presidents

Colson did not come back to full strength quickly. First he needed four months of convalescence before all traces of infection were eliminated from his bloodstream. Then, after two years of being unable to digest his food properly, he had to have another resection of the stomach. This time the surgery, carried out in Naples, Florida, was entirely successful. To make medical matters even better, at the end of his five-day stay in the hospital, Colson's doctors told him that not only was he free of cancer, he had never had cancer at all. Colson was flabbergasted. The explanation for this excellent but astonishing news was that the original diagnosis of his tumor as malignant had been a temporary one, made in the operating theater of the Georgetown hospital. It had been subsequently nullified by the results from the hospital's pathology laboratory when the removed tumor was tested and found to be nonmalignant. For some inexplicable reason this news was not passed on to the patient. Colson's rejoicings at this belated discovery were tempered by the realization that he had been heavily overpaying on his medical insurance premiums as a "cancer patient."

While Colson was away, the body politic of Prison Fellowship had also been suffering from internal troubles. Some PF staffers took the view that their chief executive officer, Gordon Loux, was becoming too demanding and autocratic in his style of management. These resentments intensified during 1987. When Colson returned to the office in full harness, two senior board members told him that the ministry was going down the drain and that it was imperative to change the CEO. However, Loux's supporters took a different view. They argued that the ministry had been very competently run by the CEO during the chairman's absence. Donor income had held up well, as had the numbers of participants in the in-prison seminars and other projects. So why did a little abrasiveness around the office matter? Colson was told it was so serious that Loux was losing the confidence of the staff. Loux, on the other hand, felt that the number of compliments paid to his interim leadership was beginning to unsettle Colson, who allegedly said to his deputy, "I can see, Gordon, that you have stolen the affection of the staff." Colson denies the quote but agrees that the situation between them was becoming untenable. "It was very sad because I really loved both Gordon and his wife, Beth. But when I got back I found there was a lot of chaos, with good people quitting the ministry and more people grumbling and unhappy. One of the board members came to me and said I was going to have to change Gordon Loux or I wasn't going to have a ministry."

The tension that was simmering between Colson and Loux was exacerbated by the latter's dismissal of John O'Grady, a senior PF vice president in charge of field operations. The episode took place while Colson was recovering from surgery. It added to his pain because just before he entered the hospital Colson had specifically told his number two, "Don't make any personnel changes while I am away." Under pressure from two Prison Fellowship board members, Loux disregarded these instructions and fired O'Grady. Regardless of the merits of demerits of the decision, Colson felt hurt by it. Personal loyalty was a virtue he had prized above most others ever since it was ingrained into him as a young marine. So his disappointment with Loux's judgment caused a rift between them. Some months later, when Loux was facing further internal criticisms of his tough style of personnel management, Colson dismissed the friend and CEO he might otherwise have protected. The departure of Gordon Loux, Colson said afterward, was "the most personally painful experience of my entire ministry."

Colson asked his old friend and prayer brother Al Quie to take over as acting CEO of Prison Fellowship. It was a temporary appointment that lasted for eighteen months. Quie improved the line management of the organization and insisted on better reporting from it, particularly in regard to statistics. At a time when PF was expanding on several fronts, this discipline was important, not least because Colson himself could sometimes be overoptimistic in his presentation of figures, based on fieldworkers' hearsay.

Between 1988 and 1989 Colson tried hard to find a permanent new president for Prison Fellowship. His big difficulty was that his preferred candidate did not want the job. On the day that Loux was fired, Colson placed a call to fifty-five-year-old Tom Pratt, who had been a nonexecutive member of the PF board since 1984.

"I am thinking about you as our new president," said Colson.

"No, Chuck. Don't think that way," replied Pratt. "I am very happy where I am." Tom Pratt was senior executive vice president at Herman Miller, a well-known office furniture company that had a turnover of $950 million a year in 1988. Pratt had been with the firm for twenty-five years and was head of sales, with good prospects of promotion to CEO. Colson's initial attempts to persuade Pratt to give up his prospects, his large salary, and his comfortable home on the edge of Lake Michigan were unsuccessful. But Colson persisted. Tom Pratt and his wife were invited down to visit the Colsons in Naples, but after a weekend of discussing the job, the answer was still no. As the visit finished, Tom and Gloria were back in their suite in the Ritz-Carlton hotel, packing their suitcases, when they both felt a powerful call from God. "Out of the blue my wife suddenly asked me, 'Are you in a different place on this than where you were this afternoon?' " Tom Pratt recalled. "So I said, 'Are you thinking what I am thinking?' 'Yes,' said Gloria, 'I think I am. I think God wants us to do this.' After she'd said that, it was just like a light going on. I knew I had to surrender to God's will."

To Colson's great delight, Tom Pratt agreed to become president and CEO of Prison Fellowship in mid-1989. He was just what the ministry needed. In addition to being a committed believer with a deep knowledge of scripture, acquired in his days as a young Baptist, Tom Pratt was a disciplined and experienced management executive. He could also be an extremely tough boss. In the early months of his fourteen-year stint as CEO, Pratt discovered that two members of Prison Fellowship's staff were having extramarital relations. He fired them on the spot, announced to the rest of the staff why they had lost their jobs, and added that everyone working for the ministry would, from now on, be held to the highest standards of moral behavior.

Not long after this episode Pratt said, only half in jest, to Colson, "Chuck, if you ever commit adultery you're going to have me to contend with." To which Colson replied, "That's never going to be a problem, but my pride still can cause me trouble."

In fact, Colson was giving the impression of having less pride and more humility in his leadership of the ministry. He was becoming a quieter and more reflective character, with fewer certitudes and demands in his approach. He was sincere in his determination to hand over all the day-to-day administration of Prison Fellowship to Tom Pratt. On this gentler wavelength the two men developed an excellent relationship, which gave them good insights into each other's personalities and achievements. "I did not worship Chuck Colson the way some people around him did but I came to love him," recalled Tom Pratt. "I saw him as a dynamo, someone who had the great ability to call people to action and somehow get them there. But I knew he was not an executive. He treated his team much more as a staff than as an organization. He was, and is, a control freak. Sometimes he would try and control things so personally that if you left him in control, he could set the organization heading toward deep tapioca. So I had to get him to trust his executives to run things and to concentrate on the areas of his real genius, which are to set out the vision given to him by the Lord and to ignite the passion of other people to follow it with their full support."

For his part Colson was quick to say that his visions and passions would not have gone very far if he had not been working in harness with Tom Pratt. "Tom saved the ministry," says Colson. "I shall forever be grateful to him for making a huge sacrifice financially and for transforming every aspect of what we did with a great combination of toughness and loving-kindness. His leadership was just tremendous. Under Tom, Prison Fellowship grew; in fact it exploded into something far greater than I had ever planned or imagined."

As is clear from these mutual compliments, Pratt and Colson complemented each other remarkably well. In the decade from 1990 to 2000, there was a quantum leap forward in the scope and scale of Prison Fellowship's ministry. This was made possible by an increase in the donor income of the organization from $12 million to $58 million a year. Although this growth took place under the stewardship of Tom Pratt, he himself gives the credit to Colson's hard work ("He is a phenomenal fund-raiser, a modern Astor") and to his spiritual vision. To understand what went on in this phenomenally successful decade, it is necessary to look at the key programs of the ministry.

The Growth of Angel Tree

Colson had been excited about Angel Tree when he heard in his hospital bed in January 1987 that ninety thousand children of prisoners had received presents over the previous Christmas. However, his excitement was tempered by his anxieties that there were many weaknesses in the administration of the program, and that some senior executives in the ministry had doubts about Prison Fellowship's capability to continue running it. Uncertain himself as to which way to turn, Colson asked Tom Pratt to report on what to do with Angel Tree.

"The first discovery I made was that there was a lot of backlash against the program," recalled Pratt, "and a lot of bellyaching too. So I made an in-depth study of Angel Tree. By the time I completed my study I had become convinced of the power of this scheme and that it had God's blessing on it." Pratt summarized his findings in a report prepared for the board of Prison Fellowship. "What started as a nice little thing to do for the kids of prisoners with whom we were working has become an opportunity for a massive ministry initiative," he wrote in his report. This initiative, as Pratt and Colson saw it, would give Prison Fellowship a new role as an enabler and encourager of churches across the country to participate in prison ministry. They also thought it would invigorate Prison Fellowship's image, donor base, and general momentum. Angel Tree, Pratt predicted, "would no longer be a ministry support program to our prison ministry; it would be a ministry to ultimately drive our in-prison program and more."

Colson shared in this vision and enthusiastically endorsed it by allocating resources, manpower, and his own time to the program. But even he was startled by the response when he issued his first public appeal for Angel Tree. The occasion for this was an appearance he made on Jim Dobson's radio show in 1992. Colson's plea to get more Christmas presents for his prison "angels" evidently struck a chord in the hearts of the audience because in the days following the broadcast they sent more than fifty thousand gifts to Prison Fellowship's new headquarters building, in Reston, Virginia. It was just as well that this new building (a generous gift from Nancy DeMoss and the DeMoss Foundation) was far more spacious than any previous PF quarters. For the presents arrived not by the sackful, but by the truckload, piling up in mountainous heaps throughout the halls, corridors, offices, and even the rest rooms of the building. As a result, huge physical and logistical problems were caused for the staff. Colson and his team had never seen a result like this from any other appeal broadcast. They were quick to see the potential for recruiting new donors to Prison Fellowship by emphasizing the ministry's wider role as a benefactor and mentor to the families of prisoners.

In the quantum leap of Prison Fellowship's donor income from $12 million to $58 million between 1990 and 2000, the Angel Tree program played a pivotal role. Other factors counted too, among them Colson's growing visibility as a national Christian leader, the rising profile of his ministry, and the impact of his radio program, *BreakPoint,* across the nation. However, the greatest story of Prison Fellowship in the 1990s was the participation of fifteen thousand churches and hundreds of thousands of individual Christian supporters in Angel Tree.

Colson was delighted by the expansion of Angel Tree but he did not regard it as a once-a-year event. He always saw it as a continuous spiritual program connecting God's people and God's churches to the hearts and minds of "the least of these my brethren" (Matthew 25:40). To emphasize the ongoing impact of the program, Colson, in 2001, launched Angel Tree

Camping. This was his response to the question he was so often asked by those who had given the presents at Christmas: "Is there more we can do to minister year round to these kids?"

Angel Tree Camping offered vacations in Christian summer camps to the children who had received Christmas presents through Angel Tree. Thanks to the generosity of two of PF's biggest donors, Rich and Helen De-Vos, camp scholarships have so far been taken up by over twenty thousand children of prisoners. The Christian message given to these children, both on their camping holidays and at the Christmas season, when they received their presents, enabled Colson to promote a wider dimension of Angel Tree. He has described the program as "fighting crime at its roots by reaching kids with the gospel. This simple program has been the biggest single invasion of the gospel into the inner cities."

"Big" is certainly one right word to describe Angel Tree, for it has now grown to a massive, nationwide distribution operation of over six hundred thousand Christmas presents to prisoners' children every year. The credit for this remarkable saga is shared by many churches and individuals, not least the originator of the program, Mary Kay Beard. However, Colson had the flair to seize on a good idea and to use his advocacy to turn Angel Tree into a great national campaign. He loves the program and his emotions are deeply involved in it. As he says, "Me a big tough ex-marine and I can't tell an Angel Tree story without getting choked up."

Another famous American whose emotions have become involved in Angel Tree is the forty-third president of the United States. George W. Bush has closely followed Prison Fellowship's programs ever since he gave his blessing to the ministry's first InnerChange Freedom Initiative (IFI) prison, in Sugar Land, near Houston, in 1997, when he was governor of Texas. The success of that project and the subsequent close relationship between Colson and Bush resulted in the latter's participation in Angel Tree at Christmas 2003.

President Bush came to Shiloh Baptist Church in Alexandria on December 22 to watch its volunteers and the Prison Fellowship staff packaging up Christmas presents for delivery to prisoners' children. The president and Laura Bush were visibly moved as they met forty children who were receiving the gifts, other members of prisoners' families, and the volunteers. After being welcomed by Colson, the president delighted his audience in this historic black church by congratulating Angel Tree for passing the milestone of 6 million presents to children since the scheme began. Mr. Bush and the first lady then gave gifts of their own to the children present, speaking to those from Hispanic families in fluent Spanish.

At the end of the forty-five-minute visit Colson introduced President Bush to Al Lawrence, a black ex-offender and ex-policeman who now works on the staff of Prison Fellowship. "Mr. President, this great guy was in prison twenty years ago when I first met him," said Colson. "He came to the Lord, and ever since, Jesus has really gotten hold of his life. Al's been working for us on programs like Angel Tree for many years. I stood up for him at his wedding. But what you'll really enjoy most, Mr. President, about Al is that he has a son who's gone to Yale as a freshman this year."

At this the president hugged Al Lawrence, saying, "Another Yale man. God bless you. Keep up the good work on Angel Tree."

The episode was an indication that this Prison Fellowship program has entered the mainstream of American Christmas care and cheer. Angel Tree, now running all the way from the jails of the United States to the president of the United States, is well set to grow even larger in its scope and generosity in the years ahead.

Operation Starting Line

In 1991 Prison Fellowship's ministry took another giant leap forward, with a program that came to be called Operation Starting Line (OSL). It has grown steadily over the last fifteen years as a nationwide prisoner evangelization campaign, and is now a huge and complex operation, bringing the gospel to over 250,000 inmates of America's jails every year. How OSL got started was through another of those coincidences, or God-incidences, that Colson insists had little or nothing to do with him.

The originator of Operation Starting Line was Aaron Johnson, the secretary of corrections in North Carolina. An African-American Baptist preacher with a heart for evangelism, Johnson had come to admire the work of Prison Fellowship. On a visit to PF's new headquarters building, in northern Virginia, Johnson was invited to lead the daily devotions for the staff. Colson was not present on that day so he did not hear the unscripted and unexpected challenge Johnson suddenly issued at the end of his sermon. The essence of the challenge was that he wanted the gospel brought to every single one of North Carolina's prisons in a huge, one-off evangelistic mission. Tom Pratt, swayed by the emotional power of Aaron Johnson's rhetoric, immediately accepted the challenge on behalf of Prison Fellowship.

When Colson was briefed on the proposal he was enthusiastic about its spiritual potential but apprehensive about its practicalities. He had a meeting with Aaron Johnson at which it was announced that the Department of Corrections and Prison Fellowship would be launching a joint evangelism program called Starting Line in all North Carolina's prisons the following year. How it would actually start was left in the air. Excited but also worried by the magnitude of the program, Colson dispatched an impassioned memo to Tom Pratt—"Tom, this thing in North Carolina is beyond belief . . . the opportunity here is absolutely unbelievable"—describing how the governor and the state legislature were fully backing Aaron Johnson's public announcement "that the doors of all ninety-five prisons were wide open, that he expected a revival statewide, and that he wanted Prison Fellowship to train every volunteer that goes into the prisons in the state of North Carolina.

"I mean this is incredible. The problem of course is that we *have to deliver*."

Delivering trained volunteers into ninety-five prisons in one state was a massive task. It would never have been achieved without Tom Pratt's management skills, acquired in twenty-five years of running big business projects. Another hero of the project was a dynamic Baptist minister, Richard Payne, whose good ole boy country drawl concealed a quicksilver mind and tremendous energy. Colson was a key player too in the planning stages of the campaign, holding public meetings with church pastors and coaching PF staffers on how to recruit volunteers on a far wider scale than anything previously attempted in one geographical area.

"Chuck had it down to a science," recalled the Reverend Myles Fish, who was one of the key managers of the Starting Line project. "He said it was just like what he had done in Boston during the Senate election campaign there in 1960. He taught us all how to go out and recruit captains in each district, who in turn world recruit prison volunteers."

Colson's campaigning techniques evidently transplanted well from politics to prison ministry, for in the week beginning September 28, 1992, when the first Starting Line swung into action in North Carolina, 2,730 volunteers had signed up and been trained in prison evangelizing. They entered ninety-four of the state's ninety-five prisons and organized 345 evangelistic events in them. The events were a combination of Christian teaching and secular entertainment provided by professional artists. Largely because of the entertainment, 20,877 prisoners attended the events. They heard well-known speakers, including Colson, and most of them received one-on-one prayer ministry during the week. Aaron Johnson and his staff at the Department of Corrections were ecstatic. So was Colson, who saw the potential for a series of similar evangelistic outreach programs in the prisons of other states.

As the first North Carolina Starting Line grew into the nationwide Operation Starting Line, Colson's leadership remained a vital ingredient, particularly when it came to securing that elusive but important element in prison evangelism—Christian unity. Uniting the churches behind Operation Starting Line was another task that Colson did well. Christian organizations and denominations are often notorious for their divisions or rivalries. However, Colson had a gift for reaching out to Christian activists across the usual barriers and mobilizing them as a united team. So, during the preparations for an Operation Starting Line week of evangelistic collaboration, it became quite normal to find Catholics, Baptists, Presbyterians, evangelicals, charismatics, and Episcopalians all training and working together. Among the best-known ministries that rallied behind Colson's banner as partners in Operation Starting Line were the Billy Graham Evangelistic Organization, Promise Keepers, Campus Crusade, the Navigators, the American Bible Society, the Moody Bible Institute, the Crossroad Bible Institute, Mission America, the North American Mission Board, the Catholic Prisoners' Aid Society, the National Black Evangelical Association, Walk Thru the Bible, the DeMoss Group, and many others.

This degree of cooperation is rare in evangelistic mission work, so it says much for Colson's powers of persuasion that he has been such a unifier of diverse groups and denominations. One of the reasons for this success is that Operation Starting Line usually creates a powerful momentum of its own. When several thousand Christian volunteers train together for weeks and then turn up on the opening day at the prisons, supported by good organization, a team of well-known professional entertainers, and big-name speakers, there is an immediate feeling of unity, purpose, and excitement. Yet it is fair to ask the question, is there a corresponding sense of excitement among the prisoners?

One way of answering the question is to offer an eyewitness description of how Operation Starting Line works on an opening day in a new target state. This author has accompanied Charles Colson on several such OSL visits to various jails all over America. One of the most memorable of these was Operation Starting Line's visit to Mississippi's Parchman state penitentiary in August 2001.

The day started at 5 A.M. as a regiment of some 250 Prison Fellowship staffers and volunteers boarded Colson's fleet of buses at a hotel in Jackson for the one-and-a-half-hour drive to Parchman. As we settled into our seats my neighbor introduced himself and his companions. "I know Chuck well. I'm a fire-eater," he began. "This guy is a juggler, this one is a drummer, and my friend here is a heavy metal man." For a moment I wondered whether these could be coded descriptions for different types of Bible Belt preachers. But it quickly became clear that they were all professional artists recruited to perform in different parts of this huge and notoriously tough jail, which has a population of over five thousand inmates. The Operation Starting Line formula is to give the prisoners in each cell block one-on-one ministry visits from PF volunteers, followed by an evangelistic entertainment event that consists of rock music, testimony stories, and finally a gospel message from Colson. By the time our buses had checked through security and reached Parchman's "worship center" (a politically correct name for the chapel), the army of PF volunteers had grown to around four hundred, drawn from churches all over the South. They were broken up into groups and dispatched with military-style schedules and itineraries to the various units spread across Parchman's sixteen-thousand-acres. Colson's tour began at Unit 32, Mississippi's death row, where sixty-two prisoners under sentence of death were waiting for execution or for reprieves from the appeals courts and sentence review boards. A prison officer equipped with a plastic shield moved into place to escort Colson with the explanation "Some of the guys in here like to throw urine or worse at visitors."

Colson and his small group of companions, who included the Reverend John Perkins, a legendary Mississippi civil rights hero, walked slowly down the line of cells. All the lights on death row were permanently dimmed, making the visitors feel as though they were on an eerie journey into a murky world of hopelessness, fear, and finality. Some of the psalmist's descriptions of Sheol as "the miry pit" or "the grave of darkness" came to mind. But Colson was there to bring a message of faith, hope, and love to any of the prisoners willing to talk to him. Most of them did. In this most artificial of settings, Colson was remarkably natural as he prayed and talked in each cell. One of his deepest conversations was with Richard Jordan, convicted of capital murder in 1975 after kidnapping Edwina Marter and shooting her through the back of the head when she tried to escape. Jordan had been on death row for twenty-six years as his case ground through the appeals system.

"Have you come to know the Lord?" Colson asked him.

"Yes sir, I have," said Jordan.

Colson recommended some gospel readings and then prayed aloud for Jordan and for his next-cell neighbor, Kevin Dycus, who had been on death row for three years after his capital conviction for robbing and killing a seventy-six-year-old woman in his neighborhood. Colson made no easy promises to these two murderers, simply praying that they would be granted God's mercy, forgiveness, and peace.

After stopping for a horrific look at the execution chamber, with its leather-strapped bed and medical monitoring equipment to measure the second-by-second consequences of a lethal injection, Colson moved to other units of Parchman. He gave an open-air talk to a large audience of under-eighteen-year-old offenders, who had been well warmed up by the fire-eater and other entertainers. Then he went to three lockdown units, where high security prevails at such intensity that any inmate who comes out of a cell to use the toilet is automatically chained and handcuffed for the ten- or twenty-yard journey along the corridor. Colson's one-on-one ministry in these units was impressively sensitive and prayerful, despite the distractions of smells, noises, and hundred-degree heat.

At the end of a long, sweltering day Colson addressed a rally of all the inmates whose low-security classifications allowed them access to the prison football stadium. Although he was visibly wilting in the scorching heat, Colson found the energy for an outstanding talk full of humor ("You should pray for your warden. I learned how to do that, although I must admit that sometimes I prayed for him to become warden of another prison") and with a strong message about the transforming power of God's love. Then he gave another talk to the PF team, headed up by the Reverend Richard Payne, inspiring them with prayer for the ministry visits they would be carrying out in twenty-four more Mississippi prisons in the coming days.

By the time the buses returned to the hotel in Jackson it was 8 P.M. Even after completing that grueling fifteen-hour schedule, Colson still had to have dinner with some major donors to the Prison Fellowship course. Was it worth it? "Some prison days are tough and this was one of them," he replied. "But bringing the gospel to prisoners is my calling. I know this Operation Starting Line effort changes lives and brings many inmates to the Lord."

BreakPoint

Colson had long wanted to expand his ministry into the work of communicating the Christian message to a wider audience than prisoners. After one or two false starts he achieved this goal with the launch of his radio program, *BreakPoint*, in 1991. It was an almost instantaneous success, winning good ratings. However, before it went on the air, searching questions were asked about how *BreakPoint* would fit in with Prison Fellowship's mission to prisoners. There were some insiders who saw the demanding schedule of broadcasts as at best a high-risk diversion from the ministry and at worst an unwanted stepchild of it.

Colson knew he had to tackle these anxieties head-on. So he explained his thinking on *BreakPoint* in a letter he sent out to Prison Fellowship's major donors and other interested parties: "I believe that for too long we Christians have looked at our faith as simply a devotional relationship or as church-going, in short just one part of our life. But the fact is our God is Lord of all, and as His people we must articulate His truth in every area of life." The letter announced that *BreakPoint* would be broadcast five days a week, tackling tough issues, pulling no punches, and confronting the secular myths of modern society. "Monday through Friday I'll be addressing a new issue, an idea or a problem from a Biblical perspective," declared Colson. "I will do this in order to challenge and equip listeners to deal with the issues of their everyday lives informed by God's truth."

This was a tall order, and Colson needed to have the key members of his team fully behind him on the project. In the past their attitudes toward his expansionist ideas had been equivocal, and occasionally hostile. A few years earlier he had launched his first series of radio broadcasts, called *Another Point of View*. After it had been on air for a few weeks, Prison Fellowship's director of communications, David Bovenizer, wrote a scathing internal memorandum recommending that "we cease and desist with the radio venture." The main thrust of the memo was that the broadcasts were exposing Colson to extraordinary dangers. The greatest of these was that he was being tempted to comment forcefully on political topics, thus giving the media an excuse for refocusing their attention on his Watergate past and ignoring his spiritual present. Bovenizer also flagged up concerns about the diversion of staff time, the intellectual integrity problem of having many of the commentaries composed by ghostwriters, and the lack of tangible benefits to Prison Fellowship. Colson's surprisingly humble response to this broadside was to write "I agree" on the top of the memo. So *Another Point of View* came off the air a month later.

Despite this disappointment Colson kept alive the idea of returning to radio commentary and resurrected it with a series of broadcasts in 1989 called *The Secularization of America*. The success of these programs brought an offer from Dr. Jim Dobson, the founder of the Focus on the Family ministry, to help Colson get established as a regular radio broadcaster. Two other leading figures in Christian media, Al Saunders of Ambassador Agency and Steward Epperon of Salem Communications, also offered to help by carrying Colson's broadcasts on their networks of radio stations. Out of these events and encouragements *BreakPoint* was born.

The first editor of *BreakPoint* was Nancy Pearcey, who had studied worldview issues under Francis Schaeffer at L'Abri Fellowship in the 1970s. "She did a superb job. There wouldn't have been a *BreakPoint* without her," recalled Colson. "She really knew how to set up the broadcasts and she did most of the early research and writing."

As the preparations for the launch of *BreakPoint* gathered momentum, some PF staffers were excited about this new development, while others were anxious about its synergy with the core activities of the ministry. Ron Nikkel, the president of Prison Fellowship International, was one in-house opponent who circulated an e-mail criticizing *BreakPoint* for using PF time and resources on matters unrelated to prison ministry. Colson's response to such criticisms was to issue a ministry-wide declaration of his commitment "that this radio program should not in any way detract from the main function of Prison Fellowship, which is to take the gospel to the prisoners. They so desperately need it behind those prison walls."

The implication that *BreakPoint* was directed at radio-listening inmates in their cells seemed disingenuous to some Colson watchers, but all such murmurings faded once the program was launched. When *BreakPoint* first went on the air, on September 2, 1991, it was an unknown quantity in terms of content, reach, and listener response. A year later it was being carried by 154 radio stations with a regular audience of over 2 million. Some three thousand subscribers were buying monthly printouts of the commentaries and two thousand new donors had started giving money to Prison Fellowship as a result of the broadcasts.

What made *BreakPoint* different from other Christian radio commentary shows was the range of topics it covered, the quality of the writing team supporting Colson, and his willingness to tackle controversial topics. An early illustration of how these ingredients combined was given by the *BreakPoint* program of September 13, 1991, entitled "Tragic Magic."

"I've held off a few days on what I am about to say today because frankly I was afraid of being lynched," Colson began as he launched into an attack on the media's hero worship of the basketball star Magic Johnson for admitting that he had contracted AIDS and that he planned to become a spokesman for safe sex. "The safe sex message is false. Condoms slip. Condoms break . . . the only real solution is sexual purity: abstinence before marriage, faithfulness within marriage." Colson concluded the commentary by urging Magic Johnson to give his adoring fans a message of true repentance and say, "Listen, I was wrong. Promiscuity is a bad thing. I realize that now. And I want to urge you not to make the same mistake."

Colson summed up: "Now that would make Magic Johnson a real hero."

Over six hundred calls jammed Prison Fellowship's switchboard on the day "Tragic Magic" was broadcast. They were the first indication, just over a week after *BreakPoint* started, that Colson's magic, or at least his ability to stir up controversy, was building an audience quickly. Perhaps more impressive than the predictable attack on Johnson's advocacy of safe sex was Colson's willingness to tackle difficult ethical issues in areas like science, law, politics, education, economics, the arts, and foreign policy, applying his Christian worldview to all of them.

To keep *BreakPoint* at the cutting edge of controversy Colson drew on outside experts in universities and think tanks. He also recruited a talented team of writers to work under the program's editor, Nancy Pearcey. Neither she nor Colson realized the complexity and the long hours of hard labor required to produce five broadcasts a week. At one point Pearcey was working seventy hours a week on *BreakPoint,* but other good writers, among them Roberto Rivera and Anne Morse, joined her on the team, whose monthly editorial meetings, chaired by Colson, were always lively and productive.

An intellectual offshoot from *BreakPoint* was created by Colson in 1995 under the name of the Wilberforce Forum. According to its own prospectus, the rationale for this new unit within Prison Fellowship was to help people "think through answers" to the pressing problems of the day by analyzing "the philosophical movements" in the arts, sciences, public policy, and popular culture. For some time the main movement of the Wilberforce Forum consisted not in analyzing philosophy but in providing scripts for *BreakPoint.* This is still partly true today, but Wilberforce also publishes papers, holds seminars, and acts as a think tank in support of Colson's Christian worldview activities.

BreakPoint has remained a fresh and innovative commentary program. Approaching its fifteenth anniversary, it shows no signs of growing stale. Inevitably it has occasional weaknesses and inconsistencies. For example, Colson appeared to get himself into a theological muddle over the Harry Potter books, which he initially applauded but subsequently criticized on the grounds that their witches and wizards did not transmit a Christian message like C. S. Lewis's tales of Narnia.

One criticism of *BreakPoint* that has surfaced with almost cyclical regularity is that some of its commentaries are too political. In the run-up to the 1992 presidential election Colson seemed to be playing so much of his old White House hardball that a Washington law firm, Gammon & Grange, was called in to advise. After analyzing nine *BreakPoint* programs, on topics such as Ross Perot's third-party candidacy, President George H. W. Bush's flagging popularity, and presidential vetoes, Gammon &

Grange concluded that some of the commentaries could jeopardize Prison Fellowship's nonprofit status because of potential violations of IRC regulation 501(c)(3)'s prohibition against political campaigning activities. The writer of the opinion suggested that legal counsel should review problematic *BreakPoint* scripts before they were broadcast.

Colson's response to this legal advice demonstrated that he had lost none of the skills he had honed in his White House years at writing incandescent memos. "Have we really been reduced to this? If it is really necessary to submit commentaries to lawyers in advance of giving them on air, then I think I ought to hang up and close down radio," his riposte began. After making the valid point that several other Christian radio commentators were far more political than *BreakPoint,* Colson insisted that he was fully aware of the law and how to avoid violating it. As he believed it was improper for a Christian spokesman to advance the cause of a particular candidate, he did not need any advice from lawyers. His memo concluded: "This is all very depressing. I'm going off into the woods to eat honey and locusts and start screaming for people to repent. The end must be near when lawyers have this much control over us."

On this occasion Colson cooled down without going on a diet of honey and locusts, and the lawyers backed off. However, from time to time his commentaries can still become politically controversial. When he got the proverbial bee in his bonnet about President Clinton's affair with Monica Lewinsky, Colson took no prisoners, as listeners to the eleven *BreakPoints* on this subject still recall. Yet on the whole his commentaries maintain their reputation for cutting-edge broadcasting because of their originality of thought and the scope of their subject matter, not because of their polemical or political content, which is rare anyway. The real test of *BreakPoint* is its growing audience and increasing influence. Today the program is carried by over one thousand radio stations and has between 6.5 and 7 million regular, daily listeners. It is also broadcast on a significant number of radio stations outside the United States. Each commentary is featured on the Prison Fellowship Web site (www.pfm.org) and receives around fifty-five hundred hits a day. An open-door reprint policy ensures that many Christian publications and some secular ones quote extensively from *BreakPoint*. One way or another Colson has clearly succeeded in his strategic ambition to "get the word out."

It might be expected that after more than thirty-five hundred *BreakPoint* broadcasts in the last fourteen years, Colson would be suffering from some degree of commentator fatigue. Far from it. Burnout has been a problem within his team of writers and researchers but not for him. The scripts, even when composed by others, bear his own unmistakably vigorous stamp of editorial authority. He records the four-minute programs in blocs, either from a specially built mini studio at Prison Fellowship's headquarters or on a switch-56 digital line from his home in Naples, Florida. The whole process of creating, editing, and broadcasting *BreakPoint* programs has become an integral part of Colson's life. By any standard of measurement this endeavor has been a major contribution to Christian broadcasting and has also made an impact on the wider culture of modern America. Whether Colson's commentaries are central or merely tangential to the in-prison work of his ministry is a debatable question. But as the flagship for Prison Fellowship's wider mission as a promoter of the Christian worldview, *BreakPoint* has kept Colson's profile and influence at a high level of national recognition.

Family Joys and Sorrows

During the years when Prison Fellowship was expanding, Colson's relationships within his family were deepening. The rock on which those good relationships were built was his blissfully contented and mutually dependent marriage with Patty. From that secure base he reached out into new dimensions of understanding with his children and grandchildren, all of whom loved and respected him as the family patriarch, even if not all of them shared his faith and religious zeal.

There was perhaps one exception to the Colson family pattern of growing serenity, and that was Diz. She fit no recognizable pattern. Mother and son loved each other, but better at a distance than in close contact. Diz's uncontrollable free spirit and eccentric excesses could never be compatible with Colson's disciplined life of Christian service. As characters they were chalk and cheese. Despite many efforts to reconcile their differences, there were always tensions, frictions, and exasperations in their relationship. Diz had remarried some years after the death of Pop (Wendell), and her second nuptials, to Massachusetts businessman George Kewson in 1979, calmed her down a little. But even in old age she was often causing worry to her only child by her financial extravagance, by her free-spirited lifestyle (not many sons have to be summoned to hotel or apartment block swimming pools to restrain their eighty-year-old mother from bathing topless!), and by her combative manner of arguing and criticizing.

Diz Colson left this world as she had lived in it—causing shocks and sensations. On May 11, 1989, she spent a happy afternoon shopping in the best stores of Wellesley, Massachusetts, as usual spending more money than she could afford. Starting up her car in the middle of a busy shopping center, she had a sudden seizure. With her foot stuck on the accelerator, she took off like a rocket. One shopper quietly putting bags into the backseat of his station wagon had the open door torn off its hinges by Diz's careering vehicle. Other passersby had to leap for their lives to get out of its way. The trail of havoc ended when Diz's car crashed head-on into the wall of a supermarket at fifty miles per hour. It was a miracle that no one else was hurt or killed.

Colson heard of his mother's death as he was coming in from a swim in the pool. It was Patty who took the fateful call and delivered the news, just as she had done when Pop died fourteen years earlier. Colson's immediate reactions of shock and sadness were softened by the happy recollection of a loving Mother's Day phone call he had made to Diz a few days earlier. He also cherished the thought that his mother would have enjoyed departing this life in such characteristically dramatic style.

After the funeral Colson sorted out his mother's personal effects and papers. One discovery that pleased him was finding that Diz had carefully treasured a ten-page letter from him dated December 28, 1978. It was one of the most important and emotional letters Colson had ever written in his life. "I have finally decided to write this letter sharing some of the deepest burdens of my heart to you," began Colson. "I probably have not been able to tell you how much I love you because our personalities clash and our conversations usually end in arguments."

The main thrust of the case Colson wanted to present to his mother was that he was totally committed to following Christ. Why couldn't she take this seriously? Why wouldn't she make a similar commitment? "You need to think about what your own life is all about," he told Diz. "I am sure you will angrily retort, 'I am a Christian and I don't need my son or anyone else to tell me what to do.' That may be; only you and God can be sure about that. All I can tell you, as lovingly as I know how, is that some things you say and do are completely the opposite to what Christ teaches." There then followed a catalog of Diz's un-Christian tendencies, coupled with filial urgings to consider her future in eternity. Colson did not expect his ideas would get a good reception.

Whenever you and I talk about these things it usually ends in a shouting match. You never take suggestions from me. But if I did not love you and did not want only the best for my mother I would not bother to write and run the risk of incurring your wrath. Any-

way, I feel that these are things I must say. I hope you know they
are written only because I'd love nothing more than for you to find
real peace and joy in your life. It is very simple but oh so tough. I
hope you'll think about it.

> *I love you,*
> *Chuck*

The impact of this letter on Diz Colson remains unknown. She never answered it or spoke about it to her son. So when he discovered it in a drawer
of his mother's desk, Colson was moved. He liked to surmise that Diz
might have taken its message to heart. As she was inclined to throw away
unwanted possessions and papers, perhaps this letter's preservation meant
something. "At least she kept it," he said hopefully.

One irony of this letter was that Colson criticized his mother for faults
that had been visible in his own preconversion personality. Getting impatient, making threats, being unwilling to forgive, intentionally hurting adversaries, and engaging in shouting matches were characteristics that had
often surfaced in the life of the old Colson. It may be speculated that Diz
would have enjoyed pointing this out in their mother-and-son arguments.
Yet since the new Colson was well aware that the toughest targets for evangelization are often to be found within the evangelist's own family, he deserves some credit for making such a serious effort to guide Diz in the
direction of a true Christian commitment.

Colson's failure to build a good relationship with his mother may have
made him more determined to stay close to his children. They had grown
up with the impression that, in their father's priorities, work came before
family. Wendell, Chris, and Emily all regarded him as a good dad but often
an unavailable one. Colson realized that they saw him as a classic example
of the overbusy-father syndrome. He did his best to compensate for the
time he had lost with them during their childhood years around the time
of his divorce from Nancy. So when his offspring were teenagers he made
great efforts to participate with them in projects, outings, sailing expedi-
tions, and trips during their many visits to Washington. "He was a great
dad even when he was under a lot of pressure from the White House with
calls flying in from the president," recalled Chris, "but we used to laugh at
his habit of scheduling everything. He'd even say things like 'Now we'll all
relax for twenty-five minutes.' "

Scheduling, organizing, and controlling were such strong characteristics
in Colson's life that he could not completely abandon them and turn him-

self into a laid-back, hang-loose father. But as the years rolled by and his children developed their own lives in adulthood, his bonds with them continued to strengthen. He took them on special overseas visits such as his journey to Britain in 1993, when he received the Templeton Prize at a ceremony in Buckingham Palace. Yet these comfortable family trips, staying with friends or in good hotels, left Colson with an anxiety. He worried that his children had never seen the conditions in which 90 percent of the world lived and where he himself was spending 90 percent of his ministry. So in 1999 Colson, with the help of his great friend and Prison Fellowship International chairman Mike Timmis, organized a trip for himself, Wendell, Chris, and Emily to Peru.

The first reactions within the family to this visit were not entirely favorable. Wendell's wife, Joanne, strongly opposed her husband's involvement in a tour focused on prisons, orphanages, and garbage reclamation projects. Nancy pleaded with her children to refuse their father's invitation on the grounds it was too dangerous. Emily evidently shared some of her mother's anxieties, since her suitcase for the journey bulged with sheets, pillowcases, towels, soap, and other comforts she thought were unavailable in the third world. But in the end Colson and his three adult children had a memorable trip, whose highlights were four missions into different prisons, two days in orphanages, several tours of the slums of Lima, and many visits to the homes of the poorest of the poor. The experiences of hearing their father preach the gospel in prison and seeing the charitable work Prison Fellowship was pioneering in the slums made a great impact on the next generation of Colsons. All three of them wrote beautiful letters of thanks to their father. Emily's was perhaps the most eloquent.

"Dad, what a wonderful trip we had together in Peru. It was nothing short of amazing. I am glad that I still feel overwhelmed when I think of the people we met and the devastating poverty," she began.

Despite the language barrier and the terrible conditions, I felt unusually at ease when the men in the prison sang. The concrete walls built to contain the men served to amplify their songs of praise, freeing their echoing voices right up to the heavens. No spikes of barbwire could keep their hearts from God. What a terrible and wondrous place to be.

It was thrilling to see the ministry that started because of just one experience you had twenty-five years ago, changing lives across the world. Dad, you have been my inspiration! You took your

*greatest hardship and allowed God to use it for good. And you have
stayed with it inspiring so many others, but I am sure there are
times when you wanted to rest. I so often think of this in my own
life with the challenges I face.*

Emily's mention of her personal challenges was a reference to her son,
Max, born in December 1990. There was an immediate affinity between
Colson and his youngest grandson, for even as a toddler Max was remarkable for his energy and his love of slapstick humor. But there was also a
mystery. Max did not seem to be interested in anything his grandfather
tried to teach him. At first Colson was determined to rise to this challenge
and redoubled his efforts to find common ground with the small boy. By
the time he was four, the mystery of Max had been solved. He was autistic. The diagnosis meant a complete rethinking by Colson of how to shape
their grandfather-grandson relationship.

An autistic child lives in a world of his own. Once Colson realized that
his grandson was never going to learn by conventional teaching methods,
he had to change his habits of a lifetime to go with the flow of Max's life.
This was a difficult experience. There is a Colson family joke that the only
person in the world who manages to get their father or grandfather to slow
down is Max. "He is not interested in other people's schedules," says his
mother, Emily. "If he goes shopping with Grandpa there is no hope for a
quick, in-and-out visit to the store to buy a couple of items. Max wants his
grandfather to share in his enjoyment of the experience of being in a shop.
This is a process which can take an hour or two. It also requires the accompanying adult to enter the autistic boy's world by playing imaginative mind
games with him at his own slow pace."

Although Colson's temperament is not naturally suited to such an ad-
justment, he has managed to make it. With infinite patience and constant
attention he has built a close and good relationship with his autistic grandson, Max. This private achievement has required more effort and more love
than many of Colson's public achievements.

Because Max is naturally very intelligent, Colson has gradually evolved
original ways of communicating with him. One of the triumphs of their communication, hugely assisted by the groundwork of Emily, is that Max has
come to know the Lord. The background to this spiritual journey through
autism is that Max, by the age of twelve, had acquired a fair knowledge of the
Christian faith from videos about Jesus, religious songs, and gospel teachings
from his mother and grandfather. Max always came to church on Sundays

when staying with the Colsons at Naples. But because crowds make him nervous he did not go into the main church. Instead it was his habit to sit out in the assembly hall area, watching the service on closed-circuit television.

During the summer of 2003 Max was watching a baptism on the screen when he turned to his mother and said, "I want to be baptized in Grandpa's pool." After much family discussion Colson called the pastor of the First Baptist Church of Naples with a request for a one-event ordination that would authorize him to baptize Max at home. The pastor consulted the church elders and Colson was duly ordained for this one baptism.

There was then a period of painstaking prebaptismal instruction, which Colson and Emily carried out with the help of drawings, visual aids, and long hours of patient talking. Max agreed that he really did want to be baptized. Colson was satisfied that Max really understood the sacramental meaning of baptism. So grandfather and grandson entered the pool. With Max holding his nose, Colson gave him a full-immerson baptism. "It was a rich, marvelous moment of great beauty. I shall never forget it," said the rejoicing grandfather.

Colson communicates well with all his grandchildren, even though he is in some ways closest to Max as both a father figure and a grandfather. "Max is a great kid and a wonderfully loving kid," says Colson. "He is marginalized by society but all of us in the family give him every bit of care we can. There are times, especially for Emily, when it is physically and emotionally taxing. But we all love Max, and in our different ways we all help."

There is perhaps a redemptive dimension in Colson's family life in which Max has played a key role. The need to care for this vulnerable, autistic child has helped to unify a family that was once divided. Nancy and Patty cooperate fully in making arrangements for Max. Wendell (now a successful inventor specializing in household blind designs) and his family support Emily in all sorts of loving, practical, and neighborly ways to meet her lonely challenges in caring for Max. So do Chris (now a well-established lending banker) and his wife and children. So it is a happy family, at peace with one another, full of mutual love and support. Colson, as always, leads from the front as grandfather, father, husband, and confiding friend. "As I look back on the rebuilding of my relationships with my family," he says, "I see that they have been more important to me than just about anything, apart from my relationship with God."

CHAPTER SEVENTEEN

New Recognition, New Horizons

The Templeton Prize

At the time when his family relationships were developing new strengths, Colson gained unexpected new recognition from the Templeton Prize, which is to religion what the Nobel Prize is to peace. In material terms it is often described as "the world's largest religious award." This was an accurate label in the 1990s, since its founder, Sir John Templeton, donated $1 million every year to the individual who he and his panel of judges decided had made "the greatest progress in religion." Three of the earliest winners were Billy Graham, Mother Teresa, and Alexander Solzhenitsyn. In their footsteps, to his great amazement, Colson was awarded the 1993 Templeton Prize. It marked a new peak of acclaim for him and his ministry.

In January 1993 Colson received a call from Wilbert Forker, a man he had never heard of, who said he was from the John Templeton Foundation, and that he needed to meet Colson to discuss an important matter. Over lunch in a Naples restaurant, Forker opened the conversation with the words "I expect you know why I'm here."

"No, I honestly do not," replied Colson.

"Well, I'm here to tell you that you have won the Templeton Prize," said Forker.

The prizewinner almost fell off his chair in astonishment. Colson had heard reports that he was going to be nominated for the award but he had not believed he was in the running for it. While trying to absorb this momentous news, Colson heard Forker saying to him, "You will have to go to Buckingham Palace, where you will receive a medal and a check for just over a million dollars. My first question is, who do you want the check made out to?"

"I have to confess that just for a moment I hesitated," recalled Colson. "I thought to myself, This is big money. It may not even be taxable, as it is an international award. All of a sudden here is someone offering $1 million in cash to a kid who grew up in pretty humble circumstances. It could fund my retirement and I would have no more worries."

These temptations were fleeting. Colson's firm and outwardly immediate response to Forker's question was "Prison Fellowship." After his inward hesitation, he gave this answer because he knew that he was being awarded the Templeton Prize not for his own achievements, but for what God had done in his life. Therefore, it was out of the question for Colson to ask for the check to be made out to himself. By the same logic he has for the past twenty-five years refused to accept speaking fees and royalties from his books, having them paid directly into Prison Fellowship's bank account. This is Colson's code of financial honor. Living by it ever since he entered full-time Christian ministry has made him Prison Fellowship's largest donor. After the decision on the check, Colson was asked to keep the news of his selection as the prizewinner a carefully guarded secret until it was publicly announced in March 1993. This announcement took place at the United Nations and was accompanied by massive national and international coverage. "Colson's high profile at the time of Templeton gave a terrific boost to his ministry," commented Tom Pratt, by now in his fourth year as president of Prison Fellowship.

The next stop on the Templeton itinerary was London, where Colson stayed for a week in Claridge's Hotel, in order to fulfill a number of engagements ahead of the award ceremony in Buckingham Palace. These engagements included attending a reception in his honor in the members' dining room of the House of Commons; giving a sermon at London's leading evangelical church, Holy Trinity, Brompton; dining with Michael and Sylvia Mary Alison; and meeting key figures in the prison world, from senior Home Office officials to ex-offenders working in the various branches of Prison Fellowship U.K. The night before his ceremonial morning at Buckingham Palace Colson addressed the Conservative Philosophy Group, a gathering of members of Parliament, academics, authors, and journalists who were political and intellectual followers of Prime Minister Margaret Thatcher.

I remember Colson's evening with the Conservative Philosophy Group particularly well, partly because I was hosting it in my home in Lord North Street, Westminster, and partly because I feared at the time of the event that the questioning of Colson by some of the group's more cerebral members bordered on the aggressive, if not the atheistic. It says much for Colson's willingness to take on a difficult dialectical challenge that he was more than ready to debate the deepest questions of belief and theology with some of Britain's leading intellectuals, among them Professors Elie Kedourie, Shirley Letwin, John Lucas, Roger Scruton, and Dr. John Casey. This was no softball evening of easy praise for Colson's work in prison ministry. What these Conservative philosophers wanted to know was why Colson was so sure of God's existence.

Leading the charge on this issue was Matthew Parris, then a Tory MP, now a renowned columnist for the London *Times.* He gave Colson a hard time from the atheistic corner, although Christian voices such as Paul Johnson's were well heard too. Whatever the host's anxieties may have been, Colson thoroughly enjoyed the cut and thrust of the debate. A week later he wrote to his friend Father Richard John Neuhaus, "When you are next in London, I will try to get you invited to the Conservative Philosophy Group. You would thoroughly enjoy the company of these high-powered intellectuals. They gave me one of the most stimulating evenings I have had in my life."

The next day at Buckingham Palace Colson received the Templeton Award from the Duke of Edinburgh. An overzealous protocol officer had sternly instructed Colson never to approach a member of the royal family, never to initiate a new subject of conversation, and to limit his exchanges with the Duke to a maximum of two minutes. Colson was almost paralyzed by these orders and missed his cue for coming forward to accept the award. But the Duke of Edinburgh seemed fascinated by Colson's work in prisons and asked many questions about it. As the courtiers, the Colson family, and Sir John Templeton fretted with worries about running over the time schedule, Prince Philip and Colson were becoming increasingly animated in their discussion, which lasted for nearly twenty minutes.

"What could we do about crime among juveniles here in England?" asked the Duke.

"Oh, that's easy. Send more young Brits to Sunday school," replied Colson. Prince Philip laughed and so did several others in the assembled company.

"No, I'm absolutely serious," insisted Colson, launching out on his familiar theme of how lack of moral teaching in youth was the cause of most criminal behavior. As he got on to worldview, the Duke of Edinburgh was becoming even more engaged, asking new questions and saying repeatedly, "That's a really good idea."

Noticing that Sir John Templeton "looked as though he was about to have kittens," Colson decided he'd better bring the royal audience to a close, even though his royal host showed no inclination to do so. "We don't want to hold you here, Your Royal Highness," said Colson. "You've been very kind to us and gracious." On that note, the visit to Buckingham Palace ended, with Prince Philip handing over the check for $1 million, saying jovially, "The sooner you get that check in the bank the better!"

Because Colson was heading off to the Cotswolds with Patty for a week's vacation, he took the Duke of Edinburgh's banking advice seriously. So Tom Pratt, who had flown over for the ceremony and was flying home the next day, was entrusted with the Templeton Prize check. On arrival at Dulles Airport, like all arriving airline passengers Pratt had to fill in a customs declaration form, answering a question on whether he was carrying any cash or monetary instruments with a value in excess of $10,000. After writing on his form that he was carrying $1 million, Tom Pratt found himself being interrogated by four agents of the U.S. Customs. He told them the full story of Colson's ministry, Prison Fellowship, and the Templeton Award. "It was a great opportunity to give witness," he said afterward.

Colson himself had a far greater opportunity to give witness when he fulfilled the prizewinner's obligation to deliver the Templeton Address to the World Parliament of Religions, in Chicago. This body was celebrating its hundredth anniversary in 1993, so the combination of Colson and the centennial guaranteed considerable public interest in the event. However, some of this interest was far from friendly. The American evangelical community had long regarded the World Parliament of Religions as the great Satan. In the view of some leading evangelicals, no self-respecting Christian could possibly address such an evil body, which diluted biblical truth by its multifaith, multicultural approach. Colson stood firm against these objections, pointing out that the World Parliament of Religions had been addressed by many respected Christians over the years, starting with Dwight L. Moody, who had given the keynote speech at the inaugural meeting in 1893. However, logic was irrelevant to the rising tide of objections, some of which turned into hate mail and others into physical protests. When he walked into Chicago's McCormick chapel on September 2, 1993, to address the World Parliament of Religions, Colson had to pass a number of protesters carrying placards denouncing him as a heretic, an apostle of the Antichrist, and an agent of the devil.

In fact, Colson was far more worried about the audience inside the Mc-Cormick chapel than he was by the demonstrators outside it. For he feared that his address might be less than warmly received by the usual attendees at the World Parliament of Religions, who included Buddhists, Muslims, Hindus, Baha'is, Mormons, Zoroastrians, Taoists, and many varieties of Christians far removed from American evangelicalism. In order to overcome the possible hostility from some religious groups within this exotic congregation, Colson decided that resurrection should be on his agenda. However, in these circumstances, the resurrected one was to be "the old Colson," using his ancient skills and tricks of the trade as a political advance man.

The first bright idea cooked up by advance man Colson was to pack the hall. "We wanted to get as many friends as we possibly could find into the McCormick chapel," he explained, "because first of all we wanted a full house and, secondly, we wanted friends to balance what we thought would otherwise be a very hostile crowd. However, this bright idea wouldn't work because the Templeton people wouldn't give us any extra tickets."

Faced with this impasse, the old Colson resurfaced and moved into Nixonian overdrive. Brushing aside warnings from a fearful Tom Pratt, who urged him to desist from political tricks, Colson gave his blessing for his assistant Tim Jewell to execute a hall-packing maneuver more appropriate to Mayor Daley's machine in the Chicago of 1960 than to the Rockefeller Chapel at the University of Chicago of 1993. What happened was that Jewell mysteriously acquired a thousand specially printed (that is, forged) passes to the World Parliament of Religion. These were distributed to Colson admirers all over Chicago, Illinois, and Indiana. Forgive us our forged passes! The Lord evidently was in a forgiving mood because the holders of the false tickets were undetected and had no difficulty in gaining admission.

"The result was that the hall was absolutely packed with a crowd split fifty-fifty between mainline World Parliament of Religion people and Colson supporters," recalled Colson. "When I finished the address there was a standing ovation, precipitated, I'm sure, by Colson friends, but the whole World Parliament lot joined in too. It was widely reported afterward that I had boldly proclaimed the gospel to a hostile audience."

Boldness was not lacking in Colson's address to his multifaith audience, many of them colorfully attired in national dress or the robes of their religions. He began on a high note of challenge: "I speak as one transformed by Jesus Christ, the living God. He is the Way, the Truth and the Life. He has lived in me for twenty years. His presence is the sole explanation for whatever is praiseworthy in my work, the only reason for my receiving this award of the Templeton Prize. That is more than a statement about myself. It is a claim to the truth. It is a claim that may contradict your own."

Ignoring the contradictions, Colson warmed to the theme of his address, which he had titled "The Enduring Revolution." In powerful phrases co-authored by his aide Mike Gerson (later to become President George W. Bush's speechwriter), Colson called on his hearers to face a momentous decision: "Each of us must decide whether to embrace the myths of modernity or to turn to a deeper, older tradition, the half-forgotten teachings of saints and sages. . . . For the West today is like Janus with a two-sided face—one offering futility, empty secularism and death; the other offering freedom, Biblically rooted spirituality and life."

Even though at least a third of his audience did not believe in biblical spirituality, Colson moved toward his peroration with an uncompromising proclamation that the Christian faith alone had an answer to the growing moral depravity of Western culture in the modern age: "Admittedly the signs are not auspicious, and it is easy to become discouraged. But a Christian has neither the reason nor the right, for history's cadence is called with a confident voice. The God of Abraham, Isaac, and Jacob reigns. His plan and purpose rob the future of its fears. By the Cross He offers hope, by the Resurrection He assures His triumph. This cannot be resisted or delayed. Mankind's only choice is to recognize Him now or in the moment of ultimate judgment. Our only decision is to welcome His rule or to fear it.

"But this gives every one of us hope. For this is a vision beyond a vain utopia or a timid, new world order. It is the vision of an Enduring Revolution. One that breaks more than the chains of tyranny; it breaks the chains of sin and death. And it proclaims a liberation that the cruelest prison cannot contain. The Templeton Prize is awarded for progress in religion. In a technological age we often equate progress with breaking through barriers in science and knowledge. But progress does not always mean discovering something new. Sometimes it means rediscovering wisdom that is ancient and eternal. Sometimes, in our search for advancement, we find it only where we began. The greatest progress in religion today is to meet every nation's most urgent need: A revolution that begins in the human heart. It is the Enduring Revolution—the Enduring Revolution of the cross of Christ."

The thunderous standing ovation that this speech received from the World Parliament of Religions must have been given with mixed motives by some of those applauding. The courage of Colson's oratory and the craft of Gerson's speechwriting may have had their appeal to the assorted Mus-

lims, Sikhs, Hindus, and representatives of other religions. The substance
of the speech may have struck deep chords with Christians, as it certainly
did with the presiding chairman of the assembly, Cardinal Bernardin of
Chicago, to judge by his congratulatory comments. Colson himself regarded the audience's response as "absolutely extraordinary. The Holy
Spirit just took over." Perhaps it was just as well that the little matter of
the extra tickets never came to light, but even so, few of his friends and followers who heard his delivery of the Templeton Address would dissent
from Colson's own assessment of it as "probably the best talk I have ever
given in my life."

Evangelicals and Catholics Together

The Templeton Prize raised Colson's status and visibility in America's
Christian community. For the first fifteen years or so of his public ministry
he had been regarded primarily as the founder and driving force of Prison
Fellowship. By the early 1990s this perception was widening. Colson's
books, his column for *Christianity Today,* and his major lectures and
speeches, of which the Templeton Address was the most important, all
enhanced his reputation. He was increasingly seen as a thinker, as well
as a doer. His outstanding intellect, coupled with his years of serious
study, gave him a grasp, occasionally a mastery, of complex issues in the
fields of apologetics, doctrine, and theology. These qualities gradually
propelled him into the forefront of Christian leadership, with a vision
that led him to take initiatives that transcended narrow denominational
boundaries.

One of Colson's most interesting and controversial initiatives in the
1990s was the launching of a theological discussion group known as Evangelicals and Catholics Together. Initially the group's purpose was to minimize hostility and maximize cooperation between these two polarized
pillars of the Christian world in the mission field. Subsequently the group
took on the scholarly role of examining, narrowing down, and if possible
reconciling the theological and doctrinal differences between Roman
Catholics and Protestant Evangelicals. How ECT started, why it provoked
a furor of negative reactions in its early days, why it cost Colson's ministry
over $1 million in lost donor income, and what it has achieved after over
twelve years of regular discussion meetings and academic publications are
issues that weave together like colorful threads in the tapestry of Colson's

life to create a fascinating picture of what may yet turn out to be one of his most enduring achievements.

The most important influence on Colson that caused him to become involved in ECT was his friendship with Richard John Neuhaus. When the two men first met, Neuhaus was a Lutheran pastor and author who was on the verge of being received into the Catholic Church and ordained into its priesthood. Neuhaus's best seller, *The Naked Public Square: Religion and Democracy in America* (1984), had made a great impact on Colson, who quoted it extensively in many of his own speeches and writings. His enthusiasm for the book led him to order many copies to distribute to friends and supporters of Prison Fellowship. However, one amusing incident made him a little more careful about exactly how and where he placed the orders. One afternoon in his office, Colson asked his secretary, Grace McCrane, to get hold of twelve copies of Neuhaus's book so that he could give them to his guests who were coming to dinner that evening. Unable to find it available in any of the local bookstores, McCrane continued her urgent search by phone. Getting through to one sales clerk she began, "Do you have Neuhaus's *The Naked Public Square?*" "Madam," came the indignant reply, "this is a Christian bookstore!" as the receiver slammed down.

In 1992 Father Neuhaus (as he had become) wrote to Colson asking him if he would be interested in attending a symposium to discuss the growing rivalry between evangelicalism and Catholicism in Latin America. Colson wrote back, "The project absolutely thrills me and I want to be as active a participant in it as possible." Quite why Colson should have been so thrilled by the prospect of attending a symposium on the minutiae of an obscure denominational turf war in Latin America was itself somewhat obscure. His admiration for Neuhaus was one factor. Another was Colson's growing international vision, which had been developing as a result of his mission trips to Latin America with Prison Fellowship International. But his deepest motivation came from an innate sense of a calling that he should be doing more for the cause of Christian unity.

Although Colson was committed to his Baptist beliefs, and to the Reformed theology he had acquired from his studies with his various professorial tutors, he had none of the visceral anti-Roman, antipapal prejudices that are found among many Born Again evangelicals. His marriage to Patty had given him an openness toward and a sympathy for Catholic believers, whose doctrinal certainties occasionally gave him twinges of envy. Moreover, his readings of the classic passages of scripture on unity, such as 1 Corinthians 12 and John 17:20–23, had filled him with a yearning to work to heal the rifts in the Body of Christ. Colson may not himself have fully understood all these latent forces behind his "thrill" to respond to his friend's invitation. They were to surface more dramatically a few weeks later during the symposium Neuhaus had convened, with a personal manifestation of the power of the Holy Spirit.

The meeting took place in September 1992 and was attended by some twenty-four participants, equally divided between prominent evangelicals and Catholics. The main focus of the first day's discussion was on a report by two British sociologists of religion, David and Bernice Martin; David was author of *Tongues of Fire: The Explosion of Protestantism in Latin America.* Colson thought that the interdenominational hostilities created by that explosion "threatened to mar the image of Christ by turning Latin America into a Belfast of religious warfare . . . there were travesties on both sides." He also took in a message from the Martins' presentation that explained why the evangelicals were doing so well in a part of the world that had traditionally been Catholic. Colson summarized this as: "The evangelicals deliver the bacon."

Colson, who in different roles had often been a successful deliverer of bacon—law clients, Senate votes, political alliances, White House victories, and now supporters of prison ministry—did not want the first ECT meeting to end in a baconless haze of academic theories limited to Latin America. So on the second day of the meeting he widened the discussion. Colson's theme was that in practical terms, here and now in the United States, evangelicals and Catholics needed to explore the possibilities for greater understanding and unity on the issues where there was common ground instead of fighting about the denominational differences that divided them. Those differences were far less important than the urgent need to champion the biblical worldview of God's creating and redeeming work against the growing postmodernist view of militantly secular naturalism.

As Colson's theme was taken up by the other participants, Neuhaus recognized that the dynamics of the meeting were changing. "It became clear that there was no thought whatever that what we were engaged in was a one-off thing. It dawned on us that we had become involved in something that was going to lead us somewhere. There was a sense that we were not so much onto something as being led."

Colson felt certain he knew who was doing the leading. As the afternoon sunlight beamed through the latticed windows of New York's Union League Club, he encountered what he believed to be "a direct personal experience of the power of the Holy Spirit." Describing this phenomenon in a letter to Neuhaus two days after the meeting, Colson wrote: "Somewhere during the second afternoon I sensed a real moving of God's Spirit. I think we all became aware that perhaps this was not just another symposium but that we might be, as you put it, on the edge of something very historic, an opportunity, a window in time if you will. Dare we believe that God is calling us to make a bold statement that could influence the course of His church in the decades to come?"

At the time of the meeting one or two of the participants observed that Colson became "visibly and audibly bolder," "suddenly very enthusiastic," and "on fire," especially when he declared in ringing tones, "You know we are really into this. Together we can do it!" He also surprised some of the staider academics and clerics by spontaneously walking over to Neuhaus, embracing him, and declaring, "You are my brother."

Although Colson put his fraternal leadership down to the presence of the Holy Spirit in the room, "inspiring us, driving us all forward," others took a more restrained view of the proceedings. The leading Catholic theologian present, Avery Dulles (now a cardinal), when interviewed for this biography ten years after the event, said, "I am afraid I am not as sensitive to the movements of the Holy Spirit as Chuck Colson. However, I would be the first to agree that we had a remarkably productive dialogue which was taking us forward to new ground."

Over the next few months an ECT drafting committee met regularly to prepare an initial statement for public endorsement by the group and other supporters. The committee consisted of Colson, Neuhaus, Kent Hill (a leading evangelical theologian), and George Weigel (the pope's biographer). They were all anxious to avoid the hedging and fudging that had characterized so many "ecumenical" statements from previous groups engaged in Protestant-Catholic dialogues. "The only unity we could seek, the only unity that is pleasing to God, is unity in the truth," said Colson, adding that he realized than any published statement would have to stand up to "severe critical examination." This was to prove an underestimate of the reception the document was soon to receive in some evangelical circles.

ECT's first public statement, released at a press conference in New York on March 29, 1994, was more a menu of subjects for future deliberation than concessions by either side of established theological positions. However the theme of the document was "convergence and cooperation between Evangelicals and Catholics." The principal subheadings of the statement—"We search together," "We affirm together," "We contend together," "We witness together"—perhaps conveyed an impression of deeper unity than might be achievable at later stages of ECT's progress. So did the sentences that were to prove red rags to a noisy herd of evangelical bulls: "We thank God for the discovery of one another in contending for a common cause. Much more we thank God for the discovery of one another as brothers and sisters in Christ."

Since the statement was endorsed by such Catholic luminaries as Avery Dulles, Cardinal John O'Connor of New York, Archbishop Francis Stafford of Denver, Michael Novak, and Bishop Carlos Sevilla of San Francisco, as well as by evangelical leaders such as Dr J. I. Packer, the Reverend Pat Robertson, Dr. Bill Bright of Campus Crusade, Dr. Jesse Miranda of Assemblies of God, and Dr. Larry Lewis of the Southern Baptist Convention, a neutral observer might have concluded that there was nothing particularly divisive in the text. The quiet tone at the New York press conference when the statement was launched seemed to confirm the anodyne nature of the enterprise. These first reactions were deceptive.

Colson realized he had got himself into boiling hot water when he read the *New York Times* on Good Friday, March 30, 1994, the day after the press conference. Under the headline EVANGELICALS AND CATHOLICS JOIN FORCES, the paper published a six-column report, accompanied by a large photograph of Colson talking animatedly to Neuhaus, who was dressed in his clerical collar. "When I picked up the *Times* I was in Albany, New York, where I had been speaking for Fred Rhodes at his alma mater Colgate University," recalled Colson. "There was snow on the ground and I stopped dead in my tracks. The presentation seemed huge—the photo of me and Neuhaus was above the fold. It was a big story, far bigger than I or anyone else had expected."

Fred Rhodes, Colson's Southern Baptist mentor, read the *Times* with grim-faced concentration. As he handed back the paper he said with masterly understatement, "I sense there may be a little trouble here, Chuck."

There was trouble aplenty. Over a quiet Easter weekend, when other news seemed to be in short supply, ECT became a major story across the nation. The first explosive reactions looked as if they would do enormous damage to Colson and to Prison Fellowship. All these explosions took place on the evangelical side of the barricades. "One had the impression that in the Southern part of the United States, many evangelicals thought that Catholics are not Christians at all and that they might even have cloven hooves," recalled Cardinal Avery Dulles. He and his fellow Catholic participants took minimal flak from their flock. Father Neuhaus had one letter from a group of Tridentine mass enthusiasts describing him as "the theological serpent in the garden," but this was mild by the standards of the attacks Colson was enduring. Because his name appeared first on the list of the evangelical participants in the ECT group and because he was such a high-profile Born-Againer, he bore the brunt of the ferocious criticism from fundamentalist pulpits and publications. The many accusations made against him included "doing incalculable damage to the cause of Christ," "overturning the Reformation," "striking the most devastating blow against the gospel in the past 1,000 years," and "betraying the doctrine of justification by faith." These onslaughts, often accompanied by scurrilous cartoons and abusive epithets, might have been dismissible as hysteria from the lunatic fringe of fundamentalism. However, two consequences of their fulminations forced Colson to take the fallout from ECT more seriously.

The first consequence was financial. All over the Bible Belt, individuals, churches, and evangelical organizations began withdrawing their support from Prison Fellowship. The net cash loss to PF's bottom line was just over $1 million, but there were other effects, such as radio stations dropping *BreakPoint*, donor functions having to be canceled for lack of support, and lower than expected responses from mail shots, which suggested that a more realistic calculation of the losses would be $1.5 million. Either figure was a serious blow to an organization that at the time had a total income of about $18 million.

As donor support ebbed and evangelical hostility flowed, Colson and his senior team at Prison Fellowship felt increasingly under siege. "We had correspondence pouring in ranging from the confused to the downright mean," recalled Karen Strong, vice president of Ministry Services. "Chuck was seriously under fire. So one morning he called together all the staff and spoke to us from his heart. When he'd finished his remarks, everyone in the room spontaneously rose to their feet and applauded our man of steel for his courage."

Colson began his remarks by quoting a line from Francis Schaeffer's book, *Mark of the Christian*. "Don't expect to evangelize the world if the world can't see us loving one another."

Colson then continued: "So let's have our disagreements in love. If we can't do that, we're name calling, pointing fingers at one another and saying 'this person is not a Christian . . . that person has betrayed the Gospel.' If we start to talk that way and the rest of the world picks it up, this controversy will destroy us. So I'm never going to answer these charges in that way. I'm going to follow the mark of the Christian, which is love."

In June 1994, Colson found it necessary to publish a personal statement answering questions such as "Have I abandoned the Reformation principle of *sola fide*?" and "Am I converting to Catholicism?" After answering both questions in the robust negative, Colson ended his eleven-page statement with a positive appeal for "a common, united defense for Christian orthodoxy, the authoritative word of God, Christian truth and the very nature of truth itself in the world today." At the end of the document he added an appendix, an essay entitled "Harmony," by R. C. Sproul, in which the eminent Reformed theologian recommended humility and an attitude of charity when Christians find themselves in disagreement over interpretations of God's Word.

The reason why Colson issued this rather curious postscript to his personal statement was that R. C. Sproul had attacked the ECT declaration in language that was a long way from being humble or charitable. This was the second serious consequence to Colson for putting his head above the parapet as a leading protagonist of ECT. He reckoned he could ride out the storm of attacks from intellectual lightweights, even if they cost Prison Fellowship significant money. But when a leading theologian of the stature of R. C. Sproul declared war on ECT and drew support from other distinguished writers and academics from the Reformed school of theology, Colson realized that he had a fight on his hands.

The fight was a particularly painful one because R. C. Sproul had been Colson's most influential mentor and tutor in the past fifteen years. Their two ministries had come close to a merger in the mid-1980s. Colson's veneration for his master was so strong that "hero worship" was not an inaccurate term to describe it. Colson himself acknowledged this in a letter to Sproul at the height of the controversy between them: "As you well know, no one has had a greater influence on my Christian growth than you. I have studied at your feet for over fifteen years, devoured everything you have written and appreciated your ministry beyond words."

In this letter and in a number of subsequent attempts Colson tried hard to reach an accommodation with Sproul, even if that accommodation merely consisted of an agreement to differ. The two protagonists held a summit meeting at Fort Lauderdale at which civility prevailed and an understanding appeared to have been arrived at to respect each other's position. But Sproul proved implacable, along with his principal theological allies, D. James Kennedy and Michael Horton. The bone of their contention against ECT was *sola fide,* the Lutheran doctrine that justification by faith alone was the true gospel of salvation and that Rome's denial of *sola fide* made Catholicism an invalid faith. In vain did Colson argue that the ECT position was less simplistic; that the Catholic and Protestant interpretations of *sola fide* could be reconciled; and that he and his evangelical colleagues were not betrayers or compromisers of the gospel of salvation. R. C. Sproul would have none of it. On one occasion he publicly declared in a lecture at Colson's hometown of Naples that "the Roman Catholic Church is neither a Christian body nor a Christian church."

This was too much for Colson, who opened fire on his former hero with both barrels. "Where does this lead us?" he asked. "There are 900 million confessing Catholics out of the worldwide Christian body of 1.7 billion. So if Rome is not a church, more than 50 percent of what the world believes as the Christian Church is gone. And to be logically consistent, of course, we would have to write off the Orthodox Church. There goes another 300 million. While we are at it, I don't know how we would hang on to the Episcopalians or the mainline Presbyterians with the way in which they have departed from the scripture. So if we are going to drum them all out of the church, there will be a very small, select group of us left to defend against the 2 billion pantheists and the 1 billion Muslims who are assaulting us."

Ridicule is a powerful weapon in the hands of an opponent as formidable as Colson. R. C. Sproul was starting to look silly. But Colson was getting damaged too. When Christian leaders of the stature of Jim Kennedy called him to say, "You will be destroyed by this," Colson feared that Prison Fellowship's future was in genuine peril. One of his evangelical ECT collaborators, Kent Hill, the president of Eastern Nazarene College, has recalled how low Colson looked after a meeting in the Union League Club. The two men shared a cab to the airport and during the ride Kent Hill expressed the hope that the controversy would not put either of their ministries in jeopardy. In an emotional moment Colson put his arm round Hill's shoulder and said, "Kent, all that matters is that we're doing the right thing—and we are."

As ECT wars rolled on, more and more good voices were raised in support of Colson for "doing the right thing." After Richard John Neuhaus, Colson's most powerful ally on the Catholic side of the battlefield was Michael Timmis, a successful businessman and an extremely influential Catholic layman in the diocese of Detroit. Timmis's enthusiasm for ECT was one of the factors that caused him to join the board of Prison Fellowship, and later to become chairman of Prison Fellowship International. The symbolism of having the Baptist Colson as chairman of Prison Fellowship working in harmonious unity with the Catholic Timmis as chairman of Prison Fellowship International sent a powerful message about ECT's practical effectiveness in the field of prison ministry. Colson was also backed to the hilt by Bill Bright, the founder of Campus Crusade, and by the leading evangelical theologian of the late twentieth century, Dr. J. I. Packer. It was Packer's stalwart support for ECT that turned the tide Colson's way in the community of evangelical academics. For Packer became disenchanted with R. C. Sproul's shrill arguments on the key issue. "RC seems to me to equate the Luther-Calvin conceptualizing of justification (with which I totally agree) with faith in Christ as Savior," wrote Packer. "This is surely Presbyterian-fundamentalist provincialism, which the New Testament won't back."

As the squabble between Sproul supporters and ECT supporters slowly petered out, ECT itself was gathering scholarly momentum. The list of both Catholic and evangelical theologians actively engaged in ECT seminars and publications grew in stature and numbers. They published papers on subjects like *sola fide, sola scriptura,* the communion of saints, the role of the Virgin Mary, the gift of salvation, scripture in the Catholic tradition, tradition in the life and thought of twentieth-century evangelicals, and sanctification.

The waves and ripples that spread out from these learned discourses made a favorable impact in unexpected places. In Colson's world ECT brought about a marked increase in cooperation between Catholic prison chaplains and evangelical prison ministry volunteers. The same was true for cooperation in the mission field in Latin America. There was also a trickle-down effect in parishes. As cooperation between evangelicals and Catholics seemed to be becoming respectable, all sorts of green shoots of greater unity started to appear. One example of this was the growth of the evangelical Alpha Course, which, in New England alone, is running in over seven hundred Catholic parishes with the blessing of the hierarchy, including its cardinals and archbishops. Not all of this progress is directly attributable to ECT. There are many other organizations promoting dialogue and ecumenical understanding, yet few, if any, have received so much positive and negative media attention as ECT. Colson, with his showman's and popularizer's touch, has given momentum to the cause in which he deeply believes.

Colson's support for ECT has not been without pain. Although Prison Fellowship's lost revenues in 1994–95 have long since been restored many times over by new donors, Colson himself continues to be surprised and sometimes hurt by old evangelical friends who feel alienated from him on this issue. He expressed this anxiety in a letter to Father Richard John Neuhaus: "I must say I continue to be amazed by the ferocity of the attack on ECT. I hadn't realized that prejudices ran so deep. But I'm more convinced than ever that what we're doing must be done even if a little of our blood is shed in the process. Some days I feel like it's not such a little amount!"

As ECT passed its tenth anniversary, in 2002, the metaphorical bloodshed seemed to be over. Calmer waters were prevailing. This author accompanied Colson to one of ECT's regular symposiums at the New York Union League Club in the fall of 2002. The subject under discussion was a draft paper on the communion of saints. It is not the easiest of topics on which to reconcile denominational differences, since evangelicals believe that all the departed faithful are saints, whereas Catholics place special emphasis on individuals who have received papal beatification or canonization. But two features of the symposium and its aftermath were impressive. The first was the quality of the theological scholarship, from both sides, applied to the narrowing down of differences. The second was the feeling, recorded in ECT's initial statement, that the participants were true brothers and sisters in Christ, working together for a common purpose. What was that common purpose? J. I. Packer referred to John 17:21, which is Jesus' prayer that we might all be one as he and the Father are one. Colson quoted his hero Abraham Kuyper, the nineteenth-century Dutch Calvinist, to the effect that Catholics and Calvinists are on the same side in the conflict against liberal secularism. In the light of these and many other comments about the drive for Christian unity, differences about definitions of saints seemed minimal. Some weeks later, when ECT's document on the saints, entitled *Communio Sanctorum,* was published, there appeared to be little or no criticism of it from any quarter. Colson would be the first to admit that he is no academic theologian himself. "There are times in these discussions when I am way out of my depth," he confided. But as his co-founder of ECT, Richard John Neuhaus, puts it, "Chuck has fulfilled many of his aspirations to understand theology. He is intellectually curious and theologically musical. He is not at all tone deaf in this area. He hears all the important tunes and themes even if he does not know every note of the score. His real talent is that he takes away the theology and applies his sanctified political skills to move it to a quite different world of discourse. Chuck thinks and prays about what he thinks. He is a remarkable man. ECT would not have happened without him."

It is still too early to judge the long-term impact of ECT. However an interesting interim judgment on it was offered by the *New York Times*. In a full-page article published on May 30, 2004, the *Times* credited ECT with providing the major impetus behind what it called "an extraordinary realignment" of religious alliances within the American Christian community. This realignment has other forces behind it, such as the gut feelings of many evangelicals who now think they have far more in common with the Catholics than they do with the Episcopalians, Presbyterians, Methodists, and other Protestant churches, which are internally divided over homosexuality issues. However, the intellectual and theological rapprochement between these two wings of Christendom has been pioneered by the leading lights of ECT. "I can see that we may be achieving a thaw in hostility between evangelicals and Catholics which is of profound importance," says Cardinal Avery Dulles. More audaciously, Richard John Neuhaus comments, "I am bold enough to believe that ECT could have historic consequences in terms of improved theological understanding. If it continues it may create a very different configuration of Christianity in America."

Colson is increasingly excited by his vision of evangelicals and Catholics as cobelligerents in the Christian battle against postmodernism and secularism. He sees ECT as a unifying force in changing the culture of Western society, swinging it back toward a biblical worldview of ethics and morality. It is this vision that causes him to say: "When all is said and done and my life is viewed in perspective, ECT is likely to be the most significant project I invested my time and capital into. It has been well worth the struggle and I think we have yet to see the great things God will do with it."

The Growth of Prison Fellowship International

When Colson delivered the Templeton Address to the World Parliament of Religions in 1993, one of the key passages in his speech was a description of a recent visit he had made as chairman of Prison Fellowship International to the Humaita Prison in the city of São José dos Campos, in Brazil. "It was," said Colson, "a prison quite different from any other that I've ever been in." The difference was that Humaita was a Christian-run prison whose inmates were all observing a regime of Christian values, teachings, and principles. Every prisoner had signed up to a chapel program, a course in character development, and was accountable to another inmate. In addition, every prisoner was assigned to a volunteer family from the outside that monitored him during his sentence and after his release.

On a spiritual level the conceptual idea of a Christian-run prison fascinated Colson. He was deeply impressed by what he saw in Humaita, for he felt that the inmates' commitment to Christ shone through their lives and behavior. Toward the end of his visit one of the prisoners escorted Colson on a tour of the older part of the jail, including a notorious punishment block once used for torture. "These days this block has only one man, in this cell," said the inmate acting as Colson's guide as they stopped at a heavy iron door. "Are you sure you want to go in?"

"Of course," Colson replied impatiently. "I've been in isolation cells all over the world."

Slowly the inmate turned the lock and swung open the massive door. Colson gazed at "the prisoner" inside the cell. It was Jesus, hanging on the cross of a large wooden crucifix that had been carved by the prisoners of Humaita. "He's doing time for all the rest of us," said the guide in a soft voice.

Colson told this story to many audiences across the world in the ensuing years, but he always linked the remarkable spirituality he had seen in Humaita Prison to the jail's no less remarkable repeat-offending statistics. For the annual records of released prisoners from Humaita over the decade since it had became a Christian-run prison showed that their repeat offending rate was 4 percent. This compared to an average repeat-offending rate of 70 percent in the other prisons in Brazil.

Colson had heard about Humaita from his close friend and Prison Fellowship board member Jack Eckerd, the founder of one of America's largest drugstore chains. It was Eckerd who persuaded Colson to make a special visit to Brazil and to study APAC—the acronym for the Portuguese Christian program that had transformed Humaita. During the 1990s, APAC started to run similar programs in other prisons in Latin America, with more good results in terms of lives transformed and reoffending rates reduced. Impressed by these results, Colson and Eckerd formed a vision of bringing a Christian program similar to APAC into the prisons of America.

Turning the vision they had seen in Latin America into practical reality in the United States was a long, hard slog. Colson, Eckerd, and their advisers from Prison Fellowship International had to work their way through nearly seven years of difficult administrative, legal, and financial discussions before the APAC concept could be transplanted to America. But in 1997 the vision succeeded, thanks in no small measure to the governor of Texas, George W.

Bush. As governor, Bush was increasingly worried by the rising cost of incarcerating prisoners in Texas (often over $60,000 per prisoner a year), most of whom were back behind bars within two or three years of their release. Colson convinced Governor Bush that the state of Texas's high reoffending rate, around 70 percent, would never change unless an attempt was made to address the moral and spiritual poverty of the reoffenders, during their prison terms. So Bush gave his approval for an experimental Christian-training prison unit run on APAC lines to be opened within the Sugar Land prison complex, near Houston. This InnerChange Freedom Initiative (IFI) unit began in 1997 and has since expanded internally as well as spawning four other IFI prisons in other states. Eight years later, the good results of IFI (see Prologue, pages 8–9) are a fine example of how Colson's international work has brought innovative new ideas into the American penal system.

In his role as chairman of Prison Fellowship International, Colson made many overseas visits throughout the 1990s, often to prisons in remote and difficult places in countries such as Japan, Korea, Fiji, and Zambia, in addition to traveling to familiar national capitals in Asia, Europe, and Latin America. Patty usually accompanied him on these testing and often physically exhausting trips. "She was a tower of strength to me," recalls Colson, "not just because of her presence but because of her discerning judgment about the people we met, her encouragement, and her obvious happiness at being with me in support of PFI."

As if to reinforce the point about happiness, Colson in the early 1990s stopped called his wife "Patty." When they were alone together his name for her became "Happy." This change was brought about by Colson's eldest grandson, Charlie, who as a toddler mispronounced "Patty" as "Happy." When Patty gently remonstrated with him, asking, "Why do you keep calling me Happy?" Charlie replied, "Because even when you get mad with me, you are happy." The boy's answer tickled Colson and he has used "Happy" as his private nickname for his wife ever since.

On his international travels there was one episode that made Colson extremely unhappy, so much so that it precipitated his resignation from the chairmanship of Prison Fellowship International. He was on a tour of the former Soviet bloc countries in 1997 that was scheduled to end with a PFI board meeting in Paris. One of the highlights of the tour was a dinner in Moscow for prominent Russian Christians who were going to be the founders of Prison Fellowship's ministry in their country. To enhance the atmosphere of the dinner, PFI's president, Ron Nikkel, arranged for wine to be served at the meal. Nikkel saw this as a natural act of hospitality for

PFI's Russian guests, who were unaccustomed to the teetotal dining habits of American evangelicals. When Colson saw the wine being poured out he seethed with anger. "It was against our strict rules and Ron knew it," he said afterward. It was not the first time that tensions had surfaced in their relationship. Although each had considerable respect for the other, Nikkel's insistence on PFI's independence from its parent organization clashed with Colson's sometimes imperious wishes for close control. Because of these differing outlooks, Colson had been thinking of cutting back on his international responsibilities. The wine incident precipitated his departure. Three days afterward, at the board meeting in Paris, Colson resigned as chairman of Prison Fellowship International.

The first person in America to know of this resignation was Mike Timmis, the businessman who had been on the board of Prison Fellowship since 1991. Timmis was amazed to get a call from Colson in Paris saying to him, "I'm standing down. Would you take over as chairman of PFI?"

Timmis's reply was, "If it was anyone else in the world asking me to do this I'd say no immediately. But since it's you, Chuck, I'll go away and pray about it."

Mike Timmis and his wife, Nancy, did pray every night for the next six months for God's guidance on the PFI chairmanship. Guidance came there none, as far as both Timmises could see. Colson, however, kept pressing his friend to accept the job. So eventually, with some reluctance, Timmis made a PFI visit to Costa Rica and Honduras. In the course of that visit Timmis felt that he could develop a good working relationship with Ron Nikkel. He also felt the tentative stirrings of a call toward overseas prison evangelism, although these stirrings were so muted that Timmis would probably not have responded to them had it not been for the intervention of Nancy.

Nancy Timmis is a reserved lady, careful in her statements, cautious in her temperament, and private in her faith. As a disciplined and committed Catholic, she is at the other end of the religious spectrum from the Baptists, charismatics, and Pentecostals, who make up the majority of Prison Fellowship's supporters. These evangelical types are familiar with personal experiences of the Holy Spirit, seeing visions, getting words, and hearing voices. None of these activities were in the style or the experience of Nancy Timmis.

And so, on the evening when Mike Timmis returned from his trip to Honduras and Costa Rica, he was astounded to be told by Nancy, "God has spoken to me. You must take the PFI chairmanship." Apparently what had happened was that in her quiet time Nancy had received the clearest message that God wanted her husband to dedicate the rest of his life to the evangelizing of prisoners in foreign countries. The message was all the more amazing because Nancy had been telling Mike for some months that he was doing too much, that he should cut back on his business and charitable activities, and that he should not take on any new appointments. But now, certain in her heart that the PFI chairmanship was a clear call from God, Nancy Timmis wasted no time in persuading her husband to accept the appointment. The following morning Mike Timmis called Colson and said, "I'll do it."

Colson was overjoyed. There was no one he admired more than Timmis, with whom he had bonded closely during the thirteen years since they had first been introduced by Nancy DeMoss. Besides being neighbors in Naples, close friends, and steadfast servants of Prison Fellowship and now Prison Fellowship International, the two men had one other symbolic link in common. As Colson put it, "Here's Prison Fellowship U.S., of which I'm chairman, and I'm a Southern Baptist; and here's Prison Fellowship International, of which Mike Timmis is chairman, and he's a Roman Catholic. Our unity has sent its own powerful message around the world, amazingly without causing any controversy in evangelical ranks. So it's a tremendous symbolic witness of what we are trying to do, and of our legacy to national and international prison ministry."

Once Mike Timmis had accepted the chairmanship of PFI, Colson restrained his control-freak inclinations and never again became actively involved in the management of PFI operations. "He left us his legacy to build on but I think he was guided by the power of the Holy Spirit to do something he would otherwise have found very hard to do—to walk away from PFI," said Timmis. "He was always supportive but never on top of us. He even cut his overseas trips down to the minimum. He let go."

One group of people who were secretly delighted to see Colson letting go of his overseas travel schedule was his devoted sisterhood of secretaries, among them Grace McCrane, Nancy Niemeyer, and Diana Longenecker. For many years they had borne the brunt of the chairman's obsession with fingertip control of his travel arrangements and his issuing detailed instructions on hotels and airlines, which ranged from the frenetic to the farcical. Air ticketing seemed to bring out the worst in Colson, particularly when the travels were to exotic foreign destinations. However, he could be just as bad when the flights were to and from his hometown of Naples. At one

Prison Fellowship summer barbecue party, Grace McCrane sent the assembled company into gales of laughter by reading this "typical Colson travel memo":

> I'd like to fly from Naples to San Francisco by whatever is the easiest, most direct, if possible nonstop way to get there. There's a 2:15 nonstop out of Miami and there may be some nonstops out of Orlando or Tampa, but what I'd really like to do is not leave Naples until midafternoon, if possible, though I could leave at noon. I should get into San Francisco no later than 9 P.M., San Francisco time, because that's midnight. I can get there by Fort Myers to Dallas, Dallas to San Francisco. I can get there by Naples to Tampa, Tampa to San Francisco. I can get there by Naples to Orlando, or Fort Myers to Orlando, Orlando to San Francisco. I can get there by way of Naples to Miami, Miami to San Francisco. What we want to do is get me there no later than 9 P.M. by the cheapest way possible, and using one of the airlines, if we have any choice, on which I can get a free or inexpensive upgrade.

In the same hilarious speech, Grace McCrane had more to say to complete her irreverent portrait of Colson the international traveler and memo dictator: "To be Chuck's secretary you also have to be a meteorologist as well, for I am often put on the spot—and feel terribly inadequate—for not knowing if it's foggy or windy in the city of his destination. More often than not, dictation is being transcribed complete with the background noise of a stewardess giving instructions, the roar of jet engines, and noisy children. For all of the precise planning we do in trying to obtain optimum airline seats, somehow there are a lot of crying babies in Chuck's immediate vicinity. And he is not restrained in choosing his place of dictation, like the time when he was in Russia and thought his room was bugged, and dictated in the closet in whispered, muffled tones."

For all such lighthearted negatives about Colson on his journeyings overseas, the enormous positives of Prison Fellowship International have shown up clearly in the results of its national ministries across the world. Under the joint leadership of Mike Timmis and Ron Nikkel, the scale and scope of PFI have grown spectacularly. This growth, and the spiritual depth underlying it, was wonderfully displayed at the PFI Convocation held in Toronto in 2003. More than eight hundred delegates from 113 countries flew in to report on what their Prison Fellowship national ministries were achieving. Stories about Rwanda's Unavumu reconciliation project, Britain's Sycamore Tree in-prison courses, the huge expansion of prison ministry across Eastern Europe and Asia, the worldwide growth of restorative justice schemes and alternatives-to-prison projects, and the results from the new Christian-run prisons in South America, New Zealand, and the United States brought tears to many eyes. Colson said in his keynote speech at the convocation that he had underestimated the magnitude of PFI's achievements. At this writing, PFI has over 120,000 volunteers helping to implement programs designed to change prisoners' lives, prison conditions, and systems of justice in six continents. All these programs are based upon, or directly copied from, the Prison Fellowship programs that were developed by Colson in the States. PFI, it seems, is one U.S. export that is universally popular. At the Toronto Convocation it was no false praise when the head of all the Canadian prison chaplains, the Reverend Pierre Allard, declared, "Mr. Colson, you are well blessed, for very few men in history have lived long enough to see their vision so richly fulfilled around the world."

Worldview and the Succession

By far the most exciting new horizon to capture Colson's imagination and commitment during the last few years of his ministry has been worldview or, to give its full title, biblical worldview. Although this term has been mentioned many times in previous chapters, it requires a more detailed explanation for readers who are not familiar with the ongoing debate on worldview issues inside the American Christian community. That debate has intensified in the early years of the twenty-first century partly, if not largely, because Colson has so energetically championed biblical worldview in his books, broadcasts, and in his new teaching project—the Centurions program. Biblical worldview is the cause of changing the contemporary culture of American society by returning it to the core values of the Christian faith as laid down by the Bible. Starting with the biblical mandate that proclaims the sovereignty of God, Colson argues that only Christianity can provide a sure foundation and framework for the life of a community whose values have so badly gone astray under the destructive cultural pressures of modernism, postmodernism, and individual autonomy.

Colson is a critic of many churches for their inward-looking teachings, which he thinks are apt to focus too narrowly on individual lives and spirituality. Worldview is a wider cause. In his advocacy of it Colson argues for a new, strategic approach by the Christian community, directed to fighting for a fundamental change in the whole culture and lifestyle of secular society.

There is a widespread impression in this Christian community that Colson's championing of worldview is a recent enthusiasm of his that effectively dates from the publication in 2000 of his major book on the subject, *How Now Shall We Live?* Although this book is seen as the seminal work on worldview issues, so much so that some bookstores display it under a poster inappropriately calling it "The Worldview Bible," it is important to understand that Colson has been studying this cause for over three decades, and writing about it for nearly two. In the week when *How Now Shall We Live?* was published, Colson gave a lunchtime lecture on it to the staff of Prison Fellowship. Among the first to congratulate him was Ellen Vaughn, a well-known Christian writer who has worked for Colson since the late 1970s as a researcher and as coauthor with him on two of his most important books, *Kingdoms in Conflict* (1986) and *The Body* (1992; revised 2003). In response to Vaughn's congratulations, Colson said, "Oh Ellen, these were the things you and I were writing about fifteen years ago. Isn't it great to see them get to this point?"

"This point," in Colson's vocabulary, means the point of challenge. For *How Now Shall We Live?* opens with a clarion call to Christian believers:

We must show the world that Christianity is more than a private belief, more than personal salvation. We must show that it is a comprehensive life system that answers all of humanity's age-old questions. Where did I come from? Why am I here? Where am I going? Does life have any meaning or purpose?

Christianity offers the only viable, rationally defensible answers to these questions. Only Christianity offers a way to understand both the physical and the moral order. Only Christianity offers a comprehensive worldview that covers all areas of life and thought, every aspect of creation. Only Christianity offers a way to live in line with the real world.

As this worldview cause is now placed by Colson at the top of his list of priorities in his Christian ministry, it is appropriate to ask, how did he come to believe in it and where is he going with it now?

Colson first came to hear about the concept of biblical worldview when he was traveling through Europe on a book promotion tour of *Born Again*. His publisher, Leonard LeSourd, suggested that Colson should visit Francis Schaeffer at L'Abri Fellowship in Switzerland. It was a name barely familiar to Colson, who had read none of Schaeffer's books. When the two men met and talked for an entire day in the Swiss Alps in the summer of 1977, Colson was very much the untutored, novice Christian, hungry for learning and guidance. Schaeffer gave him plenty of both. "I really took to the man," recalled Colson. "He spent most of the day recommending books and giving me advice. Some of it was very practical, on how to discipline oneself and how to study. I also remember Schaeffer saying to me, 'Ration your time. Every need is not a call.'"

Colson was so busy building up Prison Fellowship that he did not heed the advice about time rationing for some years. But he read all Schaeffer's books, particularly *He Is There and He Is Not Silent* (1972), *Escape from Reason* (1968), and *How Should We Then Live?* (1976). Through Schaeffer, Colson began studying the works of Abraham Kuyper, an author strongly recommended to him by his close friend and theological mentor R. C. Sproul, who was another keen champion of worldview.

In 1984 Colson became a columnist for *Christianity Today*. In its pages he began to present the arguments for worldview on a regular basis. He followed a similar pattern in his broadcasts on *BreakPoint*. This media attention given by Colson to worldview, together with many talks and lectures to influential audiences, gradually raised the profile of this previously little known Christian idea.

In 1997 the MacClelland Foundation of Tennessee invited Colson to start a Worldview Center and to teach courses in worldview there. Colson was attracted to the proposal, but after much thought and prayer, he turned it down. His explanation was that he thought his own involvement in the proposed center was premature: "I was not sure back in 1997 that I was sufficiently steeped in worldview to teach it. I was not prepared to divert my time away from evangelism in the prisons," he has recalled, "so I said, let's wait until after I have written my next book, which will be on worldview, and then maybe I will feel able to teach a course on it."

The book on worldview was *How Now Shall We Live?* Colson wrote it with a coauthor, Nancy Pearcey, in 1998–99. It was his most important and influential book since *Born Again*. In its 576 pages, the four major themes of *How Now Shall We Live?* are

—Creation: Where did we come from and who are we?

—The Fall: What has gone wrong with the world?

—Redemption: What can we do to fix it?

—Restoration: How now shall we live?

Underlying these themes is the insistence that the Christian worldview is more consistent, more rational, and more workable than any other belief system. The final chapter opens with a clarion call to action: "Christians who understand Biblical truth and have the courage to live it out can redeem a culture or even create one. This is the challenge facing all of us in the new millennium."

Colson himself faced two challenges in the aftermath of the publication of *How Now Shall We Live?* The first was how to handle a distressing personal squabble with his coauthor, Nancy Pearcey. The second was what to do in response to the widespread acclaim given to the book.

Nancy Pearcey, who had been a Colson researcher and contributor for many years, playing a pivotal role in the writing and editing of scripts for *BreakPoint,* was the acknowledged coauthor. When she began working on the book, she defined her own role in a memo of December 6, 1996: "I will be the quarterback, pulling the book togther including doing a large proportion of both the idea development and the writing." She subsequently signed a contract that assigned a substantial percentage of the authors' royalties to her.

Against this background it came as a great shock to Colson when, at the time of publication, he started to receive angry letters from Pearcey claiming that she had been treated unfairly.

The main cause of Pearcey's discontent seems to have been the size of her billing on the dust jacket of *How Now Shall We Live?* The trouble was that, on the front cover of the book, the name Charles Colson appeared in large and prominent type, whereas the ensuing words, "and Nancy Pearcey," were in much smaller type. This was the sort of squabble more usually found among Hollywood actors than Christian authors and the press enjoyed stirring it. When Pearcey expressed her grievances to journalists, the story received many column inches, some of them filled by dark hints that Colson was a plagiarist and an overbearing self-publicist.

In this row, which in reality was a storm in a very small teacup, Colson suffered in silence. He believed he had put just as much creative effort and literary productivity into the book as had his coauthor. The decisions about typeface size on the front cover were made by the publishers, Tyndale, not by Colson. Since Colson was a big-name, best-selling author, while Pearcey was an unknown one, the publishers could hardly be blamed for taking a commercial view of whose prominence should be greater on the cover. Nevertheless Colson was hurt and upset by the controversy. He approached Tyndale's chief executive, Ken Petersen, asking for his coauthor's billing to be enlarged. Colson also wrote several times to Nancy Pearcey with "as loving and gentle letters as I knew how to write," urging her to come to talk with him so that they could reconcile their differences. Pearcey replied in a far from friendly spirit. She refused to meet Colson, and in November 1999 she resigned from Prison Fellowship, severing all ties with him. Although the episode caused much mutual distress to both parties, it is difficult to see how or why Colson should have handled it in a significantly different way. He has always been transparent in his acknowledgment of the contributions made to his writings by coauthors and collaborators. Pearcey was no exception, and her contract has been fully honored. For all the recriminations and media reports about them, the dispute appears to have made no impact at all on the book's reception by the critics and the book-buying public.

The Christian and, to a lesser extent, the secular media gave *How Now Shall We Live?* an enthusiastic welcome. *Christianity Today* called it "a magnum opus in the best Shaefferian tradition . . . a handbook for today's Christians." William F. Buckley in *National Review* wrote of "the singular pleasure that comes from its absolute—learned—refusal to give any quarter to the dogged materialists who deny any possibility that there was a creator." A common theme among reviewers was that the book broke important new ground for the projection of the Christian faith in the twenty-first century and deserved a wide readership.

It got one. Over four hundred thousand copies have been sold in the hardback edition, with far bigger sales expected for the forthcoming paperback. *How Now Shall We Live?* has been translated into six languages, including Chinese and Korean. Many universities have put the book on their required reading lists for students of theology, philosophy, and ethics. Whether or not this early success is a harbinger of the change in the culture that Colson is hoping for remains an open question, but the case for biblical worldview is certainly reaching a new and far wider audience than anything achieved by its earlier pioneers, such as Francis Schaeffer.

In reaching this wider audience, Colson has made the cause of biblical worldview a central theme in the ministry of Prison Fellowship. Initially this was done through the Wilberforce Forum, a department of PF that acts

as a think tank, providing scripts for the *BreakPoint* broadcasts and material for other publications. More recently, biblical worldview has been enthusiastically championed by Colson's chosen successor, the new president
of Prison Fellowship, Mark Earley.

The story of how Mark Earley came to be appointed to his post is one
in which Colson sees the hand of divine providence. It began in the late
1990s, when Colson was a year or two short of his seventieth birthday and
supporters of Prison Fellowship were quietly starting to say, "What would
happen to this ministry if anything happened to Chuck?"

Colson himself began pondering on this question with increased attention after a medical crisis that laid him low during a visit to England in
1997. He was over there for various celebrations in honor of the hundredth
anniversary of the birth of C. S. Lewis, accompanied by a group of prominent Prison Fellowship supporters, headed by former congressman Jack
Kemp and his wife, Joanne. In the course of a ten-day speaking tour that
took him and his party to London, Oxford, Cambridge, and Cheltenham,
Colson started to feel unwell. His worsening symptoms included a yellow
complexion, white stools, and bursts of gut-wrenching pain, which caused
him to double up in spasms of agony. Despite being in the throes of what
was clearly an acute illness, Colson stuck to the tour schedule and insisted
on delivering the keynote address of the C. S. Lewis celebrations to a
thousand-strong audience in Great Saint Mary's Church, Cambridge. So
bad was the pain in his stomach on the morning of the address that Colson
nearly called it off. However, as he climbed the steps of the pulpit his pain
(which had been the subject of prayers for healing in the vestry) mysteriously vanished, and he gave an unhindered speech that many of those present regarded as a triumph. Unfortunately, however, agony struck him again
twenty-four hours later in Cheltenham, and Colson had to be rushed to the
hospital. He was diagnosed as critically ill with a bile duct blocked by gall-
stones. Surgery was scheduled, but before the operation was performed, the
stone passed. Colson, still in considerable discomfort, flew back to his doctors in Naples, who told him he had survived a close call.

This concentrated Colson's mind on the search for a successor. When
the firm of recruitment consultants engaged by Prison Fellowship started
its trawl for suitable candidates, it asked Colson if he could identify anyone who, in his view, would be an outstanding holder of the job.

"The ideal successor to me would be Mark Earley," replied Colson. "The
only trouble with him is that he's just decided to run for attorney general
of Virginia, and after that he could be the next governor. So he's out." That

was indeed the situation in 1998. Mark Earley had excellent credentials for the job of president of Prison Fellowship, both as a successful lawyer and as a Christian leader who had shown inspirational qualities as a Bible teacher in his work for the Navigators. But his political career seemed to rule him completely out of contention after he was elected attorney general of Virginia in November 1998.

During the next four years Colson and the board of Prison Fellowship searched high and low for the right man or woman to lead the ministry. Tom Pratt, who had been a superb president, was keen to retire, and Colson knew that he had to find an appointee who would be accepted as his own successor in the longer term. At least twenty-five suitable candidates were evaluated and interviewed, but for one reason or another, none of them came good. Eventually the board settled on a choice that seemed ideal in every way. Shortly before this appointment was finalized, in the summer of 2002, Colson was sitting on a bus alongside one of Prison Fellowship's senior executive vice presidents, Alan Terwilliger, talking enthusiastically about the board's choice. Halfway through this conversation the passenger who was sitting in the seat on the bus immediately behind them tapped Colson on the shoulder and said, "I'm sorry to interrupt you, but I couldn't help overhearing you talking about X. Would you mind telling me what's the context of your discussion about him?"

"Sure," said Colson. "He's likely to be appointed as my successor to head up this ministry."

"Oh my," said the man from the seat behind Colson. "We'd better have a private talk about this."

What emerged from the private talk was that X, the almost-appointed successor, was unsuitable to be president of Prison Fellowship. So it was back to square one in the search for a good candidate.

By this time it was the fall of 2002 and Mark Earley was running as the Republican candidate for governor of Virginia. After four successful years as the state's attorney general he looked a near-certain winner, but late in the campaign the Democrats surged ahead and Earley was unexpectedly defeated. Forty-eight hours later Colson was on the phone to him, asking if he would be interested in leading Prison Fellowship. In the spring of 2003 Mark Earley was appointed as the ministry's president and chief executive officer.

Colson and Earley have now been working together at the helm of Prison Fellowship for over two years. They seem to have a partnership made in heaven. For Colson has fully anointed Earley as his successor, supporting him in every possible way and giving him complete control of the day-to-day operations of the ministry. Under its new president the ministry is continuing to grow both financially and spiritually. The only discernible changes so far are that Earley puts greater emphasis, internally, on the concept that Prison Fellowship staffers are "a family," with personal and pastoral needs to which he ministers regularly. Externally, Earley is expanding Prison Fellowship's ministry to juvenile offenders and to the younger members of prisoners' families.

Although out of its executive and operational loop, Colson remains heavily involved in and totally committed to Prison Fellowship as its founder and chairman. He remains busy in certain key activities such as fund-raising from major donors, special events, and field missions of particular significance like the annual Easter weekend prison visits organized by Operation Starting Line. However, even when Colson is ostensibly playing the lead role on such occasions, he and Earley share the speaking load evenly and as equals. They are brothers and team players, making the transition of leadership in Prison Fellowship work happily, gradually, and successfully.

Colson is devoting more and more of his time to worldview, a cause that Earley supports to the hilt and participates in fully as a coleader with Colson. A new arena of worldview, in which their coleadership can be seen to be working well, is a Wilberforce Forum program called the Centurions. This was the brainchild of James Van Eerden, a member of the Wilberforce Forum's advisory council, but Colson took it up with an enthusiasm that was fully supported by Mark Earley. The thinking that propelled the program forward was Colson's belief that worldview, and the consequences that could flow from it, are so important that he must raise up a new generation of exponents of it by equipping them for their leadership role through a teaching program.

So the Centurions project annually enrolls one hundred mature Christians of intellectual ability and leadership potential to study a yearlong course in worldview subjects. Some of the course is organized by distance learning methods—lectures by e-mail and set essays. However, the core of the program is four residential weekends at which lectures and seminars are given to the one hundred students by a team of worldview experts headed by Colson and Earley.

This author spent a day with the Centurion class of 2004 assembled at a conference center in Virginia and took away three strong impressions.

The first was that the quality of the students and the excellence of the lectures were on a par with the high standards I had experienced while studying theology at Oxford University as a resident student in 2000–2002. The Centurions is no soft option course. It is an intellectually demanding and practically testing curriculum for a student body earmarked for future Christian leadership.

The second impression was that Charles Colson and Mark Earley are a teaching team whose outstanding gifts complement each other's as if they have been working together in academic harness for years. Earley is quieter, perhaps more cerebral and more didactic in style, but he is a master of biblical teaching and he communicates his scholarship to his students with deep conviction. Colson is, as always, a political performer as well as a Christian leader. So he communicates with the students by high-voltage inspiration, sparkling with wit and fine phrases, yet earthed in a passion for worldview that is both spiritual and intellectual. Perhaps the sincerest tribute I can pay to these principal lecturers is that after spending a day listening to them I longed to do the Centurions course.

The third impression I took away was that Colson has solved his succession problem. There is a clear answer now to the question, What would happen to this ministry if anything happened to Chuck? Just as Colson chose an outstanding leader for Prison Fellowship International's ministry in Mike Timmis, he has now found an exceptional leader for Prison Fellowship's ministry in the United States in Mark Earley. In both cases, Colson believes that the choices were made by God, not by himself. Either way, both Mike Timmis and Mark Earley are vitally important figures in the legacy of Charles Colson.

Epilogue

In the year 2001 Charles Colson celebrated his seventieth birthday, and Prison Fellowship its twenty-fifth anniversary. Both events were commemorated by dinners, speeches, video tributes, and letters of congratulations. Yet underlying these festivities were two intriguing questions: what is Colson's legacy, and will it be an enduring one? To answer these questions, a distinction has to be made between Colson's preconversion career in politics and his postconversion life of Christian service.

The achievements of Colson's preconversion years, as a lawyer and as a political operator, were significant at the time but are likely to prove ephemeral. A generation or so from now, who will remember that Colson and Charles Morin created a successful law firm, argued important cases, or broke the color bar in Boston's legal community? Who will recall that Colson became special counsel to the president of the United States at the youthful age of thirty-eight? Or that the White House office of public liaison, which all presidents now incorporate in their administrations, was created by Colson in 1969, exercising his unorthodox lobbying efforts on behalf of Richard Nixon? These seeds he planted in the fields of law and politics are already faded blooms.

Colson left a more permanent mark on the landscape of presidential elections. For his novel approach to building previously unheard of alliances with the power blocs of organized labor and other special interest groups did more than deliver a Republican landslide in 1972. Colson's strategy was imitated in subsequent national elections by GOP campaign managers seeking to broaden the base of their party's support. The poll victories of President Reagan and of both Presidents Bush owe something to the changed perceptions of the Republican Party among blue-collar voters, which began during Nixon's first term. Colson's originality in this area of successful vote getting was remarkable. However, the revolutionary nature of his political thinking will be remembered far less than the ruthless nature of his political techniques. For Colson's dirty tricks against the president's rivals and opponents, and his alleged tongue-in-cheek declaration "I would walk over my grandmother for Richard Nixon," have already passed into the annals of twentieth-century politics.

The same ruthlessness led to Colson's involvement in Watergate. This aspect of his career will certainly be remembered. It has much resonance with Marc Antony's lines in Shakespeare's *Julius Caesar:*

> The evil that men do lives after them,
> The good is oft interrèd with their bones.

Colson's political tricks and transgressions do not deserve the epithet "evil." However, he was such a considerable contributor to the unsavory moral climate inside the Nixon White House that he deserves his share of culpability for the environment in which it was possible for Watergate to happen. For his errors of judgment and overzealous partisanship leading up to that saga, Colson paid a heavy price. Perhaps it was too heavy, given that he had no involvement in Watergate itself. For only in the feverish political atmosphere of Washington during the last months of the Nixon administration could a prosecutor have created the unprecedented criminal charge to which Colson pleaded guilty. And only in that same atmosphere could a judge have imposed a one-to-three-year-prison sentence as the punishment for prejudicing the legal rights of a defendant whose legal rights were never in fact prejudiced. Such judicial extremism was part and parcel of the furious reaction in Washington to the follies of Watergate.

It is to Colson's credit that he has never sought to deny or even to minimize his share of the responsibility for that reaction. Alone among the leading Watergaters, he has never offered excuses or justifications for his misconduct. In a no less solitary stance he has never attacked or severely criticized his former boss Richard Nixon. Instead, he has remained conspicuously loyal to the thirty-seventh president, even when he discovered from the White House tape recordings that his loyalty was not always reciprocated. The Nixon-Colson Oval Office conversations, read in cold print, are often unedifying and sometimes distasteful. However, Colson's excessive eagerness to comply with the darker instincts of the president did not result

in many of the excesses he was reported as having committed. For Colson was a victim of numerous false allegations made against him by others. The worst of these "White House horrors" was the claim that he planned or ordered the bombing of the Brookings Institution. It was untrue.*

After his departure from the White House in early 1973, Colson, who had taken no previous interest in matters spiritual, began a religious journey that led to his conversion, repentance, and public commitment to Born Again Christianity. At that time the words "Born Again" were obscure, understood by only a narrow section of the evangelical Christian community. Colson's conversion and his international best seller describing it helped to make the term "Born Again" world famous. However, Colson himself remained infamous, at least in the eyes of secular public opinion.

In the light of Colson's eventual lionization by many Christians, it is important to recall the early demonization he encountered from many cynics. Journalists were his noisiest critics after, as well as before, his prison sentence. Following his release from jail in 1975, what seemed to provoke their anger was the public witness Colson kept giving about his newfound faith. A colorful but characteristic example of the media vilification his religious conversion received was the broadcast, in 1977, on CBS News, of a commentary by their Washington correspondent Tom Braden. Describing Colson as "a handler of dirty money, a skillful promoter of subversion, a proven liar, an instigator of burglary . . . and in the truest sense of the word, a crook," Braden made a savage attack on the bona fides of his target's spiritual sincerity.

"We do know that Colson is busy selling books about his religion, making speeches for pay about his religion, and rising at prayer breakfasts—to applause—about his religion," said Braden, rounding off his broadcast by demanding "real contrition and sincere apologies" from Colson "to hundreds of Americans including a number of newsmen of this town."

The most interesting effect of this broadcast was that it did indeed produce contrition and apology—but from Tom Braden. For three years later, the celebrated Washington commentator wrote this letter to Colson:

> *God, Colson, when I think that I actually hated you. Yes hated. I thought you stood for every single moral and political wrong that I had fought against.*

---

*For the true story of Colson's involvement in the Brookings episode, see pp. 150–53.

And now I say to myself "I'm proud I know that man," and
when I think of people who are doing worthwhile things in the pub-
lic good I think of you and my hate gives way to praise, not without
a touch of envy but of the right sort, of the "why didn't I do more
for my country?" sort.
  Well I just thought I'd tell you so. Confession is supposed to be
good for the soul.

Yours,
Tom Braden

Braden was not the only critic who confessed to changing his mind about
Colson. The acerbic columnist Jack Anderson launched an investigation
into the finances of Prison Fellowship after hearing rumors that Colson was
enriching himself from his religious activities. After establishing that Colson earned a salary of only $59,000 from his ministry, and that the far larger
sums he earned from his speaking fees and book royalties went not into his
pocket but directly to Prison Fellowship, Anderson wrote several columns
praising Colson and became a regular donor to Prison Fellowship.

These anecdotes involving journalists in the late 1970s reflected a turning
of the tide of public opinion about Colson. They also reflect an important
part of the Colson legacy, without which all the other parts would have been
undermined. It is the legacy of good example. "I pray that I will stay faithful,"
was a constant refrain in Colson's devotions with prayer groups and alone
during the early years of his ministry. There were times when he was tempted
by secular moneymaking opportunities, by resurgences of his old arrogance,
and no doubt by other snares of the world, the flesh, and the devil. His struggle to quit smoking proved particularly difficult. So did his battles against
impatience, self-centeredness, and spiritual pride. Yet his victories over such
temptations confounded his many critics, who were longing to see him fall.
Unlike some high-profile converts, Colson has maintained with full trans-
parency the highest standards of personal conduct and financial integrity. He
has worked with humility and dedication in the service of the prison ministry
to which he felt called. He has walked his talk. In that walk the dedication of
his commitment to Jesus Christ has shone out as an example to many. It is the
rock on which he has built his postconversion life.

The legacy of Colson's example has been the foundation for his legacy
of inspiration. This part of his ministry began with his authorship of *Born
Again*. Although the book became a Christian classic and is still in print
around the world, with over 3 million copies sold, many of Colson's read-

ers prefer his later and equally inspirational literary output. This has been prodigious, with twenty-seven authored or coauthored titles published so far, more in the writing or planning stages, and approximately 10 million copies sold in eleven languages.

After *Born Again,* the three Colson books that have perhaps made the most enduring impact are *How Now Shall We Live?; The Body* (and its revised sequel, *Being the Body),* which offers a new vision for the church in the face of contemporary pressure; and *Loving God*—a mixture of reportage, anecdotes, and short stories blended together by Colson in an attempt to answer the question, What does it mean to love God? This last book has made a particularly powerful impact in Russia, Eastern Europe, and the Baltic states, possibly because it opens with an analysis of Alexander Solzhenitsyn's prison writings, building on his statement in *The Gulag Archipelago* "Bless you prison, bless you. For it was while I lay on the rotting prison straw when I discovered that the meaning of earthly existence lies, not as we have grown used to thinking, in our prosperity, but in the development of our souls."

Solzhenitsyn's discovery so closely mirrored Colson's experience that he used it as the theme of *Loving God,* evidently making an inspirational impact on others in similar situations. For example, in June 1990, Prison Fellowship International received a letter from the Magadan region of northern Russia, an area notorious for its prison camps. The signatories of the letter, Semyon Garokhov and Valentin Sukonin, wrote: "In our camp there are about three thousand prisoners and everyone has read your book *Loving God.* In actuality every evening someone would read aloud while fifteen or twenty others listened. . . . When we learned that the author, Colson, had been in prison too, we understood that he knew the meaning of freedom. In other words we who hated and thought that such feelings were experienced by all people learned that it was possible to love God."

A no less surprising use of *Loving God* was made by the archbishop of Vilnius, in Lithuania, in his televised sermon on Christmas Eve 2003. In this heavily watched TV event in the Baltic state over Christmas, Cardinal Audrys Backis devoted over seven minutes of his message to quoting extensively from *Loving God,* holding up Colson's life and ministry as a shining example of how a man could stumble in his life but through Christ rise again to far higher levels.

These two examples of Colson's ability to inspire his readers across the world could be multiplied many times over by similar stories about the effect of his books. *Loving God* was first published in 1983 and is by no means Colson's most successful title in terms of copies sold (approximately 950,000). Yet twenty years later it was being read aloud in Russian prisons and preached about in a Lithuanian cardinal's Christmas sermon. As his books continue to be reprinted and as he writes new titles, Colson's legacy of inspiration through the written word seems likely to continue and endure.

Colson's success as a Christian author and broadcaster derives partly from his skill as a communicator and partly from the solid grounding of his books in orthodox theology and biblical studies. However, his legacy of inspiration through his writing derives great strength and credibility from the authenticity of his legacy in prison ministry.

Colson changed the face of prison ministry, first in the United States and then in 105 countries across the world. In 1976, when he founded Prison Fellowship, ministering to prisoners was an unfashionable, underrated, underfunded Christian activity with no national or international leadership. It was carried out on a localized, prison-to-prison basis by occasional volunteers whose organizational skills were weak. These small-time, mom-and-pop prison ministries received limited support from America's churches, whose attitude tended to be "leave it to the official prison chaplains."

Colson started Prison Fellowship with no clear vision of where he was going to lead it. He certainly intended his ministry to supplement the work of prison chaplains and other professional specialists in this field, but his ideas on how to do this were fuzzy and untested. Today Colson likes to point out that the most successful ideas and initiatives that propelled the growth of Prison Fellowship came from people other than himself. The first discipleship courses for furloughed prisoners, the in-prison seminars, Operation Starting Line, Angel Tree, Angel Tree Camping, Justice Fellowship, Sycamore Tree, restorative justice courses, the InnerChange Freedom Initiative—all are PF flagship programs, "but not one of them originated from me," says Colson. "They could only have happened because God had his hand upon them and upon this ministry."

Colson may well be understating his personal legacy to these programs for he has acted as an inspirer, popularizer, catalyst, architect, fund-raiser, and leader for every one of them. But for all the good human work he and others have done, nobody associated with Prison Fellowship underestimates the role of divine providence in bringing these projects to fruition.

Today the fruits of Prison Fellowship are enormous. In the United States alone, some 250,000 prisoners a year are introduced to the gospel by Operation Starting Line. Six hundred thousand Christmas presents a year are distributed by Angel Tree to the children of prisoners, 20,000 of whom have been to Christian vacation camps through Angel Tree Camping. Over 150,000 prison inmates a year attend PF Bible study, and 27,000 of them are connected to Christian pen pals. Fifty thousand men and women enter prisons on a regular basis doing prison ministry as PF-trained volunteers. There are now four PF-run InnerChange prisons in Texas, Kansas, Iowa, and Minnesota; their teaching and mentoring regimes show repeat-offending rates that are massively lower than the national average. All these programs cost more than $50 million a year, which is the sum raised annualy by Prison Fellowship from its supporters and donors. No comparable figures are available for the similar programs run by the national Prison Fellowship ministries in 105 countries under the auspices of Prison Fellowship International. All that can be said in the absence of reliable data is that the global activities of PFI are enormous too.

In assessing Colson's legacy of prison ministry across the United States and across the world, statistics do not begin to tell the whole story. For what Colson's postconversion life is about is opening the hearts of men and women to spiritual change through Christian evangelism. In this most personal process, which takes place deep in the soul, the results are known only to God. Colson well understands this, which is why he backs off from conversion counts or enrollment figures of the kind that are too easily recorded in the "I'm saved, you're saved" simplicities of some evangelical churches and ministries. Colson will surely leave behind him a huge legacy of change in many individual hearts and souls, but it is a legacy that cannot possibly be measured or numbered.

This part of Colson's legacy extends far beyond the community of prisoners, even though prison ministry is his primary calling. By his dedication to this cause for nearly thirty years he has helped to change hearts, minds, and behavior among men and women serving their sentences in jails all over the world—and often among their families as well. Yet for at least the last twenty years Colson's ministry has sought to change two far larger constituencies—the church and the culture.

Colson's contribution to changing the church rises above denominational boundaries. He was brought up as a nominal Episcopalian. His greatest supporters and closest prayer partners have been evangelicals. He was baptized and worships as a Southern Baptist. His theology is in deepest harmony with the sixteenth-century reform tradition of John Calvin and the nineteenth-century apologetics of Abraham Kuyper. Yet Colson also maintains close personal and spiritual relations with Catholics.

Embracing, as he does, such a broad patchwork quilt of doctrines and beliefs, it is not entirely surprising that Colson has been occasionally accused of confusion or even apostasy. Such charges cannot be made to stick. Colson possesses an ever-curious, ever-searching, first-class mind, intensely interested in both scholarly theology and the practical application of it. Perhaps it is not the mind of a pure intellectual living *for* ideas; Colson's is a highly intelligent mind living *off* ideas. He also lives for popularizing those ideas and turning them into practical Christian service.

One of Colson's strongest passions is for unity among Christians. He yearns for Jesus' prayer in John 17 to be answered. In his prison ministry he has turned that yearning into remarkable practical results. Prison Fellowship is a showpiece ministry for unity as its Christian volunteers of all denominations forget their divisions when they go about their calling of bringing the gospel "to the least of these our brethren" in jails around the world. Colson's personal leadership of that unity, sometimes in bitterly divided communities such as Northern Ireland, has been unfailingly determined.

The search for unity has taken Colson through the fire of theological controversy. When he and Father Richard John Neuhaus launched their symposium Evangelicals and Catholics Together (ECT), the reaction of some evangelicals was brutally hostile. In addition to exposing Colson to the most venomous criticism he had experienced since the era of Watergate, that symposium cost Prison Fellowship over $1 million in financial support from donors opposed to ECT. These were dark days of acute anxiety for Colson. "Maybe I'm guilty of dividing the Body of Christ," he confided to his close friend Michael Timmis, who is chairman of Prison Fellowship International. "No, you're taking flak because you're right over the target," retorted Timmis. "Just you keep on fighting against the sin of disunity."

So Colson fought against those eccentric voices of evangelicalism that regard Catholics as "not saved" or "not a church." It sounds like a bizarre battle to outsiders, but among insiders it needed to be joined. Evangelicals are the fastest-growing sector of the Christian community around the world. In America alone they number around 65 million regular churchgoers. Yet a significant percentage of them had a tendency to leave their brains outside the church door—at least on the subject of Christian unity. So when Colson and other thoughtful Protestant leaders endorsed ECT, they set off a debate of immense educational and theological importance in the evangelical community.

The consequences of this debate have been substantial. Several extremist anti-Catholic voices, sadly including that of Colson's former theological mentor R. C. Sproul, were marginalized. Some of the greatest living Protestant theologians, such as J. I. Packer and T. M. George, came out strongly in support of ECT. Several important evangelical ministries, including Campus Crusade, the Navigators, Young Life, and Promise Keepers, reached out to Catholics as never before. Leading Catholic churchmen such as Cardinal Avery Dulles, although surprised by the furor among evangelicals, have responded by continuing with constructive and conciliatory dialogue in the ongoing ECT exchanges. It is not yet possible to make a historical assessment of the spiritual and theological importance of ECT, which has moved from being a controversial to a natural process of debate. Colson believes it is the most important long-term initiative he has ever taken in his public Christian ministry, which is a remarkable claim, given the success of other aspects of his life and work. Michael Timmis agrees: "Without the leadership of Chuck there would not have been a sea change in the attitude of evangelicals and Catholics, and of Catholics toward evangelicals. It is a great and lasting achievement." If that view is correct, then Colson will also be leaving behind him in the contemporary church a legacy of greater unity.

One interesting by-product of this legacy of greater unity is a legacy of greater influence. Colson has made a serious effort to exercise a united Christian influence on contemporary politics and the culture of American society. How far has he succeeded?

On the political front, Colson's influence on presidential decision taking and policy making represents an extraordinary full circle in his life story. In the late 1960s, the young Colson exercised an influence inside the Nixon White House toward activities that had no Christian purpose or morality in them whatsoever. Yet in the early 2000s, the older Colson was having a considerable influence in a wholly Christian direction on several of the decisions and policies of President George W. Bush.

Some of that Christian influence has shown up in matters relating to prisoners. President Bush has publicly supported the IFI prisons and the Angel Tree scheme. He is the first president to ask Congress—in his 2003 State of the Union address—to allocate $300 million to help fifty thousand newly released prisoners to find jobs and housing. These policies have been directly influenced by Colson, as has President Bush's decision to set up an Office for Faith-Based and Community Initiatives. At the initial White House meeting in 2001 to launch this program, President Bush appealed to the many senators and congressmen present to give faith-based initiatives their support.

"How do we know they will work?" asked one legislator.

"Chuck Colson over here can tell you it works," replied the president, inviting Colson to outline the success of Prison Fellowship's IFI program—which Bush himself had helped PF to initiate at Sugar Land when he was governor of Texas. Colson has also been a strong influence on other faith-oriented policies of the Bush administration. On October 26, 2003, the lead story on the front page of the *New York Times,* by Elisabeth Bumiller, carried the headline "Evangelicals Sway White House on Human Rights Issues Abroad." The first name mentioned in the article was that of Charles W. Colson. Bumiller stated that Colson and other prominent religious leaders had persuaded the White House to take policy initiatives toward ending the war in the Sudan, halting sex trafficking, and preventing the global spread of AIDS. Colson, who has long championed these causes in his *BreakPoint* broadcasts and his articles, was delighted when, a few weeks after he raised these issues at a White House meeting, the president supported them in a speech to the U.N. General Assembly.

Although Colson is pleased when his Christian ideas influence public policy, he has a greater interest in leaving behind him a more permanent and more important legacy—a change in the culture of contemporary society away from postmodernism and toward biblical worldview. On the face of it, the gargantuan task Colson has set himself looks virtually impossible. For life in modern American society is so increasingly entrenched in a secular and self-centered culture that Colson's call for it to become biblical and God-centered seems like a voice crying in the wilderness. To Christian believers, however, a voice crying in the wilderness is not such a bad precedent (see Matthew 3:3). Colson has in mind the nineteenth-century precedents set by his hero William Wilberforce and his evangelical contemporaries in Clapham, London. They set out to reform the manners and morals of Victorian England. Swept forward on a rising tide of revival, they had considerable success, both culturally and politically. In the political category their greatest triumph was the passing of the Emancipation Act of 1833, which abolished the slave trade. At Prison Fellowship's twenty-fifth-anniversary dinner, Colson told the story of an attempt he made to honor the memory of William Wilberforce by visiting the church where he had been a regular worshiper, in South London. On a warm June evening Colson entered the small church in Clapham and felt sadly disappointed. Instead of the splendid monuments and inscriptions he had expected to find, the only memento of his hero was a small and dusty stained-glass window at the back of the church. On a nearby table was a small and equally dusty pile of pamphlets on sale for 50 pence (approximately $1) commemorating Wilberforce's life and his connection with the church.

Is this all? Just a pamphlet? thought Colson. He was astounded that so great a legacy had so meager a memorial. Feeling deflated, he came out of the church and began walking across Clapham Common, one of London's largest parks. An evening mist was falling as the last rays of the midsummer sunset faded away. In the hazy twilight, Colson's emotions and imagination soared into a vision that uplifted his downcast spirits. Suddenly he felt he could see hundreds upon hundreds of freed slaves walking around him on Clapham Common, throwing off their chains and shackles as they rejoiced in their liberty. "Then I understood," said Colson in his speech at the twenty-fifth-anniversary dinner. "I understood that Wilberforce's legacy consisted of living monuments—of slaves and souls and prisoners set free."

Colson's similar legacy began when he himself was set free. It started in that strange sobbing moment of crying out to God in Tom Phillips's driveway. It continued through his early stumblings of spiritual discovery with Doug Coe, Al Quie, and other prayer partners. Then his faith was tested by his ordeals in court, in prison, and in adjusting to the life of an ex-con turned evangelist, surrounded by a sea of cynicism. These processes culminated in a call from God to enter prison ministry. Colson obeyed that call and has stayed faithful to it. This faithfulness is the cornerstone of his legacy, and Colson's other legacies have been built on that cornerstone: his personal example, his public inspiration, his books, his groundbreaking initiatives and reforms launched through Prison Fellowship, his impact on the church and Christian unity, his attempts to influence public policy, and his efforts to change the culture of society—all have been made possible because Colson has stayed faithful. He is the personification of the transforming power of the Holy Spirit, which changed him from the hatchet man of Watergate into a holy man of prison ministry who has dedicated the remainder of his life to Christ's service.

In the end, Colson's legacy can be summed up in the familiar phrases Christians often use about him: "God changed him"—"God used him for good"—"Charles Colson stayed faithful." His story deserves the description: "A Life Redeemed."

Source Notes

Abbreviations for Frequently Used Sources

Aitken	*Nixon: A Life* by Jonathan Aitken
Bursaw Collection	Private Papers of Nancy Billings Colson Bursaw
Born Again	*Bom Again* by Charles W. Colson
CWC Archives	Charles W. Colson's Collected Archives at Wheaton College, Illinois
CWC Private Papers	Charles W. Colson's Private Papers
Haldeman	*The Ends of Power* by H. R. Haldeman with Joseph Dimona
How Now Shall We Live?	*How Now Shall We Live?* by Charles W. Colson and Nancy Pearcey
Hunt	*Undercover* by E. Howard Hunt
Kutler/*Wars*	*The Wars of Watergate* by Stanley I. Kutler
Kutler/*Watergate*	*Watergate: The Fall of Richard M. Nixon*, Stanley I. Kutler, ed.
Lewis	*Mere Christianity* by C. S. Lewis
Life Sentence	*Life Sentence* by Charles W. Colson
Loving God	*Loving God* by Charles W. Colson
Morin Collection	Private Papers of Charles H. Morin
Oudes	*From the President: Richard Nixon's Secret Files* by Bruce Oudes
Perry	*Charles Colson* by John Perry
PFM	Archives of Prison Fellowship Ministries, held at PFM office in Reston, Virginia
Rhodes	*Unpublished Memoirs* by Fred Rhodes, Colson Archives at Wheaton College Illinois, Boxes 102–110
RN	*RN: The Memoirs of Richard Nixon*
Safire	*Before the Fall* by William Safire

Prologue

Source Material:

> The visits to the Mountain View Penitentiary and the Carol S. Vance IFI
> Unit at Sugar Land Penitentiary were witnessed by the author, who accom-
> panied Colson on his tour of Texas prisons, 2/3/04–2/6/04
> Shakespeare quotation from Polonius's speech to Laertes, *Hamlet,* Act 1,
> Scene 2
> Henry A. Kissinger in conversation with the author, 4/3/02
> Colson letter to the author, 10/24/97
> Nixon–Colson conversation about John Kerry, White House Tapes,
> 4/17/71: quoted on *NBC Nightly News,* 3/15/04
> National Prayer Breakfast, 2/5/93: Congressional Record, 6/30/93
> Colson letter to Senator John Kerry, 2/5/93

Chapter 1: *An Unsettled Upbringing*

Interviews:

> Charles W. Colson, Chris Colson, Emily Colson, Jane Colson, Richard Col-
> son, Wendell Colson, Jr., Cathie Gill, Gordon Loux, Jonathan Moore

Source Material:

> *Born Again,* chapter 2
> *Boston Herald,* 11/9/42 and 02/4/43
> Browne & Nichols, school yearbook, 1949
> Browne & Nichols, the *Spectator* magazine (1947–1949)
> *Disraeli* by Robert Blake, p. 342 (Eyre and Spottiswoode, London, 1966)
> *Washington Post,* 12/4/79
> Charles W. Colson school essay, CWC Archives, box 2
> CWC Private Papers

Chapter 2: *Student Days*

Interviews:

> Nancy Bursaw, Charles W. Colson, Tom Glidden, Mrs. Virginia Maloney,
> General William Maloney USMC, Jonathan Moore, Robert Torok

Source Material:

> *Acton Colonial,* 16/18/53
> *Born Again,* chapter 2
> Brown University, *Daily Herald,* 6/14/52
> Brown University, yearbooks and archives, 1949–1953
> Concord Country Club Dinner Dance ticket and program, 12/18/48
> *Pippa Passes* by Robert Browning

Chapter 3: *The Marines*

Interviews:

> Nancy Bursaw, Charles W. Colson, General William Maloney USMC,
> Robert Torok

Source Material:

> *Born Again,* chapter 2
>
> Correspondence between Nancy Colson and Charles Colson, letters dated 6/8/54, 6/13/54, 6/23/54, 6/24/54, 6/25/54, 6/27/54, 7/7/54, 7/18/54, 7/20/54, 7/22/54, 7/23/54, 7/24/54, 7/28/54, 3/8/54, 5/8/54, 8/15/54, and 9/7/54 (Bursaw Collection)
>
> Letter, Wendell Colson, Sr., to Charles W. Colson, 4/17/54 (Bursaw Collection), Hunt, chapter 9
>
> CWC Private Papers

Chapter 4: *A Political Operator*

Interviews:

> Nancy Bursaw, Charles W. Colson, Wendell Colson, Jr., Jonathan Moore, Charles H. Morin, William Saltonstall, Jr., Evelyn Slater, Don Whitehead

Source Material:

> *Born Again,* chapter 2
>
> *Boston Globe,* 11/4/60
>
> Letter from Dorothy Jacobsen, 5/13/60, CWC Archives, box 3
>
> *Newsweek,* 6/18/58 and 5/5/59
>
> *Time* magazine, 5/5/59

Chapter 5: *Colson and Morin, Nancy and Patty*

Interviews:

> Nancy Bursaw, Charles W. Colson, Patty Colson, Mrs. Doris Mitchell, Justice Joseph Mitchell, Jr., Jonathan Moore, Charles H. Morin, Jr., Pat Owens, Robert Owens, William Saltonstall, Jr., Don Whitehead

Source Material:

> *Born Again,* chapter 4 (and unpublished first draft in CWC Archives, box 27)
>
> Charles H. Morin, address to Becket Fund, 11/2/02
>
> Morin Collection, file no. 8
>
> Letter, Ricky Austin to Judge Gesell, 6/1/74, CWC Archives, box 47
>
> Letter, Charles W. Colson to Charles H. Morin, 12/21/62, CWC Archives, box 47
>
> Letter, Charles W. Colson to John Murtha, 10/27/63, Morin Collection, file 22
>
> Letter, Justice Mitchell to Judge Gesell, 6/5/74, CWC Archives, box 47
>
> Letter, Elizabeth Morin to Judge Gesell, 6/9/74, CWC Archives, box 47

Chapter 6: *The Road to the White House*

Interviews:

> Charles W. Colson, Chris Colson, Emily Colson, Patty Colson, Wendell Colson, Jr., Jonathan Moore, Charles H. Morin, Jr., Richard M. Nixon, Pat Owens, Tom Phillips, Fred Rhodes, Robert Torok

Source Material:

Born Again, chapters 5, 6, 7 (see also unpublished draft, CWC Archives, box 27)

Congressional Journal, 7/14/68

Letter, Charles W. Colson to Richard M. Nixon, 11/14/68, CWC Archives, box 49

Theodore H. White, The Making of the President, 1968, p. 223

Oudes, p. 142

Aitken, pp. 307–316

Nixon on the Issues, 1968 (GOP Campaign Publication)

Wall Street Journal, 7/3/68

Letter from Brad Morse to Charles W. Colson, 8/9/60, CWC Archives, box 15

Wall Street Journal, 6/9/68

Congressional Record, 6/30/68

Wall Street Journal, 11/12/68

Washington Post, 11/25/69

Chapter 7: The President's Point Man

Interviews:

Henry Cashen, Charles W. Colson, Benjamin Bradlee*, John Ehrlichman*, H. R. Haldeman*, Herbert Klein*, Richard M. Nixon*, Ray Price*, William S. Paley*, Ron Ziegler*

Source Material:

Aitken, chapter 17

Baltimore Sun, 10/18/70

Born Again, chapters 2–6

Charles W. Colson, White House memoranda, 11/21/69, 11/24/69, 1/17/70, 3/8/70, 9/14/70, 10/12/70, 10/18/70, 11/2/70, 11/16/70, 11/21/70, 12/2/70, 1/18/71

Haldeman Diaries, 3/24/70, 5/18/70, 12/5/70, 12/28/70 (National Archives and CWC Archives)

Los Angeles Times, 3/2/72

New York Times, 1/26/70

New Yorker magazine, 3/17/75 (Shaking the Tree by Thomas Whiteside)

Oudes, pp. 72, 111–112

Perry, chapters 5–6

Safire, pp. 441–442

Washington Post, 2/5/70, 6/21/70, 7/18/70, 7/24/70

Washington Star, 6/14/71

CWC Archives, boxes 90–96

New York magazine, 12/1/69

The Making of the President by Theodore H. White, Athenaeum, 1969, p. 348

Playboy magazine, 1/10/69

Life magazine, 9/4/70

---

* Gave their interviews to the author in 1989–1991, for Nixon: A Life (1993).

Chapter 8: *Watergate*

Interviews:

Bob Abplanalp*, Henry Cashen, Jack Caulfield, Charles W. Colson, Chris Colson, Patty Colson, Wendell Colson, Jr., John Ehrlichman*, H. R. Haldeman*, Egil Krogh*, G. Gordon Liddy*, General William Maloney USMC, Richard M. Nixon*, Bebe Rebozo*, David Shapiro

Source Material:

Aitken, chapters 17–20

Born Again, chapters 1, 5–7

CWC Archives, boxes 88–117

Correspondence between Charles W. Colson and Howard Hunt, 11/18/69

Hunt, pp. 143, 150, 163

RN, p. 308

Memoranda, Charles W. Colson to John Ehrlichman, 6/28/71, CWC Archives

Oudes, pp. 279, 280, 284, 285

New York Times, 6/13/71

Newsweek, 10/2/71

Washington Post, 6/22/71–7/10/71

Wall Street Journal, 10/15/71

White House Transcripts, 7/1/71, 6/13/72 (National Archives)

The Pentagon Papers: Gravel Edition (www.pentagon/pent1.html), 1–22

Kutler/*Wars,* pp. 88, 114, 187, 194, 214–216

All The President's Men by Bob Woodward and Carl Bernstein, Quartet, London, 1974

Breach of Faith by Theodore H. White, Athenaeum, New York, 1975, pp. 176, 183, 228–299

Chapter 9: *Winning and Leaving*

Interviews:

Michael Balzano, Henry Cashen, Charles Colson, Patty Colson, John Ehrlichman, Bob Haldeman*, Steve Karalekas, Charles H. Morin, Richard M. Nixon*, Pat Owens, Ron Ziegler*

Source Material:

Aitken, chapters 18–19

Born Again, chapters 5–6

Colson: Memo to The President, 11/4/71 (CWC Archives)

Colson: Memo to staff, 8/14/72 (CWC Archives)

CWC Archives, boxes 103–117

Kutler/*Watergate,* pp. 113–115, 217, 234

Hunt, chapters 15–16

Washington Post, 8/28/72, 12/12/72

Wall Street Journal, 10/15/71

---

* Gave their interviews to the author in 1989–1991, for *Nixon: A Life* (1993).

Disraeli by Robert Blake, p. 313
RN, p. 403
Haldeman Diaries, 11/15/72
White House Transcripts (National Archives), 1/3/73
Newsweek, 3/5/73
Nixon letter on Colson resignation, 3/13/73, CWC Archives
New York Times, 4/4/73

Chapter 10: *Conversion*

Interviews:
  Doug Coe, Charles W. Colson, Patty Colson, Tom Phillips, David Shapiro,
Source Material:
  Born Again, chapters 7, 8, 9
  Lewis, chapters 8–10
  Psalm 37, New International Version
  Table Talk by Martin Luther, folio 28, p. 37
  Way of the Spirit by Evelyn Underhill, p. 146
  RN, p. 621

Chapter 11: *Prayers and Pleadings*

Interviews:
  John Bishop, Steve Bull, Jr., Doug Coe, Charles W. Colson, Emily Colson,
  Patty Colson, Wendell Colson, Jr., Seymour Glanzer, Bob Haldeman*, Egil
  Krogh*, Myron Mintz, Charles Morin, Richard M. Nixon*, Pat Owens, Tom
  Phillips, Al Quie, David Shapiro, Jerry Warren, Ron Ziegler*
Source Material:
  Letter, Charles W. Colson to Phillips, 8/20/73, CWC Archives
  Born Again, chapters 14–16 and unpublished manuscripts of *Born Again*
  CWC Archives, box 102
  Unpublished manuscript of Colson book on Watergate (never completed)
  CWC Archives, boxes 44–48
  Colson letters to Frazier, McGrory, Mollenhoff, Rosenthal, 4/73 to 9/73
  CWC Archives, boxes 117–119
  Sgt. Nathaniel Green letter to Colson, 7/27/73, CWC Archives, box 56
  Psalms 8:4, Coverdale translation
  Macbeth by William Shakespeare, act 5, scene 7
  CWC Private Papers

Chapter 12: *Prison*

Interviews:
  Michael Balzano, Henry Cashen, Doug Coe, Charles W. Colson, Patty Col-
  son, Wendell Colson, Jr., Chris Colson, Steve Karalekas, Myron Mintz,
  Charles H. Morin, Pat Owens, Al Quie, Fred Rhodes, David Shapiro

---

* Gave their interviews to the author in 1989–1991, for *Nixon: A Life* (1993).

Source Material:
   Born Again, chapters 20–27
   Letters to Judge Gesell from Richard Austin and Joseph Mitchell, Jr.
   CWC Archives, box 97
   Letter to Jerald ter Horst, 7/17/71, and accompanying Boudin Memorandum
   CWC Archives, box 102
   Newsweek, 6/17/74
   Colson speech notes for going-in party, 7/6/74
   Patty Colson to Charles Colson, 8/24/74, CWC Private Papers
   Inez (Diz) Colson to Charles Colson, 11/21/74, CWC Private Papers
   Letters from Colson to Doug Coe, Howard Hughes, Graham Purcell, and
   Al Quie, August 1974–December 1974, CWC Archives, box 134
   Letters re clemency for Colson organized by Charles Morin, August–
   September 1974, Morin Collection
   Colson letter to Morin, 9/18/74, Morin Collection
   Colson unpublished prison diaries, 7/74 to 1/75, CWC Archives, box 135
   Stonewall by Richard Ben-Veniste and George Crampton, Jr. (Simon and
   Schuster, 1977), p. 374
   Fred Rhodes, unpublished memoirs, CWC Archives, box 107

Chapter 13: *Released and Born Again*
Interviews:
   Doug Coe, Charles W. Colson, Patty Colson, Chris Colson, Myron Mintz,
   Charles Morin, Al Quie, Fred Rhodes, David Shapiro
Source Material:
   Born Again, chapter 27
   Life Sentence, chapters 1–8
   Atlanta Journal, 1/24/75
   Washington Post, 1/25/75, 1/30/75, 2/1/75, 2/4/75
   Reviews of Colson–Barbara Walters interview, 3/8/75, *New York Times,*
   Washington Post, Chicago Tribune, Los Angeles Times, Newsweek, 9/8/76
   Rhodes, unpublished memoirs, CWC Archives, boxes 108–112
   Rhodes, file of memos and letters to CWC, 1975–78, CWC Archives, box 113
   Colson, unpublished draft of untitled book on Watergate, CWC Archives,
   boxes 121–128
   Colson correspondence files with Chosen Books, CWC Archives, boxes 128–129
   Reviews of *Born Again, Washington Post,* 3/8/76; *New York Times*
   3/21/76; *Boston Globe,* 4/9/76; *Wall Street Journal,* 4/30/76; *Chicago
   Tribune,* 5/4/76
   The Cost of Discipleship by Dietrich Bonhoeffer, Fortuna Books, London,
   1972, p. 118

Chapter 14: *Starting the Ministry*
Interviews:
   Michael Alison, Sylvia Mary Alison, Doug Coe, Charles W. Colson, Patty

Colson, Wendell Colson, Jr., Michael Cromartie, Nancy DeMoss, William
Fitch, Gordon Loux, Myron Mintz, Al Quie, Fred Rhodes
Source Material:
Paradise magazine, 11/18/76
Life Sentence, chapters 5, 17–20
Time magazine, 11/18/76
New York Times, 9/23/77
Rhodes, unpublished memoirs, CWC Archives, boxes 104–105

Chapter 15: *Expanding the Ministry*

Interviews:
Michael Alison, Sylvia Mary Alison, Charles W. Colson, Patty Colson,
Myles Fish, William Fitch, Neal Jones, Walter Kautzky, Al Lawrence, Gor-
don Loux, Ron Nikkel, Dan Van Ness, Ralph Veerman
Source Material:
Life Sentence, chapters 11–12
Christianity Today, "Why Charles Colson's heart is still in prison," 9/16/83
New York Times, 7/2/81
Rhodes, unpublished memoirs, CWC Archives, box 108
Jan Kary, ed., *To God Be the Glory*, Tyndale, 1996, chapters 4–7
Crime and Human Nature by James Q. Wilson and Richard J. Herrnstein
(Simon and Schuster, New York, 1985)
Prison Fellowship International by Gordon Loux (PFI Publications, 1980)

Chapter 16: *New Developments*

Interviews:
Mary Kay Beard, Charles W. Colson, Emily Colson, Chris Colson, Patty
Colson, Wendell Colson, Jr., Nancy DeMoss, Myles Fish, Gordon Loux,
Tom Pratt, Gloria Pratt, Richard Payne, Michael Timmis
Source Material:
Veil: The Secret Wars of the CIA by Bob Woodward (Simon and Schuster,
New York, 1987, p. 474)
Letter, Colson to Richard M. Nixon, 2/1/87, CWC Archives, boxes
130–131
Letter, Colson to Billy Graham, 2/4/87, CWC Archives, boxes 130–131
Memorandum, Colson to Tom Pratt, 2/18/91, CWC Archives, boxes
130–131
Tom Pratt, report to directors of Prison Fellowship, 6/1/91, PFM Archives
Memorandum, Colson to Tom Pratt and Nelson Keener, 2/18/91, PFM
Archives
Letters, Colson to PF donors re Angel Tree, 9/91 and 9/92, PFM Archives
Memorandum David Bovenizer to Gordon Loux, 11/15/79, PFM Archives
Letter, radio proposal for *BreakPoint,* 1/12/90, PFM Archives
Video messages, Colson to PF donors re OSL, 10/01 and 10/02, PFM
Archives

Letter, Colson to his mother, Diz Colson, 12/29/78, CWC Private Papers
Letter, Emily Colson to Charles W. Colson, 11/1/99, CWC Private Papers

Chapter 17: *New Recognition, New Horizons*
Interviews:
Michael Alison, Sylvia Mary Alison, Charles W. Colson, Patty Colson, Cardinal Avery Dulles, Mark Earley, Grace McCrane, Richard John Neuhaus, Nancy Nieymeyer, Tom Pratt, Fred Rhodes, Michael Timmis, Ellen Vaughn
Source Material:
Letter from Colson to Richard John Neuhaus, 11/22/93, Neuhaus Papers
Test of Colson Templeton Prize address to World Parliament of Religions, 9/2/93, CWC Archives, box 132
The Naked Public Square: Religion and Democracy in America by Richard John Neuhaus, Eerdmans, Grand Rapids, Michigan, 1988
New York Times, 3/30/94
Rhodes, unpublished memoirs, CWC Archives, box 120
ECT correspondence, CWC Archives, boxes 131–136
ECT correspondence, Neuhaus Papers, 1993–2002
R. C. Sproul, Naples lecture text, 1995, CWC Archives, box 132
Meeting of Conservative Philosophy Group, 11/4/93, 8 Lord North Street, London SW1—CPG file, author's papers
Colson letter to Richard John Neuhaus, 10/4/97
Karen Strong memo and diary note, PFM papers, 11/3/04
New York Times, 5/30/04
Colson memo to Grace McCrane, 3/20/92
Pierre Allard, speech to PFI convocation, 9/21/03
How Now Shall We Live?, p. 22 and passim
National Review, 1/18/2000
Christianity Today, 12/9/99
Authors visit to Centurion Seminar, 10/9/03

Epilogue
Interviews:
Charles W. Colson, Michael Timmis, Ron Nikkel,
Mark Earley, Richard John Neuhaus
Source Material:
Julius Caesar by William Shakespeare, act 3, scene 2
CBS broadcast, Tom Braden, *CBS News,* 4/10/77
Tom Braden letter to Colson, 2/11/80, Morin Collection, file 14
Jack Anderson columns, *Saturday Evening Post,* 10/14/79; *Washington Post,* 2/11/80
Loving God, p. 8
Garokhov and Sukonin letter, 6/17/90, PFM Archives
New York Times, 10/26/03
CWC Private Papers

Select Bibliography

Aitken, Jonathan. *Nixon: A Life*. Washington, D.C.: Regnery Publishing, 1993.

Ambrose, Stephen E. *Nixon, Vol. II: The Triumph of a Politician, 1962–1972*. New York: Simon and Schuster, 1989.

———. *Nixon, Vol. III: Ruin and Recovery, 1973–1990*. New York: Simon and Schuster, 1991.

Bernstein, Carl, and Bob Woodward. *All the President's Men*. New York: Simon and Schuster, 1974.

Blake, Robert. *Disraeli*. London: Eyre and Spottiswode, 1996.

Bonhoeffer, Dietrich. *Cost of Discipleship*. London: William Collins, 1963.

———. *Letters and Papers from Prison*. London: Fortuna Books, 1967.

Colodny, Len, and Robert Gettlin. *Silent Coup: The Removal of a President*. London: Victor Gollancz, 1991.

Colson, Charles W. *Born Again*. Old Tappan, NJ: Chosen Books, 1976.

———. *Chuck Colson Speaks*. Uhrichsville, Ohio: Promise Press, 2000.

———. *Justice that Restores*. Leicester, England: Inter-Varsity-Press, 2000.

———. *Life Sentence*. Lincoln, Va: Chosen Books, 1979.

———. *The Line Between Right & Wrong: Developing a Personal Code of Ethics*. Uhrichsville, Oh.: Barbour Publishing, 1992.

———. *Loving God*. Grand Rapids: Zondervan Publishing House, 1983.

Colson, Charles W., with Anne Morse. *Burden of Truth: Defending Truth in an Age of Unbelief*. Wheaton, Ill: Tyndale, 1997.

Colson, Charles W., and Richard John Neuhaus, ed. *Evangelical and Catholics Together: Towards a Common Mission*. Dallas: Word Publishing, 1995.

Colson, Charles W., with Nancy Pearcey. *A Dance with Deception: Revealing the Truth Behind the Headlines*. Dallas: Word Publishing, 1993.

———. *How Now Shall We Live?* Wheaton, Ill: Tyndale, 1999.

Colson, Charles W., and Daniel W. Van Ness. *Convicted: New Hope for Ending America's Crime Crisis*. Westchester, Ill.: Crossway, 1989.

Colson, Charles W., with Ellen Santilli Vaughn *The God of Stones & Spiders: Letters to a Church in Exile*. Wheaton, Ill.: Crossways Books, a division of Good News Publishing, 1990.

———. *Kingdoms in Conflict: An Insider's View of Politics, Power and the Pulpit*. A Judith Markham Book. Grand Rapids: William Morrow Zondervan Publishing House, 1987.

Dean, John. *Blind Ambition*. New York: Simon and Schuster, 1976.

Ehrlichman, John. *Witness to Power: The Nixon Years*. New York: Simon and Schuster, 1982.

Emery, Fred. *Watergate: The Corruption of American Politics and the Fall of Richard Nixon*. New York: Touchstone, 1995.

Haldeman, H. R., with Joseph DiMona. *The Ends of Power*. New York: New York Times Books, 1978.

Hughes, Harold E. *The Man from Ida Grove*. Lincoln, Va: Chosen Books, 1979.

Hunt, E. Howard. *Undercover: The Autobiography of America's Most Famous Secret Agent*. London: W. H. Allen, 1975.

Kutler, Stanley I. *The Wars of Watergate: The Last Crisis of Richard Nixon*. New York: Knopf, 1990.

Kutler, Stanley I., ed. *Watergate: The Fall of Richard M. Nixon*. New York: Brandywine Press, 1996.

Kuyper, Abraham. *Christianity: A Total World and Life System*. Marlborough, N.H.: Plymouth Rock Foundation, 1996.

Lewis, C. S. *God in the Dock: Essays on Theology and Ethics*. Grand Rapids: Eerdmans, 1970.

———. *Mere Christianity*. New York: Macmillan Publishing Co., 1952.

Liddy, G. Gordon. *Will: The Autobiography of G. Gordon Liddy*. New York: St. Martin's Press, 1980.

Loux, Gordon. *History of Prison Fellowship International*. Reston, Va.: Prison Fellowship International Publications, 1985.

Magruder, Jeb Stuart. *An American Life: One Man's Road to Watergate*. New York: Atheneum, 1974.

Neuhaus, Richard John. *The Naked Public Square: Religion and Democracy in America*. Grand Rapids: Eerdmans, 1984.

Nixon, Richard M. *RN: The Memoirs of Richard Nixon*. New York: Grosset and Dunlap, 1978.

Oudes, Bruce. *From the President: Richard Nixon's Secret Files*. New York: Harper and Row, 1989.

Perry, John. *Charles Colson: A Story of Power, Corruption and Redemption*. Nashville, Tn: Broadman and Holman, 2003.

Price, Raymond. *With Nixon*. New York: Viking Press, 1977.

Safire, William. *Before the Fall: An Insider's View of the Pre-Watergate White House*. New York: Da Capo Press, 1975.

Schaeffer, Francis. *The Complete Works of Francis A. Schaeffer: A Christian Worldview*. Westchester, Ill: Crossway, 1982.

Solzhenitsyn, Alexander. *Gulag Archipelago, Two.* New York: Harper and Row, 1974.

Sproul, R. C. *The Holiness of God.* Wheaton, Ill: Tynedale, 1985.

Stans, Maurice H., ed. *Nixon on the Issues.* New York: Nixon-Agnew Campaign Committee, 1968.

White, Theodore H. *Breach of Faith: The Fall of Richard Nixon.* New York: Atheneum Publishers, 1975.

———. *The Making of the President, 1972.* New York: Atheneum Publishers, 1973.

Wilson, James Q., and Richard J. Herrnstein. *Crime and Human Nature.* New York: Simon and Schuster, 1985.

Woodward, Bob. *Veil: The Secret Wars of the CIA.* New York: Simon and Schuster, 1987.

Index